EXPLORING
200 YEARS OF ONEIDA COUNTY HISTORY

Compiled and Edited by
Donald F. White

Book Design by
Cynthia Long

Published by
Oneida County Historical Society
Utica, New York
October 1998
First Edition

First Edition

The following listed stories are reprinted herein with the
permission of the Observer-Dispatch for whom they were
originally written. © 1998 Observer-Dispatch

Oneida County born at right time in the right place
Farmers sowed the seed from which the county bloomed
Land, water and rail travel propelled county's prosperity
Textile industry's rise and fall shaped the fabric of the county
Oneida County nurtured great athletes, great sports
Confident, discerning leaders forged Utica's glory days

Library of Congress Catalog Card Number: 98-88654
Main entry under title:
Exploring 200 Years of Oneida County History

ISBN 0-9668178-0-X

Table of Contents

Contributors

Susan He'bert Gleason – makes her home, with three children, in Utica. She attended Utica College for a Public Relations and Journalism degree and Rochester Institute of Technology for a Masters degree in Service Management. Susan is a writer in the Oneida Indian Nations Communications Department.

Frank Tomaino – is a native of Utica who graduated from Thomas R. Proctor High School in 1949 and from Utica College in 1961 with a Bachelor of Arts degree in English. From 1951 to 1955, he served in the Air Force during the Korean War. For nearly 30 years Frank was a reporter, city editor and regional editor for the Utica Observer-Dispatch, and it was there – in a column called "Frankly Speaking" – that he first began to write about local history.

Philip A. Bean – was born and educated in Utica. He has earned degrees from Union College, Oxford University and the University of Rochester where his doctoral dissertation

focused on the history of immigrants and nationalism. He has published extensively on immigration history, as listed at the conclusion of his article. Phil is presently administrator in the Office of the Dean at Harvard College, Cambridge, MA, and a tutor in history. He is also a member of the Board of Directors of the Boston Center for International Visitors.

Richard L. Williams – is a native of Oneida County who graduated from Syracuse University and took advanced work at SUNY Albany. Dick is retired from Whitesboro Central School where he was a teacher and administrator. He also served as Mayor of Clinton, NY and as a volunteer administrator at Oneida County Historical Society.

Robert Stronach – is currently Director of Public Relations and Development at St. Elizabeth Medical Center. He worked for the Utica Observer-Dispatch and the former Daily Press as copy editor, reporter-photographer, city editor and business editor. Bob graduated with a BA degree in sociology from Siena College near Albany and is an honor graduate of the U.S. Army Military Police School.

John Pitaressi – has been reporting sports for Observer-Dispatch readers for over 26 years. He is a graduate of Hamilton College, 1970, with a major in history. He lives in New Hartford and is a member of the New Hartford Historical Society.

Joe Kelly – is a Utica native son whose contributions to Utica and Oneida County are legion. Joe is Oneida County Historian; Distance Running Hall of Fame Director; an original Boilermaker runner; book author; radio-television commentator and former reporter for the Observer-Dispatch.

Stephen S. Olney – is the Senior Planner in the Oneida County Department of Planning with a great depth of knowledge of the geological formations, mineral resources, water drainage and climatic characteristics of the County.

Florence Hopkins – a graphic artist with the Oneida County Planning Department drew the maps that outline each township and provide details that assist in orienting the history of each town.

Walter Cookenham – is a land surveyor, living in Clinton, NY, and grandson of Henry Cookinham who wrote the two-volume history of Oneida County in 1912.

Richard L. Manzelman – is Pastor emeritus of the New Hartford Presbyterian Church. He lives in retirement in Vermont.

James Parker – is a self-taught folk artist living on Clapsaddle Farm in Ilion, NY where he was born and educated through high school. He graduated from Syracuse University, as a Remington Scholar, with a degree in math and a Navy Commission. He left the Navy to start a business in carving scrimshaw and producing decorative hunting knives. In 1984 he began to paint historical views of local villages and hamlets that has led him to work for over 90 local groups among which are all of the towns of Oneida County.

Donald F. White – was born in Utica, NY, moved to Pittsburgh, PA and returned, summers, to a family farm in Barneveld, NY. He graduated in 1946 from the New York State Maritime College in the Bronx and from Cornell College of Agriculture in 1951. After a career in advertising/public relations and industrial marketing, he retired to Barneveld and is the current President of the Board of Trustees of the Oneida County Historical Society.

Acknowledgements

Published in Oneida County's Bicentennial year, this accounting of 200 years of history has a long pedigree. At least five different volumes of Oneida County histories precede this one. Pomroy Jones started it off in 1851 with Annals and Recollections of Oneida County. Judge Jones was born in 1789 in what would become Lairdsville, Oneida County, and spent an entire active life here. Samuel Durant followed with his county history in 1878. Daniel Wager in 1896 published Our County and It's People. Then Henry H. Cookinham wrote a county history covering 1700 to 1912. And finally Virginia Kelly, with a committee of active local historians produced a comprehensive county history in 1977. So it is a bit presumptuous to even hint that this book is breaking new ground. We owe a great deal to each of these earlier efforts.

However, let me just suggest that there is a new reality in these pages about what has been occurring, over 200 years, and where it all might be taking us. For that we are indebted to the contributing authors.

The Oneida County Legislature, County Executive Ralph Eannace, Jr. and County Historian Joe Kelly have been immensely supportive of a host of Bicentennial projects, of which this is one.

Through the generous cooperation of the Observer-Dispatch, articles by Frank Tomaino and John Pitaressi that appeared earlier in the Observer-Dispatch are reproduced here in edited form. In return for this privilege a portion of book sales will be donated to the newspaper's Operation Sunshine Fund for Children.

The Board of Trustees of the Oneida County Historical Society, Society volunteers, Administrator Kevin Marken and staff have provided the needed financial support and muscle to accomplish a host of chores from accounting to distribution. Without them this book would not be published.

I am indebted to Robert Montesano for his help and guidance in the early planning stages of this book.

The active involvement of the twenty-six town and city historians, together with the Rome Historical Society and the fourteen other County Historical Societies, was key to providing a depth of information on each "four corners" where we live.

In the space of twenty-one years, since the preceding county history was completed, book production has completely adopted new digital technology.

Pieshare, Inc., in the work of Cynthia Long and partner Sharon Piechowicz, made that transition and provided this volume's design, typography, photo scans, enhancements, and keyboarded a mountain of text from many different sources. They did it with unerring good judgement and good humor.

Canterbury Press, Rome, NY, is an employee-owned printer that provided a breadth of skills in fine color and black and white reproduction together with quality-conscious management throughout.

One of the unheralded strengths of Oneida County's economy lies in the capabilities and competitive skills of our graphic arts, printing and publishing companies. It is well demonstrated by the book you are now holding and the fact that we never once considered going "out of county" to achieve this result at an attractive price to the reader.

Donald F. White
October 1998

This table-top exhibit won a first place award in the 1998 History Day Competition. The work of African American students at the John F. Kennedy Middle School in Utica, it explains the history of Kente Cloth and Mud Cloth in the migration of African textile designs to the United States.

Gail Wolczanski, New Hartford School System teacher, for the past 24 years, developed a Time-Line Project program for intermediate students in Oneida County helping them to uncover history that links family, town and county events.

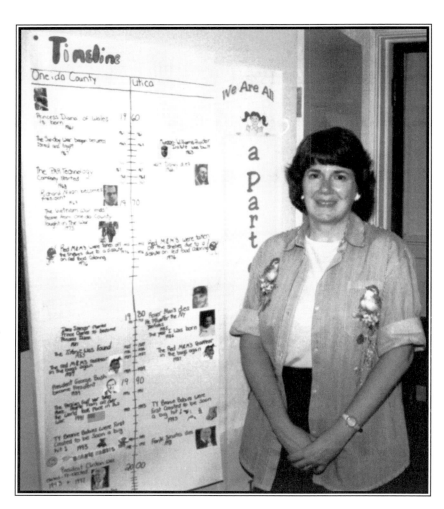

Exploring History

Donald F. White

"How will we know it's us... without our past?"

As the Okies, in John Steinbeck's Grapes of Wrath, packed to leave their dust ravaged farm and head west, they had to decide what personal belongings simply could not be left behind. Some things, they determined, are important because those possessions identified their lives up to that time...a doll, for instance, a rifle or a book. "How will we know it's us...without our past?" they asked. And that is a question that this book helps to answer for those of us living in Oneida County. It is a narrative of two hundred years of our family. What we've done. Where we've been. Why we fought. Who we loved. What we built and accomplished. What failed. How we picked up the pieces and went on. It is a story, too, about the land, the forest and the waters of Oneida County that provide crops and livestock and power for mills of all kinds, and materials to build with. But mostly, it is a story about people and what they believed. Why they came here. Why they stayed.

Like the Okie's possessions, this narrative with its pictures, drawings and maps needs to have more storytellers to carry on the history of each item of interest. A doll needs a young lady of five to give her a name and role in the family. A rifle needs a grandfather to explain the notches in the barrel...the gash on the wooden stock. And a book needs a mother or father to read from it. These kinds of storytellers are in your family. With encouragement they will throw light on the many mysteries of history that remains. Find answers about ancestors...learn new facts about what really happened...why it happened. They will become explorers of history who will tell us more of the family narrative than this book can cover. Let me tell you about several such "explorers".

A West African proverb says, "Only when lions have historians will hunters stop being heroes." So historians can change peoples perspective, just by providing a better understanding of culture and heritage. Two young African American women from John F. Kennedy Middle School, in Utica, did that by telling us about "Threads Connecting Two Worlds". They created a tabletop exhibit on African clothing that won first place in the 1998 National History Day competition among local schools. The exhibit was one of many prepared by fourth – fifth and sixth graders to explore a theme, "Immigration". The 1999-challenge theme for junior historians is "Technology". Any school

can submit entrants. National History Day is sponsored by the New York State Historical Association, in Cooperstown. Patrick Peterson of the Holland Patent School Teachers Center, is the Mohawk Valley coordinator.

President Harry Truman had a comment about why history is important. He said, "The only new thing in the world is the history you don't know." Gail Wolczanski, of New Hartford, found a way to teach that observation to intermediate grade students through a Time Line project that she developed for the County Bicentennial. The student's task is to present important happenings in their family together with events in their town and county's history, along a vertical time line. A frequent reaction from students who got involved was, "I didn't know that! I learned that my Mom and Dad met in Vietnam during the war." Or..."Now I get it!" When a new link is made connecting family happenings and town or county events. (A typical Oneida County time line chart is included in the Appendix of this book.)

Coming from a family of teachers, Gail started her work in the New Hartford School system in 1974. Her time line project builds on a unit for fifth grade Social Studies that Gail developed called ..."History – What is it?" She adds, "History is not just confined to text books. The students become historians by learning to search out and interpret new sources, formulate answers that involve research; interviewing people who lived during an event they are studying or searching out artifacts. Students get more involved today and are actually re-evaluating events as they see them in history."

Before Dr. Helen Schwartz came to Utica, she found that exploring oral history, with her students at Franklin and Marshall College, produced new and exciting links for the students with parents and older family members. Today she is using that experience to assist the Oneida Indian Nation in creating a cultural resource of traditional lore.

"The value of oral history," Dr. Schwartz pointed out, "Is in gaining understanding of the actions of people who are not necessarily figures of prominence. These are people, such as older family members, whose knowledge is too easily lost in the writing of history. Often they tell us about the things that affect our lives the most...practical knowledge and decisions that form handed-down traditions."

"One tradition that has been handed down with great meaning among the Oneidas, is the annual receiving of 'Treaty Cloth'. This stems from the Treaty of Canandaigua, in 1794. It promised rights to ancestral land and a distribution of textile cloth to each Oneida – each year – in recognition of the Nations' contribution to the colonists. Each year the price of cloth would rise, so that allotment would shrink, but the amount of cloth did not matter. The tradition of claiming the cloth was tangible proof that the Federal treaties were in full force. And so each generation learned the importance of making the claim."

"Oral history gathering," Dr. Schwartz continued, "Generates excitement in uncovering the lives of people close to us. The things that the Elders tell me about are things that enrich daily life, rather being momentous milestones. Our objective is to make this information more accessible to Oneida families who are often large, extended families and who have time constraints as we all do."

The genus "genealogy explorer" is undoubtedly the most numerous of all specie of historian in Oneida County. It is also safe to say that the personal computer, the internet and world-wide-web have put tools in the hands of the family genealogist that are exciting for even the most casually interested. In addition to more extensive access to data sources, the Web links up genealogists, nationally and internationally, who enjoy exchanging family name research. Software developments, also, have turned family genealogists into family story tellers with the ability to publish the usual birth, marriage, death statistics together with photographs, personal letters, legal documents and other memorabilia that livens family interest. Suddenly the search for ancestors becomes more interesting and a collaborative family effort.

Oneida County residents have extensive sources to turn to for family data too. The Oneida County Historical Society in Utica and the Rome Historical Society are open five days a week with paid staff to help. And there are fifteen other historical societies throughout the County in addition to the historians for each township. The County's public libraries and the Mid-York Library System provide a wide variety of data sources. In addition, the Family History Center of the Church of Latter Day Saints, located in Whitesboro, provides access to all databases at the Family History Library in Salt Lake City, Utah. For help in accessing national and international family data, the Library of Congress maintains one of the world's premier collections of reference sources. The Library's Local History and Genealogy Reading Room can be reach at (202) 707-5537, and their on-line catalog and family name index can be accessed at http://lcweb.loc.gov/rr/geneology/.

For the past twenty-four years Kevin L. Miller has been following his favorite pastime of recording family data found in small Oneida County cemeteries. Growing up in New Hartford, he started to trace his family tree as a teenager and reports tracing about 7,700 Miller-Stockbridge family members, so far. When he found the graves of his great-great grandparents covered with grass and branches in a Boonville Cemetery he decided he wanted to do something to preserve the information on grave markers in village and family plots before they were lost to acid rain and neglect.

In his summertime travels Kevin has researched over 400 cemeteries. During the winter he has begun an internet website that has grown to more than 300 pages with information on 30,000 names. Kevin says he is uploading between 2,000 to 3,000 names a month. You can access his

Dr. Helen Schwartz looks over a painting of Shako:wi's Dream at the Oneida Indian Nation Shako:wi Center. She brings her experience in oral history gathering to assist the Nation's Elders to record a heritage of experience for Oneida families.

research and leave questions for follow-up through his e-mail address: www.rootsweb.com/nyoneida.

———

"To re-awaken pride in the villages of Oneida County; that's a big reason for my painting," said Jim Parker. "Once you explore their history – study early maps – listen to some of the old-timers and current village leaders, you know what that village is most proud of," Jim continued. "Then you can re-create the way that village looked and worked at a time when it was perhaps more self-sufficient, and reinstill that pride, today."

Since 1985 Parker has worked with more than 90 village historical societies and civic groups, between the St. Lawrence and the Susquehanna rivers, to paint historic snapshots of their towns; including all the towns in Oneida County.

Jim has contributed two watercolors to this volume. The Bicentennial County Map begins the section of individual town histories. The map depicts the routes of early canal development, turnpikes and Indian trails over a period from late 1700s to mid 1800s. Bordering the map are small paintings of a key subject that characterizes each town in Oneida County.

The second watercolor is a birds-eye view of the Battle of Oriskany, on August 1777, that follows page 16. As he explains in the text, accompanying this work, Jim's ancestors took part in this battle. Two were killed and one, William Clapsaddle, who was then sixteen years old, returned to Ilion to build the farm that Jim and his wife, Hilda, now run.

"Artists, too often, don't explore history for the visual details," Jim commented. We were very careful to illustrate the dress of the different military and Indian forces as well as the weapons that they used. Most of all it was important to reflect the latest research on the location of the ambush of General Herkimer and the terrain over which fighting took place for more than five hours that day."

Joseph Robertaccio and Edward J. Kupiec, of Utica, were able to supply that research. They had been exploring the history of the battle for a number of years. Using first person accounts of survivors and aerial mapping, in black and white – color and reflective infrared, they located the path of the military road that the militia traveled toward Fort Stanwix. They were also able to determine that a high windstorm had previously leveled a swath of virgin trees on either side of the road which afforded excellent cover for the ambush; increasing its effectiveness and the confusion and vulnerability of the militia during the rest of the fighting.

"This was very resourceful research," said Jim Parker. "It altered some previously held visions of the terrain and the greater distance, two to three miles, over which General Herkimer's forces were embattled along the road. I have taken an aerial view, perhaps 1,000 feet up, to convey these aspects."

Referring to his paintings of villages, Jim remarked, "This is a wonderful way to educate kids about art and history. When I meet with fourth or fifth graders, I pick out details of the painting that I've picked up in my exploration, to describe a person who lived in that village, and we talk about what they did. I also want the kids to see there's no miracle in what I do. I just use a piece of paper and kindergarten watercolors."

Joseph Robertaccio and E.J. Kupiec, at the Oriskany Battlefield monument, used reflective infra-red aerial photography and written first person accounts to locate the most probable route of the military road along which General Herkimer's militia were ambushed on August 1777.

Oneida Arts

Oneida County has rich traditions in both folk and academic arts. It has supported native and itinerant artists since the early 19th century, when Kirkland, Trenton and Utica emerged as cultural centers. Kirkland was an early scientific and literary center because of Hamilton College. Trenton attracted many artists and writers who came to view Trenton Falls. Utica demonstrated support for the arts in its three, early museums — Stowell and Bishops Museum, the Utica Museum, and Peales' Museum. Today, county residents are enriched by several institutions — Munson Williams Proctor Institute with growing teaching facilities and student body; the Root Art Center at Hamilton College; the Kirkland Art Center; the Rome Art and Community Center; Dodge-Pratt-Northam Center in Boonville and others providing a wide range of programs to serve a public concerned with the arts.

Utica Public Library

Peales Museum opened 1828.

Munson-Williams-Proctor Institute founded in 1935; centered in this building completed in 1961 by architect Phillip Johnson.

Ed Michaels photo

Oneida Textiles

The textile industry was highly important in Oneida County, from its beginnings as a home industry to the later large spinning and weaving mills, which brought in professional weavers. James Cunningham and Samuel Butterfield of New Hartford and B. French of Waterville and Clinton were among those professionals in the first half of the 19th century. Thirty-three coverlets signed by Cunningham are known (1834 to 1848) plus table-covers and linen tablecloths. Samuel Butterfield employed the same designs, and nine coverlets signed by him have been recorded. Twelve coverlets by B. French have been recorded, most with a "parading lion" border.

James Cunningham coverlet (1842) with Geo. Washington border. Collection of Munson-Williams-Proctor Institute.

Coverlet by B. French with parading lions (1835).

Oneida Glass

Oneida County was an important early center of glass making. Fuel and good sand were abundant here. There were as many as seven factories making window glass in the 19th century and the Mount Vernon Glass Company was known for its bottles, vials, flasks and flint glass tableware. Charles P. Davis & Sons, Utica Stained Glass Works started in 1850 carried on until 1941. Today the art of stained glass has been revived by local craftsmen.

Oneida County Historical Society

Vernon Glass Decanter.

1859 advertisement of Charles P. Davis Glass Works.

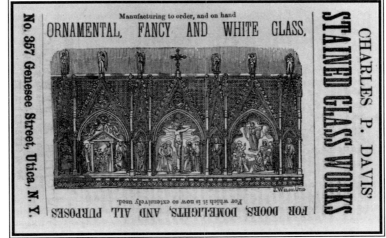

Munson-Williams-Proctor Institute

Oneida Pottery

One of the earliest potteries west of the Hudson was started in 1801 by Eastus Barnes in Clinton. Here "Redware" was produced from ordinary brick clay and fired at relatively low temperatures. With the opening of the Erie Canal stoneware "white clay" could be shipped cheaply from Long Island and New Jersey. In Utica three competing stoneware kilns were started between 1825 – 1827 that were later taken over by Noah White. By 1838 White had a monopoly in the stoneware industry. His pottery continued under family ownership until 1910. White's pottery is notable for bold use of cobalt decoration and, in the 1880s, introduction of molded, "Flemish Ware" to compete with imports.

White's stoneware jar with leaping deer, 1849-66. Collection of Munson-Williams-Proctor Institute.

White Pottery price list, 1860. Collection of Emma Freeman.

Close to 3,000 Central New Yorkers now work for the Oneidas' diverse array of businesses and governmental offices, and the area enjoys an improved economic climate due in part to the Nation's sovereign standing. Since the 1992 opening of Turning Stone Casino, the Nation has become Oneida County's largest employer.

The granite boulder known as the legendary standing stone of the Oneida People is located on the Nation's aboriginal land at Oneida today.

Pictured with the Oneida standing stone at the Nation Council House is Oneida youth Tsilos Edwards, of the Wolf Clan.

The Oneidas use tribe revenues from business operations to fund a rebuilding of their nearly-lost community in an amazing revival of a Nation.

Oneida Indian Nation

Susan He'bert Gleason

In the beginning, this place was only darkness and water until the time when a woman fell from the sky world. Water creatures dwelling here, concerned for the woman's safety, created this land as a platform for the woman with turtle agreeing to hold the land upon his back, which became known as Mother Earth.

Thus begins the ancient Oneida creation story, expressing the Oneidas' understanding of how they came into this world. The creation story continues explaining that the woman who had fallen was pregnant and gave birth to a daughter, who in turn would eventually bear twin sons and die in childbirth. The twins exhibited polarities of character — one was Dark Minded, the other of the Good Mind. From the daughter's body grew the corn, beans and squash, which are known as the sustainers of life.

The twins eventually battled and the Good Minded twin was victorious. The Dark Minded twin had favored the nomadic way of life, moving with the seasons — hunting and gathering wild foods. The introduction and cultivation of corn replaced the nomadic way of life.

Archeological studies suggest that native peoples have lived in Oneida County for approximately 10,000 years — first, as hunters and gatherers, later establishing permanent settlements in villages. Their homes were longhouses made from bark about 20 feet wide and 100 feet or more in length.

Oneida County is filled with reminders of its namesake. Numerous streets, businesses and villages bear the proud name of "Oneida". But who are the Oneida or Onyotaa:ka — the People of the Standing Stone? They have lived in this area since time immemorial and have been good neighbors, friends and allies. Oneida soldiers served in all of the wars with the United States from then up to this day. From the formation of the United States to the present day, Oneidas have played a major role in the county's and country's development.

Members of the Oneida Indian Nation have inhabited the lands comprising Oneida County and beyond for millennia. The Nation's ancestral land in New York State reached from the St. Lawrence River in the north to what is now the Pennsylvania border to the south. Together with the Mohawk, Cayuga, Onondaga, Seneca and Tuscarora, the Oneida Nation was a part of the Iroquois Confederacy — or more properly in the Oneida language, the Haudenosaunee (Iroquois is of French derivation and has a negative connotation to many Haudenosaunee people.)

The confederacy was formed centuries ago when the Peacemaker brought his message of unity to the disparate nations, creating the most famous Native American government on the continent. The confederacy had a profound affect upon colonial American history, greatly influencing the founding fathers of the United States. It is recorded that the principles of the confederacy attracted the colonial leaders because it posed as a model for a confederation which respected its members' independence while simultaneously promoting justice and equal rights for all.

The Peacemaker, who was accompanied by Hiawatha and with his aid urged the nations to be joined in cooperation, also brought the message the Haudenosaunee refer to as the Great Law. Under the Great Law of Peace, the nations became of one blood — addressing one another as family members. Chiefs of the nations became members of the Confederacy's deliberative assembly.

Through the tenets of the Great Law, members of each Nation were divided into clans which are determined matrilineally. The Oneida Nation has three clans, Turtle, Wolf, and Bear. Leaders of each clan are nominated by the women of each clan, and then presented to and approved by all the Nation's clans.

In the 1600s, when the Europeans first began to penetrate Oneida lands, the Nation sought peaceful co-existence, as the Great Law requires. Europeans were originally hoping to find gold, silver, spices or sugar — items not indigenous to the region. Beaver pelts, however, were readily available, and highly sought after in Europe for hats. The Oneidas, and other Haudenosaunee, began trading the pelts and other furs for brass kettles, spun cloth and iron tools.

Due to these interactions, a Covenant Chain was forged between the Haudenosaunee and the Dutch and later the British, which was an alliance based upon mutual respect, defense and trade.

13

But the peace was to prove short-lived, as the disgruntled colonists sought to extricate themselves from British rule. The Oneidas and Tuscaroras allied themselves with the colonists while the other members of the Confederacy sided with the British. The Oneidas were the first allies to the colonists' cause.

Oneidas fought bravely at major battles of the Revolutionary War. One of the bloodiest battles took place in present day Oneida County, the Battle of Oriskany. This battle was to prove decisive in the outcome of the war. On Aug. 6, 1777, under the command of Gen. Herkimer, a large group of Oneidas and the colonial militia were able to stop the advance of a British expeditionary force marching from the Great Lakes under Gen. St. Leger, who was attempting to move east and join Gen. Burgoyne and his forces, who were marching south from Canada. If the two forces had united, they could have successfully divided the colonies in half.

However, this union was not to be. While more than 500 people died in the opening volley of the battle, and Gen. Herkimer would meet his demise, the battle was considered a military victory for the colonists. The Oneidas and colonists prevented the British forces from joining, a pivotal event that contributed to Burgoyne's loss at the Battle of Saratoga.

Several Oneidas distinguished themselves on that August day, among them Han Yerry. This Oneida man fought valiantly, even after withstanding an injury. With the aid of his wife — who loaded his gun — Han Yerry continued to shoot at the enemy. His wife, one of his sons and his half-brother also fought with valor. Han Yerry died as a result of the battle, but his wife escaped and spread the word of the terrible slaughter. Although the colonists were defeated at Oriskany, with the help of the Oneidas, they ultimately won the campaign. They, and their colonial allies, are honored at the Oriskany Battlefield Historic Site located on Rte. 69 near the Village of Oriskany just east of Rome. But, this was not an isolated instance of Oneida valor during the War of Independence.

In the treacherous winter of 1777-78, George Washington's troops were freezing and starving at their encampment at Valley Forge. Oneida Chief Skenandoah and several other Oneidas carried 600 bushels of corn to aid their colonial allies. They were accompanied by an Oneida woman, Polly Cooper, who taught Washington's starving soldiers how to properly prepare the corn. Because she would not accept payment, a shawl and a bonnet were given to her as tokens of appreciation for her kindness by Martha Washington. The shawl remains a major treasure of the Oneida Nation today and in recent years, has been on display at least once each year at the Nation's Shako:wi Cultural Center on Rte. 46 in Oneida.

Because of their allegiance to the colonists, the Oneidas suffered retribution from the other members of the Confederacy after the war. In 1779, the Oneida fortress, which was a principal village at what now is

The clans (families) of the Oneida Nation are depicted in the Nation Seal. The Wolf, Turtle, and Bear clans are shown inside a pine tree representing the Iroquois tree of peace.

Oneida men and women fought and died at Oriskany as America's first allies. While the other Iroquois nations sided with the British, the Oneidas' loyalty was rewarded by more favorable provisions in subsequent United States-Oneida Nation treaties.

Oneida Castle, was destroyed. The Oneidas had to seek food and shelter elsewhere in the Mohawk Valley. They endured great suffering living as virtual refugees, until they ultimately returned to their homeland in 1784.

Ten years later, through the paramount 1794 Treaty of Canandaigua, the Oneidas received special protection for their lands, which included many acres in Oneida County and continued recognition of the Nation's sovereignty. The Oneidas' agreement varied from that accorded other nations of the Confederacy, due to the Oneidas' alliance with the United States from its inception. The treaty states: "Whereas, in the late war between Great Britain and the United States of America, a body of the Oneida ... Indians, adhered faithfully to the United States, and assisted them with their warriors ... And as the United States in the time of their distress, acknowledged their obligations to these faithful friends and promised to reward them ..."

This treaty is held sacred by the Oneidas and is commemorated by the yearly allocation of treaty cloth to Oneida Members from the federal government. To the Oneidas, the treaty cloth is continued affirmation that the agreement between the United States and the Oneida Nation remains intact.

Unfortunately, through a series of unscrupulous "treaties" orchestrated by New York State immediately following the Revolutionary War, the promises made by the federal government, to preserve and protect the rights of the Oneidas to their ancestral lands, were ignored. One

Oneida leader, Good Peter, made a poignant address, referring to New York State's attempts to claim Oneida lands: "The voice of the birds from every quarter cried out "You have lost your country — You have lost your country — You've lost your country! You have acted unwisely and done wrong.' And what increased the alarm was that the birds who made this cry were white birds."

The Haudenosaunee lands were considered a major stepping stone to the way west with Oneida lands especially attractive to the growing United States. One integral land area was the "Oneida carry" — a critical portage linking the Mohawk River to Oneida Lake. Access to Oneida Lake would in turn allot passage to the Great Lakes and western expansion. Gradually, the Oneidas' homeland decreased until the 6 million acre ancestral homeland diminished to a mere 32 acres. In the 1830s a large number of Oneidas relocated to Wisconsin or Canada. This exodus was preceded by individual Oneidas selling lands which belonged to the Oneida Nation — land which individual Members had no right to sell. However, many Oneidas refused to abandon their ancestral land for any price and remained in New York State with the Oneida Nation.

Years of poverty followed for the Oneidas who kept the sacred fire of the homeland burning. But a core group of committed persistent people kept the dream of regaining the lands illegally taken from the Nation alive. Mary Cornelius Winder was one of these people. Unhappy with

Reviving and preserving the distinct Oneida culture is a paramount goal of the Nation's leadership. Shown in traditional dress at the ceremonial repatriation of wampum are Oneida Nation government leaders, from left: Marilyn John, Bear Clan Mother; Clint Hill, Turtle Clan representative to the Men's Council; Brian Patterson, Bear Clan representative to the Men's Council, and Ray Halbritter, Nation Representative.

A shawl belonging to the descendants of Oneida woman Polly Cooper often goes on display at the Nation. Oral history records that Polly aided George Washington's starving troops at Valley Forge, and was given the shawl as a token of appreciation for her good will and concern.

the treatment many Oneidas endured while living on the Onondaga Reservation, Mary sought federal recognition for the Oneidas' plight and return of the Nation's lands. For over 30 years, Mary Winder persisted in an active letter writing campaign seeking to regain Nation lands. At great personal sacrifice, she traveled to Washington to try to remedy the wrongs done to the Oneida People. Because of Mary Winder, and those Oneidas who contributed to those efforts, the Nation is reacquiring its ancestral homelands in Oneida and Madison counties. In two separate decisions dated 1974 and 1985, the Supreme Court ruled the New York State treaties were illegal and that the Oneida Nation could seek to redress these illegal acts.

The Nation, after fruitless years of negotiations, decided not to wait for the land claim settlement to regain its ancestral lands and launched an economic drive that started with bingo in a trailer and has grown into the Turning Stone Casino Resort — a tourism destination that draws 3 million people to Oneida County annually. The resort houses New York State's only casino and boasts a 285-room hotel, spa, restaurants and upscale retail shops. A championship golf course and convention center are under construction.

With the Nation's new-found prosperity, it once again is involved in the area's victories, this time involved in an economic resurgence. The Oneida Nation is a major force behind the economic rebound in Oneida County and the Mohawk Valley. In an area decimated by business and military base closings, the Nation is offering Oneida County and its citizens an economic revival. The Nation remains a constant in the area — and is here to stay.

Because of the thriving Turning Stone Casino Resort located in Verona and 15 other diverse enterprises of the Nation's, the area is beginning to enjoy an economic rebound. The Nation is the largest employer in Oneida and Madison counties with an employment base of 2,850. In addition, the Nation has sparked and helped fund a four-county and Oneida Nation cooperative tourism promotion effort that already is yielding exceptional results.

The revenue from these enterprises is being used in more than 60 programs and services offered to Oneida Nation Members. Housing, education and health insurance benefits are but a few of the advantages the Nation is now able to offer its Members.

The greater community is also reaping benefits from the Nation's success. Not only is the Nation providing employment opportunities, it also is helping the surrounding communities in a monetary way. Through the Silver Covenant Chain Education Grants, the Oneida Nation compensates area school districts for tax revenues lost — because of its non-taxable status as a sovereign Nation — when the Oneidas reacquire lands. The Vernon-Verona-Sherrill District in Oneida County is just one of the recipients.

Allies in war and peace, the Oneida Indian Nation continues to hold tight to its covenants with the United States. Its interest in Oneida and Madison counties parallels the interest of the rest of the region's inhabitants — ensuring the future of the faces yet unborn.

Former Nation Clerk Gloria Halbritter, seated, and current Nation Clerk Kim Jacobs, both of the Wolf Clan, display treaty cloth provided to the Oneida Nation for distribution to Members by the United States. The cloth is the tangible symbol that the two nations still maintain the covenants of the Treaty of Canandaigua of 1794. The treaty affirms the Nation's reservation area and the Nation's "free use and enjoyment" of the land.

Mary Winder
From the time she was a young girl and throughout her life, Oneida Mary Winder worked to regain Oneida lands. She is the grandmother of the current Nation Representative, Ray Halbritter, who carries on her legacy to right the injustice of the Oneidas illegal loss of at least 300,000 acres of lands and natural resources.

The Battle of Oriskany

Folk artist, Jim Parker of Ilion, NY (German Flats) speaks about his painting, done for the Friends of the Oriskany Battle Site, from whom prints are available.

"It was a special privilege to recreate this event since our own family had four members in Colonel Bellinger's and Colonel Klock's militia who became engaged early in the battle. One member named Stahl (Steele) and Major Enos Klepsettle (Clapsaddle) were killed. William Clapsaddle, who built the home we live in was there fighting, at age 16.

"The defense of farms and villages in the Mohawk Valley brought nearly 800 Tryon County Militia and 62 Oneida Indians in answer to General Herkimer's call from Fort Dayton (Village of Herkimer). At the base of the painting participants from both sides are accurately depicted with their weapons of war.

"British forces under General Barry St Leger had laid siege to Fort Stanwix (Rome, NY). St. Leger's forces included 400 British Regular troops; 1,000 Mohawk and Seneca Indians, John Butler's Indian Department force; Sir John Johnson's Royal Regiment of New York, 400 men, plus a detachment of 100 Hessian mercenaries.

"Molly Brant, the sister of Mohawk Chief Joseph Brant, sent scouts to warn St. Leger of the Tryon county Militia's march as they left Fort Dayton, August 4, 1777. An ambush site was picked by the British and Indians, four miles east of Fort Stanwix. Here an earlier severe windstorm had leveled a wide swath of virgin trees on either side of the military road leading to the Fort. The site gave excellent cover among the downed trees, and the road had to traverse a small creek that led northward to the Mohawk River. Fully a mile beyond the creek the Hessian detachment was positioned across the road on high ground to prevent passage beyond that point. All the Indians, Butler's and Johnson's forces took cover on both sides of the road for a distance of two to three miles.

"The battle scene depicts the action on August 7, 1777, shortly after the foreguard group of the Canajoharie District Militia, under Colonel Cox, came under heavy attack, at the head of the militia column, from Indian forces. Hessian troops appeared and fired their short Yager rifles, point blank, at the surprised militia.

"General Herkimer, on a white horse, is shown galloping east on the Military Road to form other units of the militia into defensive positions. Colonel Cox and most of the forward militia are killed or wounded in this early action. The supply wagons in the middle of the column are now under full attack, on both sides, by Indians and Tories dressed as Indians. Colonel Klock's German Flatts and Colonel Bellinger's Kingsland Militias are now under attack from the north and the south. Colonel Fischer's Mohawk Militia and the Cherry Valley Militia are retreating to the north along the small creek. Shortly General Herkimer will be shot through the leg, killing his horse. Due to the length of the militia column, the fighting develops three battle areas where the militia attempt to form-up defenses, and fight in pairs.

"The battle lasted over five hours, in total, interrupted by a heavy downpour of rain. When fighting resumed no quarter was asked or given in dozens of individual combats. Men strived to kill each other with knives, spears, clubs, rifles and tomahawks. The end came as both sides, too weary to continue, disengaged.

"Over 450 of the Tryon County Militia were killed, wounded or captured. Five Seneca Indian Chiefs were killed, and many of the hostile Indians left the area, fleeing north. The Hessian and Tory forces retreated to encampments around Fort Stanwix only to find that, while they were away, soldiers from the Fort had taken their supplies, ammunition, maps and records. A few days later, on news of General Benedict Arnold's approach with a column of Colonial Regulars, General St. Leger gave up the siege and retreated in haste to Canada, leaving the western Mohawk valley secure."

Oriskany

...to preserve our land and freedom ....

777 >-

Jim Parker '98

MUSKET — American Long Rifle — PIKE

Oneidas - Chief Shenandoa   800 TRYON COUNTY MILITIA   Major General Nicolas Herkimer
German Flatts, Mohawk, Palantine, Cherry Valley, Schongrie,
Col. Bellinger, Col. Fischer, Shenandoa, Col. Cox, Col. Klock, Col. Veeder, Col. Campbell, Col. Paris, Capt. Seiber

....to those who fought so bravely......

Battle of the
AUGUST 6, 1

Officer's Sword — Knife — Ballhead War Club — Pipe Tomahawk — "BROWN BESS"

General Barry St. Leger | BUTLER'S GREENS | HESSIANS | British Regulars | Canadian Regulars | Mohawk
Col. John Butler, Sir John Johnson, Major Watts, Seneca, Onondaga, Chief Joseph Brant

Oneida County – born at right time, in the right place

By Frank Tomaino

The mid-1790s was a time of discontent for many pioneers who lived along Herkimer County's western frontier. They longed for a county of their own.

They wanted to govern themselves, enact and enforce their own laws, have their neighbors represent them in the State Assembly, set up their own fire and police protection and court system and decide for themselves where and when their roads would be built.

Most of all, they were weary of having to travel 20 miles and more over narrow, rugged dirt roads to Herkimer to conduct legal and other business.

What they did about it … and the distinctive geographical location they chose for their new county … would shape the future of Oneida County.

Hugh White, who founded White's Town in 1784, was one of the discontented. Jedediah Sanger, founder of New Hartford in 1788, was another. So was Moses Foot of Clinton and James Dean of Westmoreland.

They and their neighbors were of tough stock … strong, courageous men and women from places like Connecticut and Massachusetts who left their homes in the mid-1780s, journeyed up the Mohawk River and settled in the river's upper region. They had tamed its wild woods and harnessed the raging power of its many creeks and rivers.

Many were veterans of the just-ended Revolutionary War who left New England, marched to and fought at places like Fort Stanwix (where Rome is today) and beyond. They saw firsthand the region's fertile soil and lush forests with countless trees with which to build homes and boats, and abounding in animals large and small to hunt and trap. They spent the late 1780s spreading the news back in New England of the many attractions along New York's western frontier.

By the 1790s, though, they were a discontented lot and had begun to lobby Albany for a local government of their own.

Two hundred years ago … on March 15, 1798 … they got their wish. The State Legislature took tens of thousands of acres from vast western Herkimer County and formed an Oneida County … so named, legend has it, by a gentleman at a White's Town meeting who admired the Oneida Indians, but whose name is lost to history.

The new county … which was the home of the Oneidas for many years … was vast, too, extending north to what today is Lewis and Jefferson Counties, and west to include part of today's Oswego County.

But it was its unique geographical location and not its vastness that would influence greatly its inhabitants through the years and determine where and how many of them would work, pray, learn and socialize and the routes they would travel.

It was a location that would make Oneida County different from neighboring Herkimer, Madison, Lewis, Otsego and Chenango counties and contribute to its emergence as the region's most populated county with the two largest cities … Utica and Rome … the most manufacturing industry and the center of higher education.

River strategic

Long before permanent settlers arrived in what now is Oneida County, members of the Oneida Indian Nation lived in the region. "Onia" meant "stone" in their native tongue so they were called "Oneyotka-ono" or "Oniota-aug" since they were known as "the people of the upright stone," which alluded to a large stone that was sacred to them.

They built their villages in the region, planted their corn and squash and conducted their council gatherings around their sacred stone. They also hacked trails through virgin forests to the two most vital sites in the region … sites where later would grow the cities of Utica and Rome.

The first was a fording place in the then-very wide and turbulent Mohawk River. It was the only place in the river that was so shallow they easily could wade across and head north to the Adirondacks to hunt and fish.

In the 1750s, during the French and Indian War, the British built Fort Schuyler near the ford to serve as a supply fort and a garrison if the French tried to capture the strategic site. (They never did.)

In the 1780s, settlers also were attracted to the ford

and began to build homes, stores, inns and taverns there. The settlement grew into a village and, in 1832, into the city of Utica.

The other site important to the Oneidas was "The Great Carry"...a mile-long stretch of land between the Mohawk River and Wood Creek where one could travel west from river to creek to Oneida Lake and, via the Oneida and Oswego rivers, to Lake Ontario and the other Great Lakes. In effect, the carrying spot allowed one to travel from the Atlantic Ocean to the Great Lakes via the Mohawk and Hudson rivers.

The British also recognized the "carry" as a strategic piece of land. At the beginning of the French and Indian War, they built Fort Williams nearby and later Forts Bull, Craven, Newport, Wood Creek, Rickey and the much larger Fort Stanwix. By the 1780s, the site was attracting settlers like Dominick Lynch. Eventually, the settlements there would evolve into the city of Rome.

Whitestown's namesake **Hugh White**, *who founded White's Town in 1784, was one of the pioneers who led the fight in the 1790s for the formation of an Oneida County.*

He was born in Middletown, Conn., in 1733 and served in the quartermaster with the American Continentals during the Revolutionary War.

In 1783, he and a group of other men bought land near what is today Whitestown, and White was sent there to survey the purchase. He liked what he saw — fertile soil and an abundance of water and trees.

In early 1784, White — at age 51 — left Connecticut for good and journeyed along the Mohawk River with his family. When they reached the mouth of Sauquoit Creek, they cleared the land, planted crops and built homes. White's Town was born.

Through the years, he served as justice of the peace and when Oneida County was formed March 15, 1798, he was commissioned to "keep the peace" and was appointed one of its first judges.

Judge White died April 16, 1812, at age 79.

Many transportation routes in Oneida County today date back to pre-colonial days. Indian trails evolved into thoroughfares like the Genesee Road, Seneca Turnpike, Route 20, Route 5 and the Thruway. The flat, east-west, water level routes between Utica and Rome attracted builders of not only roads, but also railroads and canals. Even today, the Amtrak tracks, the Thruway and the Erie Canal run side by side.

And it was Oneida County's ideal location that convinced builders of the first Erie Canal in 1817 that they should build the middle section first ... the section between Utica and Rome. The soft earth and flat terrain promised no major problems in construction and quick progress, thus quieting the foes of the canal.

Water spurred industry

The strategic location of the new Oneida County also led to its first manufacturing industries ... flour, saw and gristmills operated by water power generated by the

After the close of the American Revolution, Utica was the gateway to the "Western District of New York." Egbert N. Clark painted this local historical scene in oil, watercolor and pencil in 1932.

region's dozens of rushing streams.

Early settlers like the Whites, Sangers, Foots and Deans built their mills along creeks like Oriskany and Sauquoit. They were followed by pioneers like John and Ann Bloomfield of Annsville, Christian Reall of Deerfield, Gerritt Boon of Trenton, Ebenezer Harger of Ava, James Farwell of Bridgewater, John Bellinger of Utica, Jesse Curtiss of Camden and Barnabas Mitchell of Remsen.

In the early 1800s, that same water power helped to create a textile industry... Oneida County's next major manufacturing industry.

Enterprising young people like Seth Capron and Benjamin Walcott established the first cotton and woolen mills in the state in Whitestown and soon were employing hundreds of people.

In the 1840s, local mills began to lose business to mills in New England, that had discarded water power and were operating with more efficient steam power. Once again, Oneida County's ideal

New Hartford's founder **Jedediah Sanger** *was one of the first pioneers to settle in the Upper Mohawk Region.*

He founded New Hartford in 1788 and spent the early 1790s working to convince state legislators in Albany to form an Oneida County.

Sanger was born in Sherburne, Middlesex County, Mass., in 1751.

He successfully operated several businesses in New England — including a tavern and store — until a disastrous fire forced him into bankruptcy.

He had heard about White's Town in Central New York with its fertile soil, lush forests and many streams, so in 1788 he bought 1,000 acres there for 50 cents an acre. The next year, he; moved his family to the region, founded New Hartford and erected a saw and grist mill along Sauquoit Creek.

He later spent many years as a member of the state Senate and Assembly and also was one of Whitestown's first supervisors.

When Oneida County was formed in 1798, he was appointed one of its first judges.

He died June 6, 1829, at age 78.

location came to the textile industry's rescue.

The state decided to build a canal to link Pennsylvania and the Binghamton area with the Erie Canal via the Chenango Valley. The Erie passed through the center of Oneida County, so it was decided that the new Chenango Canal would join the Erie at Utica. It was completed in 1836, just in time to carry coal from fields in Pennsylvania to Oneida County ... coal needed to produce steam for modern textile mills.

The county remained a giant in the textile industry until the 1950s, employing tens of thousands of men and women through the years and attracting thousands more from other regions ... and countries, too.

Many other industries in the county's 200-year history owed their success to the county's location. Among them was the manufacture of iron made possible by the discovery of iron ore in the early 1800s in places like Clinton, Kirkland and

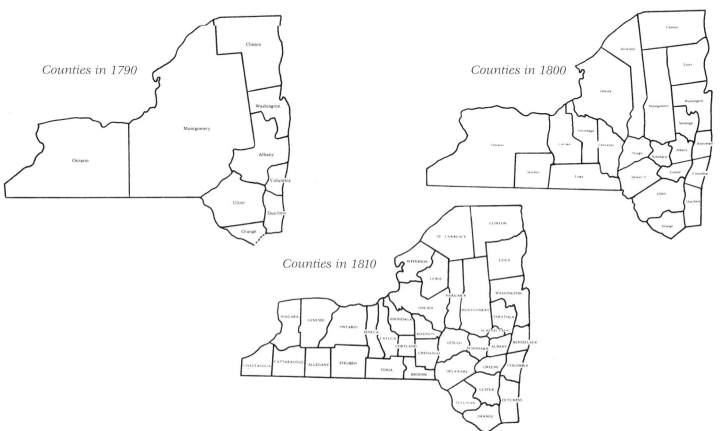

Counties in 1790

Counties in 1800

Counties in 1810

Clayville. Soon, hundreds were working in industries related to the discovery: the mining of the ore, the operation of blast furnaces that were fired up to make iron and the large number of blacksmiths needed to hammer the iron into articles like horseshoes, knives, forks, spoons, hinges and nails.

The availability of water in the region continued to play an important role in Oneida County's industrial history as late as the 1950s during the "loom-to-boom" era. Most of the county's textile mills relocated in the South and were being replaced by companies like Chicago Pneumatic, General Electric, Continental Can, Univac and Bendix. Leaders of these and other companies all agreed that one of the main reasons they had selected Oneida County as their new home was its abundant water supply.

Productive farm country

From the very beginning, agriculture was a major industry in Oneida County and, once again, the county's location played a vital role.

The region was blessed with fertile soil along rivers and streams so that, first, the Native Americans, and later the first permanent settlers could plant their corn, wheat, oats, squash and barley. The ideal climate contributed to successful crops year after year. Later in the 19th century, it supported dozens of dairy farms, sheep-raising operations and crops like hops, beans and peas.

The county's location helped farmers in another way, too. They were closer to New York City markets than were farmers in the Midwest, and that gave Oneida County farmers a big advantage when shipping milk and perishable crops in the days before refrigeration. Agriculture continues today to be an important industry in Oneida County and a major contributor to its economy.

A Bicentennial exploration of 200 years

Since the days when this region was home to the Oneida Indians, the land that now is Oneida County has seen greatness and despair, bloodshed and harmony, economic miracles and economic disasters, rapid growth and rapid population loss, important leaders and important ordinary people. This year, 1998, Oneida County celebrates its bicentennial, and Utica marks the bicentennial of its incorporation as a village.

A Bicentennial look-back at Oneida County life is the beginning for a personal exploration of events that continue to shape the future. Important themes, trends, surprises, failures and accomplishments – recounted in the following pages – are the result of the dreams and efforts of people just like you and me. We are now Oneida County, born at the right time and in the right place.

Counties in 1820

Current County outline map of New York State

Transportation

Land, water and rail travel propelled county's prosperity

By Frank Tomaino

The Erie Canal in the 19th century, looking west toward the Genesee Street bridge. The 363-mile canal cost $7 million. The section between Utica and Rome was opened October 22, 1819. The canal was complete in 1825.

Traveling on roads in Oneida County 200 years ago was an adventure to be undertaken by only the strongest and sturdiest of pioneer, wagon and beast. The few roads that did exist in the 1780s were narrow trails filled with deep holes and ruts and made impassable by the slightest rainfall.

As a result, by the time Oneida County was formed March 15, 1798, more than 90 percent of its inhabitants used rivers and other waterways, not roads, to move people and goods.

It wasn't until the Erie Canal was completed in 1825 that Oneida County began to grow and prosper.

The impact of the canal … and the railroads that followed … on Oneida County's economic, social and political life was great and continued through the first half of the 20th century.

Today, it's the region's transportation systems that greatly influence the well-being of the county.

"A good transportation network is essential in building a foundation for regional economic growth," said Steven J. DiMeo, executive vice president of The Oneida County EDGE (Economic Development Growth Enterprise).

A consultant's economic development strategy prepared for EDGE, in 1997 concluded that highway access was one of Oneida County's strengths, but its weakness was the lack of a north-south expressway.

That certainly was not a problem 200 years ago when families in New England preparing to journey to and settle in Oneida County were more concerned about the safest east-to-west routes rather than those that went north and south.

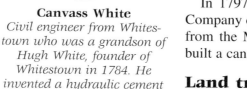

Canvass White
Civil engineer from Whitestown who was a grandson of Hugh White, founder of Whitestown in 1784. He invented a hydraulic cement (hardens under water) in the early 1820s for builders of the Erie Canal. He also was the canal's chief lock designer.

They usually chose the Mohawk River and traveled in small boats … heavier cargoes went by flat-bottomed boats called batteaux, designed for shallow waters … until they reached Old Fort Schuyler (Utica) or "The Great Carry" near Fort Stanwix (Rome).

Those who wanted to head west beyond Ft. Stanwix carried their boats from the river for a mile to Wood Creek and proceeded to Oneida Lake and from there to Lake Ontario and the other Great Lakes.

Travel on swift rivers and streams was as treacherous as it was on land, though, so by the early 1790s, settlers were demanding improvements in transportation.

In 1797, the Western Inland Navigation Company eliminated the need to carry boats from the Mohawk to Wood Creek when it built a canal across the portage.

Land travel improves

The success of a highly profitable turnpike in Pennsylvania between Philadelphia and Lancaster prompted New York state in 1800 to charter the Seneca Turnpike Co. and build an improved road from Utica's Bagg's Square south to New Hartford and then west to Vernon and Oneida Castle … along the route of today's Route 5.

The turnpike made Utica the fastest-growing community in the region as it began to attract not only westbound travelers, but also permanent settlers who ran stagecoach companies and entrepreneurs eager to build hotels, taverns, blacksmith shops and wagon repair shops.

The business of accommodating travelers became Utica's first major industry.

The county got its second turnpike in the early 1800s when the Great Western Turnpike was built through the towns of Sangerfield and Bridgewater along a path that Route 20 follows today.

Turnpikes made traveling a bit more comfortable, but transporting heavy freight to and from the county was expensive and made the prices of goods produced in the region prohibitive in Eastern markets. That problem was solved by the Erie Canal.

The Erie Canal

When talk of building a canal from the Hudson River to Lake Erie via the Mohawk Valley began in earnest, in about 1810, many powerful politicians opposed the project.

Thomas Jefferson said, "Making a canal 350 miles through wilderness ... it is a little short of madness. Perhaps in 100 years."

But in 1815, the state Legislature ... prodded by political leader DeWitt Clinton ... voted to survey the route an Erie Canal would follow. Two years later, the survey concluded that the 363-mile canal could be built for $6 million. It eventually cost $7 million.

Clinton ... by then governor of the state ... decided that work on the 94-mile middle section of the canal from Utica west to the Seneca River would be completed first since the terrain was flat and the earth soft. That meant the greatest progress could be made in the shortest time ... thus silencing opponents.

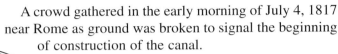

Benjamin Wright
Civil engineer from Rome who, in 1817, was picked to build the middle section of the Erie Canal between Utica and the Seneca River area to the west.

A crowd gathered in the early morning of July 4, 1817 near Rome as ground was broken to signal the beginning of construction of the canal.

Two years later, Oct. 22, 1819, the section between Utica and Rome was opened. Thousands cheered as the first boat to travel on the Erie ... the 60-foot "Chief Engineer of Rome" named for Benjamin Wright of Rome, who was the middle section's civil engineer ... left Rome for Utica towed by one horse.

When the canal was completed in 1825, it became an immediate success. Revenues poured in as 218,000 tons of freight were carried the first year. The cost of shipping cargo from Albany to Buffalo dropped from $100 to $7. The value of land along the canal increased greatly. And Utica and Rome became boom towns with Utica's population exploding in 1820-30 from 2,972 to 8,323 and Rome's from 3,569 to 4,360.

The county's population grew in that decade, too, from 50,997 to 71,326. Many of its new residents were Irish immigrants who helped to build the Erie and most were Catholic. This led to the organization of the first Catholic parish west of Albany. It was called St. John's and still exists today in downtown Utica.

The success of the Erie prompted the building of two lateral canals in Oneida County: the Chenango in 1836

Charles S. Mott
Utican who manufactured bicycle wheels and rims in Utica from 1900-05. Later began to make wheels and axles for "horseless carriages." He moved his company to Michigan and later sold it to a young company called General Motors in exchange for stock. He continued to reinvest the stock and soon owned the largest number of shares in the firm and became its richest stockholder. He was a billionaire when he died in 1973 at age 97. He founded the Automobile Club of Utica, one of nine such clubs in the United States. In 1902, he represented the city at a meeting of the other eight auto clubs in Chicago to form the American Automobile Association.

The late Charles S. Mott at the wheel of his Utica-built Remington automobile, circa 1901.

and the Black River, begun the same year.

The Chenango … from Binghamton to Utica … came at an opportune time for Utica. It was converting its textile mills to steam power and needed coal from Pennsylvania to produce that steam. The Black River began in Rome and proceeded north to the Black River in Carthage.

The Erie was ideal for hauling freight, but hauling passengers was another matter. Packet boats were small and usually over-crowded. Travelers complained about long delays as captains and crews frequented the many saloons that lined the canal. Women passengers often were accosted by "canawlers" … violent men who drank hard, fought hard and, when in need of money, would board a boat, knock a passenger on the head, rob him and then throw him overboard.

Riding the rails

It's not surprising then that the Erie lost most of its passenger business in the early 1840s when the railroads came to town.

The first railroad in the state was the Mohawk and Hudson between Albany and Schenectady. It opened in 1831. Five years later, the Utica and Schenectady began operations with six locomotives and 50 cars each with a 24-passenger capacity.

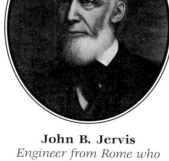

John B. Jervis
Engineer from Rome who became superintendent of construction of a large section of the Erie Canal from 1819 to 25. He later became chief engineer for construction of the Chenango Canal from Utica to Binghamton.

In 1839, the Utica and Syracuse was completed as were other short lines to the west. In 1853, Albany merchant Erastus Corning consolidated all the small railroads into the New York Central.

Although the railroad passed through Utica, it did the city more harm than good. The city's lucrative stagecoach business slowed to a standstill. When westbound passenger trains began to pass through the city instead of stopping as had the stages, many of Utica's hotels, taverns and stores closed their doors for good.

Farmers in Oneida County benefited greatly from the railroad, though, as they began to grow more and more crops for far-away markets.

Between 1850 and 1895, nearly a dozen smaller railroads originated in the county or passed through it … including the West Shore.

Many of the workers who built the West Shore in 1883 were Italian immigrants who liked what they saw in Utica and … like the Irish who had built the Erie Canal 65 years earlier … decided to settle in the city.

Railroads weren't the only modes of transportation to use tracks. Since 1860, horse-drawn trolleys had been used throughout the county. In 1890, the Utica Belt Line began to use electric trolleys from the city to places like

Jason Parker
Began the largest stagecoach operation in the settlement of Old Fort Schuyler in 1795, which later became Utica. He delivered mail and carried passengers between Whitestown and Canajoharie. In 1810, started a daily stage between Utica and Albany and later to Buffalo and Niagara Falls. At the time of his death in 1830, his company was originating eight stage runs a day to east and west destinations and 12 daily running north and south.

Canal packets were more comfortable, but for the traveler who wanted speed in 1832, the stagecoach filled the bill. Pioneer stage operator Jason Parker published this schedule the year Utica became a city, just four years before the first railroad came to town. Courtesy, Buffalo & Erie County Historical Society.

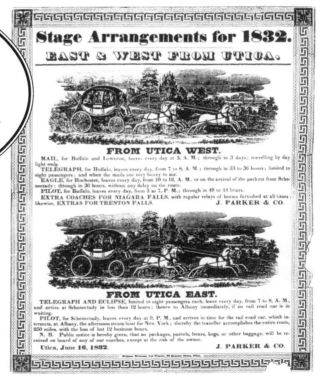

Clinton, Deerfield and Oriskany. Many thought: "Travel between communities can't get much better than trolleys."

Automobiles begin many changes

They were wrong, for at the turn of the century the automobile came to town.

In April 1900, the Saturday Globe ran a photo of Dr. Willey L. Kingsley of Rome in his Locomobile runabout and identified him as the first Oneida County resident to own a horseless carriage.

By 1901, so many others did that they formed the Automobile Club of Utica ... only one of nine such clubs in the United States.

In 1902, representatives from Utica and the other eight clubs met in Chicago and formed the American Automobile Association.

The first half of the 20th century saw many changes in transportation in Oneida County.

In 1914 New York Central opened its magnificent Union Station in Utica and made the city one of the largest freight centers in the country.

The Erie Canal was closed and the larger Barge Canal was opened in 1918.

In the second half of the century, the Oneida County Airport opened with Robinson Airlines inaugurating scheduled passenger service in 1950.

And in 1954, the Thruway opened.

John Butterfield
Utican who established the Overland Mail Company in the 1850s — the first stage to deliver U.S. mail and passengers from Missouri to California in fewer than 25 days. In Utica in 1863 he started the first horse-drawn trolley line to connect the city with New Hartford and Whitesboro.

Transportation today

Today, the county's transportation picture is a mixed bag. Planners say its limited air and rail services are an obstacle to attracting certain ... but not all ... industries. Commercial use of the Erie (Barge) Canal is on the decline, but recreational and tourism use is up.

Ridership on the county's public transit systems increases each year and planners say the trend will continue for the next 20 years. For many ... including senior citizens and people with disabilities ... buses and other transit vehicles will continue to be the only means of transportation available. Additional funds, say planners, will be needed to maintain their operations in the future. Many of their operations ... like purchasing and scheduling ... should be consolidated to save money.

While the county has an advantage over other regions with its easy access to the Thruway and other highways, its well-maintained roads and its absence of serious traffic congestion, the county's lack of a good north-south expressway puts it at a disadvantage when competing with Syracuse and its Route 81.

"It is not critical when attracting most businesses seeking new sites in the county," DiMeo said. "However, it would be a definite plus if we did have one." Traffic experts say the problem can be alleviated by improving Routes 8 and 12 south and Route 12 north.

Car 502 led the first train when the Oneida Railway "third rail" service was inaugurated between Utica and Syracuse on June 15, 1907. A group of "Utica Boosters" chartered this car in May 1910 for a promotional tour as far west as Indianapolis and Detroit, a trip made entirely over electric interurban railways.

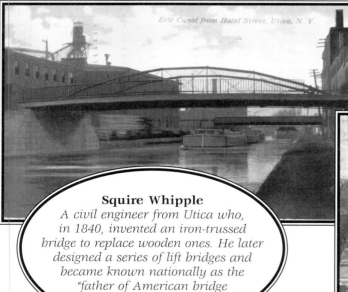

Erie Canal from Hotel Street, Utica, N. Y.

Squire Whipple
A civil engineer from Utica who, in 1840, invented an iron-trussed bridge to replace wooden ones. He later designed a series of lift bridges and became known nationally as the "father of American bridge building."

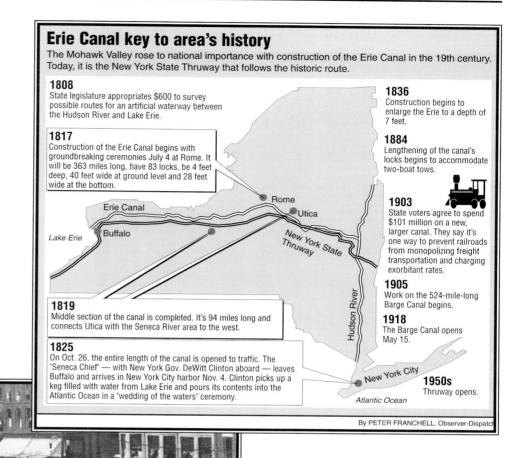

Erie Canal key to area's history

The Mohawk Valley rose to national importance with construction of the Erie Canal in the 19th century. Today, it is the New York State Thruway that follows the historic route.

1808
State legislature appropriates $600 to survey possible routes for an artificial waterway between the Hudson River and Lake Erie.

1817
Construction of the Erie Canal begins with groundbreaking ceremonies July 4 at Rome. It will be 363 miles long, have 83 locks, be 4 feet deep, 40 feet wide at ground level and 28 feet wide at the bottom.

1819
Middle section of the canal is completed. It's 94 miles long and connects Utica with the Seneca River area to the west.

1825
On Oct. 26, the entire length of the canal is opened to traffic. The "Seneca Chief" — with New York Gov. DeWitt Clinton aboard — leaves Buffalo and arrives in New York City harbor Nov. 4. Clinton picks up a keg filled with water from Lake Erie and pours its contents into the Atlantic Ocean in a "wedding of the waters" ceremony.

1836
Construction begins to enlarge the Erie to a depth of 7 feet.

1884
Lengthening of the canal's locks begins to accommodate two-boat tows.

1903
State voters agree to spend $101 million on a new, larger canal. They say it's one way to prevent railroads from monopolizing freight transportation and charging exorbitant rates.

1905
Work on the 524-mile-long Barge Canal begins.

1918
The Barge Canal opens May 15.

1950s
Thruway opens.

By PETER FRANCHELL, Observer-Dispatch

Circus Parade on Genesee Street.

A look at the railroad freight yard in 1914. The first railroad in the state was the Mohawk and Hudson between Albany and Schenectady. It opened in 1831. The Utica and Schenectady began five years later with six locomotives and 50 cars each. The Utica and Syracuse was completed in 1839. Between 1850 and 1895, nearly a dozen smaller railroads originated in the county or passed through it.

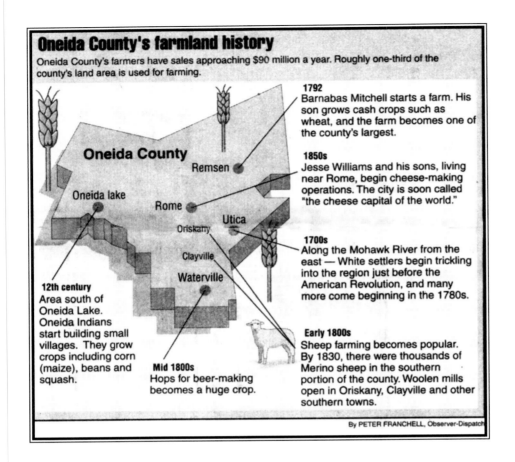

Oneida County's farmland history

Oneida County's farmers have sales approaching $90 million a year. Roughly one-third of the county's land area is used for farming.

Oneida County

Remsen

Oneida lake

Rome

Utica

Oriskany

Clayville

Waterville

12th century
Area south of Oneida Lake. Oneida Indians start building small villages. They grow crops including corn (maize), beans and squash.

Mid 1800s
Hops for beer-making becomes a huge crop.

1792
Barnabas Mitchell starts a farm. His son grows cash crops such as wheat, and the farm becomes one of the county's largest.

1850s
Jesse Williams and his sons, living near Rome, begin cheese-making operations. The city is soon called "the cheese capital of the world."

1700s
Along the Mohawk River from the east — White settlers begin trickling into the region just before the American Revolution, and many more come beginning in the 1780s.

Early 1800s
Sheep farming becomes popular. By 1830, there were thousands of Merino sheep in the southern portion of the county. Woolen mills open in Oriskany, Clayville and other southern towns.

By PETER FRANCHELL, Observer-Dispatch

Hop pickers in Bridgewater. During the late 19th century, hops were an important cash crop in Oneida County.

Agriculture

Farmers sowed the seed from which the county bloomed

Delivery of milk at a cheese-factory. Utica, NY 1878

Throughout its 200-year history, Oneida County has had no better friend than its good, rich soil.

It nurtured crops and forests to sustain Indians, hunters and trappers in pre-Colonial times and did the same for pioneers who first began to trickle into the region in the early 1770s and arrive in larger numbers in the mid-1780s.

It made possible hilly, grazing pastures necessary for dairy farming and sheep-raising to be profitable during the first half of the 19th century and, after the Civil War, made the farm and the growing of cash crops a major part of the county's growing economy.

That rich soil continues today to make agriculture a major industry, with the value of its farm products sold each year reaching $90 million ... ranking Oneida County eighth among the state's 62 counties. Suffolk and Wyoming counties top the list ... a list whose figures show Herkimer County at more than $55 million and Madison and Lewis counties at about $75 million each.

Agriculture contributes much more to the local economy than $90 million, though. Farmers are consumers, too, and their purchases link dozens of businesses to the farm ... businesses such as insurance, farm machinery, feed, fertilizer, seed, electricity, banking and building supplies.

"Every dollar made on an Oneida County farm generates six to seven dollars in the local economy," said Joseph Walsh, assistant director for agriculture, the environment and economic vitality at Cornell Cooperative Extension of Oneida County. "Our farmers tend to spend their money locally so one can begin to realize the importance of agriculture to the county's economy."

Because of the fertile soil, it is not surprising that the region ... as early as the 12th century ... began to attract Indians, especially the Oneidas, who built small villages south of Oneida Lake.

They felled trees to clear the land and then, using pointed sticks to break up the ground, planted crops, starting with corn or maize. When the corn began to sprout, they planted pumpkin, squash and beans.

By the 1700s, it remained for the early settlers to tame the wilderness.

Most of them were from Connecticut and Massachusetts who, in the mid-1780s, headed for New York's western frontier that they had heard so much about.

The families of Barnabas Mitchell and James Wilson were typical of those who journeyed along the Mohawk River to Old Fort Schuyler (Utica). They stayed for a day or two in one of the settlement's many inns, resting and buying supplies for the final leg of their journey into the wilderness fraught with danger: wild animals, malnutrition and winters in primitive dwellings. Some would not survive.

The Mitchells, who arrived in 1792 in what today is the town of Remsen, and the Wilsons, who settled in Marcy two years later, did survive.

They, like all first settlers, could not become farmers until they first became woodcutters and cleared the land.

After a cabin was built, it was time to plant their important first crop. Their survival depended on it.

The Mitchells, Wilsons and their neighbors quickly discovered that the climate and average rainfall, too, was ideal to grow a variety of crops ... corn, oats, barley, potatoes, beans, squash, pumpkin, carrots and wheat.

It wasn't easy, though, for plows and farm tools were wooden and unwieldy. Families were able to grow enough food for themselves, but not much more. Farmers worried about surviving and not about producing food for market.

Development slow

Between 1785 and 1800, agriculture in Oneida County certainly was no industry.

"In spite of all (the) favorable conditions, agriculture (as an industry) was slow in developing in the county," comments Dr. Virgil C. Crisafulli, Utica College professor emeritus of economics. There were two main reasons for the slow development:

• A handful of landowners owned large tracts of land ... people like John Bleecker, Nicholas Van Staphorst, Christina Coster, James Dean and Philip Schuyler. Many of them did not farm their land, hoping it would increase in value. Sometimes the speculators would lease small plots to tenant farmers. That slowed the development of agriculture since tenant farmers had little incentive to improve the land.

• The early settlers ... like the Indians before them ... were limited farmers.

Land was plentiful so it usually was worked until the soil was exhausted. Then, the farmer would move to another piece of land. Crop rotation was unheard of and little, if any, fertilizer was used.

Gradually, though, more and more settlers were able to buy their own farms. Farm tools and methods of planting and harvesting improved, too. Some Oneida County farmers, by 1800, were beginning to farm to make a living.

Milo Mitchell, son of first settler Barnabas Mitchell, began to grow cash crops like wheat and soon was operating the largest farm in the Remsen area. James Wilson and his family did the same and soon they were the wealthiest people in Marcy.

Prosperity falters

During the first decade of the 19th century, many Oneida County farmers began to grow cash crops like wheat, barley and rye for markets in New York City and Europe ... a Europe embroiled in the Napoleonic Wars and in desperate need of food from breadbaskets like Oneida County.

Then, in 1808, the farmers' prosperity came to an abrupt end.

In December 1807, Congress passed an Embargo Act, hoping to deprive England and other European countries of U.S. products and force them to stop attacking U.S. ships. The embargo forbade U.S. merchant ships from carrying goods to Europe.

Angry Oneida County farmers ... led by Jonas Platt and Thomas Gold, two prominent lawyers from Whitestown ... joined the Federalist Party in waging a fight against President Thomas Jefferson, his Democrat-Republican Party and their embargo.

Eventually, the embargo was lifted, but the damage was done and the agriculture industry in Oneida County was at a near standstill.

But it didn't stand still for long.

When foreign markets disappeared, farmers in the county turned to raising sheep and dairy farming. There were advantages. The county's fertile soil provided lush hilly pastures for sheep and cows to graze in. Women and children in farm families could help with butter-making and milking to reduce labor costs, and butter and cheese could be stored easily before being taken to market.

Also, local dairy farmers were closer to important New York City markets than were farms further west. In those days before refrigeration, they easily could deliver milk and other products downstate before spoilage began.

By 1830, there were thousands of merino sheep in the county, especially in the Sangerfield-Bridgewater area. Merinos, originally raised in Spain, were famous for their fine wool.

Sheep farmers had dozens of markets nearby, too, as woolen mills sprang up in Oriskany in 1809, Clinton in 1810, Sauquoit in 1812, Clayville in 1844 and Utica in

---

Jesse Williams, *a mid-19th century Rome resident, was responsible for what many today consider one of the most important developments in agriculture in the history of Oneida County, and beyond.*

Williams founded the cheese factory system in 1851, which made it possible, for the first time, to take milk and convert it directly into large quantities of high-quality cheese.

Previously, small amounts of cheese were made on individual farms. The small number of cheese manufacturers who did exist at the time bought curd - that was separated from milk in farmhouses - and then made cheese from that curd.

Williams' plan was to buy milk in large quantities from farms in the vicinity and transport it to a factory he erected. There, using a machine he invented, he would convert the milk directly into high-quality cheese of uniform sizes - with some blocks weighing as much as 150 pounds. This had never been done before.

Williams opened his cheese factory - the first such factory in the world - May 10, 1851. It quickly revolutionized the cheese-making industry in the United States and abroad.

Williams was born near Rome Feb. 24, 1798. His father, David, and three uncles were with Col. Peter Gansevoort at Fort Stanwix during the siege of August 1777 that led to the Battle of Oriskany.

Jesse Williams and Amanda Wells were married in 1822, and 12 years later they inherited David Williams' 265-acre farm near Rome. They then owned 65 head of cattle, three horses, 72 sheep, and 27 hogs.

They made their own cheese - a New England-type cheddar.

After his cheese factory became successful in 1851, his fame spread throughout the land. Soon, factories, following his design, were built in states like Wisconsin, Michigan, and Ohio and countries in Europe, including a large number in France.

By 1864 Rome had become the cheese-making capital of the world and that year cheesemakers from throughout the country met in Rome and formed the New York State Cheese Manufacturers Association.

George Williams, Jesse's son, was elected its first president. It later evolved into the American Dairymen's Association.

Jesse Williams died Dec. 20, 1864 at age 67.

1846. By then, there were more than 200,000 sheep in Oneida County.

Cheese market grows

At the same time, dairy farms were booming, with butter- and cheese-making being a profitable part of the industry.

In 1851, Jesse Williams and his sons, living near Rome, invented a method to convert milk directly into cheese in large quantities, something that never was done before. They erected cheese factories where they used milk from their neighbors' farms to produce superior quality cheese. Soon, Williams was labeled "father of the cheese factory system" and Rome was "the cheese capital of the world."

By 1860, Oneida County farmers were growing cash crops in large quantities for markets throughout the Northeast. Agriculture slowly was developing into an important industry.

Livestock needed feed and fodder so county farmers began to grow oats, barley and rye. The latter two also were sold to breweries. So were hops, first planted in the county in about 1820 and by 1850 a major crop, especially in the Waterville-Sangerfield-Bridgewater area. Oneida County hops were a major factor in World markets where it was a key ingredient in brewing beer.

Other cash crops at the time were potatoes, beans, peas and apples.

With the coming of the Erie Canal in 1825 and railroads a little later, wheat farming in the county grew rapidly and large shipments were sent weekly to New York City markets.

Agriculture booms

Right after the Civil War, agriculture became a major industry in the county.

Organizations such as the Oneida County Agriculture Society, American Dairymen's Association and state fairs began to educate farmers in the sciences of soil, plants and livestock, and the benefits of fertilizer and crop rotation.

Tenant farmers were being replaced by men and women who owned their own land and were eager to improve it. They invested in farm tools and machinery and learned how to conserve the soil.

By 1875, agriculture in Oneida County was booming. "Farmers were a majority of the population and they dominated the economic, political and social life of the area." Virgil Crisafulli wrote.

Nearly 90 percent of the county's 800,000 acres were being farmed ... more than 700,000 acres mostly used for livestock, hay, oats, corn, potatoes, apples and hops.

Beginning in the 1890s ... farmers were learning how to produce more with less farmland, and the number of farms began to decrease.

Agriculture is Oneida County's "invisible industry," said Joseph Walsh of Cornell Cooperative Extension.

"It's not like the electronics or insurance industries," he said. "We can see that they are large industries for every

Cows crowd behind a gate waiting to be milked. Milk meters are used to weigh the milk, and the information is processed into a computer system, which makes it easier to spot health problems by tracking individual cow milk production on a daily basis.

Joe Van Lieshout drives the feed truck through the free-stall barn built in 1980. It houses about 500 cows which are fed three times a day.

day we drive by their plants and tall buildings with parking lots filled with workers' cars."

The county's agriculture industry today, in contrast, has 1,170 farms scattered across 1,250 square miles. But it is a major industry nevertheless, said Walsh.

About 260,000 acres of the county's 806,000 acres are being farmed today by about 2,800 farm owners, and full-time and part-timer workers.

Agriculture not only is a major industry in Oneida County today, it is a changing one, too, Walsh said.

The number of farms continue to decrease every year, mainly because of decreasing profits, increasing taxes and the high cost of tools and machinery.

Many older farmers quit because they cannot find young people to take over. For example, 4-H, a youth component of Cornell Cooperative Extension of Oneida County, still is very active with 451 members in 66 clubs, but the number of members has decreased over the years.

While the number of farms decreases – 1,170 today compared to about 1,560 in 1983 – the amount of field crops and vegetables and the milk and dairy products produced each year in Oneida County increases.

The county has lost about 60 dairy farms since 1993 – there's about 390 today – but in most cases, the cows were sold to other dairy farmers in the region. So, many of the dairy farms that survive actually are growing larger.

Other branches of agriculture are growing, too – horticulture, for example – but dairy farming remains today the heart of Oneida County's agriculture – and has for many years.

More than one-third of the county's farms produce dairy products.

There are about 25,000 milk cows and they contribute to the sale of more than $60 million a year in dairy products. That places the county seventh among counties in the state.

There are problems for some dairy farmers, though, especially the smaller ones State Sen. John R. Kuhl, R-Hammondsport, chairman of the Senate Agriculture Committee, recently said

that unless New York farmers joined those in New England to form a coalition to raise prices they get for milk, many would not survive. Those prices have dropped to their lowest level in many years.

Most farmers credit farm organizations for much of the progress and development on their farms.

Pat Van Lieshout, Oneida County Farm Bureau president, said his group's aim is to "enhance the quality of rural life."

Cornell Cooperative Extension – funded here by Oneida County, state and federal governments, and grants, fees and contributions – aims to "help people identify and find solutions to improve their homes, families, farms, businesses and communities through education, experience and research."

They and other farm groups through educational programs and support, are among the main reasons that today's Oneida County farmer is able to produce more on less farmland and make agriculture what many say is Oneida County's "No. 1 Industry."

Oneida County farming

Over the years, Oneida County has seen a decrease in the number of farms and the land they occupy. However, the value of the products they sell has risen. Here's a look at the figures:

▶ **Number of farms**

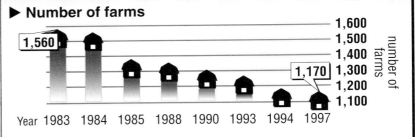

| Year | 1983 | 1984 | 1985 | 1988 | 1990 | 1993 | 1994 | 1997 |

1,560 ... 1,170

number of farms: 1,600 / 1,500 / 1,400 / 1,300 / 1,200 / 1,100

▶ **Acres of farmland**

In 1875, 84% (704,363 acres) of all the land in Oneida County was used for farming.

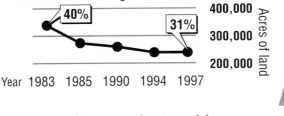

40% ... 31%

| Year | 1983 | 1985 | 1990 | 1994 | 1997 |

Acres of land: 400,000 / 300,000 / 200,000

▶ **Value of farm products sold**

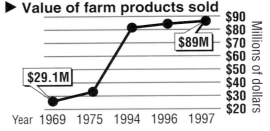

$89M ... $29.1M

| Year | 1969 | 1975 | 1994 | 1996 | 1997 |

Millions of dollars: $90 / $80 / $70 / $60 / $50 / $40 / $30 / $20

Source: Cornell Cooperative Extension of Oneida County, State of New York Agricultural and Market Statistics

Observer-Dispatch/KF

Industry

Textile industry's rise and fall shaped the fabric of Oneida County

By Frank Tomaino

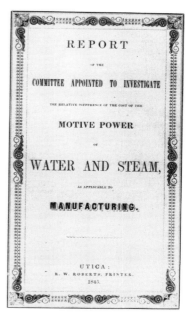

Farming, metal, electronics, and defense industries major components of county business

The early morning sun shone brightly as three men … the future of Oneida County in their hands … boarded an eastbound train at the depot at Utica's Bagg's Square.

The date: April 3, 1845.

Their mission: Visit New England's textile mills using power looms run by steam and determine whether it was practical to use similar looms in Oneida County to replace ones run by hand and water power.

The county's textile industry was a shambles. It could not compete with New England's steam-powered looms that wove faster and produced superior goods.

The decline was happening at an inopportune time, for another of the county's major industries also was reeling.

Trains were fast replacing stagecoaches … stagecoaches whose passengers, especially those heading west, usually stayed overnight or longer in places like Utica and Rome before continuing their journey. An industry employing hundreds had sprung up to accommodate the travelers … hotels, taverns, supply stores, blacksmith shops, wagon-repair shops, etc.

By 1845, most of them had gone out of business, for trains only stopped long enough to pick up and discharge passengers.

There were, of course, other industries in Oneida County.

Clayville had a shovel factory, for example, and there were blast furnaces in Taberg and Paris smelting iron ore mined in Kirkland. Camden factories were turning out china closets and bedroom furniture and many communities near streams used water power to run saw and grist mills. Farms scattered throughout the county were just beginning to produce cash crops and using the Erie Canal and railroads to reach out-of-county markets.

But the county was not growing as fast as other areas on the Erie Canal or the railroads.

Utica, in particular, was limited in its ability to manufacture goods because the Mohawk River did not flow fast enough to turn the machines and wheels of industry.

For the first time since Oneida County was formed on March 15, 1798, some communities were losing population. Between 1840 and 1845, for example, Utica's population dropped from 12,000 to 10,000.

Something had to be done, so on an April morning in 1845, three men … selected at a mass meeting of county residents … headed for New England for a close look at looms and other machines powered by steam.

Attorney Edward Graham, merchant Spencer Kellogg and industrialist Andrew Pond returned with a plan to get Oneida County's stagnant economy moving again.

Coal could be used to produce steam, they said, and the county had a large supply readily available via the recently completed Chenango Canal that connected the county with the coal fields of Pennsylvania.

Money was needed, too … capital to be raised locally to start companies and build mills designed to use steam power.

Within a year, a fund-raising drive … headed by wealthy local entrepreneurs like Alfred Munson and Theodore Faxton … raised enough money to build companies such as the Globe Woolen Mills, the Utica Steam Cotton Mills and the Utica Steam Woolen Mills.

True, the region had textile mills for years. The first cotton mill in the state was erected in 1809 in Yorkville led by industrialists like Seth Capron. A mill in New York Mills was started by Benjamin Walcott in 1812, and there were mills in Clinton, Clayville and Sauquoit at the same time. But not until the late 1840s when the steam-powered looms came to town did the textile era begin in Oneida County.

For the remainder of the 19th century, dozens of mills were built and prospered in places like Oriskany Falls, Camden, Kirkland, Sangerfield, New Hartford, New York Mills and Whitesboro. The textile industry reached its peak in 1918 during World War I when nearly 22,000 in the region worked at producing knit goods for companies like Oneita Knitting and Avalon Knitwear.

The giant of the industry, though, was the Utica Knitting Co. It was founded in 1872 by Quentin McAdam and in 20 years made Utica the knit goods capital of the world. Besides its several mills in Utica, it had plants throughout the region in places like Oriskany Falls, Clayville and Sherburne.

Other industries were growing at the same time.

Farming industry

Farming flourished when canals and railroads ... before refrigeration ... were able to transport local crops and dairy products to New York City markets, something Midwest farmers were too far away to do without their products spoiling.

Dairy farmers found profits increasing after 1851 when Rome's Jesse Williams founded the nation's first cheese factory system and began to produce high-quality cheese in large quantities.

The hundreds of acres of peas, beans and other vegetables grown in the county led to large canning factories in places like Annsville, Camden, Rome and Verona. New York state, by 1880, was producing 90 percent of the nation's hops and a large chunk of that percentage was being grown in Oneida County's Waterville-Sangerfield-Bridgewater area.

Forest to furniture

The region's lush forests provided the lumber needed for the many furniture manufacturers.

In the early 19th century, for example, Truman Yale started a chair factory in Forestport. One hundred years later, Frank Harden founded the Harden Furniture Co. in McConnellsville, town of Vienna, which continues today its reputation as one of the country's finest furniture makers.

Metals forged businesses

During the first half of the 20th century, Savage Arms in Utica employed hundreds making sporting rifles and, during the two world wars, machine guns.

Today, companies like Utica Boilers and Utica Cutlery continue to provide jobs for many ... as does Oneida Silversmiths in Sherrill. That company dates back to 1848 when John Humphrey Noyes founded the Oneida Community, which, among other things, taught that people must share all personal possessions.

The Community began several successful businesses, silver knives, forks and spoons. When the community experiment ended in 1881, it reorganized as a joint-stock company to continue some of the businesses.

The largest metals industry in Oneida County history, though, has been the copper and brass industry of Rome.

It began in 1878 when railroads began to use steel rails instead of ones made of iron. So Jonathan S. Haselton converted the Rome Iron Works into a brass-production firm. In 1891, it began to make sheet copper and changed its name to the Rome Brass and Copper Co. It eventually merged with Revere Copper and Brass.

Rome became known as the Copper City, and by 1925 nearly 3,000 men and women were working in the industry, the second-largest nonagricultural industry in Oneida County after textiles.

War signals decline

After World War I, though, the textile industry was poised on the brink of a sharp decline. Owners were

Oneida County had textile mills for years, but it wasn't until the late 1840s, when the steam-powered looms came to town that the textile era began in Oneida County. For the remainder of the 19th century, dozens of mills were built and prospered in places like Oriskany Falls, Camden, Kirkland, Sangerfield, New Hartford, New York Mills and Whitesboro. Pictured is the Alliance Knitting Mill in Whitesboro.

tempted to head south where labor was cheaper and cotton fields closer.

Dr. Virgil C. Crisafulli, Utica College professor emeritus of economics, said, "The popular view of the economic decline of the Utica-Rome area is that it was caused by the flight of textiles to the South and that it happened all of a sudden after World War II. This is a vastly oversimplified view.

"The peak of the 19th-century industrial expansion was reached about 1910," Crisafulli continued. After that, there began a long decline that was postponed by World War I orders, hidden from view by the national prosperity in the 1920s, by the depression of the 1930s and postponed again by World War II demands.

"Thus, to the general population, the collapse after World War II seemed sudden. But industry leaders knew all along that local industry was sick."

The reasons for the decline were many: customers turning from cotton and wool goods to silk and nylon; factories and machinery growing old and inefficient and poor management.

By the mid-1950s, most of the textile mills in Oneida County were gone. Other industries ... like Savage Arms and Griffiss Air Force Base ... began layoffs within weeks of the end of the war. The "loom-to-gloom" era had begun.

But it did not last long.

Leaders throughout the county had begun laying the groundwork for an industrial recovery by forming industrial development corporations.

They were prepared to provide land and underwrite other costs for new businesses interested in building in the county.

And those companies came: Chicago Pneumatic Tool in 1948, Bendix in 1951, General Electric in 1953 (although it had had a small operation in Utica during the war) and Sperry-Rand's UNIVAC in 1957. Businesses already in the county began to grow: Mohawk Airlines, Utica Drop Forge and Tool, Special Metals, etc.

Griffiss Air Force Base became a major employer with nearly 10,000 military and civilian workers.

The '50s era was appropriately labeled "loom-to-boom."

Good labor-management relations helped economy

Good labor-management relations always played an important role in past economic recoveries in Oneida County.

During the "loom-to-loom" era in the late 1940s and early 1950s – when textile mills moved out and manufacturing and electronic firms moved in – the new companies usually cited the region's history of excellent relations between local unions and companies as one of the main reasons they

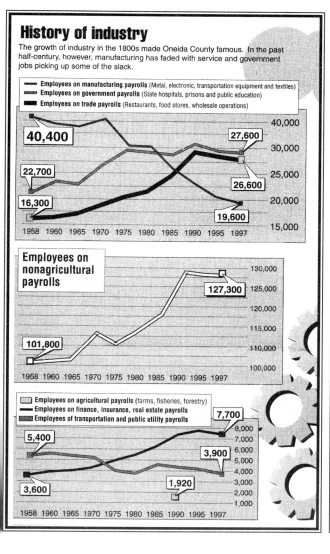

History of industry

The growth of industry in the 1800s made Oneida County famous. In the past half-century, however, manufacturing has faded with service and government jobs picking up some of the slack.

Oneida County's lush forest – such as this old logging camp at Verona Beach in 1908 – provided the lumber needed for many furniture manufacturers. In the early 19th century, Truman Yale started a chair factory in Forestport. One hundred years later, Frank Harden founded the Harden Furniture Co. in McConnellsville in the town of Vienna.

had decided to relocate in the Oneida County area.

Unions first appeared in the county in the early 1800s. There were dozens of them by 1870 representing a variety of workers from locomotive engineers and printers to bricklayers and cigar makers.

Dr. Virgil C. Crisafulli, Utica College professor emeritus of Economics, said, "The record of collective bargaining was a good one in the Mohawk Valley after World War II. The number of workers involved and the number of worker-days lost in stoppages was among the lowest in the country."

Edward J. Morgan, secretary-treasurer of the Mohawk Valley Building and Construction Trades Council, said that labor-management relations in the region is "much better today than it was 10 years ago."

He said that there are about 6,500 members within the trades council's jurisdiction radius of 50 miles – carpenters, plumbers, painters, iron workers, etc. – and one of "our primary responsibilities is to work with management to keep our work force well-trained and up-to-date as to the latest ideas and techniques."

"When a company decides to build in the region," he said, "it wants an adequate supply of skilled labor who not only will do a good job in the construction, but also will bring the project in on time.

"Our members help to provide our region with that skilled work force, and they also have a strong work ethic to go along with those skills. That's something the region can be proud of."

Growth, prosperity hinge on economic diversity

"One of the lessons I've learned from local history is never to put all your economic eggs in one basket," said Oneida County Executive Ralph J. Eannace Jr. "The textile industry dominated our economy for decades and when its mills left town, there were not many major, nontextile industries her to absorb jobs lost. Later, the region repeated the mistake by becoming too dependent on the defense industry.

"Our hopes today and in the future lie in having a diversified economy, one that not only includes businesses already here, but also new ones in a variety of categories from industry and agriculture to tourism and high technology."

"Economic diversification is they key," Rome Mayor Joseph A.Griffo said. "We must develop an economic climate that attracts a variety of businesses and industries."

One way to accomplish that, he said, was to have a good industrial development team in place to work with the state in developing reasonable mandates and regulations that don't overwhelm out-of-state businesses. Reasonable taxes, too, are powerful tools in any strategy designed to bring in new industries.

Utica Mayor Edward A. Hanna said that not only did the region's economic hopes lie in diversification, but also in ending "once and for all parochialism that has plagued our area for years."

"We must erase all border lines between communities," Hanna said. "I look at the Mohawk Valley from a businessman's point of view and consider it one community. When one city or town is successful in attracting a new business, the entire region benefits."

Eannace agrees that another lesson he learned from local history was that any successful industrial development strategy had to be regional in design.

He added a third lesson: "Government can't do it alone."

It can contribute to creating the proper climate needed to retain and attract businesses, he said, but more important, it must work with the private business community to make the local economy grow and prosper.

Mark Barbano, Department of Labor regional economist in Utica, agrees that diversity is the key to the region's economic success in the future and is optimistic about that future.

He said that many business services – such as security guards – added jobs from 1993 to 1997 as did the wholesale and retail trade sector. Amusement and recreation multiplied nearly five-fold as the Oneida Indian Nation opened the Turning Stone Casino Resort with more than 2,000 workers.

Many, but not all, the new jobs were full time with better-than-average pay, Barbano said.

"The civilian payroll and the average weekly pay for workers in the Mohawk Valley rose each year from 1993 to 1995," he said, "and more recent data for the first six ;months of 1996 show the trend continuing."

Eannace, Griffo and Hanna agree that a positive attitude about the region and future is vital to an economic recovery.

"Oneida County is a wonderful place to live," Eannace said. "We should be proud of our quality of life. We've got to get excited again about living here. Once we are aware of what we have here, we more easily can make prospective businesses aware of the advantages of moving to the Oneida County region."

From the six-pound "Number One" furnace have come successive generations of larger furnaces. The one shown here is Special Metals' "Number Nine" furnace with a capacity of 30,000 pounds.

Leaders

County's heavy hitters wielded power and clout

By Frank Tomaino

John C. Devereux was co-founder of both St. John's Roman Catholic Church and The Savings Bank of Utica. A pioneer merchant from Ireland, he became the first popularly elected mayor of Utica.

People of influence left mark locally, nationally

Roscoe Conkling had it.

So did Rose Cleveland, Gerrit Smith, Horatio Seymour, Theodore Faxton, Henry Highland Garnet and a handful of other giants who walked Oneida County in the 19th century.

And in the early 20th century, few possessed more of it than did Elihu Root and James Schoolcraft Sherman.

What they had was power. Influence. The ability to control events and people. Good old-fashioned clout.

When they talked, ears in Albany, Washington and company headquarters across the nation wiggled, waggled and snapped to attention.

Their action and achievements not only affected events and people in Oneida County, but often changed the course of U.S. history.

Today, local politicians and community leaders exert some power and influence at state and national levels, but not as much as their predecessors. It's not their fault. They just were born about 100 years too late.

"Oneida County in the early and mid-19th century was a growth center," said Dr. Virgil C. Crisafulli, Utica College professor emeritus of economics. "It was a leading producer in the United States of farm goods, dairy products, textiles, lumber and furniture, canned goods and many other products. The county was prospering and growing rapidly and needed strong leaders to represent its interests in Albany, Washington and in the business world.

"History shows that when there is a need in a region for leadership, its citizens find the right people to fulfill it."

Gentler times

Dr. Crisafulli said many of Oneida County's leaders today are able men and women with high ability, but must operate in a world much more complex and competitive than was the case 100 to 150 years ago.

While Oneida County industrial and political clout began to decline in the 20th Century, it still had great leaders, especially after World War II. Leaders such as mayors Vincent Corrou and Boyd Golder; men like James Capps and Henry Dorrance, Charles Hall, Walter Matt and William Murray led the County in its successful drive to attract industry and higher education. They were able to establish Utica College and Mohawk Community College and bring in new businesses such as Chicago Pneumatic, General Electric and Sperry UNIVAC. But local politicians lacked the clout in Albany and Washington to get the Utica area a north-south expressway, desperately needed to compete with Syracuse and Albany. Those two cities did get the expressways in routes 81 and 87.

Today's local politicians must battle politicians from other areas for state and federal dollars and programs. Local business and industrial leaders struggle daily to survive in the beleaguered Northeast against companies in warmer climates and on other continents.

The road to power and success had fewer bumps and steep hills to climb in the 19th and the early 20th centuries.

Oneida County in 1798 - the year it was formed - was on the nation's western frontier.

It fortunately had the Mohawk River - and later railroads and the Erie, Chenango and Black River canals - flowing through its veins and was located ideally within easy reach of New York City, Boston, Montreal and other major markets.

Its farmers and manufacturers were able to compete successfully with regions to the east - especially in New England - and had a giant head start over the small number of communities and companies that existed at the time to the west.

Oneida County was fortunate, too, that entrepreneurs like Theodore Faxton, Alfred Munson, John Butterfield and Silas Childs were able to start businesses with their own money and local capital. Today's circumstances among communities often depends on growth from new businesses moving in and using mostly outside capital and management.

Oneida County soon was producing more than it needed and began to export its excesses. Its farms and factories grew and made much money - sometimes millions - for its local owners and investors. That, in turn, attracted outsiders with ideas for new businesses, but in need of capital.

Men of enterprise

In 1845, for example, inventor Samuel F.B. Morse developed the world's first successful electric telegraph, but needed money to begin operations and string lines. In New York state, he turned to Oneida County where, wrote James D. Reid in his "The Telegraph in America," there was "a circle of solid, somewhat rough and practical men, always wide awake to enterprise...a kind of frontier man, quick, impetuous, daring, ready for any new thing which had in it the necessity of pluck and the probability of success."

Utica's Theodore Faxton was such a man.

He was a self-made millionaire who made his money operating packet boats on the Erie Canal and Lake Ontario and in steam cotton mills and banks. He was a stagecoach driver in Utica's early days and loved speed - fast boats, fast horses and fast stagecoaches.

He was attracted to Morse's telegraph that could send messages rapidly across the nation, so he obtained the rights from Morse to establish a telegraph line between New York City, Springfield, Mass. and Buffalo via Oneida County and formed a company with $200,000 capital.

He established headquarters at Genesee and Whitesboro streets in Utica and hired hundreds to string lines and to work in his offices.

Utica became the home of the first commercial telegraph company in the world.

Theodore Faxton

It is not surprising then that in that kind of positive atmosphere that pervaded Oneida County throughout the 19th century grew an outstanding crop of astute, able and ambitious men and women.

Oneida County inhabitants were gaining a reputation as a tolerant people, too, who welcomed foreign-born, especially those with skills needed by the expanding textile mills and other industry. As early as the 1830s Oneida County became the center of movements advocating social change. Gerrit Smith, famed abolitionist, led the fight against intemperance and slavery. In 1843 the first hospital in New York State to care for the mentally ill opened as Utica State Hospital.

"Today we have men and women who are just as capable as the industrial and political giants of the 19th century.

"In the early 1800s, Utica was on the western frontier and with its excellent transportation facilities was able to compete with regions to the east. There was very little, if any, competition to the west to be concerned about because regions there were just beginning to develop.

"And while Utica began to decline in the 20th century, it still had great leaders, especially after World War II

"If they had lived in the 19th century, their names would now be on the pages of our local history books as

A view of Bradish Block on Genesee Street between Elizabeth and Bleecker Streets in 1835.

Oneida County Historical Society

Roman Catholic priest from Albany celebrated some of the first Masses in Utica in the John C. Devereux house on Broad Street at Second Avenue. Later occupied for many years by the Lowry Brothers cotton business, this historic home was torn down about 1972. A bronze plaque on a boulder remains to explain the significance of the site. Photo by Carl K. Frey

Oneida County's movers and shakers from the past

Roscoe Conkling was elected to public office for the first time in 1858 when he became mayor of Utica. He was, at the time one of the top trial lawyers in the Northeast.

He was born in Albany on Oct. 30, 1829, educated in Auburn and, at age 17, moved to Utica, where he read law in the offices of prominent attorney Joshua Spencer.

For most of his life, he was one of the country's leading Republicans and served in the House of Representatives in the 1860s and in the U.S. Senate from 1867-81.

Today, Conkling is remembered as one of the most powerful, influential senators of his time and a close friend of President Ulysses S. Grant, but he also had an outstanding career as a congressman.

He dominated the House from the moment he first stepped onto the floor; a 6-foot-3-inch, powerfully built giant with reddish blond hair and a well-groomed beard.

He strutted like a peacock and attracted attention with his fancy pants and waistcoats, dark cutaway coats and loud ties. He was a great orator and when he spoke, all eyes turned to him.

It came as no surprise then when, in early 1862, President Abraham Lincoln – a fellow Republican – picked Congressman Conkling to introduce the president's resolution which offered financial aid to any state that passed or had a law which gradually abolished slavery. It was an important bill and Lincoln said he wanted the "House's great orator" to guide it through.

Many opposed the bill, but Conkling fought hard for it and in the end it passed 89-31.

Henry Highland Garnet was an educator and clergyman who was born a slave in 1815 in Maryland and, at age 9, escaped via the "underground railroad" to New York City.

At 21, he enrolled at the Oneida Institute of Science and Industry – located off Main Street in Whitesboro – which was one of the few colleges in the country at the time to admit blacks.

After graduation, Garnet went on to become one of the foremost black abolitionists in the United States and spent a lifetime encouraging blacks to fight slave owners and demand equal rights.

In 1881, he was appointed U.S. minister and consul general to Liberia on Africa's west coast.

When he died, a colleague wrote that Garnet had influenced the lives of thousands of blacks and that "he fought for his race as no other man could."

Gerrit Smith, wealthy 19th-century philanthropist and reformer, was born in Utica in 1797 and spent a lifetime opposing slavery, building churches for needy parishes, donating money to schools and colleges and supporting prison reform and women's suffrage causes.

He gave thousands of dollars to the operation of the "underground railroad" which helped slaves flee the South to northern states and Canada.

He once purchased thousands of acres in Northern New York and gave them to blacks.

When he died in 1874, the New York Times called him one of the most influential Americans of the 19th century.

Horatio Seymour, who lived in Utica and Deerfield, was elected governor of New York in 1852 and again in 1862.

He was one of the most respected, influential Democrats in the 19th century in the United States and in 1856 was the keynote speaker at the Democrat Party National Convention in Cincinnati that picked James Buchanan as its presidential nominee. Buchanan was elected the country's 15th president in November.

In 1868, Seymour was his party's choice to run for president against Civil War hero Ulysses S. Grant.

Seymour was defeated narrowly, and for the rest of his life Democrats young and old from across the country visited him in his home on Whitesboro Street and magnificent farm house in Deerfield for advice and counsel.

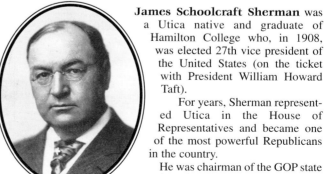

James Schoolcraft Sherman was a Utica native and graduate of Hamilton College who, in 1908, was elected 27th vice president of the United States (on the ticket with President William Howard Taft).

For years, Sherman represented Utica in the House of Representatives and became one of the most powerful Republicans in the country.

He was chairman of the GOP state committee in 1895, 1900 and 1908 and chairman of the Republican National Committee in 1908.

the men and women who led the city of Utica during its glory days."

Confident, discerning leaders forged Utica's glory days

Early one morning in the summer of 1846 in the Central New York community of Auburn, 17-year-old Roscoe Conkling boldly faced his father and said, "I have decided not to go to college, sir. I am, instead, moving to Utica to read law in the offices of Joshua Spencer."

Obviously, Alfred Conkling ... a federal judge in the Northern District of New York ... was disappointed, but did nothing to dissuade his intelligent, ambitious and sometimes rebellious son. After all, Spencer was one of the most respected lawyers in the state and Utica was booming ... a fast-growing city whose hard-working citizens were making it an industrial giant and whose political and civic leaders were beginning to make friends in high places in Albany and Washington.

Elihu Root

Young Roscoe Conkling had chosen the right city to begin his career.

Conkling's Utica had an abundant supply of skilled and unskilled labor reinforced almost daily by immigrants from northern and western Europe.

And while many communities had the Erie Canal, Utica had both the Erie and Chenango canals.

The Chenango, completed in 1836, connected Utica with the coal fields of Pennsylvania and that coal enabled the city's textile mills to convert from hand-operated looms to more efficient and faster steam-powered looms.

Leaders were giants

But the city's most valuable asset was its leaders. They truly were giants of politics and industry.

Theodore Faxton was one such giant.

In the 1830s, he ran packet boats on the Erie Canal and later organized the first American line of steamers to operate on Lake Ontario and the St. Lawrence River. He invested in Utica's textile mills, banks and railroads and helped Samuel F.B. Morse finance his new invention called the telegraph.

Soon, a Faxton-led company, with headquarters near Bagg's Square, controlled all telegraph lines in the state and others strung up as far west as the Mississippi River.

Faxton and other Utica industrialists like Alfred Munson, John Butterfield and Silas Childs also had enough influence to get state and federal governments to spend tens of thousands of dollars on roads, canals and railroads in Oneida County.

Utica was fortunate, too, that those "giants" started businesses with their own money and local capital (which differs from today's trend among communities that depend on outside companies moving in using mostly outside capital and management.)

Those 19th-century industrialists lived in Utica, loved the area and built their companies to stay put and not move away after a few years.

So, Utica continued to grow as the years of the 19th century passed by.

It didn't hurt, either, to be the home of two of the century's greatest political giants ... Democrat Horatio Seymour and his brother-in-law, Republican Roscoe Conkling.

Seymour, governor of New York in the 1850s and again in the 1860s, was chosen by his party in 1868 to run for president of the United States. He was defeated narrowly by Ulysses S. Grant, but Utica still gained a friend in the White House because Grant was one of Conkling's closest friends.

Conkling also was the political boss of the powerful, influential state GOP at the time.

Seymour, Conkling and other political leaders in Utica opened many doors in Albany and Washington for the city's business leaders.

During the Civil War, for example, Utica workers supplied the Union Army with much clothing, underwear, caps, shoes and military equipment.

Wielding power

It's the spring of 1875 and President Ulysses S. Grant is talking with Utica's Roscoe Conkling - who is the president's close friend, the U.S. senator from New York and the boss of the state's Republican Party. They are alone so their exact conversation never will be known, but it probably went something like this:

Grant: "The Army of the Cumberland is having its reunion in September, Roscoe, to celebrate its many victories in the Civil War. I'll be there as will Vice President Wilson, Generals Sherman and Hooker, most of my cabinet members and several Supreme Court justices. It's going to be the social event of the year and already dozens of major cities have invited us."

Conkling: "Why not have it in Utica, Mr. President? After all, the majority of Oneida County voters supported you in 1868 and 1872.

Grant: "Can Utica handle such a large delegation, Roscoe? You know there also will be more than a hundred state officials and mayors from many cities and villages."

Conkling: "I'm sure that Bagg's Hotel and the Butterfield House will be able to accommodate everyone and the ceremonies can be held in our luxurious opera house. You, Mr. President, are welcome to stay at my house at Rutger Park."

Grant agreed and the event took place in Utica Sept. 16 and was a great success.

One man rivaled Conkling in power and influence was Clinton-born Elihu Root, an 1864 graduate of Hamilton College.

His list of achievements and influence on U.S. history is a long one.

As President William McKinley's Secretary of War from 1899-1904, he set policies for the administration of Cuba and the Philippines which the United States acquired after the Spanish-American War in 1898.

One of his most challenging tasks, though, was the reorganization of the Army which, since the Civil War, was dominated by bureaucrats fighting for power and who, in the process, were ignoring the needs of soldiers. The Army's old seniority system also had become a problem with bright, capable younger officers being bypassed for promotion.

Rose Cleveland

Root stomped on the bureaucrats and sliced through the red tape.

One day, President Theodore Roosevelt (who became president after McKinley was assassinated and kept Root in his cabinet) recommended that the son of a large contributor to the Republican Party be promoted in the Army. Root refused and replied: "This officer man cannot be promoted without violating established and necessary rules."

Root also created the Army War College, which presented advanced studies for lieutenant colonels, colonels and other officers on national security and war planning.

During World War I, Secretary of War Newton D. Baker said: "Elihu Root's creation…was not only the outstanding contribution to the national defense o the country, but the outstanding contribution made by any secretary of war from the beginning of our history. Without that contribution from him, the participation of the United States in the World War would have been confused and ineffective."

Woman of influence

Another 19th-century Oneida County giant was Rose Cleveland, who spent most of her life in Holland Patent, but greatly influenced the lives of many young men and women.

She completed studies at the Houghton Seminary in Clinton and became a teacher. Women in her day were not encouraged to write or lecture - so she wrote and lectured, attracting large crowds and always emphasizing a woman's right to an education, to vote and to work at any job she was capable of doing.

Her "George Eliot's Poetry and Other Studies" went

through 12 editions in its first year and earned her $25,000 - a fabulous sum in her day.

She attained her greatest power, though, in 1884 when her brother, Grover Cleveland, was elected the 22nd president of the United States.

He was a bachelor and asked his sister to become the chatelaine or official mistress of the White House.

Historians later wrote that she made an impressive "First Lady" and one, Allan Nevins, wrote that she was one of the most cultivated women to ever control the operations of the White House.

Her first important challenge came March 21, 1885, at President Cleveland's first official reception. Members of his cabinet and their wives, congressmen and senators and their wives and the entire diplomatic corps were invited as the press stood by to report the results. Could the bachelor president, they asked, run the White House in a dignified, proper manner?

The no-nonsense Rose Cleveland answered that question when she reigned over a perfect reception and dinner, although some o the wives later said they were "terrified" by her energy and strong personality. She told them, for example, that her White House would no longer serve whiskey although she would permit wine.

Cleveland later admitted that she had relieved the boredom of shaking hands in the reception line for more than an hour by conjugating Greek verbs while smiling properly.

In June 1886, the president and Frances Folsom were married and Rose returned to Holland Patent.

Faxton, Conkling, Root and Cleveland obviously are at the very top of any list of powerful influential giants who walked Oneida County, affecting events and people in Albany, Washington and across the country.

There were others, but not many.

Some of them had names like Seymour, Garnet, Smith and Sherman and what they said and did throughout their lives changed forever their country and their Oneida County.

Beginning of decline

Dr. Virgil C. Crisafulli, Utica College professor emeritus, said, "The great expansion in Utica from the Civil War to World War I was carried forward by several industries, including textiles, transportation, metal products, tools and gun manufacture. They were growth industries in the 19th century and became declining industries in the 20th century."

Crisafulli offered several reasons why that happened.

Utica's textile mills produced mostly cotton and woolen goods and consumer tastes in the 1920s began to change to fashions dominated by clothes made of nylon, silk and similar materials.

Utica, once a transportation leader in the Northeast because of its many railroads heading in all directions, the Mohawk River and the Erie and Chenango canals, became less important when cars, trucks and airplanes leveled the playing field for other communities.

The city's old, multi-storied factories became dependent on aging machinery and cumbersome elevators and had difficulty competing with cities with modern plants which usually were only one-story tall and used fast, efficient horizontal conveyors to move goods from one work station to another.

Many of the city's family owned businesses were clos-ing or moving away as the founders died and younger family members ... eager to seek a career and fortune of their own ... had no interest in the business.

And it did not help that Utica was in the Northeast, a region whose industry was having difficulty competing with warmer regions and foreign countries.

"We must accept that fact that Utica can never return to its glory days," said Crisafulli. "We must concentrate, instead, on making sure that there are jobs available for the young people who love the area and want to live and work here.

Oneida County Historical Society

Washington and Genesee Streets in 1838, looking north. Washington Street is on the left with the steeple of the First Presbyterian Church in the background. Genesee Street is on the right.

Sports & Recreation

Oneida County nurtured great athletes, great sports

By John Pitarresi

The Utica Curling Club was organized in 1868 and preserved an ancient Scottish winter sport, played on ice with brooms and round granite stones. Among the many tournaments hosted by the club, the most prestigious was the 1970s Men's World Championship (the Silver Broom), the first time it was held in the United States. Photo by Edward Michael.

The post-World War II Utica Blue Sox baseball team and the Clinton Comets of the 1960s still live happily in the memories of thousands of Oneida County sports fans.

Those teams and their 1980s successors ... the Mohawk Valley Stars hockey team and the "new" Utica Blue Sox ... produced championships that thrilled fans and still spark plenty of nostalgia.

But the residents of Oneida County were a sporting breed long before those teams ever were imagined, and well before the dawn of the 20th century. Sports were enjoyed soon after pioneers from New England pushed into the area more than 200 years ago and interest intensified in the days preceding the Civil War.

Eventually, the county would turn out its share of great athletes and teams, from the 1886 International League baseball champions, to the 1947 Utica Blue Sox team whose core soon became the Philadelphia Whiz Kids, to the 1983 Blue Sox team that inspired a popular book by baseball journalist Roger Kahn.

Team sports did not really begin to develop until the middle of the 19th century. Before that, horse racing ... trotting, more than anything else, by most accounts ... was a major recreation.

And the horses of those days were a tough breed, apparently. In 1860, Broker, a well-known Central New York trotter, was the favorite of local aficionados in a 10-mile race, the result of which is unknown. In 1857, Broker had lost a 100-mile race from Albany to Whitesboro to a New York City horse.

Hunting and fishing also were common pastimes for the early residents of Oneida County, and they remain so today. Even then, Oneida Lake was a favorite destination of anglers, although in colonial times the most desirable fish sought there were landlocked salmon. The lake later was dominated by northern pike and then by walleyes, which continue to be the favorite of most visitors,

although many other species abound there.

The county also was blessed with many fine trout streams ... the upper portions of the Mohawk River, Oriskany Creek, West Canada Creek, Fish Creek and the Black River are just a few ... although many of them suffered for decades because of dams, mills and sewage.

In many ways, some of the creeks are in far better shape today than they were a century and more ago.

Still, in the earliest days, the waters were known for trout. In 1789, Dr. Samuel Hopkins wrote that the Oriskany "contained plenty of trout." The fish still are there, and thousands of anglers avidly pursue them.

Eventually, team sports did become important in the county, as they did throughout the nation in the years surrounding the Civil War.

The "Star of the West" cricket club, founded by English, Welsh and Scottish immigrants in Utica in 1845, probably was the county's first organized sports club. Games were played off Columbia Street between Cornelia and State streets in downtown Utica, later, on Grove Place and then at Utica Park, where the Masonic Home is now.

Curling

Newcomers from Great Britain also brought curling to the area when they arrived to work in the Mohawk Valley's burgeoning textile industry at mid-century. They began playing on a pond in Clark Mills in 1854, and the Utica Curling Club was founded in 1868, when Benjamin Allen laid out two rinks in the ravine of Ballou's Creek on Rutger Street. The club moved to Francis Street in 1915 and then to Clark Mills Road in Whitestown in 1997, after the downtown building burned.

Golf

Golf has been extremely popular for more than a century in Oneida County, and the Utica-Rome area has a great many courses, one of the highest per capita rates in the country. The Sadaquada Golf Club and the Yahnundasis Country Club were founded in the 1890s, and are among the oldest golf clubs in the nation.

The area has produced many standout golfers, including 1998 touring pros Wayne Levi and Moira Dunn. Levi was the PGA's Player of the Year in 1991, and Dunn, in her fourth season on the LPGA Tour, recently had her best finish ever with a fourth-place tie in the Rochester International. It was the late Ed Furgol, however, who made the biggest single splash, winning the 1954 U.S. Open at Baltusrol Golf Club in New Jersey.

Furgol, who came out of the great golf tradition at Twin Ponds Country Club in New York Mills, enjoyed a productive professional career, winning five times on the PGA Tour, finishing second six times and being named to the 1957 Ryder Cup team, all despite a boyhood injury that caused his left arm to be shortened and crooked.

Olympians

Oneida County also has been represented in the Olympics from time to time since the modern games were inaugurated in 1896, most recently by discus thrower Anthony Washington of Rome and wrestler Jason Gleasman of Boonville.

Former Utica Free Academy athlete Irving K. Baxter won the high jump and pole vault in the 1900 Paris Olympics and finished second in three other events. Speed skater Val Bialas was an early star of the Winter Olympics

... ice skating became popular in the county before the turn of the century, and Oneida County also was the home of another great skater, former world record holder Patty Sheehan.

Bicycling

Bicycling is a sport that rose to prominence in the 1890s, part of a national craze resulting from the invention of the "safety" bicycle, which made the sport available to just about anyone. Many important races were held in the area, which developed some outstanding athletes, including Emil Georg. Georg's daughter, Ruth, a longtime Utica educator who died recently, preserved his glittering collection of silver trophies, gold watches and other awards for his many victories in the early days of the century.

Football & Basketball

Football and basketball have been played and followed religiously by Oneida County residents for more than a century. A signature football event occurred when the fabled Carlisle Indians played Hamilton College at Utica Park in 1899.

There were many outstanding basketball teams through the decades at the high school, college and professional levels, including two versions of the Utica Olympics, in the New York State League, during the 1940s and the Continental Basketball Association in the 1980s.

Hockey

Hockey has been a local passion since A.I. Prettyman

The Utica Utes were members of the New York State League in 1913. The team was known as the Pent-Ups and the Asylums from 1898 to 1909, then became the Utes and disbanded, along with the league, after the 1917 season. The team originally took the name Pent-Ups from the county's first championship team of 1886.

brought the game to Hamilton College around World War I. The Clinton Hockey Club played its first game New Year's Day, 1928, marking the birth of a tradition that led to the Clinton Comets, the scourge of the Eastern Hockey League of the 1960s. The game's fortunes have known many ups and downs since … one of the ups being the 1982 Atlantic Coast Hockey League championship the Mohawk Valley Stars won under late coach Bill Horton … and hopes are high again now that a United Hockey League team will return to the Utica Memorial Auditorium next winter.

Baseball

Baseball was a focal point of Oneida County sports scene for more than a century. From Little League, Babe Ruth League, high school, American Legion and college teams, through the amateur teams that nearly every village and town once supported, and to professional teams like the Rome Colonels and Utica Braves and Utica Blue Sox, it has remained a primary focus of sports interest.

Oneida County has turned out a large number major league players, starting with Warren "Juice" Latham in the 1870s and Mike Griffin in the 1880s to present big leaguers Mark Lemke, Archi Cianfrocco and Chris Jones. Andy Van Slyke of New Hartford recently retired after a long and solid career, and Dave Cash, who starred for the Pirates, Phillies and Expos into the 1980s, now is a coach with the Rochester Red Wings.

The area's baseball history goes back to at least 1860, when the Utica Baseball Club was founded. There also was a baseball club in Whitesboro, and the teams met in June of that year, with Utica winning 39-8 in the county's first game for which there is a record.

Professional baseball made its debut in 1878, when the Crickets of the New York State League moved to Utica from Binghamton. Pro ball moved in and out of the area many times over the years, with teams in Utica and Rome. The first championship was won by the Utica Pent-Ups. The origin of the name is lost but local baseball historian Scott Fiesthumel believes it referred to the emotions of players or fans, or the fact that Utica was home to a large insane asylum … who won the International League title in 1886.

During that season, hundreds of fans would take the train to Syracuse to see their heroes play their arch-rivals, and July 4 they shuttled between the cities for a morning-afternoon doubleheader. A crowd of about 10,000 saw the teams play at Star Park in Syracuse, watching Utica win 10-2 after the Stars won the morning game 5-4.

Champions or not, the Pent-Ups moved to Wilkes-Barre in the middle of the next season, and there were many moves and franchise shifts in succeeding years. There were no more pennants, however, until the Utica Blue Sox won the Eastern League crown in 1945 and again in 1947. Manager Eddie Sawyer, future Hall of Famer Richie Ashburn and many of the rest those who would become the Philadelphia Phillies Whiz Kids of 1950 who won the Eastern League crown.

The Blue Sox were sold down the valley to become the Schenectady Blue Jays in 1951, and there was no more

Utica produced several champion bicyclists during the late 1880s and early 1890s. Among them were Frank Jenny (back right) and Emil Georg (front left). Courtesy, Miss Ruth Georg.

Wheelmen's Fountain in Cassville.

professional baseball in Oneida County until the Utica Blue Jays joined the New York-Penn League in 1977. The team caused a stir that season with future big leaguers, Jesse Barfield and Boomer Wells, in the lineup, along with fan favorite Rocket Wheeler.

Renamed the Blue Sox in 1981, the team won the NY-P championship in 1983, the "Good Enough to Dream" season that resulted in the book of that name by Roger Kahn, the team's president and noted author of "The Boys of Summer."

High schools

Today, Oneida County's sporting passion is reflected in high school sports. Rome Free Academy has had a long and storied football history, and still draws thousands of fans to its Friday night home games. Whitesboro and New Hartford have enjoyed standout football success, as well, in the last decade. Many of the area's boys and girls basketball teams have competed successfully on the state level, with the New York Mills boys and the Notre Dame girls winning state championships in the 1980s.

The long-standing passion for hockey has reached down to the scholastic level as well, with RFA, Clinton and New Hartford maintaining strong programs and a number of state titles in the last dozen years.

Boilermaker Keeps Utica Running

By Joe Kelly

Oneida County Historian

In 1999, more than 10,000 people are expected to sign up for the 22nd running of the Boilermaker Road Race, which has become Oneida County's biggest participatory event. No other Mohawk Valley athletic event comes close to the size of the Boilermaker.

The Boilermaker is also Oneida County's big spectator event. Thousands of people line the racecourse, which starts at Utica Boilers in east Utica and finishes at the F.X. Matt Brewing Company in west Utica. The athletes run through a tunnel of cheering spectators.

The Boilermaker is a race, yes, but it is much more than that. It has a million-dollar impact on Oneida County's economy. The Boilermaker brings former county residents home for family reunions, which are tied to the race. And the Boilermaker has improved the physical and mental well being of untold numbers of participants.

The Boilermaker has become the biggest 15-K (9.3 miles) race ever held in the United States. Not bad for a city the size of Utica and a county the size of Oneida.

There are some 15,000 races in this country, ranging from short ones to marathons. No matter what the size of the race, there are only 40 or so in the country bigger than the Boilermaker.

Quality wise, the Boilermaker is rated as one of the country's "top 100 races." That judgment is made by the editors of Runner's World magazine.

The reputation of the race is the reason why runners come to Oneida County from 45 states, and several foreign countries.

We once used the phrase "Boilermaker Sunday."

Then we started referring to it as "Boilermaker Weekend" because two days were packed with activities of one sort or another. Now we call it "Boilermaker Week," and it is filled with things such as a golf tournament, a children's run, and a pasta dinner.

By the way, local charities have linked up with the Boilermaker. The partnership has resulted in many thousands of dollars being raised for a wide variety of good causes.

But wait, there's more. The Boilermaker has spawned the newly created National Distance Running Hall of Fame on Genesee Street in downtown Utica.

The Hall of Fame has attracted the attention of the national news media. Articles about the Hall have appeared in USA Today, the New York Times and in other major newspapers.

Because of the Boilermaker, the Hall of Fame, America's Greatest Heart Run & Walk, the Falling Leaves Road Race and other running events, Utica is being referred to as the "running capital of New York State.

For the record, the Boilermaker was started in 1977, with $500 donated by race director Earle Reed's company, then called Utica Radiator, now called Utica Boilers. Some 800 runners signed up for that first Boilermaker.

We've come so far since then. The Boilermaker is a success story that all of us – runners and non-runners – can point to with pride. Think of the good things that never would have happened here in Oneida County if it weren't for the Boilermaker.

Migration and Ethnic Development

By Philip A. Bean

When the textile workers of New York Mills went on strike in 1916, the company retaliated by evicting them and their families from the company-owned houses. Photographic postcards of poignant scenes such as this were made and sold to arouse sympathy and raise money to aid the strikers. Courtesy, New York Mills Historical Society.

The Pioneer Era

The ethnic landscape of Oneida County has been transformed periodically since the seventeenth century by global population shifts. European colonialism, the migration of people of African descent, and immigration from Europe, the Caribbean, Asia and the Middle East have all shaped and reshaped the ethnic, social, cultural, political, and even economic history of the county; likewise, various groups have been drawn to the county by economic change both here and abroad. The history of Oneida County can therefore be seen as the story of the arrival and settlement of progressive waves of peoples, with some groups dramatically altering the ethnic composition and other aspects of the county at intervals that often coincided with the assimilation or declining presence of earlier inhabitants of the area.

As its name might suggest, Oneida County was once home to only one group of people, the Oneida Nation. At the time of their first contact with Europeans, the Nation consisted of perhaps as many as 4,000 people who settled in the southwest of the present county. However, the Oneidas experienced a series of misfortunes associated with the extension of European political and economic power into the Upper Mohawk Valley. To begin, an epidemic – presumably a result of the introduction of diseases to which Native Americans had no resistance – wiped out about 50 percent of the Oneida population in the 1630s. Epidemics of various kinds continued to hit the Oneidas and weaken the Nation throughout the remainder of the seventeenth century; by 1700, the Oneida population had been reduced to probably fewer than 2,000 individuals. In the closing years of the century, the French subjected the Oneidas and the other Iroquois to a series of punishing raids, which likewise took their toll. In addition, the Oneidas unfortunately became bitterly divided over Christianity, another import from Europe.

These religious divisions were, in turn, mirrored by political dividing lines in the Nation that would lead to a profound split among the Oneidas over the American

Revolution. While the vast majority cast their lot with the colonists, many of their leaders preferred a policy of neutrality in the conflict. In supporting the revolutionaries, these Oneidas were influenced considerably by the Rev. Samuel Kirkland, one of the first white settlers in what would become Oneida County. In addition to being a missionary among the Oneidas, Kirkland was also an enthusiastic and effective agent for the Revolutionary cause in the 1770s and 1780s.

Although the bulk of the Oneidas had been staunch allies of the former colonists, the government of New York State helped to force most of them progressively out of the state and into Wisconsin. By 1840, there were only 178 Oneidas in all of New York State, whose land holdings shrank progressively from 1,388 acres in 1840 to a mere 32 acres in 1920.

However, although the overwhelming majority were progressively pushed out of the county, the Oneidas remained a presence in the county to the present day. In addition, they left a lasting mark on the local agricultural landscape. The corn that still covers much of the rolling hills of the county was the most important of Oneida crops. Indeed, the Oneidas taught the first white settlers how to process this corn. Pomeroy Jones, the first county historian, wrote in 1851 that "the early settlers in many instances had to resort to the samp mortar, the pattern of which they borrowed from the Oneidas, to reduce their corn to a proper consistency for making of hominy." In addition, the influence of the Oneidas can be seen in some place names. The present community of Oneida Castle, for instance, is so named because it was the site of a fortified Oneida village. The name Oriskany was derived from the Oneida village named Orisata-aak, which was another Oneida "castle" at the time of the American Revolution.

As the first known inhabitants of Oneida County suffered a series blows that progressively eroded their presence in the region, the number of white settlers expanded slowly but steadily throughout the last decades of the eighteenth century. In the earlier part of the eighteenth century, settlers from the Palatine region of western Germany had settled throughout the Mohawk Valley. Even before the Revolution, a small handful of these German settlers are believed to have moved to what would become eastern Oneida County, as reportedly did a handful of Dutch settlers from the Lower Mohawk Valley (the Albany-Schenectady area having been part of the Dutch Colony of New Amsterdam before the British takeover in 1662).

The American Revolution disrupted, if not temporarily reversed, this first, limited flow of settlers of European stock into Oneida County, but the cessation of hostilities in 1782 opened what was then the western frontier to further settlement. The vast bulk of settlers in the first half century after the Revolution were migrants from neither the Mohawk Valley nor Europe. New immigration from Europe was largely disrupted by two decades of warfare set off by the French Revolution and Napoleon, only a decade after the end of the American Revolution. European immigration to America and to Oneida County would not resume significant levels until the second and third decades of the nineteenth century.

Instead, New Englanders were the chief beneficiaries of the opening of the western frontier to settlement. Many of these Yankees had gotten their first look at the land that would later become Oneida County during the Seven Years or French and Indian War (1756-63) and the American Revolution (1776-83); in both wars, troops from New England were garrisoned in the fortress at present-day Rome. For instance, Major Benjamin Hinman of Southbury, Connecticut, was stationed at Fort Stanwix during the Revolution, and was reportedly "so pleased with the character of the country...that he determined on the expiration of the war to settle there." In 1787 he moved to Little Falls; in 1797 or 1798, he resettled in Old Fort Schuyler (Utica); some years later, he established himself at Deerfield.

Almost 90 percent of the first wave of settlers in Whitestown (which then included all of the present county) came from either Massachusetts or Connecticut. As late as 1845, settlers from New England, and their children and grandchildren, accounted for almost half of the population of the county. Many of these early Yankee migrants came to Oneida County as a result of a phenomenon referred to as "chain migration" –that is, the process by which individuals entice their relatives and former neighbors to follow in their footsteps and settle in a new land. Pomeroy Jones wrote of Hugh White, the founder of Whitestown:

> "As a means for inducing his acquaintances in New England to emigrate, Judge White used to send to them, when opportunities offered, the largest and handsomest stalks of wheat, corn, oats, etc., also samples of his best potatoes and onions, as evidence of the productiveness of the soil."

As a result of White's efforts, many of the earliest settlers of the county came from Middletown, Connecticut. This type of story was repeated many times in the succeeding centuries, with each wave of migrants from other lands having come in greater numbers in reaction to encouraging news from former neighbors who settled in Oneida County.

The imprint of the migrations of the last two centuries and more can also be seen in the evolution of Oneida County's religious landscape. Given the fact that New Englanders constituted the bulk of the early migrants into Oneida County, it should not be surprising that Yankee religious sensibilities set the tone for much of the life of the county well into the eighteenth century. The first churches in the county were Congregationalist, the denomination that had dominated religious life in Puritan New England. Fittingly, these churches were established in Clinton and in New Hartford in August 1791 by Jonathan Edwards of New Haven, Connecticut, the son one of the most celebrated Yankee evangelicals of the eighteenth century, also named Jonathan Edwards. Congregational and Presbyterian churches, which effectively merged in Upstate New York and New England in the early nineteenth century, spread through the county as both the numbers and prosperity of settlers grew.

Government, church, family, and even business were frequently intertwined in the early days of the Oneida County. For instance, when Hugh White, the founder of Whitestown, was negotiating a contract with a neighbor in 1797 concerning the use of water from the Sauquoit Creek, he insisted that the other party "would become a Presbyterian, and join the congregation under the charge of the Rev. Bethuel Dodd." The first charters of Whitestown and Utica contained provisions requiring the local government to enforce the strict sanctity of the Sabbath. Church members were encouraged to monitor one another, to admonish, persuade, and guide brethren they deemed to have gone astray, and to report repeated or gross violations of moral codes to church authorities. Indeed, church courts initially wielded significant social influence in local communities, helping neighbors to ensure that church standards of day-to-day conduct were enforced. However, this practice of summoning people to face charges of violating the moral standards of the community ended in the early nineteenth century. As would happen in succeeding generations, an immigrant was a pivotal agent of this cultural change. In 1834 Alexander Bryan Johnson, a locally prominent resident from England was charged by the First Presbyterian Church in Utica with having "dishonored religion and truth" by publishing an essay in defense of delivery of mail on Sundays. Unlike earlier "respectable" residents of Oneida County, Johnson simply ignored the charges, did not show up at the church court hearing, and instead defected to Utica's Grace Episcopal Church. Not too long there-after, such trials ceased.

Welsh Immigration

Although European immigration to Oneida County did not reach peak levels until the opening of the nine-teenth century, members of other groups, notably the Welsh, came here in significant numbers beginning in the 1780s. By 1812, there were over 700 Welsh settlers in Oneida County; by 1855, Welsh immigrants and their chil-dren and grandchildren accounted for ten percent of the population of the county. In time more people of Welsh heritage would reside per capita, in Oneida County than in any other county in the United States. The Welsh were attracted to the county for the same reason as the New Englanders and the Mohawk Valley Germans and Dutch: the abundance of cheap land. Many came under the lead-ership of land agents, armed with at least a down payment for a homestead. "I have bought land here with a house on it and a place for all you to work your own land – if I have my health and life, within six years I will have paid for it all," wrote one local Welsh immigrant to his son in Wales. (He added in a post-script to his son: "If you do not come this summer I shall say goodbye to you all for ever.")

Welsh immigrants carved out an agricultural enclave in eastern Oneida County, in Remsen and the town of Steuben, between the 1780s and the 1840s. The historian Pomeroy Jones wrote in 1851: "The descendants of the ancient Cambrians form a hardy, industrious, and frugal, and of course thriving population. Their butter dairies, for which they are far famed, are carried on to great perfec-tion..." A Welsh immigrant in Trenton described life in his corner of the county in 1816 in slightly less poetic terms:

"There are plenty of shops and plenty to be had for money or goods. There is a good school within half a mile of our house...There are good woolen and cotton mills nearby...Welsh butter is going to many merchants in New York who make thousands of dollars every year...Many of the Welsh who did not have a pound are now worth many thousands."

There were also many skilled workers among the Welsh, many of whom settled in Utica (indeed, by 1800, the Welsh outnumbered every group in the village other than the New Englanders). The county – particularly Utica – became the center of the Welsh book publishing indus-try in America. As many as twelve firms operated locally at one time or another in the nineteenth century; much of the output of these ethnic presses consisted of collections of sermons and other books that catered to the profound religious piety of the Welsh.

Although the Yankee settlers of the county for some time maintained a high level of religious discipline, the early Welsh sometimes considered the Americans around them to be barely religious (one might note that I am speaking of the period before the great religious revivals of the 1820s and 1830s). "Religion is weak compared with the Old Country and the preachers are few," wrote one Welshman from Utica in 1818. Another Welsh immigrant wrote from Utica in 1832:

"When I came here first about twenty-eight years ago there was not one religious meeting house but soon after I arrived the Welsh built one for use in their language and that was the first!!! Now there are fifteen houses of worship of different denominations and three of them belong to the Welsh. There are more than forty Welsh preachers here."

Welsh immigrants were Methodist, Baptist, or Presbyterian, but all protestant; "A Welsh Catholic would

Capel Cerrig, Prospect Street, Remsen, 1831

be an anomaly, and they are peculiar in their hatred of all that appertains to Popery," wrote Pomeroy Jones. Both the first and second churches of any kind in Utica were Welsh (one Baptist, the other Congregational). By 1850 there were ten Welsh chapels in Remsen alone, most of which were Methodist, although there were also Baptist and Presbyterian congregations. In fact, in 1828 Welsh immigrants organized the "Oneida County Presbytery (Welsh)" at Penycaerau church, two miles east of Remsen. As a sign of the vibrancy of the Welsh ethnic community in Oneida County this Welsh presbytery did not merge with the English-speaking Utica Presbytery until over a century later, in 1936.

The Welsh established a string of institutions that, like churches, were to become characteristic elements of nearly every other immigrant community in the subsequent ethnic history of the county. The Welsh community produced one of the first of a long and rich line of local ethnic newspapers. In 1854, a group of investors in Utica established Y Gwyliedydd Americanaidd ("The American Watchman"), one of the earliest Welsh-language newspapers in the United States. In 1855, this publication was bought out by Y Drych, which had itself been established in New York City in 1851. In the early 1870s, Y Drych was purchased by Thomas J. Griffiths, a local Welsh printer, who moved it to Utica. Y Drych eventually became the only national-circulation Welsh-language newspaper in the United States. In 1814 the Welsh established the Ancient Britons' Society, probably the first ethnic organization of any kind in the county and certainly the first of many mutual aid societies established by various immigrant groups to provide insurance against sickness, death, and unemployment.

Choral societies were yet another distinctive contribution of the Welsh to the County's ethnic history. Pomeroy Jones wrote in 1851 that the Welsh are "a nation of singers, and in this part of public worship nearly the entire congregation join." Welsh singing societies held great annual singing competitions called Eisteffods. Such choral societies were not characteristic of all subsequent immigrant groups, although the German Gesangvereine (to be discussed below) were the equivalent of these Welsh choral societies in the history of the county.

Although Welsh immigrants continued to come to Oneida County and were to be a lively local presence into the twentieth century, by the 1840s the heyday of Welsh settlement in the county was over. In some regards, declining influx of Welsh farmers (not to mention farmers from New England, Germany, and other places) was a reflection of the success of Oneida County as a gateway to the West. In fact, by 1825 Oneida County was second only to New York County (i.e., Manhattan) in population, largely as a result of the power of the Erie Canal to draw thousands of migrants westward through Utica, Rome, and other local communities. Reflecting on the extent to which rural Oneida County had been settled, one Welsh immigrant in New York City stated bluntly in 1844: "the land has become dearer than usual...I am against [the Welsh] settling in mountainous districts where the land is covered with snow for five months of the year when the fertile lands of the Mississippi are much cheaper and have a more pleasant climate."

African-American Pioneers

While settlers of British parentage or descent – the New Englanders and the Welsh – dominated the first half century of settlement, a handful of people of African descent were also among the very earliest settlers. For instance, three African-Americans were brought to Utica in 1797 as slaves of Benjamin Walker, an Englishman who had served as Aide-de-Camp to Baron Friedrick von Steuben and George Washington during the American Revolution. Slavery was abolished in New York State in 1827, and even before then there was also a number of free Blacks in the county. Much of the county's still small African-American population would make its home in Utica, where slave sales probably ended in 1815, and where only one black person would remain enslaved by 1820. By 1840, there were 242 blacks in Utica, and 402 in the rest of the county.

By 1860 the number of African-Americans in the county had diminished, as had the black population in Utica. At this point, Blacks constituted only six-tenths of a percent of the overall population of the county and just under one percent of Utica's population. The local African-American population would not experience significant growth until nearly a century later. Although Oneida County would become a center of anti-slavery sentiment, many local residents undoubtedly shared the sentiment of Alexander Coventry, first President of the Oneida County Medical Society. He wrote that "free blacks are a great nuisance to the country: they are lazy, dishonest and profligate." Such attitudes undoubtedly did not make it easy for these black pioneers to establish themselves.

Nevertheless, this fledgling African-American community in Oneida County made progress during the nineteenth century, sometimes with the help of white residents. In 1815, local residents started giving Bible classes for African-American children in Utica, a mission taken on formally by the First Presbyterian Church in Utica in 1825. This constituted not just the first signs of black religious life, but the origins of efforts to provide education to local Blacks. In 1840 a school for black children had been started in Utica, by a student from Whitesboro's Oneida Institute, because they were excluded from local schools. By 1851, this special school was no longer required, as the Utica schools evidently became integrated.

African-Americans also established their own institutions for the improvement of their community. In 1826, local Blacks established one of the first ethnic mutual aid societies, which was succeeded in 1830 by the African Union Benevolent Society. An "African Church" was known to have existed as early as 1840, but the first formal religious congregation of which we know was Hope Chapel African Methodist Episcopal (A.M.E.) Zion Church, established in Utica around 1865 with the financial assistance of Theodore Faxton and other prominent local white residents. At the end of the twentieth century, Hope Chapel, is the oldest surviving black institution in the county.

The Arrival of the Irish and the Germans

Settlers from New England, the Mohawk Valley, immigrants from European lands, and the small handful of African-Americans, were sufficiently diverse that a frequent visitor to the county wrote, in 1802 that Utica "appears to be a mixed mass of discordant materials. Here may be found people of ten or twelve different nations and of almost all religions and sects..." However, Oneida County at this point was getting just its first taste of diversity. In the second decade of the nineteenth century, immigrants from Ireland became an increasingly prominent element of the local population. The first significant influx of Irish immigrants took place in 1817-25, when many came to dig the Erie Canal. The construction of the canal (the first spur of which was opened between Utica and Rome in 1817) brought thousands of Irish laborers to local communities. Once the canal was opened, many more Irish came to Oneida County in search of work, and they found the area going through a vigorous expansion. By 1830, only five years after the opening of the canal, the county's population had grown 23 percent, thus continuing to be the second most populous county in New York.

Irish immigrants and others were also brought to Oneida County by the Industrial and Transportation Revolution which the canal had helped to nourish. In 1832, the Mohawk and Hudson Railroad opened between Albany and Schenectady. In 1833-37 the Utica and Schenectady Railroad was built. In 1834-39, the Utica and Syracuse Railroad was constructed. The process continued throughout Upstate New York until it reached Buffalo. In addition, the railroads and canals themselves became sources of large numbers of permanent jobs, particularly in the county's urban areas. Finally, the middle decades of the nineteenth century witnessed the emergence of the powerful local textile industry, centered chiefly around Utica and the surrounding communities (like New York Mills and New Hartford). Between 1809 and 1847 some 34 textile companies opened in eastern Oneida County, and this was only the beginning. All of this created a powerful and continuing local demand for unskilled labor, the only work for which the sparsely educated mass of Irish

and later European immigrants were qualified.

Irish immigration to Oneida County was therefore well under way for decades before the famous Irish Potato Famine of 1845-49. Although the Famine helped to push more Irish people – who had been reluctant to leave their homeland – to come to the United States, it was the abundance of suitable work that persuaded thousands of Irish immigrants to settle in Oneida County. By 1855 Irish immigrants accounted for over ten percent of the population of the county, with the majority residing in its cities and other mill towns.

The arrival of the Irish began one of the great alterations in the religious life of the county. Previous to the first influx of Irish immigrants into the county in the early nineteenth century, Oneida County was solidly Protestant. However, by 1819 there were enough Irish immigrants in Oneida County to warrant the establishment of Utica's Saint John's Church, the first Roman Catholic parish in New York State west of Albany. Known initially as "The First Catholic Church of the Western District of New York," Saint John's included trustees from as far away as Johnstown, Auburn, Syracuse, Rochester, and the Genesee Valley, as well as from Utica and New Hartford. Utica's Nicholas and John Devereux, the two early Irish immigrants who founded the Savings Bank of Utica, were among the earliest benefactors of Saint John's. In fact, the first Catholic mass in the western part of the state was celebrated in John Devereux's home on Broad Street in Utica.

The early- and mid-nineteenth century also witnessed an influx of German immigrants into the county. Between the 1760s and the 1830s, the people of German descent who settled in the county were primarily from the Mohawk Valley. However, beginning in the 1830s, growing numbers of immigrants from Germany and Austria, along with significant numbers from Alsace-Lorraine (which was part of France until 1871) and Switzerland, began to settle in Oneida County. Like the Irish, German-speaking immigrants tended to settle in the county's urban areas and its larger towns and villages. However, unlike the Irish, the Germans had already lived in towns and even cities in Germany, and had brought a wide range of skills with them. Some were unskilled or semi-skilled, and these often found employment in local textile and woolen mills, particularly in West Utica. For instance, Barbara Koob, a young German immigrant who later became known as Mother Marianne of Molokai for her work among the lepers in Hawaii, evidently worked in the woolen mills of West Utica for about five years in the 1860s. Many were skilled craftsmen, making everything from wallpaper to pipe organs, and some were farmers. By 1855 German-speaking immigrants constituted over six percent of the population of the county.

The German community was divided into two principal religious groupings: Catholics and Lutherans. The German Lutheran community in Oneida County was nurtured by the preaching and organizational efforts of the Rev. Andrew Wetzel (1808-1880), a native of the German state of Wuerttemberg who came to the area in 1832. At the time of his arrival, only five German Lutheran families are known to have resided in the area, but by 1842 there were 259 communicants in Utica alone, enough to warrant what later became known as Zion Lutheran Church. The local Lutheran community was distinctive for the bitter disputes that sometimes erupted in the late nineteenth and early twentieth centuries over proposals to introduce or shift entirely to English language services. The local German Catholic community developed pretty much in tandem with the Lutheran community. In 1835, German Catholics established a chapel in West Utica; in 1842, they formally established Saint Joseph's Church, which at the time was the only German Catholic parish between New York City and Buffalo.

The Germans made a number of distinctive contributions to the social and cultural life of the county. In 1853, the local German community produced the first local immigrant newspaper, the Central New York Demokrat, which changed its name soon thereafter to the Utica Deutsche Zeitung. The Zeitung was edited and published for most of its existence by one man, John Schreiber, who died at his desk in 1907 after 50 years of service. The Zeitung thereafter maintained Schreiber's high standards, but circulation began to decline as a result of the growing assimilation of younger German-Americans and the aging of the German-speaking population in the early twentieth century. The Deutsche Zeitung ceased publication in February 1934. Germans were also fond of choral music societies, called Gesangvereine, the earliest of which was the Utica Liederkranz, founded in 1852. The Utica Maennerchor, founded in 1865, was long one of the leading such organizations in Central New York. At the close

of the twentieth century, the Maennerchor is the only Gesangverein, indeed, the last German ethnic organization left in the county.

German immigrants also established gymnastics clubs known as Turnvereine. The so-called Turner Movement was started in Germany in the early nineteenth century in reaction to Napoleon's conquest and humiliation of Germany. The "Turners" believed that the French had been able to bully Germany because the German nation was then divided into hundreds of small political units. The Turners in Germany believed that by keeping themselves in prime physical shape, they might someday help Germany become a united, progressive, and therefore powerful and respected land. When the American Civil War broke out, many Turners in Oneida County believed that American unity should be defended because promoting unification anywhere was progressive and inherently good. As a result, the Utica Turnverein, founded in 1854, ceased to exist during the American Civil War, its German immigrant members having volunteered in such great numbers to fight for the American Union. The Utica Turnverein was not re-established thereafter until 1882, at the height of German immigration to the county and the United States.

Jewish Community

Jews constituted another significant group of immigrants to the county in the 1840s and beyond. The very first Jewish immigrants who settled in the county came from Poland, but many of the hundreds who came here in subsequent decades were born in Germany. The vast bulk of the local Jewish community was and remained established in the urban areas of the county, particularly in Utica. In the late 1860s, for instance, only two Jewish farmers are known to have lived in the countryside (one in

Founded in 1882, the Utica Turn Verein or Turner Society was a local branch of a German organization devoted to physical and intelletural culture. This ladies' class, photographed about 1919, was directed by Fritz Nicke, standing in rear.

Trenton, the other in Rome). However, although they favored urban areas, early local Jews were familiar sights in the rural areas of the county, as the bulk of them were peddlers who traveled with carts of dry goods that they sold to farmers who were unable to get into town frequently. Between 1849 and 1871, 155 of the 225 Jews whose occupations were known in Utica were peddlers; 22 others were store owners, and virtually all the rest were skilled workers, including 14 cigar makers, five tailors, four cap makers, and two shoemakers. By 1848 the Jews in Utica were sufficiently numerous as to constitute a minyan ("quorum"), and they consequently founded the first Jewish congregation in the county, Beth Israel, near the corner of Whitesboro and Hotel Streets.

Nativism and Machine Politics

As Oneida County became ethnically most diverse than ever before, the reaction of more established residents was generally positive. The American or Know-Nothing Party, which promoted a nativist or anti-immigrant political agenda, enjoyed relatively limited support in Oneida County. Only ten percent of the voters of the county voted for the Know-Nothings, an average that was among the lowest in the State of New York. This is not to say, however, that the European immigrants who came to Oneida County in this period were never subjected to prejudice, quite the contrary. The Irish immigrant community sometimes had to contend with abusive treatment at the hands of the American-born Protestant majority. The popular activity of "Paddy baiting," for instance, was known in Oneida County in the early years of Irish immigration. One Irish immigrant recalled in 1872 how anti-Irish ruffians used to hang a Paddy, a dummy dressed like a stereotypical Irishman (decorated with a rosary of potatoes and a codfish), in an effort to goad Irish immigrants into a fight. He described one such incident that occurred at the Erie Canal Weighlock many years before:

"[The Weighlock] affords a capital place to display Paddy one fine, windy St. Patrick's day...it dangled in a reproachful contiguity to the Hibernian precinct...Then a strong party issued from Paddy Nichols' restaurant...and, meeting the enemy in open field, defeated him, with great effusion of blood on both sides."

However effective and gratifying such retaliatory violence might have seemed, poor Irish immigrants were to discover that there were more effective ways to master their opponents and to make their lives a tiny bit easier… become a political force.

The Irish motive for organizing politically went well beyond their need to defend themselves from nativist attacks. Many early nineteenth century Irish immigrants had had experience in political organization in rural Ireland, long before coming to America. Furthermore, in America they were restricted to the lowest paying jobs in an age in which there was no minimum wage, no unemployment insurance, no workmen's compensation, and no retirement pensions of any kind. Much of the Irish-American community therefore lived in dire poverty, particularly in the first decades of the local immigrant community. Political machines were organizations dedicated solely to winning elections so that the tools of local government could be used to help loyal needy voters. (Some argued that early machine politicians were also careful to help themselves, as well!) In return for their votes, the "faithful" or their friends or relatives were rewarded with jobs or other favors financed by local government.

A local man of New England stock, rather than an Irishman, was the first pioneer of machine politics in Oneida County. In the 1850s and 1860s, Orsamus Matteson operated a primitive form of machine that

Ancient Order of Hibernians, Ball Team Clambake, Clinton, NY – September 15, 1912

secured him a seat in Congress and a powerful voice in the politics of Central New York (it was "primitive" because Matteson used money out of his own pocket to fuel this machine, and eventually went broke doing so!). Nevertheless, the Irish seem to have been the pioneers of modern machine politics in Oneida County, in that they used government resources, rather than private ones, as the main source of the patronage and favors they used to secure and maintain power. This first modern political machine emerged in the the 1880s under the leadership of Thomas Wheeler, a Republican from Utica. The son of Irish immigrants, Wheeler served as Sheriff of Oneida County from 1889 until 1891, and remained a great influence in local politics until his death in 1916. Thereafter, two Irish-Americans likewise led a Democratic organization in the early twentieth century, again centered in Utica: M. William Bray and Charles Donnelly. Bray, an attorney, served as Lieutenant Governor of New York under Herbert Lehman in 1932-38; Donnelly succeeded his father as Sheriff of Oneida County in 1914; was elected as Mayor of Utica in 1929, and was later appointed Postmaster of Utica. These men would help cultivate the Italian political leaders who would dominate much of the urban political life in Oneida County between 1920 and 1960.

The Development of the Italian Community

The arrival of the Italians in the late nineteenth century began a shift in the predominant ethnic flavor of the county. As the numbers of Northern European immigrants, notably the Irish and the Germans, peaked and began slowly to diminish, immigrants from Southern and Eastern Europe were beginning to trickle into Oneida County. A handful of Italians had already settled in the county before the 1870s, most, if not all of whom were from Northern Italy. John Marchisi settled in Utica in 1817, where he became a successful pharmacist and a respected member of the local community. Another early settler, Alessandro Lucca, who arrived around 1853, made plaster images of famous people that he sold from his canal boat (which he was allegedly strong enough to pull from Utica to Rome in his periodic search for customers). However, only a few of Italian immigrants came to Oneida County before 1880, and the bulk of the thousands who came thereafter were unskilled peasants from Southern Italy.

As with other ethnic groups, southern Italian immigration into Oneida County was dominated in the early years by immigrants from identifiable villages. These pioneers then became the first links in chains of immigrants drawn from the Old World to the new, just as Hugh White's success had helped to induce some of his former neighbors to move from Middletown, Connecticut, to Oneida County in the 1780s and 1790s. The earliest Italian immigrants in Utica, for instance, came from the village of Laurenzana, in the southern region of Basilicata. The original chain of migrants from Laurenzana began with the Pellettieri brothers, one of whom married the daughter of the early local Italian settler, Alessandro Lucca. The Pelletieris became prosperous, and their success became a great inducement to other ambitious Laurenzanesi to come to Oneida County. A boarding house and saloon operated by the Pelletieris also became a temporary home and safe community center for Laurenzanesi who subsequently decided to join their friends in Oneida County.

In addition to immigrants from Basilicata, the remainder of the county's Italians came from Lazio (the region around Rome), Apulia (the "heel" of the "boot"), and Campagna (Naples and the surrounding region). Although Sicilians accounted for one-quarter of all Italian immigrants in the United States, they seem to have constituted a smaller proportion of the Italian population of Oneida County – probably as little as five percent of the Italian immigrant community in Utica, for instance.

Southern Italians, like the Poles and other groups that came to America between the end of the Civil War and 1920, were pushed from the land of their birth by shortages of affordable, fertile agricultural land. However, these immigrants were not drawn to places like Oneida County in search of land (which was then no longer so cheap or abundant as it was in the nineteenth century). They instead came in response to the demand for industrial labor, particularly in the county's growing number of textile and copper mills. Many of the Italians who first came in the 1870s and 1880s were drawn to the county by a major transportation construction project, the building of the North Shore Railroad. Many also came to Oneida County to work on urban paving projects and in the building industry. Since these lines of work were not carried on efficiently during the winter, many of the early Italian immigrants often spent their winters in New York City, where at least some of their families are known to have lived, before settling permanently in Oneida County.

Many southern Italians displayed a marked talent for small business, particularly in fields related to food processing and retailing. By 1902 Italian immigrants operated nearly ten percent of grocery stores in Utica even though less than five percent of the population of the city was Italian; by 1940, 95 of Utica's 311 independent grocery stores were owned by Italians. Especially in Utica and Rome, Italian immigrants engaged in a wide range of business activities, including baking, pasta making, olive oil packing and food importation, printing, furniture dealing, and real estate sale and development. In 1880, there were only 529 Italians in the county, but by 1900, over 2,000 Italians resided locally. By 1920, this number had risen to over 11,000, or more than six percent of the population of the county; more than 7,000 of these Italians had settled in Utica alone, and much of the remainder lived in

Rome. As late as 1970, Italian immigrants and their children constituted the largest group of foreign parentage in the county.

Like the Irish, Italian immigrants sometimes had to endure prejudice in Oneida County, ironically often from the Irish themselves. An Italian who came to Utica in 1882 later stated:

We were treated worse than dogs. We could not get a house to live in. We could not walk on Bleecker Street without having a fight with the gangs of Irish boys that stayed around the street corners.

Another local immigrant similarly commented that "we Italians had plenty of fist fights with the Irish or the Germans who used to like to call us 'dagos'." Nevertheless, relations between local Italians and other ethnic groups, particularly the Irish, were not always bad. Indeed, to some extent the reaction of other local ethnic groups to the Italians seemed to vary according to socio-economic status. While the Italians just cited were talking about the troubles they had with working-class Irish-Americans, more prosperous Irish-Americans were responsible for notable acts of charity toward the Italians. Just as more enlightened local Yankee-stock protestants donated the land on which Saint John's Roman Catholic Church was built in Utica, well-to-do Irish-Americans were generous in their donations to the first Italian church in the county…Utica's Saint Mary of Mount Carmel. Part of the credit for this generosity, though, needs to be assigned to the Kernan family, particularly Celia Repetti Kernan, who came from a wealthy New York City Italian family to marry Michael Kernan and became an effective and, by all accounts, charming advocate for her fellow Italians.

The bulk of Italian immigrants put great emphasis on the festa or feast of their patron saint, which was celebrated annually with colorful street festivals, special religious services, and even special foods. The highpoint of every festa was a parade in which a statue of the saint, decked with ribbons on which the faithful often pinned money, was carried through the streets of the neighborhood for all to see; the especially devout would walk barefoot in such parades in gratitude for a special favor granted by the saint.

Although Italian immigrants were Catholics, a small handful also became Baptists. In fact, Utica's Rev. Anthony Perrotta was a leading figure in the Italian Baptist movement in the United States. This tiny, but interesting minority of Italian immigrants were highly critical of the Pope and considered the feste to be distasteful, almost idolatrous displays. For several decades in the first half of the twentieth century, the national newspaper of the Italian-American Baptists, L'Aurora, was published in Oneida County.

The Italian Baptists did not by any means publish the only Italian-language newspaper in Oneida County. In fact, the county produced more Italian-American newspapers per capita than communities in which Italians settled throughout the United States. This distinction probably stemmed from the fact that the city of Utica had more Italian immigrants per capita than almost any community in New York State and, indeed, the country. In 1900 Utica's L'Avvenire ("The Future") became the first Italian-language newspaper between New York City and Buffalo. Between 1900 and the cessation in 1948 of the last local Italian-American newspaper, The Messenger (successor to the Messaggerodell'Ordine or "Messenger of Order," founded in 1921), over a dozen Italian-language publications were printed at one time or another in Oneida County, many of which have been preserved on microfilm.

In time, the Italians, like the Irish before them, learned that much could be accomplished through political action coordinated by an Italian political leadership. The great local Italian political leaders of twentieth century Oneida County became powerful forces in local politics. In Utica, for instance, the pioneer Pellettieri family organized local Italians under the ultimate leadership of the Irish Republican Wheeler machine beginning in the 1880s. As allies of Wheeler in a multi-ethnic, if Irish-controlled, political organization, Italians helped to influence county politics. By 1910, even prominent mainstream local politicians found it necessary to reckon with the "Italian vote." For instance, in gratitude for the help he received from local Italians, Congressman James S. Sherman (later Vice President of the United States) used his influence on Capitol Hill to have Utica named a Port of Entry, which was advantageous for local Italian food importers.

In time, Utica's many Italian Republicans came under the leadership of an immigrant named Alfred Bertolini, who was known as the "unofficial Mayor of Utica" by the early 1920s. However, the 1920s also witnessed the rise of a local Democrat Italian-American leader who would become a force in Utica and county politics for the better part of four decades: Rufus Elefante. The Italian Democratic and Republican political organizations fought an intense struggle for the Italian vote throughout the 1920s and into the early 1930s. On the eve of the elections of 1929, however, Bertolini died prematurely, leaving Italian Republicans in disarray and Democrat Rufus Elefante the single most significant political force. In the decade that followed, the bulk of Utica Italians shifted toward the Democratic Party, which provided many poor residents of the county with desperately needed assistance during the Great Depression.

Eastern Europeans

Just as the Italians were beginning to come to Oneida County in increasing numbers in the late nineteenth century, the Poles and Ukrainians were also arriving. The first wave of Polish immigrants came from the German-controlled West Prussia and Austrian-occupied Galicia. By 1900, there were 1,125 Poles in Oneida County, and this number rose dramatically to 7,073 by 1920. Of these, 4,091 resided in Utica, and much of the remainder of the Polish immigrant community was centered in the village of New York Mills. After 1905, Polish immigrants were also coming in large numbers from the Russian-controlled portion of Poland, including at least some who allegedly were avoiding conscription into the Russian Army during the Russo-Japanese War. A very large proportion of the Polish population worked in local textile mills and other factories; as with the Italians, some were also employed by various railroads.

The Poles were Catholics, and like the Italians, the local Polish community produced a minority who dissented from the majority religion. Rather than join a Protestant denomination, as did a handful of local Italians, some local Poles instead joined the Polish National Catholic Church, which had broken with the Vatican and placed considerable emphasis the need to preserve not just the faith, but also the language and national identity of the Polish people. Two parishes of the Polish National Church, Holy Cross and Sacred Heart of Jesus, were established in Utica and New York Mills, respectively; the two parishes merged in 1988 following the destruction of Holy Cross by fire.

Another distinctive Polish contribution to the ethnic life of Oneida County was the establishment of local lodges, or "nests," of the Polish Falcons, a group very similar to the German Turnvereine. The Falcons, like the Turners, were dedicated to gymnastics and to the libera-

tion of their homeland from foreign domination, by force of arms if necessary. Many Falcons joined the Polish Army in World War I in order to expel the Germans, Austrians, and Russians who had occupied Poland since the late eighteenth century.

Like other immigrant communities, local Poles produced their own newspapers, the most notable of which was Utica's Slowo Polski ("The Polish Word"), which was published from the first decade of the twentieth century until 1966. Like many other local ethnic newspapers, Slowo Polski was a nationalist newspaper which defended Poland's right to independence from the time before Poland's recreation in 1918-19, through the period of Nazi domination, and well into the era of Communist and Soviet domination.

In the same period that witnessed the influx of the Poles, significant, if relatively small numbers of settlers, came from the western Ukraine to settle in Oneida County. There are reports that a small number of Ukrainians had migrated to the area by the end of the nineteenth century; what became of these immigrants is not known, and some might very well have melted into the local Polish population. By the time of the First World War, however, sufficiently large numbers had come to warrant the establishment of Ukrainian Catholic churches in Utica and in Rome. The Ukrainians fell religiously into one of two general groups, the Ukrainian Rite Catholic church and the Eastern Orthodox Church. Which church one belonged to depended largely on which part of the Ukraine one came from, with the Catholics coming from the western part closest to Catholic Poland.

Tomaino's Grocery (above) and a store run by Gennaro & Albert Domeneione, 944 Mary Street, July 1983.

Casimir Pulaski, celebrated Polish originator of American Cavalry.

The Syro-Lebanese and the Jews

In the mid-1890s, the local Syro-Lebanese community also began to emerge. The core of the early community were immigrants from the town of Baskinta, in central Lebanon, although there were also immigrants from what would become Syria, principally the city of Aleppo (Syria and Lebanon were one unit in the Turkish Ottoman Empire. In addition, most Lebanese and Syrians considered themselves a single people into the 1930s, when more distinct group identities began to develop, hence the expression of "Syro-Lebanese". Like the early local Jewish community, a large proportion of the earliest Lebanese settlers were peddlers. These immigrant peddlers were part of a Lebanese business network that acquired its merchandise from Butrus Saad, a fellow Basinktan merchant who lived in Brooklyn. About one-third of Syro-Lebanese immigrants were settled at the turn of the century in New York Mills and Whitesboro, where they, like their Utica counterparts, found work in textile mills. By 1910, the number of Lebanese immigrants who had settled in eastern Oneida County had grown to approximately 600, up from an estimated 100 ten years previously. In 1920, by conservative estimates, at least 2,500 Lebanese-Americans (that is, immigrants and their children) were living in the county. In time, some of them also went into farming, particularly around Clinton. Small business remained an important feature of the Lebanese immigrant work world in the urban areas into the post-World War II era. By 1920 there were 47 Syro-Lebanese grocers in the Utica area, up from 13 in 1910; this number would grow steadily up to a peak of over 60 in the 1940s. Syrians and Lebanese in Oneida County were members of one of three Eastern churches: the Maronite Catholic, the Melkite Catholic, and the Orthodox. The Maronites, by far the largest of the three groups, drew members from the Lebanese community; Syrians were either Melkite Catholics or Orthodox.

The local Jewish community, first established in the 1840s, did not experience significant growth until 1870, when there was a new influx of Jewish immigrants from Russia (including Poland) and Germany. The number of Jewish immigrants increased in the 1880s as a result of the Russian Pogroms. By 1920, several religious congregations had been established in Utica and one in Rome. By 1930, there were some 2,500 Jews in Utica alone, which was home to a lively Jewish quarter in the lower downtown and a growing middle-class community in Corn Hill. As in many Jewish communities, the local Eastern European Jewish immigrant community produced its fair share of socialists, some of whom joined Utica's Jewish Arbeiter Ring ("the Workers' Circle"). Established in 1906, the Arbeiter Ring maintained a reading room stocked with Yiddish literature, and sponsored lectures, literary discussions, and Yiddish theater productions. However, Jewish organizations such as this often consisted of artisans and other skilled or educated men, and as its members became increasingly prosperous in the 1920s, the Arbeiter Ring slowly dwindled.

The historical concentration of particular immigrant groups, like the Jews, in cities and larger towns of the county after the Civil War was a result of several factors. Work was most available in the cities, and most immigrants did not come with enough cash to establish themselves as farmers in the rural areas of the county. In addition, some immigrant groups were not interested in farming even though they had been overwhelmingly peasant in Europe. The Southern Italians, like the Irish, had experienced considerable unhappiness and suffering because of their ties to agriculture in their homelands, and were usually not eager to become farmers again (however much the Italians were great urban gardeners). In addition, some groups, like the Italians, came from societies in which peasants lived in small, compact villages, from which they went out to their fields to work. In contrast, American farmers lived in relatively isolated farmhouses and often had to make an effort to "go into town" in search of company and necessities. The Italians and the Irish were among those who would have considered the daily life of the American farmer to be profoundly lonely and therefore unappealing, even if they were in a position to buy farmland. Other immigrant groups, like the Jews and many of the Germans, had been craftsmen and merchants, not farmers, back in Europe; such immigrants had little interest in agriculture even if they had served rural areas before they migrated to America.

By 1910, the settlement patterns of the various immigrant groups in Oneida County were pretty much as they would remain for much of the twentieth century. Although the number of European immigrants who settled locally continued to increase until the 1930s, the heyday of European immigration to the United States was disrupted irrevocably by the outbreak of the First World War. As each country in Europe went to war in 1914-15, each put a halt to the migration of men of draft age (precisely the group most likely to emigrate). At the same time, the German policy of using submarines to harass shipping across the Atlantic made emigration to America in 1914-18 dangerous and therefore distinctly unappealing. However, the war was to have an immense impact not just on those who might have come to Oneida County, but on those who had already settled locally.

World War I and the Red Scare

Oneida County's ethnic life was turned upside down by the First World War and its aftermath. When the conflict began in the summer of 1914, various groups came to the aid of their homelands. For instance, German-speaking immigrants and their children organized efforts to help Germany supposedly defend itself against its enemies. Indeed, the day that Britain declared war on Germany, German immigrants from throughout the county were gathered in Utica to dedicate a statue to Baron Friedrich Wilhelm von Steuben, whom they considered a symbol of both their German and American identities. The dedication ceremony turned into a rally in support of their Vaterland; as enthusiastic German-Americans proclaimed their support for Germany, few probably suspected that this moment, which was to have been one of the most joyous in the history of the Germans in Oneida County, was the prelude to tragedy.

At the same time, hundreds of British and Canadian immigrants flocked to the British Army recruiting stations in Canada (a British recruiter became active in Utica only in February 1918). For instance, much of the county's Welsh-American community responded enthusiastically to the British call to arms. "Militarism must be met with and crushed by militarism," wrote the local Welsh publication, the Cambrian, "right is helpless and hopeless against might." Among the British immigrants who attained distinction in defense of their homeland against Germany were Stella Jenkins, a nurse who was awarded the Royal Red Cross by King George V for "valuable services with the armies in France and Flanders," and Reginald Heath, who boasted that he had flown 32 different types of aircraft during his career in the Royal Air Force.

The local Polish and Italian communities were likewise inspired to support the causes of their nations. The county's several thousand Poles raised over $100,000 for the Polish cause, despite the modesty of their economic means. Hundreds of Poles also volunteered to fight for the freedom of their homeland under the banner of a newly established Polish Army in France during the war; these same volunteers also defended Poland from the Soviets immediately following the war. At least some of these Polish volunteers had been involved with the nationalistic Polish Falcons organization before the war. As many as 1,000 or more local Italians voluntarily returned to Italy to fight in the Alps, a region that was more foreign to most of these southern Italians than was Oneida County. Many thousands of those who remained behind in Oneida County participated in fundraising events, rallies, and other demonstrations of their love of their homeland. For example, over 3,000 Italians in Utica marched in an one impromptu parade in 1916 to commemorate the Italian conquest of the city of Gorizia, a key Austrian stronghold.

While local Jews had no homeland to defend, many were profoundly moved by the suffering that the war was causing fellow Jews in Eastern Europe. In fact, the war began to intensify interest in Zionism, the movement to establish a separate homeland for the Jews. A speaker at a Jewish relief rally held in Utica in 1916 expressed this feeling that fellow Jews were being used as pawns in a war by rulers who were either anti-Semitic or not concerned about the interests of their Jewish citizens:

> Three and a half million Jews are being offered up to preserve royalty in the old World. When the war is over the countries will care for their own – all have their own countries to return to, but the Jews have no country.

Similarly, the war helped to intensify local Lebanese, Syrian, and Armenian demands that their compatriots be liberated from the control of Turkey, which was fighting on the side of Germany in the war.

All of these immigrant demonstrations of devotion to their homelands did not go over well with much of the population of the county, particularly those who had (or believe they had) no ethnic affiliation. Many local residents became concerned that, in permitting so many foreigners to settle in the county (not to mention the rest of the country), Americans had permitted their land to become an extension of the battlegrounds of Europe. Indeed, many residents of the county began to question the loyalty of immigrants, arguing that immigrant demonstrations of love of their homelands during the war indicated clearly that immigrants were incapable of becoming "real" Americans.

The first group to feel the effect of the growing anti-immigrant backlash were the German-Americans, who had put themselves in the unenviable position of defending and supporting a country for which a very large portion of the county had little or no sympathy. The attacks of the German-American community, especially the county's German newspaper, the Deutsche Zeitung, on President Wilson also did not sit well with many residents of the county. When America entered the war against Germany in April 1917, the reaction against the local German-speaking community was ugly. The Utica School District banned the teaching of German on the grounds that the German language somehow supposedly brain-washed the young, turning them into unthinking, war-mongering, pro-German maniacs. The Sheriff of Oneida County published a statement in English and German in the Deutsche Zeitung warning German immigrants to "keep their mouths shut" or face "severe penalties"; indeed, several German-Americans in Oneida County were arrested under the provisions of the American Sedition Act for criticizing the American war effort in 1917-18. Out of fear of being associated with supposedly disloyal institutions, many German-Americans abandoned their social organizations and canceled their subscriptions to the Deutsche Zeitung.

Thousands of immigrants and their children had fought in the United States armed forces or in those of countries fighting side-by-side with America; thousands more worked in factories in the Utica-Rome area manufacturing weapons for the United States and other countries fighting against Germany. Despite this contribution to the American and Allied victory in 1918, after the war the hostility that German-Americans had borne in 1917-18 now focused on immigrants in general. Many American-born residents began to regard their foreign-born neighbors — and not just the German-Americans — with suspicion.

Much of the American public was concerned that the Bolshevik Revolution in Russia could spread and lead to unrest and even upheaval in this country. Prejudicial attitudes toward European immigrants, including the not uncommon belief that immigrants from the Mediterranean and Eastern Europe were "racially inferior" (an idea that had started to become popular during the war), intensified fear that immigrants were especially susceptible to "dangerous" doctrines like Communism.

In Oneida County, these concerns were fed by the considerable labor unrest that followed the war. In the summer of 1919, copper workers in Rome, the great bulk of whom were Italian immigrants, went out on strike for better wages and working conditions. The atmosphere in Rome was tense, and at times the dispute took unpleasant turns, including the discovery of a bomb built by unknown individuals allegedly associated with the strike. However, a major disruption of local life was headed off by the intervention of Governor Al Smith, who sent Francis Perkins (who would later serve in the Roosevelt Administration as the first female Cabinet member) to mediate a settlement of the disputes between workers and management. No sooner had the Rome strike ended with a settlement favorable to the workers but an even more intense dispute broke out in the Utica textile industry. The strike, which lasted from July until December 1919, centered in Italian-dominated East Utica, although workers from the quarter's small Polish community also played an active part in the dispute. The struggle took an especially nasty turn in October, when policemen fired over 250 rounds at workers protesting against the arrest of one of their leaders outside the Oneita mill on Broad Street.

In the aftermath of the October 1919 shootings, many members of the wider local community became concerned that the strikes in Utica and Rome were parts of a vast attempt to bring about a workers' revolution in the United States. Local newspapers carried full-page advertisements claiming that "the Red Flag of Revolution" had been raised by immigrant radicals in Oneida County. Editorial writers commented that immigrants had to learn that they should shun "un-American" doctrines and ideas or "go back from whence they came." Similar concerns, along with long-standing prejudices toward immigrants, led to the passage of federal legislation in 1924 that permanently restricted immigration, particularly by such "inferior" peoples as the Southern and Eastern Europeans.

Era of Immigration Restriction

As a result of immigration restriction imposed by Congress after World War I, Oneida County was affected far less by European immigration from the 1920s until the later part of the twentieth century, and the composition of the population began to settle. European immigrants still continued to trickle into the county, but immigrant populations began to age and decline throughout the first half of the twentieth century. The Italians, Poles, Jews, Syro-Lebanese, and others reached their peak numbers in the 1920s and 1930s. The most notable demographic change became apparent by 1940, when the Italian and Polish immigrant populations started to decline; as old settlers began to disappear, they were not being replaced by sufficient numbers of newcomers.

However, the local Polish and Ukrainian communities experienced an influx of newcomers after World War II, as people displaced by war, the shifting boundaries in Eastern Europe, and the rise of Communism came to America as refugees. Many were drawn to Oneida County because they were aware that they would find established communities of older immigrants, many of whom not only welcomed them, but would help them get established in the county. This influx of "new blood" helped to reinvigorate these Eastern European groups, which became active and vocal critics of the post-war Russian domination of Eastern Europe. For instance, Poles and Ukrainians were prominent in anti-Communist demonstrations locally in the 1950s. As late as the 1980s the local Polish-American community raised tens of thousands of dollars to help the Solidarity movement in Poland survive the Communist repression. On one occasion, the "Mohawk Valley Supporters of Polish Solidarity" sent $2,000 to the wife of Lech Walesa after the resistance leader was arrested by the Polish authorities.

Migration of southern African-Americans

The arrival of thousands of African-Americans constituted the single most significant change in the county's ethnic make up in the decades following the Second World War. As late as 1940, there were only 951 African-Americans in the county, 514 of whom lived in Utica, which has been the center of black life in Oneida County since the early 1800s. By 1950, however, there were 1,500 Blacks in Utica alone. These black Southerners had much in common with earlier waves of migrants. Many African-American migrants came to Oneida County in this period initially in search of seasonal work, as pickers, particularly for local bean growers. In the years following the Second World War, as many as 6,000 of these migrant workers were in Oneida County during picking season, which stretched from May until October. In this can be seen a parallel to the history of other immigrant groups whose the pioneers originally came to Oneida County for seasonal work. Just as the early migratory history of some local ethnic groups was dominated by immigrants who came from one town or region, a large proportion of early black migrants came to Oneida County from one community: Belle Glade, Florida.

These temporary communities slowly transformed themselves into a permanent local presence in the 1950s and 1960s. Searching for entertainment and other community amenities, these early, periodic visitors to the county were drawn from the farm lands and into Utica, where they made friends and learned about possible job and housing opportunities. Long closed out of educational opportunities in the still segregated South, they also found that local schools were open to all, regardless of race. The racial barriers that had kept Blacks out of the local textile mills had begun to fall during the Second World War, when labor came at a premium. New employers of the post-World War II era began to hire black settlers in increasing numbers. For many African-American migratory workers, Oneida County seemed to offer as promising a future as it did to earlier immigrants. Even though they found an environment that was in some ways more congenial from the one they left behind in the South, African-Americans, like many of the immigrant groups that settled in Oneida County, often encountered prejudice and discrimination.

Just like earlier waves of European immigrants, black migrants had come to Oneida County with relatively few skills in hope of finding industrial work. However, the exodus of the textile mills (to the South, ironically) and the contracting importance of the Rome copper industry occurred at precisely the time when this new African American migration was under way. This issue of the timing of their arrival constitutes one of the chief, if not the key distinguishing characteristic between the black migrants of the late twentieth century and the European immigrants who came in the nineteenth and early twentieth centuries.

In the closing decades of the twentieth century, the ethnic character of Oneida County was again altered by the influx of more refugees, many of whom, like their predecessors in the 1950s, had fled Communist oppression. Most notable among these were refugees from Viet Nam, Cambodia, and Laos who came to the county, particularly Utica, in the decades following the end of the American war in Viet Nam. However, many more refugees came as a result of the collapse of the Soviet Empire in Eastern Europe after 1989. Chief among these refugees were numerous Russians, many of whom are evangelical Christians who had been subjected to religious discrimination in their homeland, and Bosnians, many of whom are Muslims had suffered as a consequence of the disintegration of Yugoslavia. The stories of these groups, and of

the Puerto Ricans who had started coming to the area decades earlier, are yet to be told. They await community historians who will record and interpret the experiences of the pioneers of their communities, just as George Schiro chronicled the history of local Italians in 1940 and Rabbi Kohn recounted the history of local Jews in 1959. If these relative newcomers are able to preserve the stories of their local ethnic communities they will set the groundwork for some historian in the third century of Oneida County.

Bibliography

Bagg, M.M., *Memorial History of Utica, N.Y.,* Syracuse: D. Mason and Company, 1892.

Bean, Philip A., *"Germans in Utica,"* Utica: Utica College of Syracuse University, 1990.

_____, *Fatherland and Adopted Land: Irish-, German- and Italian-American Nationalism,* (1865-1950), doctoral dissertation, University of Rochester, 1994.

_____, *"The Great War and Ethnic Nationalism in Utica, New York, 1914-20,"* New York History, LXXIV (4), October 1993, pp. 382-413.

_____, *"The Irish, the Italians, and Machine Politics,"* Journal of Urban History, 20 (2), February 1994, pp. 205-239.

_____, *"The Role of Community in the Unionization of Italian Immigrants,"* Ethnic Forum, 12 (1), 1992, pp. 36-55.

Briggs, John W., *An Italian Passage: Immigrants to Three American Cities,* 1890-1930, New Haven: Yale University Press, 1978.

Campisi, Jack, and Laurence M. Hauptman, *The Oneida Indian Experience: Two Perspectives,* Syracuse: Syracuse University Press, 1988.

Clarke, T. Wood, *Utica for a Century and a Half,* Utica: The Widtman Press, 1952.

Conway, Alan, ed., *The Welsh in America: Letters from Immigrants,* Minneapolis: University of Minnesota Press, 1961.

Ellis, David M., *The Upper Mohawk Country,* Woodland Hills, California: Windsor Publications, 1982.

Goldenes Jubilaeum: Utica Deutsche Zeitung, Utica: Utica Deutsche Zeitung Company, 1903.

Hanley, Sister Mary Laurence, *A Song of Pilgrimage and Exile: The Life and Spirit of Mother Marriane of Molokai,* Chicago: Franciscan Herald Press, 1980.

The History of Oneida County, Utica: C.L. Hutson Company, 1977.

Jones, Pomeroy, *Annals and Recollections of Oneida County,* Rome: A. J. Rowley, 1851.

Kohn, S. Joshua, *The Jewish Community of Utica,* New York, New York: American Jewish Historical Society, 1959.

Moses, John G., *The Lebanese in America,* Utica: John G. Moses, 1987.

Moses, John G., *How the Lebanese Advanced Civilization,* Utica: John G. Moses, 1998.

Pula, James, ed., *Ethnic Utica,* Utica: Ethnic Heritage Studies Center, 1994.

Ryan, Mary, *Cradle of the Middle Class,* New York: Cambridge University Press, 1983.

Schiro, George, *Americans By Choice,* Utica: Thomas Griffiths' Sons, 1940.

Rocks & Rills

Natural Characteristics

By Stephen S. Olney
Oneida County Department of Planning

Trenton Falls Gorge

INTRODUCTION

Oneida County contains the upper reaches of streams which flow eastward to the Hudson River, westward to Oneida Lake and Lake Ontario, north to Lake Ontario, and south to the Susquehanna River. It is characterized by a broad lowland in the central part occupied by the Mohawk River to the east and the Oneida Lake plain to the west. North and south of this central lowland is hilly terrain.

The height of land in this east-west lowland became the site of the City of Rome. Here was located the Carrying Place between the Mohawk River flowing to the east and Wood Creek and Oneida Lake flowing to the west. This divide at about 419' elevation provides the easiest route of travel from the East Coast around the Allegheny Mountains to the interior. During the Colonial Period the major travel route was the river system and the Carrying Place became the site of a series of fortifications culminating in construction of Fort Stanwix in 1758. It was also the site of the first canal construction of the Western Inland Lock Navigation Company in 1791 and the site of the first work on the Erie Canal in 1817. In later years the developing railroads also utilized the "water level route" and to this day the Hudson-Mohawk Valleys and the Lake Ontario and Lake Erie plains provide the most energy-efficient travel route between the East Coast and the interior, whether by water, rail, or highway. Thus the east-west lowland passing through Oneida County was a key factor in its early military importance, its early settlement, and the development of commerce. In contrast, the hilly terrain to the north and south provided obstacles of varying intensity which were overcome in time by construction of turnpikes, the Chenango and Black River Canals, and railroads. Compared to the east-west route, the north-south routes were characteristically higher in cost to build and operate, and produced far less revenue.

On the following pages notes are presented on the topography, geology, water, and climate of the County.

TOPOGRAPHY

The topography of Herkimer-Oneida Counties has been shaped primarily by glacial action, including water erosion as the glaciers retreated, and by present drainage of snow and rainfall. These natural processes have given the area a highly varied surface both in elevation, which varies 1,575 feet, and slope, which ranges from the flat sand plains around Rome to the precipitous walls of Boonville Gorge and Trenton Gorge.

Overall, the land tilts downward from the Adirondacks in the northeast to the Mohawk River-Oneida Lake valley, rising again towards the south and the Appalachian Plateau. Low points occur in the valley corridor at Oneida Lake on the west, 370 feet, and where the Mohawk River leaves Oneida County on the east, 390 feet. Between these points, an elevation of 419 feet at Rome divides the Mohawk and Oneida Lake watersheds. Tassel Hill, the highest point in Oneida County at 1,945 feet, occurs along the ridge dividing the Mohawk and Susquehanna River watersheds. Much of Oneida County is level, particularly the triangle bounded by the Cities of Utica, Rome and Oneida; and below 1,000 feet in elevation. Only a few exceptional hills protrude above 1,500 feet.

GEOLOGY

Three broad aspects are considered in the following geological analysis of Oneida County: (1) surface geology which deals with the earth-molding events of various time periods; (2) bedrock geology covering bedrock and soil building material; and (3) mineral resources and reserves, which are summarized for both past extractive activities and present reserves.

Surface Geology. "The enormity of geologic time is difficult to comprehend. If we could compress the span of geologic history, a time interval extending from the birth of our planet, some 4½ billion years ago, to the present, into a motion picture lasting a full year, man would make his first appearance at 11 p.m. on New Year's Eve." So says John Broughton in The Geology of New York State. Because of its vast scale, geologic time is not measured in precise years but rather in eras and periods. More than a billion years ago during the Precambrian era, an interval spanning seven-eights of geologic time, the original rock crust of the earth was formed. The Adirondack mountain region still exposes these ancient rocks on its surface although elsewhere in New York Precambrian formations are now buried under thousands of feet of younger sedimentary rocks. The present Adirondacks in northern Herkimer County and elsewhere represent the worn remains of an ancient mountain system which has been slowly eroded through the years.

The next era, the Paleozoic, about 420 million to 600 million years ago, brought submergence under vast seas extending to the uppermost Adirondack peaks. Not one flood, but repeated rising and falling of both water bodies and land masses caused many layers of sediment to be deposited and compressed into hard rock. Fossils and other records give evidence of this action. Many local streams have exposed these fossil records in the rock strata along their banks. In general, the Paleozoic Era developed much of what is now New York State, while later time periods were spent in reorganizing, moving, and eroding its formations.

During the Mesozoic Era, about 20 million years ago, very gradual erosion of mountain ranges relieved pressure from the earth's crust, causing the old Appalachian mountain area, as well as the Adirondack, to move slowly upward, exposing their Precambrian roots or basement rocks. Other than this very slow action, the higher elevations were free of violent change; their primary experience was of gradual erosion by wind and water which carried quantities of surface material to the lower plains.

Not all of the relatively short Mesozoic Era was quiet. Volcanic activity occurred within the state but little can be traced to Oneida County. The Palisade Cliffs along the Hudson River are an example of an igneous mass dating from this period. Very limited dark-colored dike rocks found in the county may relate to activity of this time.

The familiar landforms which we see today were largely formed during the current Cenozoic Era which started about 63 million years ago. The deeply eroded Adirondacks and the eastern seaboard of North America again uplifted. These renewed peaks were in turn subjected to erosion which washed their sediment onto the continental shelf of the Atlantic coast.

The Ice Age of the continent has had several reoccurrences, the last about 10,000 years ago. The force and power of its mobile ice sheet, which marked even the highest peaks, first broke loose and then deposited vast quantities of surface material. The pattern of material left during its melting is very evident today. As the rate of

Mineral Resources
figure 1

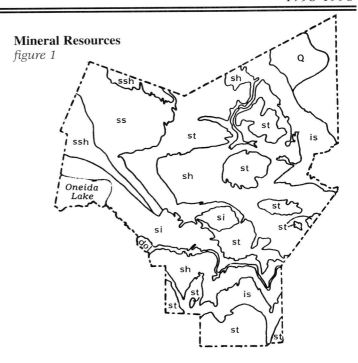

dol DOLOMITE principally (Ca,Mg) CO 3 uses: flux, bldg stone; on GMNYS* Si, Css

is LIMESTONE uses: flux, bidg stone, aggregate, agstone, cement; on GMNYS Obr, Otbr, Dhg, Don

st SHALE & SILTSTONE uses: shale light weight aggregate, cement; on GMNYS Of Dh, Dhm, 01

sh SHALE uses: light weight aggregate, cement; on GMNYS Ou, Sbs, Sbc, Sv

ss SANDSTONE uses: aggregate, source of silica; on GMNYS Oo

ssh SANDSTONE & SHALE uses: same as sandstone and shale; on GMNYS SmOq

si SANDSTONE, SHALE, & HEMATITE uses: same as sandstone and shale; hematite uses: paint pigment, iron ore; on GMNYS Scl

mu METASEDIMENTARY ROCKS UNDIFFERENTIATED includes quartzite, marble biotite-quartz-plagioclase paragneisses uses: source of silica, bldg stone, and talc.

Q UNCOLSOLIDATED PLEISTOCENE & RECENT ALLUVIUM (shown only where bedrock geology obscured) uses: sand and gravel for aggregate, clay for brick and ceramics, peat, on GMNYS Q

GEOLOGIC RESOURCES *figure 2*

MINERALS	ROCKS	
Garnet	Granitic gneisses	Limestone
Quartz	Marble	Sandstone
	Dolomite	Shale
	Granite	Quartzite
ORGANIC MATERIALS	Sedimentary hematite	Gneiss
Peat		(Leucogranitic)
Natural Gas (small amount)		
	UNCONSOLIDATED MATERIAL	
	Clay	Gravel
	Sand	Fuller's Earth

summer melting exceeded the winter's accumulation of snow and ice, the ice sheet retreated, leaving behind a layer of jumbled rocks, sand and soil, and drainage lines which changed direction or disappeared altogether as the water source melted. In places the ice sheet acted as a dam, later melting away and draining the imponded lake but leaving the sand and silt of the lake bottom. Oneida County contains outstanding examples of glacial forms which have been studied and described at length. Slowly these glacial landscapes are being eroded and leveled.

Glacial deposits may be divided into materials remaining where the ice left them, and materials which were later washed away by water and dropped where the current slackened on more level ground. The former deposits are evident in many of the area's hills and ridges which contain sand and gravel mixed in various sizes. Field boulders and rocky soils out of which the area's stone fences were built are also examples of these morainal deposits or glacial drift. Generally this "dropped" material is completely unsorted with sand and large rocks found together. In contrast, water-deposited material was dropped according to particle size as silt, sand, gravel or large rocks.

Preglacial topography was accentuated in some areas, blurred in others by the ice sheet. The Tug Hill Plateau and Adirondack Mountains provided obstructions to the creeping ice flows, diverting the glacier's power into existing lowlands and making them even wider and deeper.

The present Mohawk Valley was widened and deepened by the ice but later partly filled with sediment. The Sauquoit and Oriskany Valleys seem to have experienced more destruction on their eastern slopes, as well as a general increase in size. Boonville Gorge north of Rome is an outstanding example of a melt-water channel or valley, formed by retreating glacial action. As the ice sheet temporarily blocked the Black River, water which would normally drain into the St. Lawrence Valley spilled over into the Mohawk basin. Much greater than the present flow of the Lansing Kill and the old Black River Canal, the overspill cut this dramatic gorge faster and steeper than others such as the valleys of the East and West Canada Creeks in Herkimer County. The sudden loss of discharge when the Black River's ice dam broke prevented layers of sediment from accumulating and filling the valley bottom. Trenton Gorge is a post glacial channel formed after an earlier valley was blocked by glacially deposited sediment.

Extensive mucklands, sandy deltas, beach ridges, and wavecut terraces are evidence that many parts of Oneida County were once the beds of lakes. These lakes were formed during the recession of the continental ice sheet. The largest of these lakes stretched across central New York, bounded by the ice sheet to the north and hills to the south. Dubbed Lake Iroquois by geologists, this lake had its outlet at the Rome divide and drained down the Mohawk Valley. Several recessional stages of Lake Iroquois occurred as the lake waters found successively lower outlets. The Rome sand plains and the extensive mucklands in Rome and Verona are associated with Lake Iroquois. The large potholes at Little Falls and the series of rockcut channels in the Syracuse area lead us to believe that, during the recession of the ice sheet, melt-waters from what is now the Great Lakes Basin found their outlet in the Mohawk and Hudson Valleys.

Today, glacial deposits with their water and ice-formed valleys are important factors in man's occupation in this area. The current distribution of these soil materials has set the pattern of plant life: pine forest on sand, hemlock and cedar on muckland, hardwoods on the rocky slopes, and the fertile grasslands on the valley floors. Sand and gravel deposits are of value for building aggregate, highway material, and as a source of ground water. Exposed limestone and sandstone deposits are also of value in construction. Valleys cut by melt-water or accentuated by ice are often used as transportation routes. Route 46, for example, follows the Boonville Gorge while the former Chenango Canal followed an old path of either the Sauquoit or Oriskany Creek. Similarly, Erie Canal and railroad engineers found the best routes for their facilities along old waterways.

Bedrock Geology. The Geological Survey of the New York State Museum and Science Service summarized years of work with publication of the Geologic Map of New York State-1961 in which Oneida and Herkimer Counties appear on the Adirondack, Finger Lake and Hudson-Mohawk sheets. Formations are mapped in color at a scale of 1:250,000 or about four miles to the map inch. The reader is referred to this publication for a more technical discussion.

The following description of Oneida County's bedrock or subsurface geology is confined to the dominant rock types either exposed at the surface or inferred to exist beneath an unconsolidated cover of till and sediment. Material of a more detailed and technical nature is listed in the References. In general, the shale, limestone and sandstone beds dip toward the southwest. Moving from northeast to southwest, one encounters successively younger rocks. It is assumed that a well drilled in Bridgewater would pass through all of the rock formations outcropping farther to the north and finally come to granites and gneisses like those of the Adirondacks.

The Town of Forestport in northeastern Oneida County is underlain by very old Precambrian granitic gneiss, part of it covered by recent deposits of sediment. Exposed sections of granitic gneiss occur largely in wooded areas within the Adirondack Forest Preserve. Most of Oneida County-the area enclosed by Hinckley Lake, Utica and New London north to Lewis County-is underlain by siltstone and black shale. A sedimentary rock rich in iron oxide and known as the "Clinton Formation" outcrops on a line extending through New Hartford, Westmoreland and Vernon. The Towns of Camden and Florence in the northwest corner of the county are in an area of sandstone with some red and green shales. Oneida Lake lies in an east-west band of sandstone-shale-hematite which narrows at Utica. South of Route 5 from New Hartford to Sherrill, various red and green shales and limestone are irregularly banded together along the plateau margin. The Towns of Sangerfield and Bridgewater are largely made up of undifferentiated shales and siltstone which continue southward into Madison County.

Mineral Resources. Figure 1, *Mineral Resources*, shows very generally how mineral deposits are distributed throughout the area. These resources are listed in the following table, Figure 2, *Geologic Resources*. In the following discussion, mineral reserves differ from mineral resources in that reserves are deposits proved to have economic value while resources are materials which may be generally useful but have not been sufficiently studied to prove or disprove their suitability for commercial exploitation. In a general sense, most geologic materials may be considered mineral resources until proven to be reserves. The likelihood of resource development depends upon the absence of impurities, nature of uses, demand, market price, distance to market and other factors. Because a rock or mineral is economically exploitable in certain areas does not mean that it is developable commercially everywhere.

Hematite. Mining of a sedimentary hematite deposit containing 48.5% metallic iron ore took place in the 19th century near Clinton and Franklin Springs in central Oneida County. Good fluxing limestone was also found nearby. First local charcoal, later Pennsylvania coke, was used in the furnaces as the iron ore was smelted into pig iron. Most of this activity ended about 1880. However, hematite was produced for pigment until 1962. The hematite deposits associated with shales and sandstones in this central Oneida County area are present in thin, discontinuous strata. These deposits do not appear suitable for commercial extraction of the ore at this time. Perhaps some locations could be used as red pigment sources.

Sandstone. The southern portion of Oneida County is rich in sandstone, which has potential as a silica source in glass manufacturing. Another use for well cemented sandstone is as crushed aggregate. Use of a red sandstone as architectural building stone has recently increased. Old stone buildings and the stonework of the old Erie Canal locks bear witness to the quality of the local rock, traditionally a reddish sandstone but including some gray limestone. Field stone, particularly glacial boulders, has also been popular in the past for residential construction.

Limestone. The area's many limestone deposits, again mainly in the south, were used many years ago for flux in the manufacture of pig iron, and have been employed more recently for concrete aggregate production and agricultural lime. The last two are still, and are expected to remain, important local industries; commercial quarries for crushed rock are now operating in several locations, road construction materials being the prime product. Use for flux, however, has been seriously handicapped by distance to markets and associated transportation costs.

Shale. Extensive shale deposits in central Oneida County could be used for light-weight aggregate or such ceramic uses as bricks; however, much sampling and analysis would first be necessary.

Sand and Gravel. Sand and gravel deposits of uneven quality are abundant in Oneida County. These include glacial monrainal deposits which offer sand, gravel, and silt in mixed layers of till, and water-deposited materials which are segregated by particle size. At present, several glacial kames and eskers are exploited commercially for their sand and gravel content. While many of these deposits are satisfactory for road foundation and fill, gradation and permeability make most deposits unsatisfactory for use as fine aggregates in concrete. Sand deposits near Cleveland on Oneida Lake have been used in the past for glass manufacturing. Deposits near Rome have been a source of Fuller's earth, a fine-particle clay or sand used as a filtering material. Sand is currently mined at McConnellsville for use in metal casting.

Clay. Until about 1940, clay taken from the flood plain of the Mohawk River near Utica was used in the manufacture of several million bricks each year. Other small clay pits are on record in the valley bottoms of the Mohawk River and West Canada Creek. These clay deposits remain but increasing use of other building materials has reduced the demand for bricks. Considerable face brick is currently imported into the counties. Study of the firing properties of local clay might demonstrate suitability for ceramic uses other than brickmaking.

Other Minerals. Agricultural peat is not uncommon near Rome where muck farming has been the primary use of these deposits.

Mineral Fuels. Several natural gas wells have been drilled in Rome, Verona, Vernon and Marcy. After a small amount of gas was extracted, the wells became unprofitable and remain capped today. Central New York is continually prospected for petroleum mineral wealth and land mineral rights may be purchased.

WATER

Three major river basins divide the county: the Black River to the north, the Oswego to the west and the Upper Mohawk to the east. That portion of each basin lying within the county is shown on Figure 3.

Black River. Part of northern Oneida County drains

into the Black River which flows northward through Lewis County and on into Lake Ontario at Watertown. The basin encompasses all or portions of five counties, 18 incorporated villages and 43 towns. Detailed information on the river and its tributaries has been published by the Black River Basin Water Resources Commission.

Although it is the second largest basin in Herkimer-Oneida Counties, the Black River's upper reaches, particularly the Beaver River and Moose River sub-basins, lie mainly within the Adirondack Forest Preserve and so encompass a limited population. Visitors make up a significant addition, however, increasing the Moose River watershed's permanent population of 2,500 to an estimated 12,000 during the summer season. The basin's primary importance to Oneida County is as a year round recreation area, offering fishing, hunting, camping, hiking, swimming, boating, skiing and other outdoor recreational opportunities. Most of these activities depend directly or indirectly on the upper valley's water resources. Low seasonal flows are downstream problems during dry years. Black River waters originating upstream from Forestport may be diverted into the Mohawk River Basin through the Lansing Kill Feeder for Barge Canal supply.

Oswego River. The Oswego River basin comprises portions of Madison, Onondaga, Cayuga and Oswego Counties and all of Oneida County west of Rome including the City of Syracuse. Basin population is estimated at over 675,000. The Oneida County portion, which contains the City of Sherrill, surrounds the eastern end of Oneida Lake. On the Oneida County side, the Oneida Lake is fed by Oneida Creek, Sconondoa Creek, Fish Creek, Wood Creek and the Barge Canal. The shallow lake is troubled by pollution and by the growth of algae, both of which interfere increasingly with the recreational use of the lake itself and its shores. Relief is in sight in the form of sewage systems spanning the lake's southern shore from the Oneida River to the Village of Bridgeport on the Madison-Onondaga County line, and a system on the east shore in Verona, Sylvan Beach and Vienna. Accumulation of nutrients which support annual algae blooms remains a problem, however, since many of these nutrients occur naturally in south shore streams.

The City of Rome utilizes the east branch of Fish Creek as water supply and diverts waste water to the Mohawk River. The City of Oneida obtains water from Florence Creek in the Fish Creek basin. The Oneida system serves Sherrill, Oneida Castle, and Vernon.

Dairy farming and muckland cultivation are other important uses of the basin's land in Oneida County. Both depend to a great extent on surface water for cattle watering and irrigation. Increasing competition for the basin's water among urban, rural and recreational uses has led its constituent counties to participate in an overall study and plan for the basin's resources. The Eastern Oswego Basin Water Resources Plan was published in 1973.

Upper Mohawk River. Most significant to Oneida County is the Mohawk River which rises north of the City of Rome and joins the Hudson River at Albany, 130 miles eastward. The so-called Upper Mohawk River stretches upstream from the Mohawk's confluence with East Canada Creek. In Herkimer-Oneida Counties, the valley is heavily urbanized and industrialized, containing the Cities of Utica, Rome, and Little Falls, a number of urban towns and villages and housing a population of a quarter of a million persons. The valley also picks up parts of Hamilton and Fulton Counties and minor parts of Montgomery, Lewis and Madison. These, however, contribute only 10 per cent of the total population.

The dairy industry of the Upper Mohawk is the largest in the New York City milkshed. Field crops and pasture are found wherever soil and slope permit. Some of the mucklands near Rome have been partially drained and are now used for truck farming. The valley floors along the

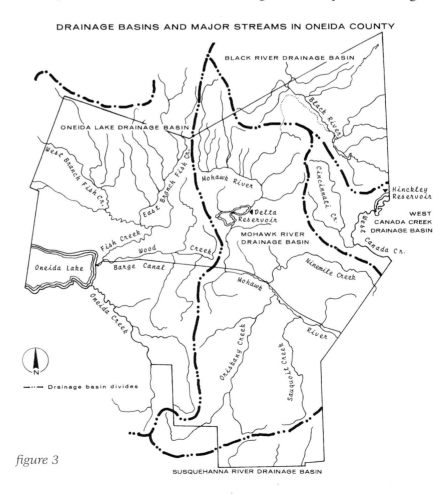

DRAINAGE BASINS AND MAJOR STREAMS IN ONEIDA COUNTY

figure 3

Mohawk and West Canada Creek are used for field crops. Headwater areas are largely devoted to woodland. Water-based recreational uses are concentrated in the state parks under development at Hinckley and Delta Reservoirs.

The major sub-basins of the Upper Mohawk are the East and West Canada Creeks in Herkimer County, and the Sauquoit, Oriskany and Nine Mile Creeks in Oneida County. The main stem and many of its tributaries are plagued by problems of pollution, fluctuating reservoirs and occasional flooding. To fully document these problems and to reconcile the many conflicting demands upon its resources, the Upper Mohawk should be the subject of a basin-wide analysis.

Barge Canal. One of the major water users in Oneida County is the New York State Barge Canal System. The historic Erie Canal was the forerunner of the present Barge Canal System which provides the only east-west water route from New York City to the Great Lakes except for the St. Lawrence Seaway which accommodates larger vessels. The legal and actual demands for water supply to the Barge Canal are substantial. Both Delta and Hinckley Reservoirs provide quantities of canal water during the summer months as well as holding amounts specified as reserve. A major water input is needed near Rome where the Barge Canal reaches its highest point in elevation between Albany and Oneida Lake.

To insure that a sufficient supply of water would be available at Rome, canal engineers developed three systems of reservoirs and feeder canals.

1. *Delta Reservoir.* North of Rome the Upper Mohawk River was impounded behind Delta Dam. To supplement Mohawk waters, part of the abandoned Black River Canal was retained to carry water from Forestport Reservoir and Kayuta Lake on the Black River, to the Mohawk River.

2. *Hinckley Reservoir.* Hinckley Reservoir was constructed on West Canada Creek, and a canal dug to carry West Canada Creek water to Nine Mile Creek and thence to the Canal.

3. *Old Erie Canal.* The old Erie Canal from New London to Syracuse was retained as a feeder to bring water to the Barge Canal from Butternut Creek, (Jamesville Reservoir), Limestone Creek (De Ruyter Reservoir), and Chittenango Creek (Cazenovia Lake and Erieville Reservoir). Canal traffic in recent years has been insufficient to require use of these latter water sources, and their present value lies primarily in their potential for recreational use. The feeder canal was established as the Erie Canal State Park in 1967.

An additional feeder carries water from Lake Moraine to Oriskany Creek and the Mohawk River. This water enters the canal at Frankfort where the river and canal merge. It is interesting to note that these systems were designed to divert water to the canal from the Black River

Basin, the Oneida River Basin and the Susquehanna River Basin.

Like its predecessors, the original and enlarged Erie Canals, the Barge Canal is owned and operated by the State of New York. No charge is made for its use. Although constructed for commercial use, pleasure boating has increased in recent years. Because of a long-term decline in commercial traffic and mounting maintenance costs, several alternate proposals for management of the canal have been studied. These range from closing the canal completely to enlarging it to accommodate larger tows of barges, or even oceangoing ships, and transferring the system to the federal government. Whatever the disposition of the Barge Canal's future, it will be significant to the water resources and particularly the Mohawk River Basin in Oneida County.

Flooding. Because Oneida County serves as headwaters for several river basins, water volumes here are lower and so less likely to cause large-scale flood hazards than in otherwise comparable areas downstream. However, the Mohawk River near Utica and the West Canada Creek near the Village of Herkimer have caused localized flooding in the past. Unusually high freshets in the Oriskany and Sauquoit Creek are on record but have incurred little damage. Ice dams on the lower sections of West Canada Creek and several smaller creeks flowing into the Mohawk have also caused some local flooding where constrictions such as bridges and culverts accumulate broken ice flows and form ice dams.

The Mohawk River between Rome and Herkimer drops in elevation only 32 feet over the 35-mile distance. The resulting flood plain, built up through the years, is considerable in size and affects development of the valley. Annual spring submergence of this marshy flood plain is routine, and urban development has not taken place for this reason. While flooding is largely a springtime occurrence on the Mohawk River, the Utica area established a high water record in October of 1945 as the result of heavy rains.

Railroad, highway and various Barge Canal construction projects have largely defined the present flood plains of the Mohawk River. Regulatory devices such as Delta Reservoir and the parallel channels of the Barge Canal-Mohawk River further limit the Mohawk's flood potential. The Barge Canal is a parallel channel from Rome eastward to Frankfort where the Mohawk River becomes channelized and doubles as the Barge Canal much of the way to Albany.

In 1975 the U.S. Army Corps of Engineers completed a series of flood plain information reports on the Mohawk River from the Herkimer County line to Delta Dam. Using maps and river profiles these reports indicate the area that would be flooded in a "100-year" flood such as that of October, 1945. In 1974 the Oneida County

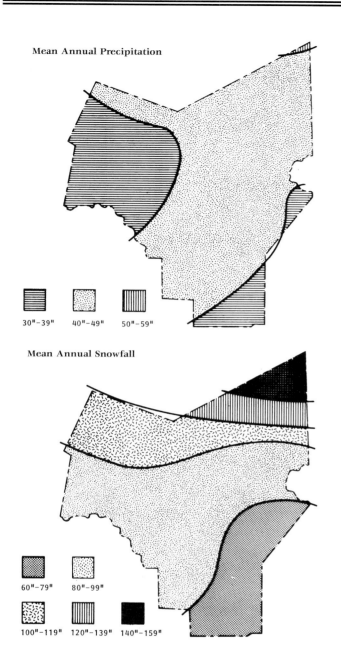

Mean Annual Precipitation

30"-39"　40"-49"　50"-59"

Mean Annual Snowfall

60"-79"　80"-99"

100"-119"　120"-139"　140"-159"

Department of Planning completed "A Plan for Management of the Mohawk River Flood Plain." The land use control measures recommended reflected studies of hydrology, ecology and archaeology as well as existing and potential land use.

CLIMATE

Oneida County is characterized by a variety of micro-climates influenced by land configuration, elevation, and location relative to Lake Ontario and Oneida Lake. The climate of the county has been recorded at comparatively few weather stations and generalizations about the climate derived from the records of these stations necessarily overlook many unique local situations.

The northern towns in the county have more rainfall, more snowfall, and a shorter growing season than the Mohawk Valley and the Appalachian Plateau to the south. Annual precipitation in these northern towns is 45 to 50 inches, compared with a range of 40 to 50 inches in the valley and 30 to 40 inches in the Appalachian Plateau. The heaviest precipitation occurs on the fringes of Tug Hill, especially in Florence and northern Annsville. Tug Hill also influences the climate of other northern towns. This is especially noticeable in higher snowfalls than the rest of the region. Northern and western towns are especially subject to "lake effect" snowfalls resulting from air carrying moisture picked up over Lake Ontario which is forced to higher altitude by the Tug Hill plateau and drops its excess moisture on the plateau and in the area to the southeast. In northern towns mean annual snowfalls range from 100 to 140 inches. In the valley snowfall ranges from 80 to 100 inches and in the southeastern towns in the county the range is 60 to 80 inches. See Figure 4.

The parts of the county with significant agricultural activity have a growing season of 135 to 150 days. The northeastern towns, which contain no significant agriculture, have a season of 120 to 135 days. In agricultural areas, on the average, the last killing frost in the spring

LENGTH OF GROWING SEASON

	Period	Length (days)			Proportion less than (per cent)			
Stations	(Yrs.)	Longest	Average	Shortest	120 Days	130 Days	140 Days	150 Days.
Bouckville	20	190	139	98	15	30	60	70
Little Falls No. 1	48	190	150	121	0	8	29	48
McKeever	11	122	94	63	80	100	100	100
North Lake	45	148	117	65	50	74	89	100
Rome*	17	177	143	106	6	24	53	65
Salisbury	48	162	121	64	40	67	85	95
Stillwater Res	18	141	119	97	44	72	94	100
Utica	17	179	144	126	0	18	47	65

*Old station where records have been discontinued.

SOURCE:Bulletin 764, "The Climate of New York State" by R.A. Mordoff

occurs in mid-May and the first killing frost in the fall occurs the first week in October. Figure 5 shows length of growing season at various weather stations in the region.

A measure of cloudiness is the percentage of possible sunshine experienced in the county. During the growing season (May 1 - September 30) Oneida County receives 55 to 60 per cent of possible sunshine. In New York State the Lake Ontario shore west of Rochester receives the largest percentage of possible sunshine during the growing season (65%). The smallest percentage is in the Binghamton area (52%). During the winter considerably less sunshine is experienced and in January Oneida County receives 35 per cent of possible sunshine; the southeast shore of Lake Ontario only 20 per cent. New York City and Long Island receive over 50 per cent of possible January sunshine, the highest in the state. These percentages indicate, among other things, a low potential in the area for direct utilization of sunshine for heating pur-

poses. During the growing season, however, the combination of sunshine and precipitation is favorable for a variety of field crops.

Selected References

Dale, Nelson C., Ph.D., Geology and Mineral Resources of the Oriskany Quadrangle, New York State Museum Bulletin No. 345, (June 1953).

Delthier, Bernard G., Precipitation in New York State, Cornell University Agricultural Experiment Station Bulletin No. 1009, (July 1966).

Kay, Marshall, Ph.D., Geology of the Utica Quadrangle, New York, New York State Museum Bulletin No. 347, (July 1953).

Mordoff, R.A., The Climate of New York State, Cornell Extension Bulletin No. 764 (1949).

Natural Characteristics, Herkimer-Oneida Counties Comprehensive Planning Program (1965).

SUMMARY OF NATURAL CHARACTERISTICS OF ONEIDA COUNTY

Government Unit	Acre (in acres)	Underlaying Geology	Elevation Range (in feet)	Slope (% of area)				Mean Precipitation (inches per year)	Mean Snowfall (inches per year)	Mean July MaxTemp (°F)	Mean January MinTemp (°F)
				0- 5%	6-10%	11-20%	21%+				
ONEIDA COUNTY	727, 077		330 to 2000	35	30	20	1 5	30 to 49	60 to 1 59	76-86	8-16
Annsville	36, 693	Sandstone and Shale	330 to 1450	65	20	10	5	30 to 49	80 to 119	80- 84	10-12
Augusta	16,602	Limestone, Shale, Sandstone	750 to 1750	30	35	30	5	40 to 49	80 to 99	82-86	10-12
Ava	20,738	Siltstone	1000 to 1750	40	35	20	5	40 to 49	100 to 139	78-82	10-12
Boonville	40,151	Glacial Deposits Shale	1000 to 1750	50	20	10	20	40 to 49	100 to 159	76- 80	8-12
Bridgewater	16,008	Shale and Limestone	1000 to 2000	20	25	45	10	30 to 39	60 to 79	80-82	12-14
Camden	32,737	Sandstone and Shale	330 to 750	45	45	10	-	30 to 39	100 to 119	80- 84	10-14
Deerfield	20,000	Shale	330 to 1500	50	20	20	10	30 to 49	80 to 119	80- 84	10-16
Florence	32,421	Sandstone	750 to 1250	55	20	15	10	40 to 49	100 to 119	80- 82	10-14
Floyd	19,588	Siltstone	330 to 1500	50	40	10	-	40 to 49	80 to 99	80-84	10-12
Forestport	46,386	Glacial Deposits, Gneisses	1000 to 1750	50	30	10	10	40 to 49	100 to 159	76-80	6-10
Kirkland	19,631	Shale, Limestone	705 to 2000	30	40	20	10	40 to 49	60 to 99	82-86	10-14
Lee	27,869	Siltstone, Shale	350 to 1250	45	30	15	10	40 to 49	80 to 119	80-84	10-12
Marcy	18,556	Shale, Siltstone	330 to 1250	40	30	20	10	40 to 49	60 to 99	80-84	10-14
Marshall	19,814	Limestone, Shale	750 to 2000	40	25	25	10	40 to 49	60 to 99	80-84	10-14
New Hartford	13,303	Sandstone, Shale, Limestone	500 to 1250	30	35	25	10	40 to 49	60 to 79	82-86	10-14
Paris	19,215	Limestone, Shale	750 to 2000	25	25	40	10	30 to 49	60 to 79	82-86	12-14
Remsen	20,880	Limestone, Gneisses	1000 to 1500	55	20	15	10	40 to 49	80 to 119	76-80	8-10
Rome	43,760	Shale	330 to 500	100	-	-	-	30 to 49	80 to 99	80-86	10-12
Sangerfield	19,007	Shale, Siltstone	1000 to 2000	30	20	40	10	30 to 49	80 to 99	80-82	10-14
Steuben	25,009	Siltstone, Shale	1750 to 2000	25	35	25	15	40 to 49	80 to 119	76-82	8-12
Trenton	25,465	Limestone, Shale	500 to 1250	55	25	20	-	40 to 49	60 to 99	78-82	8-14
Utica	10,387	Shale	330 to 750	70	15	10	5	40 to 49	60 to 79	82-86	12-16
Vernon	23,458	Shale, Limestone	330 to 1250	55	25	15	5	40 to 49	80 to 99	82-86	10-14
Verona	41,426	Sandstone, Hematite, Shale	330 to 750	95	-	-	5	30 to 49	80 to 99	82-86	10-14
Vienna	37,139	Sandstone, Shale	330 to 750	60	20	10	10	30 to 39	80 to 99	82-86	10-14
Western	31,443	Shale, Siltstone	500 to 1500	20	20	30	30	40 to 49	80 to 119	78-82	10-12
Westmoreland	26,241	Sandstone, Shale, Hematite	500 to 1000	70	15	5	10	40 to 49	80 to 99	82-86	10-12
Whitestown	14,018	Sandstone, Shale	330 to 750	50	35	15	-	40 to 49	60 to 99	82-86	10-14

Sherrill's figures are included with the Town of Vernon.

Land Development

By Walter Cookenham

*Land surveyor and grandson of Henry Cookinham,
who wrote the two volume* History of Oneida County

In 1492 Christopher Columbus made his journey across the Atlantic and discovered a new world. Word of his discovery spread like wildfire in Europe and only five years later John Cabot, a native of Venice, but sailing under the flag of England, explored the northeast coast of North America. Upon his voyages and the patent issued to him rested the English claim to North America. We quote from this letter patent:

"Henry by the grace of God, King of England and France, and Lord of Ireland, to all to whom these presents shall come, Greeting.

Be it known that we have given and granted, and by these presents do give and grant for us and our heirs, to our well beloved John Cabot, citizen of Venice, to Lewis, Sebastian and Santius, sonnes of the sayd John, and to the heirs of them, and every of them, and their Deputies, full and free authority, leave and power to saile to all parts, countreys and seas of the East, of the West and of the North, under our banner and ensignes, with five ships of what burthen or quantity soever they be, and as many mariners or men as they will have with them in the sayd ships, upon their owne proper costs and charges, to seeke out, discover, and finde whatsoever isles, countreys, regions or provinces of the heathen and infidels whatsoever they be, and in what part of the world soever they be, which before this time have been unknown to all Christians: We have granted to them, and also to every of them, the heirs of them and every of them and their deputies, and have given them licence to set up our banners and ensignes in every village, towne, castle, isle, or maine land of them newly found. And that the aforesayd John and his sonnes, or their heirs and assignes may subdue, occupy and possesse all such townes, cities, castles and isles of them found, which they can subdue, occupy and possesses as our vassels, and lieutenants, getting unto us the rule, title and jurisdiction of the same villages, towns, castles, and firm land so found. ..."

Armed by similar letters of authority, adventurers and explorers of many European countries crossed the ocean, sailed up the various rivers, set up trading posts, made small settlements and claimed the lands for their respective sovereigns.

Thus, in the case of New York, we find Verrazano in 1524, sailing under French orders, discovering New York Bay; Henry Hudson, under Dutch flag, exploring the Hudson River in 1609 and the French also exploring the state from the St. Lawrence River Valley. Samuel de Champlain, the great French leader, doomed the land claims of France to failure by his attack against the Iroquois on the shore of Lake Champlain.

The Indians never forgave him for this attack and were enemies of the French thereafter in spite of the many French Jesuit priests who tried to convert them to Christianity. The story of Father Isaac Jogues, whose memorial is at Auriesville, Montgomery County, is a fascinating (and horrifying) account of the life of a captive of the Iroquois.

Van den Bogaert, a Dutch trader, came through what is now Oneida County in 1634. Other Dutch traders and explorers from Albany and Schenectady also traveled this area to the settlements of the Oneidas.

Following Hudson's exploration the Dutch established settlements in eastern New York and formed a colony originally called New Belgium which was later called New Netherlands. They had very friendly relations with the Iroquois. In 1664 the English sent a fleet to New Amsterdam, forced the Dutch to surrender, and changed the name to New York.

The King of England, Charles II, granted the conquered colony to his own brother, James, Duke of York and Albany. This was done, to quote the patent, "in the same manner as our Manor at Westminster." Thus James became, in his own eyes, lord of a feudal manor in the New World. As a manorial lord he was ruler as well as land owner subject only to his sovereign, King Charles. This grant was done between the brothers so that the English Parliament would have nothing to say as to the governing of this colony.

In 1673 during the second Anglo-Dutch War, a Dutch fleet recaptured New York and restored Dutch rule. At the conclusion of that war New York was returned to English hands.

The English Parliament immediately claimed partial

control over New York as a result of this second treaty. When James succeeded his brother as king he insisted on sole rule of the colony. He also instructed his map maker to produce a chart of the royal colony showing as large borders as possible. The accompanying map shows New York at its greatest extent: bounded east by a line 20 miles east of the Hudson River, south by eastern Pennsylvania and extending down through the center of modern Pennsylvania, to the north line of Virginia, thence running west including western Pennsylvania, Ohio, Indiana, Michigan, Illinois, Iowa, Nebraska, Wisconsin, Minnesota, North and South Dakota, southern Manitoba and southern Ontario below the 50th degree of latitude and the Ottawa River.

The King wanted to include all of the old Dutch colony, all of the lands of the Iroquois and also all of the beaver trapping lands of Lake Superior in his own private domain. He had at least four treaties with the Iroquois to back up his claim. A treaty negotiated by Royal Governor Thomas Dongan extended the protection of the King's sovereignty to the Indians during the series of wars the Iroquois fought with the French and Algonquins. In 1701 agents for King William III also made a treaty with the Iroquois in which they acknowledged British sovereignty.

During King William's War, Queen Ann's War and the French and Indian War, British troops passed and repassed through the Mohawk Valley and built several forts at strategic locations. These were the Royal Block House at present day Verona Beach, Fort Bull, Fort Williams and the famous Fort Stanwix at Rome (a reconstruction of which has been built) and Fort Schuyler at present day Utica. Garrisons at these posts explored the surrounding countryside so that knowledge of the land of Oneida County was much more-widespread than we today realize.

The first grant of land in Oneida County was the area right near the forts and covered the end of river navigation on the Mohawk and the land portage (Carrying Place) to Wood and Fish Creeks. Called the Oriskany Patent it was granted April 18, 1705 to five close friends of the colonial governor: George Clarke, the royal secretary of New York colony; Peter Schuyler, a member of the colonial council; Thomas Wenham, colonel of the King's troops at Fort George, the governor's headquarters; Peter Fauconnier, receiver of customs of the port of New York (who was reputed to be in league with the pirate, Blackbeard); and Roger Mompeson, chief justice of the colony. By virtue of this grant of 32,000 acres to wealthy and powerful people, the land from Rome to Oriskany on both sides of the Mohawk River two miles wide on each side and from Oriskany up the Oriskany Creek for four miles also two miles wide on each side was effectively closed to settlement and purchase. This was the case for more than 80 years. It was not until after the Revolution that a division of the land and a sale to settlers took place. At that time the

most prominent and hated Tories had their land seized by an Act of Attainder. The new State of New York was short of cash money and having these lands available, immediately (and gleefully) auctioned them off. To pay for the partition and auction of the Oriskany Patent a large section of 697 acres was surveyed in what is now the historic district of Rome. (Expense Street is one of the bounds of this Expense Lot.) This was sold to Dominick Lynch who called his settlement Lynchville. His name is preserved in East Dominick and West Dominick Streets of Rome.

The next patent granted was the famous Cosby Manor of 1734. In following regulations for obtaining land from the Indians it was necessary for settlers first to obtain a license from the Royal Governor, then meet with the Indians and get them to agree to sell, have the Indians convey to the British Crown, have the Surveyor General of the Colony survey the tract, have the Governor petition the Crown to issue the patent, secure approval, and finally to have the Governor issue the Patent. This was all to be done at the expense of the purchasers.

In 1725 Nicholas Ecker and other German Palatine associates went through this procedure only to be stopped at the last by not having enough political influence to secure the final patent. They sold their interests to close friends of Governor William Cosby. Cosby had a plan to build a great colonial manor for himself and as he was prevented by his appointment orders as governor from conveying land to himself, he merely set up his friends as primary grantees. He granted them the land he wished and six days later they granted the land back to him. This huge tract of 43,000 acres covers the area from Frankfort on the east to Yorkville and Maynard Road, Marcy on the west; and from Pleasant Street and the Parkway in Utica on the south to Smith Hill by Station WKTV on the north.

Many difficulties of ownership arose after Cosby died and thus this tract also was in effect closed to development for many years. In 1772 just before the Revolution it was sold to Philip Schuyler, John Bradstreet, Rutger Bleecker and the heirs of John Scott. After the Revolution the area developed rapidly as the City of Utica grew. Now nearly half the people in the county live in the patent.

The Patent was divided into great lots, each of which had frontage on the Mohawk River and extended either north or south from the river to the bounds of the tract. They were very long and very narrow strips of land and because of this subdivision there has always been a great deal of difficulty in arranging east-west streets in the areas of Utica particularly in northeast and northwest parts of the city. You can still see these old great lot lines as today's property lines marked by fences by traveling east on the Utica-Ilion highway and looking across the valley at the south slopes of Deerfield and Smith hills.

Next the Sadequahada Patent was granted to Frederick Morris and his friends. At the time of the grant he was the

Royal Secretary of the Colony of New York, having succeeded George Clarke. This tract consisted of the remaining valley lands lying between Oriskany and Cosby Manor and today is the Whitesboro, New York Mills, and Yorkville areas, and lands adjacent and north of the Mohawk River. About 6000 acres in all, this tract was owned in 1775 by Hugh Wallace, a prominent Tory whose lands were attained during the Revolution. The purchasers of the land were the only people interested in selling land to settlers in the valley. Thus Hugh White, founder of Whitestown and one of the purchasers, was able to attract people to live at his settlement. This is the reason why Whitesboro became the center of settlement in Oneida County.

The great increase in population of the English colonies caused many people to push westward into Indian territory. Naturally the Indians became very bitter, and fighting and massacres took place. The British King, in order to maintain peace, commanded that Sir William Johnson, his agent in the Americas for the Indian Tribes, arrange a treaty to define a line of property beyond which no English settlement was to be made. In the Fall of 1768 at Fort Stanwix, Johnson, the Governor of New Jersey and other prominent officials acting on behalf of the Crown, after much discussion and debate, agreed with the assembled chiefs and sachems of the Indians on the Great Line of Property.

This line in Oneida County leaves Wood Creek at the mouth of Canada Creek and runs southerly across the towns of Rome, Westmoreland, Kirkland, Marshall, and Paris to the headwaters of the west branch of the Unadilia River. Some years ago the author of this article during the course of his surveying business had the pleasure of resetting a marker in the middle of a tiny stream marking the south end of this line. Johnson states in his reports that he did not have as much trouble getting the Indians to agree to the line as he did in stopping the Puritan Congregational ministers, acting as missionaries to the Indians, from stirring up trouble. He complained bitterly against these New England troublemakers. They wanted the line just as far to the east as possible so as to enlarge their own mission fields. This Great Line of Property is the most important property line in the county as almost all subsequent land patents were affected by it.

In the February following the treaty at Fort Stanwix, a patent for 2000 acres of land was granted to Peter Servis and others. This is a tract lying next to West Canada Creek

Stone on College Hill Road near Route 233, Town of Kirkland, marking the Line of Property between Indian and white men's lands, fixed by the Treaty of Fort Stanwix, 1768.

THE LINE OF PROPERTY BETWEEN THE AMERICAN COLONIES AND THE SIX NATIONS

FIXED BY TREATY AT FORT STANWIX NOV. 5, 1768

and containing the eastern part of the Town of Trenton, the northeast corner of the Town of Marcy and the south end of the Town of Remsen. Sir William Johnson wanted more land so he persuaded Servis and others, who were all servants or tenants of his, to obtain the land. Shortly after the patent was granted Sir William had a great feast for them at Johnson Hall and they deeded the land to him.

These deeds were part of the papers that his sons, Guy and John, buried in the orchard when they fled to Canada during the Revolution. When they returned they found the papers ruined so they could not be read. In the subsequent legal proceedings to prove that these deeds as well as others covering many thousands of acres of land existed, oral testimony was accepted. This was a most unusual procedure, since the Statute of Frauds in 1672 required written proofs of land transfer. The man whose oral testimony was accepted as proof was the black fiddler at that feast.

The Right Honorable Henry Lord Holland was granted a large tract of land now called Holland Patent and surrounding the Village of Holland Patent. He was the lord of a Holland which is a section of northeastern England that is similar to the country of Holland. This patent was named after the man and not after the famous Holland Land Company which in later years purchased most of the tract. As

was customary, when the surveyor general of the Province of New York, Alexander Colden, had the tract surveyed by his deputies, Hendrick Fry and Christopher Yates, the Oneida Indians sent observers along with the survey crew to make sure that what was surveyed was what they had sold. The Indians had learned from bitter experience that this was necessary.

General Thomas Gage, His Majesty's Commander of troops in North America, also was granted land in our county. He is mostly remembered as the British Commander of the port of Boston during the Revolutionary War. His grant is the bulk of the town of Deerfield. He saved his land from expropriation by Attainder by conveying it to Peter Kemble, his father-in-law.

Immediately following the Fort Stanwix treaty a scramble was on for the remaining unpatented land. A typical petition for a grant of lands follows:

_____

To His Excellency Sir Henry Moore, Baronet Captain General and Governor in Chief in and over the Province of New York and the Territories depending thereon in America, Chancelor and Vice Admiral of the same
                                                     In Council,
The petition of Lieut. Abernathy Cargill late of the Raingers, Humbly Sheweth,

That there is a certain tract of vacant Land Lying in the County of Albany of the South side of the Mohawk's River and on the East side of the Orhriskanie Creek bounded Northeasterly by a line running Northwest by Southeast between Orhriskanie Creek and Sadaquada Creek from the distance of two miles up the Sadaquada Creek above the westernmost corner of Cosby's Manor: as laid down on the map annexed: two thousand acres of which lands your Petitioner prays to have granted him on the east side of and adjoining the said Orhriskanie Creek on the terms of the royal proclamation of the 7th of Oct. 1763.

And your Petitioner as in duty bound shall ever pray.
                                   Simon Metcalfe Attorney for
                                     Lt. Abernathy Cargill

_____

Peter Lansingh petitioned from the tract bounded west by the Great Line of Property and Canada Creek, east by Holland Patent, and Oriskany Patent and southeast by Oriskany Creek (spelled Orhriskanie in the above petition) while Charles Nicholl, John Lamb, William MacKinley, Nathaniel MacKinley, William Howe or Kane, John Taylor, Robert Stewart, Abraham Leggit, John Miller, William Young, Andrew Myer, Samuel Boyer and George Willis, Sr., all noncommissioned officers of his Majesty's Forces in a joint petition also prayed for land. Another petition of John Gregg, Corporal, Henry Freaker and Benjamin Robeson also Corporals, John Brusel and Thomas Lang, Drummers, all late of the 55th Regiment was filed for lands near Oriskany Creek.

All of the above petitions were denied. Instead the land comprising some 47,000 acres was granted to Daniel Coxe and associates to compensate him for losses in trying to settle his ancient grant in the southern United States. This ancient grant consisted of "all the lands lying between the thirty first and thirty six degrees of Northern Latitude inclusive on the continent of North America and extending westward to the South Seas" (a truly astonishing patent).

The Revolutionary War brought about major changes in land ownership in Oneida County. The state took the place of the King, the loyalists fled north and west to Canada or to Nova Scotia or England. Their lands were lost to the new state, many of the settlers were killed and the Indian tribes were decimated by the conflict. The Oneidas had tried to stay neutral although most of them sided with the colonists through the influence of Chief Skenendoa, the Rev. Samson Occum, the Rev. Samuel Kirkland and Judge James Dean. A little mentioned Indian called Colonel Louis should also be given credit, as well as one known as Plattcopf, for swaying the Oneidas to back the American side.

After the end of the fighting, the state wished to reward those men who had rendered outstanding services. As the government had almost no money, it gave large land grants instead. Thus Baron von Steuben received a large grant, which is located in the present town of Steuben. Marinus Willet, the American commander at Fort Stanwix when the British and Indians under St. Leger besieged it, was granted land in northern Oneida County. Thomas Machin, the American army engineer who, under General Washington, erected the chain across the Hudson River at West Point so that the British fleet could not carry troops upriver and surprise the American force, received about 40,000 acres in northern parts of the county (Boonville and Forestport).

Jelles Fonda, who ran a trading post at present-day Fonda, Montgomery County and was a major in British service during the French and Indian Wars, was known to be the man most in charge of intelligence work for the Americans. As a result the Loyalists did their best to kill him. They did succeed in ruining him financially and as a reward for his invaluable services the state granted him 40,000 acres around present-day Rome and Western. Many others received lands or purchased them for very small amounts. The fullest description of these later patents is found in Wager's History of Oneida County.

George Clinton, the last royal governor and the first state governor, was a man respected by all groups in the state. In 1788 he negotiated a purchase of a large section of Indian land in the southern part of what is now Oneida County which, with adjacent lands in Madison and Chenango Counties, was referred to as the Governor's Purchase. By subsequent treaties the Oneida Indian title was extinguished in the balance of the county. It is however, of great interest and importance that after almost 200 years the Oneida Indians have commenced a lawsuit in federal court to reclaim some of these lands. This suit was heard at Auburn, New York in January 1976 and has not been decided.

Selected Reference

See historians David Cosick, Parker, Schoolcraft and Morgan as well as the January 1976 issue of the New York Conservationist.

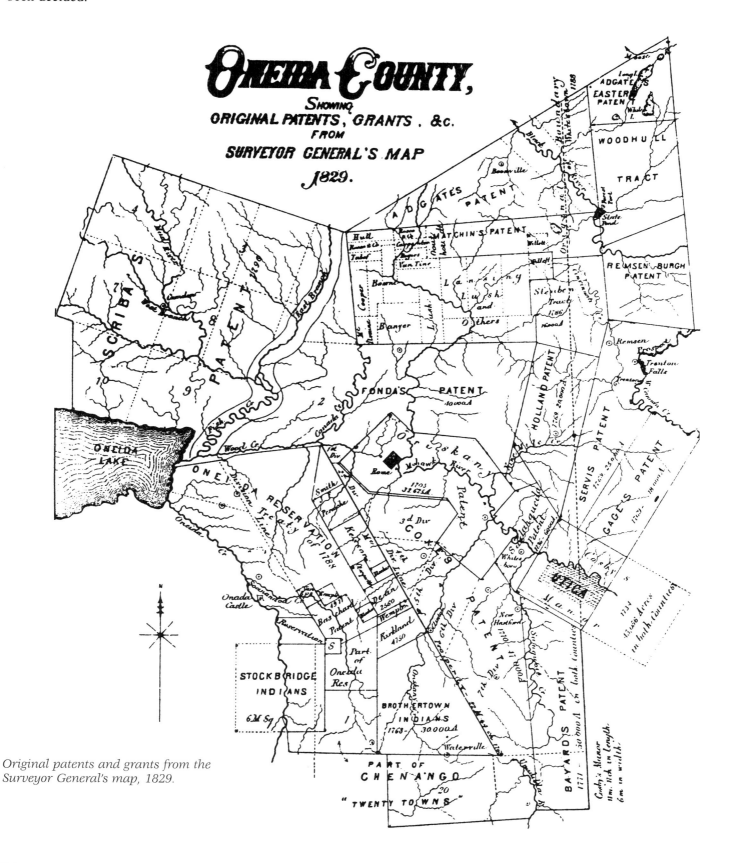

Original patents and grants from the Surveyor General's map, 1829.

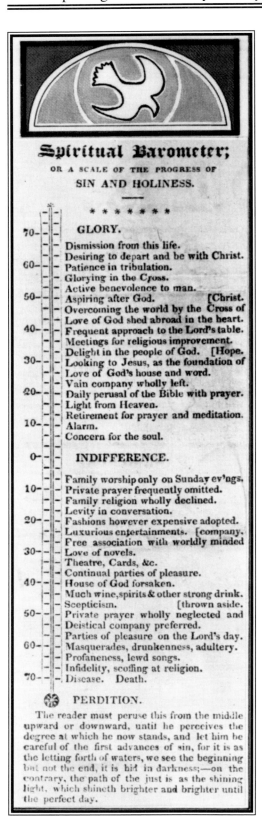

Spiritual Barometer;

OR A SCALE OF THE PROGRESS OF
SIN AND HOLINESS.

———

* * * * * * *

GLORY.

70—
— Dismission from this life.
— Desiring to depart and be with Christ.
60— — Patience in tribulation.
— Glorying in the Cross.
— Active benevolence to man.
50— — Aspiring after God.   [Christ.
— Overcoming the world by the Cross of
— Love of God shed abroad in the heart.
40— — Frequent approach to the Lord's table.
— Meetings for religious improvement.
— Delight in the people of God. [Hope.
30— — Looking to Jesus, as the foundation of
— Love of God's house and word.
— Vain company wholly left.
20— — Daily perusal of the Bible with prayer.
— Light from Heaven.
— Retirement for prayer and meditation.
10— — Alarm.
— Concern for the soul.

0—   **INDIFFERENCE.**

— Family worship only on Sunday ev'ngs.
10— — Private prayer frequently omitted.
— Family religion wholly declined.
— Levity in conversation.
20— — Fashions however expensive adopted.
— Luxurious entertainments. [company.
— Free association with worldly minded
30— — Love of novels.
— Theatre, Cards, &c.
— Continual parties of pleasure.
40— — House of God forsaken.
— Much wine, spirits & other strong drink.
— Scepticism.   [thrown aside.
50— — Private prayer wholly neglected and
— Deistical company preferred.
— Parties of pleasure on the Lord's day.
60— — Masquerades, drunkenness, adultery.
— Profaneness, lewd songs.
— Infidelity, scoffing at religion.
70— —. Disease.   Death.

☠ **PERDITION.**

The reader must peruse this from the middle upward or downward, until he perceives the degree at which he now stands, and let him be careful of the first advances of sin, for it is as the letting forth of waters, we see the beginning but not the end, it is hid in darkness;—on the contrary, the path of the just is as the shining light, which shineth brighter and brighter until the perfect day.

This Spiritual Barometer was featured in the March 22, 1825 issue of the Western Recorder that was printed in Utica by Merrell & Hastings, 40 Genesee Street.

The constitution of the Female Missionary Society set forth the ideals on which the group was founded.

Many women who belonged to the Female Missionary Society (1814) had husbands who maintained business addresses separate from their residences. These ladies had both time and freedom to experiment with new roles. Eunice Camp, for example, ran a school for black children. The ladies also contributed to the support of missionaries who were bringing the Gospel to pioneer homes. Educated women began to write memoirs and stories for the evangelical magazines published in Utica.

Converts to the cause of temperance swore an oath or signed a form such as this in which they renounced the use of intoxicants.

CONSTITUTION

&c.

****

THE subscribers, believing that a portion of the bounties of Providence can be applied in no better way than in administering to the spiritual necessities of our fellow creatures, and convinced of the utility and importance of Missionary Societies, by whose benevolent exertions the glad tidings of redemption are carried to multitudes who are perishing for lack of knowledge: and wishing to contribute our mite towards the advancement of so good a cause, do agree to associate ourselves for that purpose under the following REGULATIONS:

I. The society shall be composed of females, associated under the name of the *Female Missionary Society of Oneida.*

II. There shall be an annual meeting of the members of the society for the purpose of choosing trustees, who shall be elected by a majority of the votes of those present: The meetings to be on the first Tuesday of September, at two o'clock in the afternoon, at the place to which the previous meeting shall have adjourned.

III. The society shall appoint ten trustees, whose duty it shall be to manage and transact all business relative to the institution, for which purpose said trustees shall meet at least twice a year, at such times and places as they shall agree.

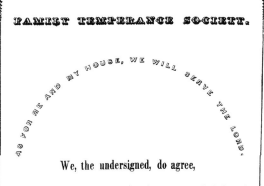

FAMILY TEMPERANCE SOCIETY.

AS FOR ME AND MY HOUSE, WE WILL SERVE THE LORD.

We, the undersigned, do agree,

that we will not use intoxicating liquors as a beverage, nor traffic in them; that we will not provide them as an article of entertainment, or for persons in our employment; and that in all suitable ways we will discountenance their use throughout the community.

This little band do with our hand,
The pledge now sign, to drink no wine,
Nor brandy red, to turn our head,
Nor whisky hot, that makes the sot,
Nor fiery rum, to turn our home
Into a hell, where none can dwell,
Whence peace would fly—where hope would die,
And love expire, 'mid such a fire;
So we PLEDGE perpetual hate
To all that can intoxicate.

*Sophia Converse
George C. Powell, of Arkansas
Sarah Maria Roberts
G. Wetmore.*

Revivalism & Reform

By Richard L. Manzelmann

Pastor Emeritus, New Hartford Presbyterian Church

"Oneida County has been completely overthrown by the Holy Spirit," reported an eastern paper in 1826, "in consequence of this display of divine power the theatre has been deserted, the tavern sanctified, court business has fallen off and jails are empty." The religious excitement and social impact implied in that report drew the attention of the entire nation to this spot in upper New York State. The zeal it generated, and both the religious and social influence it set in motion, went way beyond the boundaries of the county. It spread like a fire from this county to the next and finally to the nation at-large. For good reason, this section of New York State is called "the burned-over district," meaning burned-over with religious enthusiasm. If Northampton, Massachusetts, was the birthplace of the First Great Awakening with Jonathan Edwards in the 18th century, Oneida County was the birthplace of what has been called the Second Great Awakening with the Rev. Charles Grandison Finney. If the First Great Awakening influenced the founding of the nation, this Second Great Awakening helped to determine the great reform movements of the 19th century and influenced dramatically the great debate on slavery which ended in the Civil War. 1826 in Oneida County was a portentous moment for the history of the United States.

Not everyone, however, would have agreed that this moment was a work of the divine spirit. Some in the area and beyond thought it the work of a very unholy spirit. A Rev. William Weeks of Paris Hill was not shy about describing it as the work of the devil himself and wrote several vicious pamphlets condemning it. Lymon Beecher, a famous New England preacher and father of the even more famous Beecher clan, wrote to his friend Nettleton, a more staid evangelist, about what was going on in Oneida County. "The mask must be torn off from this Satan coming among the Sons of God and transforming himself into an angel of light." The debate raged locally. It divided churches, families, friends, and institutions, including the Board of Trustees of Hamilton College. Some abandoned words and took action to prevent and destroy the revivals. In a description of revivals in New Hartford, the Universalists were blamed for trying to disrupt the revivals by stoning the meetinghouse, by shooting off guns during the meeting, or by organizing young rowdies from the community to shout down the services.

The chief agent of this important commotion in the county's history, Charles Finney, made more modest claims for its effectiveness. Needless to say he did not blame it on the devil, but he did not credit –at least all of it – to the Holy Spirit either. He said quite bluntly, "a revival is not a miracle … it is plainly the philosophical result of the right use of means." To Finney a revival was not the work of God, although it could not succeed without the "blessing of God," it was rather the work of man, a question of a very definite set of techniques that could be used to raise the consciousness of congregations to the point of decision. He developed these techniques in Oneida County. He later wrote them down in a treatise on revivals which has become something of a handbook for the evangelistic movement. For this manual Finney is called the father of modern revivalism.

Revivals were not peculiar to the Mohawk Valley nor to the country at large. The Great Awakening in New England still lived in memory and church membership was not only a matter of formal confession but had to include an experience of the divine. Oneida County, at least at this early stage of its history, was mainly an accumulation of immigrants from New England. They brought the thought and practices of that area with them to this frontier settlement. Local historians indicate that hardly a year went by without a revival somewhere in one or more of the churches. The people liked and expected revivals. They added numbers to their churches. They also added a bit of color and excitement to the traditional worship of the day, which was formal, rigidly doctrinaire, and long, very long. They provided some diversion in a society that worked very hard and did not have many public diversions, except the tavern, especially in the winter when farm chores were light and canal traffic was at a standstill.

But there were differences between the early revivals and the ones that Finney instigated. It is important for us to probe these differences in order to capture the impact of this epochal moment and to understand the significant religious and social consequences that came out of them.

Chief among these differences between the old and new revivals was the main figure himself, Charles Finney. Whereas the old evangelists were rather formal, cold, distant figures; the new evangelists, Finney among them, were more down-to-earth, warmer, enthusiastic persons. William McLoughlin of Brown University, the most profound student of this era, says that Finney "deserves to be ranked with Andrew Jackson" as a cultural hero of that democratic period.

Oneida County can lay claim to Charles Finney at least during this formative stage of his career and influence. Although he was born in Warren, Connecticut, in 1792, and returned to that state for some education, he spent his boyhood in the county, returned to Whitesboro for a wife, was sponsored by the Female Missionary Society of Utica in his first efforts as a preacher, and met his first success as a revivalist in several communities here. It was while he was working as a law clerk in Adams, New York in 1821 that Finney was converted from a conventional faith to a more enthusiastic espousal of it. After some months of meditation on this experience he decided for the ministry. He felt that normal and orthodox training for the ministry at such a bastion of tradition as Princeton was not helpful and so he spent three years working on the farm and studying theology informally with his Adams pastor, the Rev. George Washington Gale, who had moved for reasons of health to Western (which later became Westernville) within the county. It was in the small church of Western as well as a few other rural churches that Finney discovered his powers as a preacher.

Rome heard about his preaching in Western, and invited him to conduct a revival there. He created such excitement in Rome that the Utica area churches invited him to come down for a season of preaching. And so his meteoric career was launched. He was tall and spare, a handsome and commanding figure in appearance. He had a voice that could reach, penetrate and stir, and a tongue that could shape words and images easily. He was master of the appropriate gesture; in fact his whole body expressed his preaching. It was especially his eyes, often remarked on, that could pierce the individual and compel the masses. He had the uncommon ability to control and sustain the attention of his congregations for hours on end. He had, in short, what we call "charisma." A local account reports that during one sermon at the First Presbyterian Church in Utica part of the roof gave way, but Finney kept on preaching and the congregation kept on listening.

Charles Finney
was raised in Oneida County and became an outstanding preacher whose sermons sparked social reform and change.

Finney was, of course, not the only preacher in these Oneida County revivals. He had assistants and followers who sought to emulate him, but Finney provided the model. It was his success that gave others the courage to break through the traditional image of preacher and evangelist and set in motion the new style.

The "means," or "new measures" as they are sometimes called, were, of course, at the heart of Finney's success. William McLoughlin marks the difference between the old and the new: whereas the old revivals were "prayed down," the new revivals were "worked up." It is worth noting in some detail the measures that Finney devised to work up his congregations to the point of decision. Preaching was, of course, the primary means of a revival but with significant differences from traditional preaching. It was more direct with simple language and short, urgent sentences. It was personal. Instead of addressing "sinners" in the third person, Finney addressed them as "you." He always tried to match a scriptural text to a particular congregation so that it carried a "present obligation." Illustrations were chosen from the common life and not from the literary. Most important, the sermon must be extemporaneous. Finney preached from an outline only and not from a manuscript.

All these innovations were drastic departures from the traditional preaching of the day which was viewed as elegant and doctrinaire discourse. The intent of the new was, of course, different. It was meant to move, compel, excite the listener and not just stimulate. The difference can perhaps be symbolized through church architecture. The New Hartford Presbyterian Church renovated the interior of its sanctuary under the impact of Finney's preaching. It changed its interior seating from a meetinghouse to an auditorium. It replaced its high wineglass pulpit to a platform with a speaker's stand and it changed its seats from little cubicles and balconies to rows of pews; they were called "slips," on a raked floor so that all could see.

Prayer was another essential means of these revivals- not that prayer had not always been a common element of religious services- but here it was used with a new intensity, urgency, frequency and, above all, with what was called, "the new system of particularity." The new evangelists prayed throughout the day and the night, alone, together, and with the community. They prayed in common language both in public and in private. At prayer meetings they prayed endlessly, urgently and passionately. The new warmth commanded in revivalistic praying is expressed by Finney in a letter to a preacher, "Your prayers are so cold that they do not rise more than 6 feet off the ground. You must groan, you must agonize, why you must pray until your nose bleeds."

Father Nash, one of Finney's closest assistants, had a reputation for his praying in these revivals. He prayed so loud that neighbors complained that he disturbed the peace of the community and he prayed so powerfully that it was said he could pray his horse into the neighboring pasture. Both men and women were encouraged to pray not only in private but in public as well. The inclusion of women in this invitation was considered a controversial innovation, for it was not traditional for women to speak out in public. Some scholars mark this innovation as one of the first small steps toward the liberation of women from their traditional role.

Most controversial in the subject of prayer was "the new system of particularity." The revivalists thought it "an offense against true religion to ask of the Lord any vague request." Prayers should be specific, as specific as a person's name and sin. It is easy to see how this could become not only controversial but also create a highly pressured environment.

In addition to preaching and praying, pastoral visitation played a part in revivals. Before Finney, it was common practice for the settled pastor to make calls on his parishioners and to chat informally about friendly, social things. It was not common practice for a minister to call on the entire community to determine the specific spiritual state of each household. The Whitesboro Presbyterian Church has in its archives a fascinating notebook of its pastor, the Rev. John Frost, during this period. It lists all his calls within the community indicating the state and stage of salvation for each person, their denominational sympathy, and incidental information such as whether or not they had a horse. The evangelist and his accomplices also accosted people on the streets, in the tavern, in shops and at work to investigate the spiritual condition of as many as possible in the community. here is record of Finney invading a mill in New York Mills and throwing the factory into such a turmoil that production was halted for several days.

Later additions to these essential means were the enquiry meeting, at first merely a meeting after church for interested persons, later a separate meeting in the church or in a home for all those who wanted to probe salvation and their feelings about it. The most notorious innovation, "the anxious bench," a seat set apart for those on the brink of decision in the front of the church where they could be exhorted and prayed over at length, was not introduced until Finney hit Rochester. It was used in Oneida County after this, however, and was part of the furor over revivals.

Some, if not all, of these practices may seem extrava-

Some scholars mark the inclusion of women in public prayer as the first small step toward the liberation of women.

gant. They were certainly considered as such by critics in their own day. They were viewed by some as a definite threat to the normal practice of the church. The more conservative New England ministers, Beecher and Nettleton, called Finney to account for these extravagances at a conference in New Lebanon, New York, during the summer of 1826. It was widely reported on in the press. The informal preaching, the praying, especially by women, the visitation program, were all subject to vigorous debate. A corps of ministers from Oneida County accompanied Finney to New Lebanon to help in his defense.

The seeming extravagance of these measures should not, however, lead us to view these revivals as wild, insincere, or mindless. They were definitely not as wild as some reports indicated. Whitney Cross, who has written the best book on the history of the period entitled The Burned Over District, writes, "No more impressive revival has occurred in American history ... the exceptional feature was the phenomenal dignity of the awakening. No agonized souls fell in the aisles, no raptured ones shouted hallelujahs. Rather, despite his doses of hell-fire, the great evangelist, 'in an unclerical suit of grey' acted like a lawyer arguing before a court and a jury." Lawyers, real estate magnates, millers, manufacturers, and commercial tycoons led the parade of the regenerate. In the less expert hands of some of Finney's followers, then and now, some of these methods were cheapened and carried to extremes, but the initial impulse with Finney was a very decent, honest, studied effort to make a difference to the person and the community.

Nor were these revivals insincere. They were, of course, criticized as being manipulative and opportunistic. The revivalists would have defended them against this criticism, however, mainly because the techniques seemed to work. They were evolved out of experience and they validate-I themselves through continued use. The end, conversion of the individual and the stirring of an entire community, seemed to justify the means chosen. If they didn't seem to have much to do with God at times, they at least hoped that they served Him. As Nathaniel Beman of Troy wrote, "I hope we look to God, but we must have means."

These revivals were not mindless either. A reading of some of Finney's sermons and books demonstrates that a clear and very logical mind was at work. They were not just emotional gibberish. The sermons are impressive in both their language and in the logic of the development of ideas. These are sermons that appeal not merely to the emotions but to the mind as well, or as one person remarked, ". . . he pressed the anxious sinners with closely reasoned truth."

And behind Finney's preaching and teaching there was a very well thought out theology. It was very different from the traditional theology of the time. Finney quarreled, along with many others of the time, with the rigid theological formulations of the day. To put it in its simplest terms, the traditional Calvinism of New England insisted that a person couldn't really do anything about his salvation until God wanted to do something about it and sometimes God didn't want to do anything about it. Finney rebelled against this. He loved to quote a satirical jingle about this brand of Calvinism:

> You can and you can't
> You will and you won't
> You're damned if you do
> And damned if you don't.

Finney insisted that you didn't have to wait around for God to do something, but that you could change your own heart and mind now. "If the sinner ever has a new heart, he must ... make it himself." If Finney did not invent this new theology, as is sometimes claimed, he certainly gave it currency and put it to work more effectively than others. It is the basic assumption that underlies all his "new measures." "Mankind will not act until they are excited .... How many there are who know that they ought to be religious, but they ... are procrastinating repentance until they have secured some favorite worldly interest. Such persons will never relinquish their ambitious schemes till they are so excited that they cannot contain themselves any longer."

Orthodox Presbyterians and Congregationalists tried to hold the line against this new theology even though it meant sacrificing the unity of the church for a time. The Presbyterian Church actually became two churches for a number of years as a result of this theological difference.

Finney's importance not only in the ecclesiastical struggle, but in helping to move the entire mind of the nation cannot be overestimated. He helped to break the back of rigid Calvinism and set new impulses in motion, social as well as religious. Not only did he say that man could change his own heart, but he could and must change his society as well. Calvinism had made personal salvation the end of all belief. Finney made salvation the beginning of religious experience instead of its end. Rather than use religion as an escape from life, Finney felt all Christians, once converted, should begin a new life, "in the interests of the kingdom,. . . they should set out with a determination to aim at being useful in the highest degree possible. " They should give practical expression to their faith and set to work to reform the church and society. "It is the business of the church to reform the world, to put away every sin." Thus he encouraged his ardent followers to join together and make a difference. This new focus of religion unleashed a powerful impulse for reform and its importance to the entire nation cannot be overstressed.

Frequently history books name this period of the 19th century in the United States "the Age of Reform." It is only fair to say that there were many influences that helped to create this mood, among them the inherited philosophy of the Enlightenment of the 18th century with its faith in progress and human capability, its traditions of benevolence. But most scholars agree that it was revivalism as it came out of Oneida County with Charles Finney and his cohorts that played the crucial role in the 19th century. Revivalism added an urgency, an energy, a moral and theological imperative to reform that the cool and general philosophy of the Enlightenment could not supply. Part of that urgency was supplied by the fact that many of these converts thought they could build the kingdom, the perfect society, and inaugurate the millenium, not just eventually but in a reasonable length of time. "If the church will do her duty," wrote Finney in 1835, "the millenium may

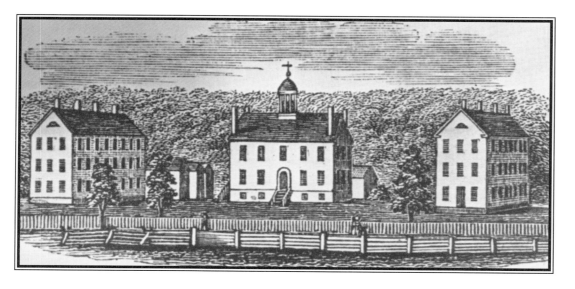

Oneida Institute in Whitesboro combined manual labor with studies to train poor young men for the ministry. This school was the first institution of higher learning in the country to admit blacks.

come in this country in three years." And so men, women and children joined together to eradicate sin and to effect change with an enormous enthusiasm and optimism.

The instrument chosen to accomplish reform was the voluntary society, an organized group of like-minded individuals who together hoped to exert more influence and effort than any individual could alone. There were societies against every imaginable sin known to man-dueling, flogging in the navy, the theatre, prostitution, frivolity, profanity, warfare, tight corsets. Then there were also societies to help the insane, handicapped, blind, deaf, orphans, prisoners, the poor, sailors, etc., etc.

Newspapers, pamphlets, and books of the period tell us that Oneida County was as busy if not busier than most areas of the country in trying to bring in the kingdom. What gave the county a special prominence in this activity was not only the fact that this was the birthplace of revivalism, but that this was an important center of the printing industry, third after New York and Boston. Every society had its publications, news sheets, and tracts. Many of them had their printing and editing done here. Recent advances in the mechanization of printing created a mass audience and enabled the wide dissemination of information and propaganda for the various causes.

The year 1826 itself saw the establishment of several important societies in Oneida County. The Western Education Society was founded to encourage ministerial studies and it sponsored along with Auburn Seminary an important weekly, the Western Recorder, which was edited for a time by Thomas Hastings, a Finney convert who later wrote the famous hymn "Rock of Ages." There was also a Female Missionary Society which underwrote the expenses of evangelists to the smaller villages and encampments to the north and west. Both the Utica Bible Society and the Welsh Bible Society were founded in 1826. They were local, but important, chapters of a larger movement that attempted to place the Bible in every home.

Tracts were a favorite device of the reformers and a tract society was started here in 1826. They were printed here and elsewhere by the millions and distributed free by pious folk to anyone who could read. They provided quick, one-page remedies to all the various social and spiritual problems of the day. Looking at them today we are forced to wonder whether their lurid descriptions of some of the more personal sins repelled or enticed their readers. The Sabbatarian Movement, an effort to curb commerce and traffic, including the delivery of the mails, gathered many supporters.

Theodore D. Weld
led Oneida County in a
radical reform movement for
the abolition of slavery.

This, as well as many of the other reform movements of the day, worked not only to persuade but to legislate. It was common in the 19th century for ministers and other Christian people to express themselves politically. In contrast to most evangelical religion today, Charles Finney blessed political involvement and said that politics was an indispensable part of religion. "No man can possibly be benevolent or religious without concerning himself to a greater or lesser extent with the affairs of human government." The Sabbatarian Movement lobbied for laws to preserve Sunday as a day of rest and sadness. Many of our blue laws, still on the books and so flagrantly ignored today, reach back to this effort.

The temperance movement recruited an enormous amount of support in the area as well as nationally. Evidently it was a needed reform. The hard-drinking habits of the 18th century spilled over into the 19th century. Alcoholic overindulgence was more or less socially accepted. Innkeepers held rather high social status and there were well-known alcoholics in positions of public trust. Cider, beer, wine and whiskey were incredibly cheap. It was considered normal to drink and even drink to excess. Captain Basil Hall, traveling in the United States in 1828, observed that Americans had "the practice of sipping a little at a time every half-hour to a couple of hours during the whole day." One church record in the area indicates that their preacher should not only be paid a certain amount of cash and firewood for his salary but also be given a keg of whiskey a year.

Such drinking produced its inevitable disasters and so good Christian people went to work to correct it. The history of this concern dates earlier than 1826, but its organized and crusading stage received a major injection of urgency and zeal from the revival movement which spread out from Oneida County. Instead of defining drinking as a social problem, it was now defined as a sin and the existence of intemperance in American society came to be considered the major hindrance to the revival of spirituality which was to inaugurate the millenium. The temperance movement became, in the words of one of its leaders, "Christ's work ... a holy war, and every true soldier of the Cross will fight it."

The various "means" of the revival with preaching, praying, visiting, meetings, and tracts, were devoted to this crusade. As far as the county was concerned it saw the founding of one of the earliest chapters of National American Temperance Union. Alexander Bryan Johnson, a distinguished citizen, banker, and philosopher, whose wife was a member of the famous Adams family, was the first president. In his address before the society on July 29, 1829, Johnson painted a lurid picture of the problem in Utica: "Even now in this orderly town, I have heard the cry of infant distress issue from the abodes of intemperance; and seen, more than once, some pitiable youth fleeing from his miserable home, and the ferocious father stumbling after him with maniacal fury."

During the 1830s Johnson parted company with the leaders of the temperance crusade who insisted on teetotalism and legal prohibition. The county contributed many leaders and preachers to the temperance crusade. Most of the young converts of the revivals joined the cause. The Independent Order of Good Templars, an international temperance society which once had more than 600, 000 members, was founded in Castor Hollow near Utica. Its rituals, regalia, discipline and secrecy had a romantic appeal and it was viewed as an alternative fellowship to those who were suspicious of the Masons, Odd Fellows and other mysterious orders.

All of the above represent rather conservative moral reforms. The major contribution of Oneida County to the reform movement of the nation was not, however, conservative. It was, strange as it may seem for the area today, radical. Its main theme was the abolition of slavery and its leading personage was a young man named Theodore Weld. In this matter of abolition, with Theodore Weld leading the fight, Oneida County can be said to have made significant contribution to the social and political life of the nation.

Weld was a gifted and popular student at Hamilton College in 1826. He was not, however, in sympathy with the revivals then going on in the area. His reluctance to succumb to Charles Finney's charms worried his aunt, not only because she was concerned about the state of his soul but also because of his influence among fellow students. In collusion with Finney, she deceived him into attending a revival meeting at the First Presbyterian Church of Utica where Finney directed his entire sermon on the text, "One sinner destroyeth much good," at the young man squirming with discomfort in the first pew. Weld's first reaction was one of angry resistance to the Finney effort but after several days of wrestling with his thoughts and after a couple of encounters with the evangelist, he capitulated. He became one of Finney's strongest supporters. For a time after this he joined "the Holy Band," preaching and helping in the revivals throughout the area. To his evangelistic labors Weld brought tremendous physical energy and personal charm. He was especially effective in helping to convert young men. This ardent host of young converts, including Weld, needed further training if they were to

Henry Highland Garnet, *educated at the Oneida Institute, was one of the most outstanding black leaders of the abolition movement.*

continue their ministerial labors.

At this moment, in February of 1827 to be exact, George Washington Gale who had converted Finney and tutored him in theology, enlisted the aid of the Presbytery of Oneida in sponsoring a school in Whitesboro for the preparation of poor young men in ministry. It was based on a somewhat new idea of combining manual labor with studies, which grew out of Gale's experience in training Finney and some others on his farm outside of Western. First called the Oneida Academy, it later became the Oneida Institute. It had a great success and gathered the financial and moral support of many leaders of the evangelistic movement. Some of its educational ideas were considered radical, such as the substitution of the biblical language Hebrew for the classical Latin. Its unique combination of work and study became the model for many schools of its time including Oberlin in Ohio and Knox College in Galesburg, Illinois. It was very widely studied, written about and visited.

The main contribution of the Institute, however, was to the abolitionist cause. A few historians tell the story that in the early days of its history, the students, along with all other citizens of the area, had to pay a road tax. Since the students were poor and could not afford the tax, they could substitute their labor instead. So one fine day the student body went out to spread gravel. The gravel, however, had not yet been delivered to the site, so to use the time constructively-as every good Institute student was called to do-they devised a debate on the hottest issue of the day. One side argued the cause for colonization, a very popular solution to the slavery problem which called for the return of the slaves to their homeland in Africa. The other side argued the less well-known case for abolition, immediate emancipation. The latter solution won the day and the students of the Oneida Institute were "converted" to the more radical position. This is known as the famous "Gravel Debate."

Whether the story is true or not, it still symbolizes an important union between evangelical religion and social cause. Instead of being just a social problem that could eventually be negotiated away, slavery became "a sin" that had to be purged from the body politic immediately. Evangelical zeal and all the revivalistic practices were now devoted to the cause of abolition. The students of the Oneida Institute, especially Weld, preached, taught, prayed, traveled, wrote tracts, pamphlets, published a newspaper called A Friend of Man, visited, confronted friends and strangers, demonstrated on the green in Whitesboro and organized in the cause of abolition. They changed the character of the Institute itself.

By this time Gale had departed the school and a new head, Beriah Green from Western Reserve in Cleveland, had been brought in. The school adopted an open admission policy and is considered the first institution of higher learning in the country to admit blacks. By its critics it was called "that Negro school." It educated a significant number of blacks, among them Henry Highland Garnet, one of the most outstanding black leaders of the abolition movement. Green himself wrote widely on the problem of slavery, was a close friend of the poet and abolitionist John Greenleaf Whittier, and became a president of the AntiSlavery Society in 1833. The Institute founded the first Abolition Society in New York State and was a stop on the underground railway.

For these and many other reasons Utica, New York was considered the logical place for the first meeting of the New York State Anti-Slavery Society in 1835. It was to meet in the courthouse, but a group of prominent citizens protested this use of public facilities for so radical a cause. The meeting was shifted to the Bleecker Street Presbyterian Church, but a mob instigated by "gentlemen of property and standing" in the community invaded the church and broke up the meeting. It was forced to adjourn to a farm owned by the land baron and supporter of many causes, Gerrit Smith. This was not one of Utica's most glamorous moments, although the city redeemed itself, partially at least, a year later when it mobbed a lawyer's office to prevent the return of a runaway slave to his southern owner who had come north to claim him. A series of lectures on abolition by Theodore Weld at the Bleecker Street church may have helped to change the mind of the community from injustice to justice. Utica's destructive mob action against slavery has been widely studied. It's constructive mob action at the lawyer's office is seldom remembered. Nevertheless the overriding memory, at least among historians, is that Utica and Oneida County made a significant contribution to the great debate on slavery.

Credit for this positive reputation belongs largely to these students, especially Weld, from the Oneida Institute. As they left or graduated from the school they fanned out in every direction carrying the message of abolition. Inflamed by Finney but informed by abolition, they confronted the nation with the necessity to purge this sin from its midst. The urgency of their convictions and the ardor of their devotion to the cause hastened the coming of disunion to the nation. It is not always easy to recognize the work of these students because their work of evangelical abolitionism took place in halls and churches in thousands of communities throughout the nation. Many of them remain nameless, but their effective presentation of the cause brought the urgent issue of slavery to the masses. Weld, incredibly gifted but terribly modest, was the mas-

Located at the corner of Bleecker and Charlotte Streets, Utica, this church was Presbyterian and later Baptist. In the 1830s and '40s anti-slavery and temperance groups met here.

ter and sometime leader of this movement. There is enough documentation available about his career and achievements to name him one of the primary social and political figures in American history. Ultimately the impulse for this important movement can be traced back to Oneida County and this strange wedding between revivalism and reform.

Selected References

Barnes, Gilbert Hobbs, *The Anti-Slavery Impulse 1830-1844,* with a new introduction by William G. McLoughlin, a Harbinger Book (Harcourt, Brace and World, Inc. paperback, 1964). The best survey of the abolition movement rescuing the work of Theodore Weld from his own modesty.

Cross, Whitney R., The Burned Over District: The Social and Intellectual History of ,Enthusiastic Religion in Western New York 1800-1850, (Cornell University Press, 1950, Harper Torchback 1965). Excellent survey of the entire scene in paperback.

Finney, the Rev. Charles G., Memoirs, many editions; Lectures on Revivals of Religion, many editions, but a modern one has been published by the Belknap Press of Harvard University with an introduction by William McLoughlin.

McLoughlin, William G., *Modern Revivalism,* (Ronald Press, New York 1959). The best book an revivalism in American history.

McLoughlin, William G., *"Revivalism In The Rise of Adventism, A Commentary on the Social and Religious Ferment of Mid-Nineteenth Century America,"* edited by Edwin Scott Goustad, (Harper and Row, New York, 1974). Superb essay which puts revivalism in an historical context.

Manzelmann, Richard L., *The Revival Heard 'Round the World,* pamphlet, (Auburn Theological Seminary, New York City, 1975). The script of a service put on at the New Hartford Presbyterian Church.

Richards, Leonard L., *Gentlemen of Property and Standing: Anti-Abolition Mobs in Jacksonian America,* (Oxford University Press, 1970). A paperback study of the famous 1835 mob in Utica. Highly recommended.

Rome

By
E. Stevens Wright
and
Dr. William Forbes

Rome City Hall

D. F. White

Rome began as dry land between two streams, one turning east and the other west near the center of New York State. Here Wood Creek was separated from the Mohawk River by a mile of woods. The Indians knew that Lake Ontario was linked to the Hudson River and the Atlantic Ocean via these waterways. The Oneida Indians called this spot Deo-Wain-Sta, by which was meant the place where a canoe is carried between two streams. The path beaten by their feet ran along the north shoulder of a cedar swamp, which bounded the area on the south. It became known as the Carrying Place.

While it is not known when European eyes first glimpsed what would be Rome, whether the explorer was from the French colonies of Canada or the Dutch and English settlements along the Hudson, an agent of the Dutch West India Company, Harmen Van den Bogaert,

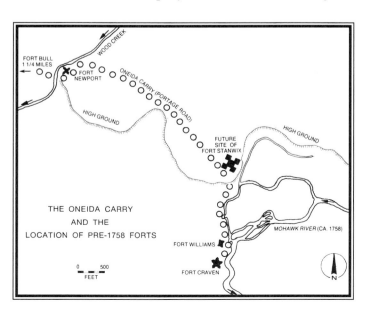

THE ONEIDA CARRY
AND THE
LOCATION OF PRE-1758 FORTS

describes a trip made with Indian guides as early as 1634 to an Oneida Indian settlement just southeast of Oneida Lake. Traveling on foot from the Dutch settlement Fort Orange (Albany), it is clear that he did not traverse the Carry because in a sketch of the area he represents the Mohawk River as flowing from Oneida Lake directly to Albany.

Soon horse-drawn wagons were transporting boats and their cargoes across the wooded plateau where Rome would begin to grow. In the summer months they would back up to the low river banks near martin Street, Bateaux, planked heavy-duty versions of the Indian canoe, would be loaded upon the specially adapted wagons and brought along the southwest bank of the Mohawk and across the higher ground, along a route touched by present-day Martin, East Whitesboro, Dominick and Liberty Streets. Connection with Wood Creek was made at the present site of Fort Bull or more distant juncture with Canada Creek, which were the only practical launching sites for all vessels but canoes. The transportation of boats and goods became Rome's first business and induced a handful of colonists to dwell there.

The Oneida Carry, because of its strategic position on what had additionally become an important military route, probably sprouted many forts as well. To secure this initial trade route linking the ports of the east with Ontario and the Great lakes, the British build Fort Williams in 1755 near the east end of the Carry Road. Fort Bull was built the same year at what was called the middle landing of Wood Creek. Later came Forts Craven, Newport, Wood Creek, Stanwix and Rickey. Fort Stanwix, much the superior of any of these, was rebuilt by the Americans at the Revolution and successfully withstood a 21-day British siege in 1777. Here at this dirt and log outpost, tradition holds the Stars and Stripes first flew in the face of an enemy.

The Revolution and two subsequent Indian treaties, signed by the Iroquois at Fort Stanwix, made possible a far greater influx of settlers to Central New York than had been practical before. Those who brought their families and belongings to the Carrying Place found an established water route embracing fertile land stretching north and east from the eroding bastions of a memorable fortress. To their chagrin they also found that the best land for business and mercantile interests had been bought by wealthy speculator Dominick Lynch, who lived in remote New York City.

After the Revolution, the colonial Oriskany Patent, upon which Rome sits, was divided into allotments with one lot set aside to pay for the expense of the surveying. This expense lot of 697 acres was sold at auction in 1786 to Dominick Lynch. By 1800 he had accumulated about 2,000 acres. Lynch correctly perceived that lands on and adjacent to the Carrying Place would soon support a thriving community. He was not interested in letting others develop it for themselves, so the lands were leased to settlers. Many settlers preferred to move west or north of Lynch's lands at what quickly became Wright Settlement and Ridge Mills. The Carry, with a tavern or two, George Huntington and a few other merchants, was referred to by these settlers as the Fort.

The speculator from New York began developing his dream in the wilderness. A gristmill was built on Wood Creek in 1795. The Carry Road, as it ran west from under the ramparts of Fort Stanwix past this mill, was laid straight for a distance on a map labeled Dominick Street.

A small grid of streets was attached to this, which he proposed to name Lynchville. By 1797 the Western Inland Lock Navigation Company, which was formed to improve navigation along the Mohawk-Wood Creek route to Lake Ontario, completed a small canal connecting for the first time the waters of the above streams and supplanting horse and wagon conveyance of boat and cargo over the Carry. The canal brought larger craft called Schenectady and Durham boats directly through the village on the south side of Dominick Street.

Mr. Lynch dug a millrace bisecting the eastern bend of the Mohawk River (Race and Mill Streets); and a woolen mill was erected in what was to be his "factory village." Several structures were erected by Lynch and Rome's first local developer, Jebediah Phelps, in the present down town area attracting traders and artisans. In spite of these efforts, Lynchville was not a great success. Dominick Lynch had never intended to sell, but rather to rent his lands to settlers. In so doing, he misjudged the mood of the new American citizen who wanted to own his own land free and clear.

Prominent among those early settlers who did stay under Lynch's terms prior to 1800 were: Jebediah Phelps, John Barnard, George Huntington, Joshua Hathaway, Dr. Stephen White, Henry Huntington, Roswell Fellows, Matthew Brown, Matthew Brown, Jr., Bill Smith, Seth Ranney, David Brown, Ebenezer and Thomas Wright, Daniel W. Knight, Thomas Selden, Solomon and John Williams, Peter Colt, Colonel William Colbrath, Abijahj

The relocation of the Erie Canal about 1844 along present-day Erie Boulevard stimulated new growth in Rome. This view taken about 1900 at South James and Erie Boulevard looking north. Stanwix Hall on the corner.

Chester Williams

and Clark Putnam, Caleb Reynolds, Rufus Easton, Thomas Gilbert, Moses Fish, Stephen Lampman, Jeremiah Steves and John Niles.

Historian Daniel Wager says in 1810: "There were then no sidewalks or paved streets, hardly a planked walk the entire length, no gas to light the streets and stores, but instead tallow candles shed their…rays in store and dwelling, tending to make darkness visible, and when business closed for the night and 'tallow dips' were extinguished, Rome repose, as it were, in a cloud of midnight darkness."

When the first shovelful of earth was turned for the commencement of the Erie Canal in 1817. Romans had lost an important battle to secure the route of the new canal along that of their former waterway, the western Inland. Flowing one-half mile south of Dominick Street through swampy land, it meant much less to Rome than to other communities through which it passed.

The name Lynchville did not endure. Rome was the name of the township that was established from the Town of Steuben in 1796 and Rome's first merchant, George Huntington, may have suggested it for the name of the village incorporated in 1819 from a portion of the township. Village boundaries were described in part as running "thence on a line of said farm to a poplar tree south of the old canal, thence to the east corner of Fiero's barn, thence

Jesse Williams was the first in America to use a factory system for making cheese.

to the north corner of Jacob Tibbitts' farm…"

The village languished for a time then started to fight in the 1830s for the right of way of the Syracuse and Utica Railroad. The first train to pass through the village was in the early summer of 1839. The same strong-minded Romans succeeded in 1844 in relocating the Erie Canal along present-day Erie Boulevard. With a railroad and canal providing fast and economical transportation for Rome's goods, the village's first industries could begin to grow.

The village's surrounding farmlands contributed a great deal to the success of Rome. The wagons rumbling into town laden with produce traveled from several adjacent settlements, one of which, Ridge Mills, could boast a gristmill, sawmill, woolen mill and fulling mill. A little north of the Ridge was Elmer Hill, named for Hezikiah Elmer who came from Vermont in 1792. Rolling up to the Mohawk from the east beneath the Ridge were the fertile acres of Wright Settlement. This neighborhood brought Rome's first religious society into being in the confines of a tavern. It was this settlement which had lured many o f Rome's earliest settlers away from Lynchville. Most of its inhabitants and those of adjacent Canterbury Hill and Selden Neighborhood were of Connecticut lineage. To the southwest of Rome lay Greenway and Hatch's Corners. To the southeast, after the digging of the Erie, grew up Stanwix.

Rome Brass and Copper Company, formerly Rome Iron Works. Today the company is known as Revere Copper and Brass, Inc.

New York Central Station, 218 South James Street, is still standing.

Chester Williams

The dry house and portion of foundation of Jesse Williams' cheese factory. Photo from Souvenir of Rome, NY, 1894.

Chester Williams

Home of John B. Jervis, superintendent of construction for a 50-mile section of the Erie Canal, chief engineer for the Chenango Canal, the Croton Aqueduct and the Hudson River Railroad. His home was donated for the Jervis library.

Possibly Rome's greatest year occurred in 1851. Great strides in transportation were made with the completion of the Watertown and Rome Railroad and the Black River Canal. The consolidation of the various railroad lines connecting Buffalo at Lake Erie with Albany into the first New York Central Railroad greatly streamlined cross-state rail service, while plank roads, then a mania sweeping the country, were completed connecting Rome with Whitesboro, Taberg, Bouckville, Boonville and Oswego.

A new public school of brick was constructed in 1850 on the 300 block of Liberty Street where Barringer School now stands. Richard Upjohn designed and finished Zion Episcopal Church, and the First Presbyterian Church at Court Street was started. The new Rome Savings Bank opened; and to bring all this progress into historical prospective, Judge Pomroy Jones of Westmoreland had just published his Annals and Recollections of Oneida County.

Not to be outdone by these considerable events, Rome's farming community in 1851 contributed, through the efforts and genius of Jesse Williams, a factory system for the manufacture of cheese, hitherto an unpredictable item as to quality and availabili-

Calvert Comstock in 1870 became first mayor of Rome.

ty. This achievement had not been accomplished before in America. By 1864 Rome was the world center of the cheese market.

Rome started to build its industrial base after the expanding Rome, Watertown and Ogdensburg Railroad moved its building shops to west Rome in 1863. Three years later Addison Day, superintendent of the railroad, joined with local men to organize the Rome Iron Works. In 1868 the Rome Merchant Iron Mill was formed by the well-known engineer John B. Jervis of this city. An extensive boot and shoe factory was built in the same year by Messrs. Kingsbury, Abbott and Hale. Rome got a start in the food processing business in 1872 when Homer T. Fowler established the Rome Canning Company. Lumber processing businesses, knitting mills, breweries and a locomotive works were all enjoying steady growth before the turn of the century.

The entire Rome Township was incorporated in 1870 as the City of Rome, resulting in zoning control within the 73 square miles of the township. The first mayor, Calvert Comstock, stated to Edward L. Stevens, retiring president of the village trustees: "This change has happened at an auspicious time.

The first Rome Academy, northwest corner James and Court Streets. Formerly a private school built in 1848, it became in 1869 Rome's first "free" school. Francis Bellamy, author of the Pledge to the Flag, graduated here 1872.

Chester Williams

Sign mounted on the Mill Street bridge over the Barge Canal boasting "one-tenth of copper used in the United States manufactured in Rome." (Send-off for World War I soldiers).

Chester Williams

We are free from debt. Manufacturing enterprises have recently sprung up in our midst which have given a large accession to our population and a healthy tone to every branch of business."

Rome justifiably became known as the Copper City. Rome Iron Works converted to the production of brass in 1878 when iron railroad rails, the principal product were supplanted by steel. By 1890 it had become Rome Brass and Copper Company, with sales covering three-and one-half million pounds of copper. This company merged with others and today is Revere Copper and Brass. In 1892 Rome Manufacturing Company was established and was soon producing specialty items such as copper tea and coffee pots, wash boilers, basins, and the like.

Pioneered by Nicholas Spargo, who came to Rome in 1883, a wire a cable industry took hold in 1904 when Herbert T. Dyett founded the Rome Electrical Company, specialists in insulated wire for the winding of transformers. Through the acquisitions and mergers of this company, General Cable Corporation was launched in 1927. Later, Mr. Dyett formed the Rome Cable Corporation as the corporate heir of Rome Metallic Bedstead Company organized in 1886.

By the second decade of the 20th century Rome proudly proclaimed, "One-tenth of copper used in the United States in manufactured in Rome" on a huge electric sign mounted on the Mill Street bridge over the new Barge Canal, in plain view of the New York Central System's relocated trackage. Passing under this sign several times a day and along the east side of martin Street ran the cars of the New York State Railway System's electric trolley line which connected the people of Rome with those towns and cities along its route to the railway's terminus at Little Falls.

July 4, 1887 marked the beginning of the first street railway in Rome. These horse-drawn cars of the Rome City Street Railway operated on a leisurely and accommodating basis until 1900, when the notion of cars (locally manufactured) driven by compressed air was entertained, reviewed, and scrapped. In 1903 electric trolleys came to stay, and eventually could take a rider from the American Corner at James and Dominick Streets to Charles Street on the west; to St. Peter's Cemetery on the east; up James Street to Linden and thence to Madison, Thomas and Expense Streets. One could travel out Floyd Avenue as far as the fairgrounds and the Oneida County Home and also to the New York Central Station on Martin Street. The line served Romans until 1932.

As the close of the 20th century approaches, Rome can no longer make boasts about its copper and wire production. Revere has downsized and closed much of its operation in Rome; the Pettibone plant has been closed,

1887,
Floyd Avenue
street railway.

Chester Williams

In 1899, this French chateau-styled high school on James and Court replaced the original Academy building. Present site of the Justice Building.

Chester Williams

and the Spargo Wire Company has been taken over by International Wire Company of Camden. However, these blows to the economy have been softened somewhat by the formation of the 1212 Corp., an "incubator" for new businesses, and the Rome Locomotive Works on E. Dominick Street.

Rome's first public school, constructed in 1850, was a pleasant-looking two-story brick structure of classical design. Its location at the 300 block of Liberty Street gives an idea of the size of the village at the time. The "free" or tax-supported school system, after a struggle, had its debut in Rome in 1869. Its first structure was the Rome Academy building, formerly a private school built on James and Court Streets in 1848, site of the present Justice Building. This edifice and its successor, a handsome French chateau-styled building completed in 1899, have both disappeared, and later giving way to the present Rome Free Academy building in 1926. Used thereafter as a junior high, the old James Street building was demolished in 1960.

In 1957 the area district schools, many of them old country schoolhouses, were consolidated into the city school district and several new elementary schools were built to accommodate the pupils. A handsome addition to Rome's parochial school system, Rome Catholic High School, opened on Cypress Street in 1963.

The aforementioned senior high building was gutted by a disastrous fire, which was fought by the entire Rome Fire Department with additional assistance from Utica on April 28, 1938. Earlier fires in Rome did more damage. Rome's first great fire is said to have occurred in 1844, followed closely by a second major fire two years later which swept away all the buildings on and adjacent to the northwest corner of the American Corner. Hand-drawn and pumped fire apparatus of that time was grossly outmatched by most fires of any consequence. Alarms were sounded by the bell atop the meetinghouse of the First Religious Society of the Town of Rome. Fires were located by the "shine" i.e. the shine of the fire seen in the night or on the horizon.

Rome's first fire company was founded in 1827. By 1881 two horse-drawn steam fire engines, hooks and ladders, hose carts and about 2,000 feet of leather hose could be summoned by a steam whistle at the old Rome Gas and Electric plant on South Madison Street on the north bank of the canal. It was said that the whistle could be heard 25 miles away. The device was supplanted in 1903 by a large bell hung atop Rome's City Hall building. Fire fighters would listen to the tolling count of the bell then speedily ascertain the pull-box location.

During World War II a Rome Sentinel page two headline blares incredulously, "Old Fire 'Gong' (whistle) Sought For Blackout Turns Up As Signal In Herkimer."

Provision for the election of a police constable was made in 1835. Police regulations created in the same act mandated that the constable "...arrest any and all persons in the village guilty of any crime, misdemeanor or offense against the peace or good order of society." A village

Chester Williams

Rome Gas and Electric Light & Power Co., home of the famous "steam whistle."

St. Peter's Roman Catholic Church and City Hall.

Chester Williams

police department was created in 1853. The police station, located on East Whitesboro Street, moved into quarters on the ground floor of the new four-story red stone city hall in 1896. At the rear were men's and women's cell blocks. Motorcycles replaced horses but the force must have achieved an apex in style in 1918 with the purchase of a Cadillac patrol car. During these times, traffic in the downtown business district was regulated by stop-and-go devices known as "silent policemen" set in the center of intersections and hand-operated by patrolmen.

Under "An Act to revise the Charter of the City of Rome" May 9, 1904, the city was divided into seven wards, with one alderman representing each of the wards, In 1954 Rome decided to adopt the Council-Manager form of city government. In this system the aldermen were replace by nine councilmen elected at large. The one receiving the greatest popular vote was designated as mayor and presided over the Common council. In 1959 Rome citizens elected to return the Mayor-Council form of government to the city. Charles T. Lanigan Jr. was elected mayor with one alderman representing each of the seven wards.

In 1941, while Mayor Ethridge was out of town, four men paid an unexpected visit to city hall telling the Public Works Commissioner they were looking over possible sites for an Air Force repair and maintenance depot to serve the entire northeastern section of the nation. In 82 days, with the help of state, county and Utica officials, railroad and utility officials, Rome City Hall, Chamber of Commerce and the Rome Sentinel, Rome was announced as the site of the $13,200,000, two-thousand-acre depot. The first plane touching down at Griffiss less than a year later was an unscheduled flight landing on the runway before it was completed.

Griffiss Air Force Base, which was built on those beginnings, became a city within a city occupying 4,000 acres of land and accommodating as many as 4,000 military and an equal number of civilian personnel serving four major Air Force organizations which were eventually housed on the base.

Unfortunately for the City of Rome and the immediate surrounding area, after the Cold War ended, the Federal Government decided to downsize the military bases in the United States. On September 22, 1995, at the recommendation of the Base Closure Commission the 416th Bomb Wing, the hot mission of Griffiss, was inactivated, the base was closed and the property turned over to the city.

The base closing, with its resultant loss of about 5,000 jobs had an immediate, negative impact upon the local community. Schools were closed because of the loss of student population with the subsequent reduction in the teaching staff; stores closed from lack of business, and many homes were thrown on the real estate market all at the same time, causing a drop in property values in the city.

To combat this economic downturn, the Oneida County Economic Development Growth Enterprises (EDGE), and the Griffiss Local Development Corporation (GLDC), were formed to attract new business and to mar-

Chester Williams

The American Corner at the north side of Dominick Street looking west.

Oneida County Fair, Rome.

Chester Williams

ket the properties on the now defunct base. High technology enterprises were sought to tie into the Air Force Information Directorate (formerly the Rome Lab) which had remained at the base after the closing. Other overtures went to heavier industrial business, sports enterprises and medical organizations that could bring jobs and payrolls back to the Rome area. Housing subdivisions on the former base were also considered as a means of bringing people back to the center of town.

A further boost to Rome's economy was given by the establishment of the Rome Industrial Park in West Rome with its huge Rite Aid warehouse, and the subsequent building of Wal Mart and K Mart stores adjacent to this facility. In 1995, the city transferred the Rome Memorial Hospital to private ownership after years of operation in the red, and allowed the city to end this strain on the taxpayers of the city.

In 1935, Fort Stanwix National Monument was authorized by an act of Congress. This legislation was introduced at the request of the Rome Chamber of Commerce, which was interested in having the fort rebuilt as an emergency public works project. The fort did not materialize at that time due to lack of funds in Depression years, but in 1963, the site of Fort Stanwix was designated a Registered National Landmark, and in 1964, the National Park

Service agreed to help work the fort site into the city's proposed urban renewal project.

The outcome of this project was complete reconstruction of Fort Stanwix built on the original site by B.S. McCary Co., Inc. of Rome for the sum of $4,288,000. The formal dedication of this addition to the National Park Service was on May 22, in the Bicentennial Year of 1976, and it continues to be great drawing card for visitors to the city.

The Fort Stanwix Central Business District was the name given to the beginnings of an almost completely new downtown Rome, extending west from the Fort Stanwix Park to George Street, and between Erie Boulevard and Liberty Street. The area was created as a pedestrian mall with circumferential traffic circulation and parking. An earlier renewal project of the fifties, Midtown Plaza, on the south side of Erie Boulevard, was then connected with the mall by an enclosed shopping bridge, called the Living Bridge.

The establishment of Fort Stanwix and the Business District caused downtown Rome to lose part of its past identity, and the establishment of malls outside the Business District drew shoppers away from downtown Rome. The shops on the Living Bridge disappeared, along with the customers, and in 1997, that part of Dominick

The Living Bridge, left center, is a pedestrian crossing over Erie Boulevard in the area of the old Erie Canal bridge at Washington Street. Photograph taken May, 1977.

Chester Williams

Street which had been closed to traffic, was repaved and reopened in an attempt to bring customers back to downtown.

Recreation and tourism have replaced heavy industries as major sources of income for Rome. Along with Fort Stanwix National Monument, such attractions as the Erie Canal Village, Fort Rickey Game Farm, and the nearby Turning Stone Casino bring visitors and tourist dollars to the area. Local sporting events also bring visitors, and several statewide events, especially hockey tournaments, are regularly held at Kennedy Arena.

In a city that boasts the first American flag to fly in battle (over Fort Stanwix in 1777), the same determined spirit that was displayed by the garrison is shown during the Honor America Days, which incorporates the older Fort Stanwix Days. It shows that, despite recent economic setbacks, the spirit of the City of Rome remains optimistic about its future.

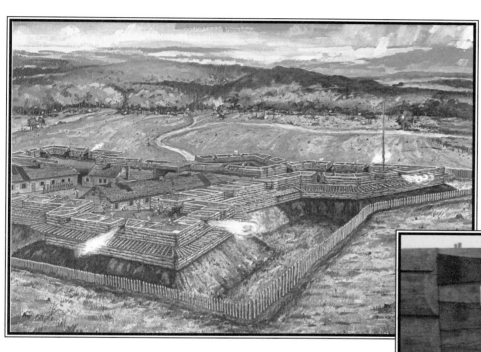

"The stronghold that would not surrender," Fort Stanwix, August 1777, at the time of siege by British, Indian and loyalist forces under General Barry St. Leger. Painting by Tom Lotta, commissioned by Marine Midland Bank.

Guide wearing uniform of Third New York Regiment at Fort Stanwix National Monument. Photo by Paisley & Friends.

Utica National Insurance Group

Fort Stanwix National Monument, reconstructed by the U.S. Department of the Interior on the site of the original fort, was opened to visitors in 1976. Photo by Paisley & Friends.

Utica National Insurance Group

Selected References

Fort Stanwix – A Master Plan, (National Parks Service, 1967).

Haggerty, Gilbert, *Massacre at Fort Bull,* (1971).

Lake, Robert, *Industrial Development of Rome,* (1969).

Rahmer, Frederick, *Jesse Williams, Cheese Maker,* (1971).

Rome *Daily Sentinel,* June 26, 1941, and February 20, 1942.

Rome, New York – Centennial History, (Rome Historical Society, 1970).

Scott, John Albert, *Rome, New York – A Short History,* (1945).

Scripture, Parker F. and Williams, Chester, *Photographs of Rome, New York, 1880 – 1930,* (Rome, 1975).

Wager, Daniel E., *Our City and Its People,* (1896).

D. F. White

Entrance to Griffiss Air Force Base, former home of the 416th Bomb Wing, and current site of the Air Force Information Directorate.

The Erie Canal Village reconstructs village life along the canal. At Rome on July 4, 1817 the first earth was turned to begin construction of the canal.

Siringo Studio photo

Sherrill

*By
Ruth C. Park
and
Dwight Evans,
Mayor*

The "smallest city in New York State," as Sherrill proudly calls itself, is a modern community with well-planned parks, a swimming pool, grade school, bank, library, churches, Clubhouse, municipal building complex, post office, tree-line streets and tremendous community spirit. It is located on Route 5, a few miles south of Interstate 90 between Utica and Syracuse.

According to an 1855 map of Oneida County, "Turkey Street" (Sherrill) was a small settlement situated on a creek, not far from the Village of Vernon. About 30 families lived on a sort of crossroads, most of who were farmers; but there was also a sawmill, a gristmill, a woolmill, a wheelbarrow factory and a plaster mill. There were toll houses operated to help defray expenses of the upkeep of the Seneca Turnpike tollroad (Route 5).

A small hotel, owned by Joe Williams, had a long barn with doors on either end so that a stage coach could drive in one end, change horses, and drive out the other end. The town water pump was also on the hotel property. Joe Williams' father owned the sawmill as well as the little store. He would shut down the mill in order to take care of store customers.

There are many stories about Turkey Street and how it got its name. One tells of the white men who stole turkeys, corn and other meal from the Indians at Oneida Castle. The Indians called it "Tu-ri-kes-re-et" (The Place of the Thief).

Turkey Street was located on the Seneca Turnpike tollroad, later called the Great Plank Road, now Route 5.

John Humphrey Noyes and his followers, who founded the Oneida Community in 1848, came from Putney, Vermont to an area a mile south of this small town called Turkey Street. They came to establish a home and practice their religious beliefs in privacy. John Noyes had many ideas about religion, which appeared to the Calvinist elders in Putney at that time to be radical. So they had to leave Putney.

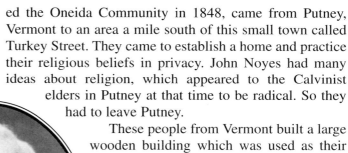
*John Humphrey Noyes,
founder of the Oneida Community.*

These people from Vermont built a large wooden building which was used as their main house until 1870, when it was torn down, and a huge brick building was erected in four parts between 1861 and 1878. This is now known as the Mansion House and is in use today.

At first the members of the Oneida Community called themselves Perfectionists. They taught that Christ had already come for the second time, so it was no longer possible to alternate sinning with repentance. They must sin no more, and eliminate selfishness.

They believed that there must be complete spiritual equality. Not only must personal property be sacrificed to the good of all, but also rights over the lives of others, i.e. marriage. They began to substitute for the small unity of home and family, the larger unit of a group family.

Their neighbors in Oneida, seeing that they were honest and kind, did not censure them, but let them live as they wished.

In the 1850s, the Community became interested in business and started to invent products for resale. They canned fruits and vegetables, made traps and chains, and traveling bags. They also found out how to make silver knives and forks and spoons. One item, the Newhouse animal trap, became well-known and was profitable.

At its peak the Community had 200-300 people. Mr. Walter Edmonds has written, "As far as possible, the men and women shared equally in the work of barns and fields and of pantries and kitchens. One result was the characteristic dress of the women whose bobbed hair, short skirts, and pantalettes created so much comment in their day.

Another was that men, confronted by a term of household chores, began to invent labor-saving devices. 40 years before such things came into general use, the Community laundry and kitchen had been equipped with washing machines, dish washers, a machine for paring apples, and another for washing vegetables.

The Oneida Community had a fundamental belief in the dignity of work...A man who did his work well received the same recognition and respect whether he was a kitchen assistant or a factory superintendent."

The Community system of child care was interesting. All babies, from the age of one year, were cared for in what they called the Children's House: a series of large apartments in the Mansion House, where, from babyhood to 12 years, they lived, were tended and taught by a selected group of men and women called Mothers and Fathers of the Children's House. These children were allowed to see their own parents once or twice a week, were well taught, and had freedom to play. Their health was carefully guarded. Testimony of people who "graduated" from the Children's House, said that they were not spoiled but were especially happy children.

The Community encouraged reading, and there was enthusiasm for every kind of education. They published a weekly journal telling of their ideas and activities.

From 1848 to 1880, the Community prospered. Then, as their leader became older, and were criticized by local church groups, the group voted to end their experiment. A joint stock company was formed to carry on the businesses it had developed. It was called Oneida Community, Ltd.; later changed to Oneida Ltd. And now commonly known as Oneida Silversmiths. It has grown to 3000 employees, many of them descendants of the old group and thus still close friends. The Community still prides itself on its feeling of family and working together.

Although the Community didn't believe in fighting in wars, after it dissolved, men fought in World War I and during that time Oneida Community made a wide range of surgical instruments. During World War II a wide diversity of war production items were manufactured.

Today the mansion House looks from the outside much as it did a hundred years ago. Oneida Silversmiths now manufactures silver knives, forks and spoons, silver

*Pea-shelling bee
at the Oneida Community.*

*Oneida Community women
with their famous short hair,
short skirts, and pantalettes.*

holloware and, recently, stainless steel tableware, plus Melamine dinnerware, and metal polishing supplies such as buffs. It does the silver plating of wire for electronic and communications systems. The company has factories in Niagara Falls, Canada; Bangor, Northern Ireland, and Tolucca, Mexico.

By 1888 the town of Turkey Street had grown because of the establishment of the Oneida Community Trap Shop so a post office was needed. The first post office was in a small store located in the James Graves home. Mr. Graves' father drove the stage between Oneida Castle and Vernon Center and also carried the mail and some passengers. As the post office grew, it was moved to other homes and finally to a site on East Seneca Street which it occupied from 1921 to 1960. The present Sherrill Post Office achieved first class status in 1935 and now occupies a handsome brick building on Sherrill Road.

Along with the need for a post office, the people of Turkey Street felt a need to change the name of their town. But in order to do so they had to obtain the consent of the postmasters of the Villages of Vernon and Oneida Castle, as well as the consent of the stage coach driver. The consent was obtained and Congressman James S. Sherman (later vice-president of the U.S. 1901-1912) was instrumental in obtaining permission for the change in 1888. As a result, he was given the privilege of naming the town. He chose the name of Sherrill, after his small son.

The City of Sherrill is a thriving community because of the hard work and foresight of the Perfectionists. As the town experienced growing pains, the areas once occupied by grazing cows, abundant apple trees and well-tilled farms, gave way to well-kept homes on wide, tree-lined streets.

Sherrill's school system was once self-contained with two elementary schools, one on Willow Place for kindergarten through third grade and the Kenwood Park School – grades four through six. After sixth grade, pupils attended Sherrill High School on Kingsley Street. However, that school burned in 1942. After the fire, school centralization was considered. However, since Sherrill was a city, a special act of the state legislature was necessary for eligibility to centralize, which was eventually granted. In June 1950, 31 districts consolidated to make up the Vernon-Verona-Sherrill Central School. The new junior-senior high school located on Beacon Light Road was dedicated in 1955. By 1961 a new elementary school (E.A. MacAllister) stood on the site of the old Sherrill High School. The two original elementary schools have been demolished.

There are four churches in Sherrill established at various times. St. Helena's Church, Catholic, was started in September 1917. The Church of the Gethsemane

Community members playing croquet.
Oneida Silversmiths

The Mansion House was built to house members of the Oneida Community. It is located in Madison County adjacent to the Oneida County border.

Oneida Silversmiths

Oneida silversmiths have been crafting table silver for one hundred years.

Oneida Silversmiths

(Episcopal), in the hamlet of Hampton in Westmoreland, was given to a Sherrill-Kenwood church group. It was therefore moved to Sherrill, rebuilt, and formally opened in 1922. Christ Church, Methodist, was built in 1923 and 1924. Plymouth Congregational Church was built in true New England style and dedicated in 1922.

The City Commission form of government for Sherrill is unique. Originally, all of the five commissioners were elected every two years, in odd-numbered years. This has been amended so that two commissioners are elected every two years, thus insuring that the board will not be replaced completely at each election. Any resident may have his name on the ballot by securing signers on a petition representing a small percentage of voters. The member of the commission receiving the most votes is appointed mayor by the commissioners themselves.

Sherrill is an industrial community with the majority of residents working for Oneida Ltd. However, the Westmore Ltd. Milking Machine Company, established in 1940, is a large manufacturer of milking machinery for dairy farmers and employs over 100. It started in the annex of Park Methodist Church and now occupies a modern plant on West Hamilton Avenue with worldwide distribution. Miller Plating Company, organized in 1950, does industrial plating of customer's goods, which require cad-

mium, zinc, copper or nickel plating.

Marshall-Houseman, located on Route 5, builds, repairs and sells truck tractor units and busses.

For a short time the weekly Sherrill *Sentinel*, founded in 1924, was edited and published by J. Howard Tupper and Vern B. Smith. This was the only newspaper wholly edited and published within Sherrill and ceased publication in 1929.

The Sherrill-Kenwood Library started as a cupboard of books set up in the machine shop of the Trap Factory about 1900. Over the years it was moved from place to place as usage, interest and circulation grew. It occupied a building on East Noyes Boulevard from 1921 until 1970 when it again outgrew its space. The library is now located across from the post office in a new, modern building with the most modern facilities.

There are several clubs and fraternal organizations in Sherrill. The Sherrill Grange #1567 is the largest grange in Oneida County. The Clubhouse, a community landmark, once a barn on the Community Farm, has been converted for use by company employees. It contains 12 bowling alleys, a youth center, a health center and sauna, billiard tables, a meeting room, as well as an auditorium. It is a center for recreational activity for all residents.

As one travels along Route 5, it is not apparent that a

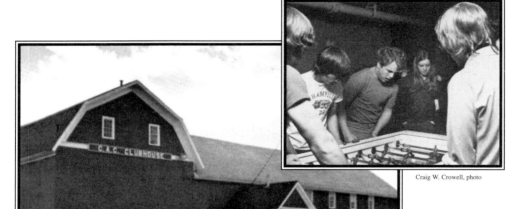

Youth Center operated by city in the CAC building owned by Oneida Silversmiths.

Craig W. Crowell, photo

Craig W. Crowell, photo

left, Community Associated Clubs building, formerly an Oneida Community barn.

Fishing derby sponsored annually by Sherrill Rod, Gun and Conservation Club at the Sherrill Pond, located adjacent to Oneida Silversmiths and the Sherrill American Legion.

Craig W. Crowell, photo

whole city lies on one side, and the largest tableware manufacturing plant in the U.S. on the other side. Riding through the city, street names attest to the people who were responsible for the establishment of the city: Noyes, Leonard, Wayland-Smith, Campbell, Kinsley, Skinner, Hinds, Park, Life, Gordon, Allen, Hamilton, Primo, and many more. Many of the original streets are reaching out to Betsinger Road with new homes. Young people who have left here for college and careers in other cities often come back to bring up their families; to work at the Community or in the surrounding territory, and to take an active interest in keeping Sherrill a thriving, modern, community-minded city.

(Information on the Oneida Community and Walter D. Edmonds' quote was taken from a pamphlet on the Oneida Community by Constance Noyes Robertson).

Selected References

Onions, Tomahawks, and Spoons, (1960).

Robertson, Constance, *Golden Anniversary*, (Sherrill, 1966); *History of Oneida Community; The Oneida Community, An Autobiography, 1851-76*, (Syracuse University Press, 1970); *The Oneida Community, The Breakup, 1876-81*, (Syracuse University Press, 1972).

Plymouth Congregational Church on Kinsley Street, dedicated in 1922.

D. F. White

Municipal complex on Sherrill Road combines city administration, police and courts, and public works garage.

D. F. White

Gazebo, center for weddings and community activities, adjoins the municipal complex.

D. F. White

To determine the tolls for canal boats, the state built several weighlocks, including one on the south side of the canal near John Street in 1829. The canal was wider here to allow boats to maneuver. Courtesy, Savings Bank of Utica.

Utica

By

Frank Tomaino

The city of Utica and the county of Oneida have marched hand in hand through the 19th and 20th centuries, their histories inextricably connected by their people, places and events.

Their first permanent settlers arrived at about the same time (the 1780s), mostly from the same place (New England) and for the same reasons (a plentiful supply of available land, water, trees and fertile soil).

Many of those pioneers had learned firsthand about the lush Upper Mohawk Valley region when, as soldiers with the American Continental Army during the Revolutionary War, they had marched through the valley past Old Fort Schuyler (today Utica) on their way to Fort Stanwix (today Rome) and beyond.

They had seen the fording place in the then very wide Mohawk River at Old Fort Schuyler and had marveled at "The Great Carry" – a mile-long stretch of land between the Mohawk and Wood Creek near Fort Stanwix where one could travel from the river to the creek to Oneida Lake and from there on to Lake Ontario and the other Great Lakes.

Both Fort Stanwix and Fort Schuyler had been built by the British in the 1750s during the French and Indian War – Stanwix being named for its builder, Brigadier General John Stanwix and Schuyler named for Colonel Peter Schuyler, a well-decorated officer.

In 1772 – three years before British regulars and Massachusetts farmers fought at Lexington and Concord and fired the shots that began the American Revolution – four men purchased the land surrounding Old Fort Schuyler on which Utica is now located,

The estate of the late Governor William Cosby – who in 1734 had been granted 22,000 acres in the Upper Mohawk Valley region by King George II – had failed to pay back taxes on the property. The four men bought the land for about 15 cents an acre. They were: General Philip Schuyler; General John Bradstreet; John Morin Scott, a New York City lawyer, and Rutger Bleecker, a wealthy man from Albany.

After the war ended in 1783, a small settlement began to grow around Fort Schuyler.

But most of the pioneers who emigrated to what is now Oneida County in the late 1780s and early 1790s chose places like New Hartford, Whitestown and Clinton to build their homes.

Land in the vicinity of Fort Schuyler was too swampy for most pioneers,

Eventually, though, Fort Schuyler began to grow. After all, it was located at the only shallow spot in the Mohawk River for miles and each month hundreds of westbound pioneers would travel on the river as far as Fort Schuyler and there use the ford to cross the river and head north to the Adirondacks or south on roads leading to territories to the west.

To accommodate those travelers, enterprising citizens of Fort Schuyler began to build and operate hotels, inns, taverns, blacksmith shops and wagon repair shops. They also built stores of all kinds for the visitors were eager to fill their wagons with supplies before the long trek to the vast wilderness to the north and west.

The pioneers Fort Schuyler attracted were a hardy group, eager to make their community the best in the region.

One of the first of those pioneers was Major John Bellinger, who had fought side by side with General Nicholas Herkimer at the Battle of Oriskany on August 6, 1777. He arrived in Fort Schuyler in March 1788 in four feet of snow and built a house on what later became the corner of Whitesboro and Washington streets. At first he farmed, but later he erected the settlement's first hotel. It became known as "The New England House."

Among those who came the next year was Peter Smith. He established a general store where Bagg's Square is located today and became the settlement's first merchant.

He later built a large house on Broad Street, just east of Mohawk Street, and there was born his son, Gerrit, who went on to become a nationally known abolitionist in the years before the Civil War. Peter Smith became a very wealthy man for he traded with the local Indians for furs and later became a partner with John Jacob Astor, founder of the Astor fortune who at one time owned much of the land that is now New York City.

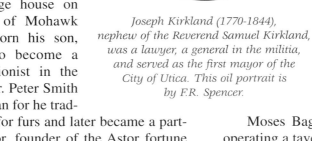

Joseph Kirkland (1770-1844), nephew of the Reverend Samuel Kirkland, was a lawyer, a general in the militia, and served as the first mayor of the City of Utica. This oil portrait is by F.R. Spencer.

In the spring of 1790, John Post, his wife and three children left Schenectady, traveled west on the Mohawk River and arrived at their destination eight days later – Old Fort Schuyler. He was a veteran of the Revolutionary War who had been present in 1777 when British Gen. John Burgoyne surrendered his army to the Americans at Saratoga and four years later was at Yorktown when Lord Cornwallis surrendered to Gen. George Washington, thus ending the war.

Soon after arriving at Old Fort Schuyler, Post built a house on the west side of Genesee Street near Whitesboro Street and from that house sold to Indians in the area and to settlers in the vicinity tobacco, blankets, ammunition and whiskey.

In 1791, he built a store on Bagg's Square just north of his house and soon became a very wealthy merchant.

The year 1794 saw several families move into the area.

James S. Kip became a merchant and later a banker.

Moses Bagg arrived as a blacksmith, but soon was operating a tavern at the square that later would be named for him and his family. In 1812, his son, Moses Bagg Jr., erected a large hotel on the site and a Bagg's Hotel

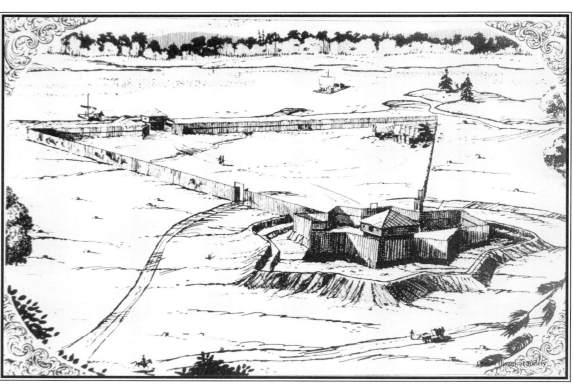

Drawing of Old Fort Schuyler.

remained there until the 1930s.

Jason Parker first settled in New Hartford then moved to Fort Schuyler. He got a job carrying mail on horseback between Whitestown and Canajoharie. In 1795, he began a stagecoach business along the same mail route. It was a huge success and by 1811, his stages were running between Utica and Albany and west to Buffalo and Niagara Falls.

Apollos Cooper built his house on Whitesboro Street and, being a carpenter, proceeded to build a bridge over the Mohawk River.

The next three years saw several industrious families settle in Fort Schuyler. Nathan Williams went on to become village president, an Oneida County district attorney and a member of Congress. Benjamin Walker, who was an aide to General George Washington during the Revolutionary War, built a magnificent mansion on Broad Street, east of Mohawk Street, and later represented the area in Congress.

These pioneers were joined by others – mostly Yankees from New England – so as the 18th century was drawing to a close, Fort Schuyler was ready for the 19th.

By 1800, the Mohawk River was able to accommodate larger boats than before since the state – through the Inland Lock Navigation Company – had built several locks at Little Falls to allow boats to travel through that community and head directly to Fort Schuyler. Previously, boats had to be unloaded at the rapids at Little Falls and pulled through the water with ropes. It had been impossible for larger boats to make the journey – until, that is, the locks were built.

At the same time, roads were being built throughout the area. The Seneca Turnpike, for example, started at Utica's Bagg's Square and headed south to New Hartford and then onto Kirkland, Vernon and Oneida Castle.

And Jason Parker's stage lines were making Fort Schuyler one of the state's busiest transportation centers.

There's no doubt that Fort Schuyler was in an excellent position when the 19th century began – a position that promised prosperity and growth.

Before it prospered and grew, though, something had to be done about its name.

Its inhabitants complained loudly and often that the name was too long and too clumsy to pronounce so in the spring of 1798 they gathered in Bagg's Tavern to select a new name.

One citizen suggested that the settlement be called "Washington" – for obvious reasons.

Another favored "Skenandoah," in honor of the great Oneida chief.

And yet another spoke up for "Kent," that splendid English region that had sent many of its sons and daughters to the Americas.

The debate continued for hours until it was suggested that the new name be chosen by lot. Those who wanted to would write their choice on a slip of paper and deposit it in a hat that had been placed on a table. The name on the first slip of paper drawn would be the new name of the settlement.

Oneida Historical Society

Bagg's Square 1850. Bleecker House was adjacent to Bagg's Hotel. Bleecker later merged with Bagg's Hotel.

So on that day in the spring of 1798, 13 citizens of Fort Schuyler wrote their choices on slips of paper and placed them in a hat.

One of the 13 was attorney Erastus Clark. He had been born in Lebanon, Connecticut in 1763 and later had graduated from Dartmouth College and admitted to the bar.

He studied the classics and was familiar with the history of the ancient city of Carthage in North Africa. He knew that in about 1100 B.C., the Phoenicians had built a city near Carthage and that later, after the Third Punic War, that city had become the capital of Rome's territory in the region. It soon rivaled Carthage as a powerful city and religious center.

That city was called "Utica" and that's the name Clark wrote on his slip of paper.

And that's the slip of paper that was drawn.

On April 3, 1798, the state Legislature proclaimed that Fort Schuyler was no longer a settlement. It was incorporated as a village and that new village would be called "Utica."

There were about 200 people living in about 50 houses in Utica at the time. They elected Talcott Camp as their first village president.

As the new century arrived, westbound pioneers on the Mohawk River and the road from Albany continued to pause in Utica for a night or two before heading south on the Seneca Turnpike and then to the great unsettled territories to the west.

From 1810 to 1815, the village's population increased by 70 percent – to nearly 2,000.

The village had a fire department, banks and a newspaper, but it did not have many large manufacturing plants. Those plants depended on water power to turn their machinery and the Mohawk River did not flow fast enough to generate the power needed. The large plants, instead, were being built in Utica's neighboring villages – Clinton, New Hartford, Whitesboro, New York Mill and Oriskany, for example. Those places had the fast-flowing Sauquoit and Oriskany Creeks to provide water power.

Many of the large businesses Utica did have concentrated on goods that could be produced with hand power – wagons, furniture, wagon wheels, for example.

The owners of those businesses – and those involved with transportation and the accommodation of weary travelers – were becoming wealthy. In fact, most Uticans were working and making a good living.

By 1815, most of them were convinced that the village would someday grow into one of the largest cities in the country.

It did not, but it did become one of the most important.

From the very beginning, Uticans were convinced that

The Marquis de Lafayette, French hero of the War for Independence, visited America in 1825, "The nation's guest" rode into Utica in an elegant carriage driven by Theodore Faxton and accompanied by a military escort. Entering the village on Fayette (now Lafayette) Street, the party passed under a triumphal arch erected over the canal bridge on Genesee Street. The general visited the home of Alexander Bryan Johnson, whose wife was the niece of President John Quincy Adams. Then, with the militia firing a 24-gun salute and small boys throwing flowers from canal bridges, the French nobleman departed on his packet drawn by three white horses. Courtesy, Savings Bank of Utica.

the education of their youth was vital to their community's success.

As early as 1797, Fort Schuyler had its first school and its first teacher.

The small school building was on Main Street, between First and Second Streets, and the teacher was Joseph Dana. It was not your typical school for the classroom had no desks, just benches without backs for support. But, the pupils learned and soon most young boys in the settlement knew how to read and write. It would be several years before young girls were allowed – and encouraged – to get an education.

On March 28, 1814, the Utica Academy was incorporated by the Regents of the University of the State of New York and eventually Uticans erected a school building on Bleecker Street, between Academy and John Streets – a building the school would share with a county courthouse. By 1827 Utica's young boys had several schools to attend including a high school that opened that year. **See attached article Utica "Public Schools" on page 117.**

In 1837, a group of parents asked; "Our sons are being educated, but what about our daughters? They deserve an education too." So that year, the Utica Female Academy – with Urania E. Sheldon as principal – opened classrooms in the United States Hotel at Genesee and Pearl Street. In 1839, the young ladies moved into a new building on Washington Street at Genesee (about where the YMCA is located today.)

In 1817, the village received a third charter from the state Legislature. (A second one had been issued in 1805 which enlarged the boundaries of the village.)

The third charter extended the village boundaries as far east as Turner Street and west to Schuyler Street. It also removed the village from the town of Whitestown and created a town of Utica. Nathan Williams was appointed the first president under the new charter. Williams was born on December 19, 1773 in Williamstown, Massachusetts and emigrated to Utica in about 1797. The following year he was admitted to the bar.

The year 1817 was memorable for other reasons, too. The village got its first directory and it listed 2,861 citizens.

And construction began on the Erie Canal – a vital waterway that would change the village of Utica forever. It would help it to grow and prosper at a rate much faster than most cities in the state.

The first and middle section of the canal – between Utica and Rome – was completed in the fall of 1819 and on October 23 the first boat to ever sail on the Erie left Rome and headed for Utica. When the "Chief Engineer of Rome" – named in honor of Benjamin Wright of Rome, the middle section's chief engineer – reached Utica, it was

The imposing Greek Revival Utica Female Academy, built in 1838, stood on the site of today's YMCA. Burned in 1865, it was replaced by a Mansard-roofed structure later known variously as the Balliol School and Mrs. Piatt's School.

Oneida Historical Society

greeted by ringing bells, exploding cannons and thousands of spectators.

The entire length of the canal – 363 miles of water linking the Hudson River with Lake Erie – was opened in October 1825.

The year 1825 marked another great celebration in the village when the Marquis de Lafayette paid a visit. The Frenchman – who had joined the American cause during the Revolutionary War and had helped the Continental Army defeat the British – entered the village from the west along Rome Street, which was later renamed Fayette Street and finally Lafayette Street.

Traffic on the canal both hurt and benefited the village. Canal traffic took customers away from many businesses along the Seneca Turnpike and on other roads in and out of the village, while businesses right on the canal prospered. The impact of the canal was immediate and great. Before the canal, the center and busiest section of the village was the Bagg's Square area. After the canal was completed, much activity moved south two or three blocks for that's where the canal was located (along the route of today's East-West Arterial or Oriskany Street). Businesses moved there to be close to canal traffic and soon stores, taverns, hotels and warehouses dotted the area.

And, of course, like all communities on the canal, Utica's population grew rapidly – from 5,041 in 1825 to 8,330 in 1830 to 10,183 in 1835.

In 1832, Uticans decided it was time to petition the state Legislature for a city charter.

The Legislature approved the request and on February 3, 1832 passed an act that incorporated the city of Utica.

Its population at the time was 8,323 and Joseph Kirkland was elected by members of the Common Council as the new city's first mayor. (In 1840, it was decided that the people should elect the mayor and the people chose John Devereux.)

According to Dr. T. Wood Clarke in his 1952 history, "Utica for a Century and a Half," the city in 1832 had 44 dry goods stores, 63 groceries, 10 hardware stores, six jewelry stores, five bookstores, 20 blacksmith shops and 79 cabinetmakers.

The years that followed were exciting ones.

Several major industries were started, including the Munson & Hart Company, which made millstones. Alfred Munson (the founder of the fortune that evolved into the Munson-Williams-Proctor Institute) and Martin Hart were two of the city's most prominent citizens. Other industrialists began to manufacture such items as oilcloths, cigars and other tobacco products, wheels for railroad cars and steam engines.

In 1839, John and Nicholas Devereux, longtime Utica merchants, founded a bank that still exists today: The Savings Bank of Utica.

From its very beginning, Utica had been a leading

Utica's third fire engine was purchased secondhand fron New York City in 1823, served Utica until 1834, and then was used in Sauquoit until 1876. Perserved first by the Veteran Fireman's Association and now owned by the Oneida Historical Society. Photo by Douglas M. Preston.

After a series of incendiary fires in the early 1850s in which some volunteer firemen were implicated, the city attempted to start a part-time paid fire department, one of the first in the country. This proved unworkable, however, and the volunteer system was reinstated in 1857. One of the elite units formed in 1857 was the Tiger Hose Company, seen on parade on Broad Street just off Genesee in 1866. They served until the establishment of a full-time paid department in 1874. Courtesy, Richard M. Lockwood.

transportation center and two events in the 1830s made it one of the busiest in the country.

In 1836, the Chenango Canal was completed. It connected the Erie Canal in Utica to Binghamton and the coal fields of Pennsylvania. Those fields, during the next decade, would play an important role in rescuing the city from a serious decline.

The second event was the coming of the railroad.

In 1837, the Utica & Schenectady Railroad was completed and, at the time, the 72-mile line was the longest in the world.

At first, Uticans were enthusiastic about their railroad. Freight and products could be moved to market faster and cheaper than on canal boats and citizens could travel to faraway places in shorter periods of time. But, there was a problem.

For nearly 40 years, westbound stagecoach passengers had stayed in Utica a night or two before continuing their journey. An industry had grown to accommodate those passengers – an industry made up of hotels, taverns, inns, blacksmith and wagon shops and dozens of stores that sold a variety of goods.

Trains, however, stopped in Utica only for an hour or two, and not overnight. Unlike stagecoach passengers, train passengers did not need hotels, shops or stores. Fast-moving trains carried them right by Utica.

For the next seven or eight years – from the late 1830s to the mid-1840s – Utica stood still. In fact, the census of 1845 showed that for the first time in its history, the city's population actually had decreased.

"We need new industries!" cried out the Utica Daily Gazette.

"Something must be done! Where are our leaders?" shouted Uticans.

At the time, not only were the city's transportation-related businesses suffering because of the railroads, but its textile industry was suffering, too.

Its cotton and woolen mills were still using hand and some water power to operate looms and other machines. They suddenly were faced with competition from New England's new steam-powered mills. Those mills not only could produce goods at a faster-than-ever rate, but they were high-quality goods.

Utica's mills began to lose business at an alarming rate.

One thing Utica did have in 1845 were leaders and industrialists with money. They decided to push and shove Utica back on the road to growth and prosperity.

Three men were picked to travel to New England and determine the feasibility of using steam power in Utica's textile and other industries.

Spencer Kellogg, Andrew S. Pond and Edmund A. Graham visited cooperative mills in places like Newburyport in Massachusetts and Newport in Rhode

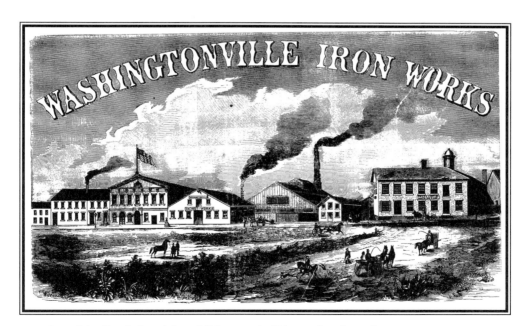

Oneida Historical Society

One of the first industrial establishments in Utica and perhaps the oldest factory is the building at the right of this circa 1862 print. Built by Philo C. Curtis in 1832 at Whitesboro and Lafayette Streets, it housed part of the Utica Steam Engine& Boiler Works up to 1982.

Island and upon their return published a pamphlet titled: "The Relative Difference of the Cost of the Motive Power of Water and Steam as Applicable to Manufacturing."

What it said was that Utica's wealthy citizens should give the city a boost by paying out of their own pockets to convert the Utica's textile mills to stream-powered mills and build new woolen and cotton mills, too.

"But how can we produce the steam needed to run those mills?" asked the cynics and pessimists.

The Committee of Three replied: "By using coal, my friends. And that coal is easily and cheaply available via the Chenango Canal that connects the city with coal fields of Pennsylvania."

Within weeks, the city's wealthy citizens – industrialists like Theodore Faxton – answered the challenge. Within two years, the city had the Utica Steam Cotton Mills, the Utica Steam Woolen Mills, the Globe Woolen Mills and dozens of other industries using steam to run their machinery.

The city's "Textile Era" had begun and it would be the city's major industry for the next 100 years, employing thousands of men and women and making Utica "the knit goods capital of the world."

So by 1848, Utica was booming again!

The mills began to attract immigrants, especially skilled machinists and workers from Germany who settled in West Utica and found jobs in the many mills nearby. There were others, too, mostly from western and northern Europe – Great Britain and Ireland, for example.

And Utica became the home of the world's first commercial telegraph company.

John Butterfield, Hiram Greeman and Faxton had convinced a group of area investors in 1845 to finance Samuel F.B. Morse's newfangled invention called the electric telegraph. Their company strung lines from New York City to Buffalo via Oneida County and soon owned most of the lines in New Jersey, Pennsylvania and west to the Mississippi River.

Utica was becoming a fast-growing, modern city.

Among its citizens were many skilled physicians.

The first doctors had arrived with the earliest pioneers – Dr. Francis Guiteau and Dr. Alexander Coventry in 1796, for example.

Others followed and most of them were recent graduates of the College of Physicians and Surgeons which had opened in 1810 in the Herkimer County hamlet of Fairfield. Uticans were a healthy and hardy group, though, so some of the doctors began other ventures to supplement their income. They owned drug stores, manufactured bottled water and a few even opened taverns.

Uticans who did become ill, however, were well-cared for and soon the settlement had a reputation as a leader in medical treatment and care – especially in the case of the mentally ill.

On January 16, 1843, the first patient was admitted to the new Utica Lunatic Asylum (later called Utica State Hospital). For the first time in the state, patients with mental disorders were being treated instead of being chained

St. John's first church, completed in 1821.

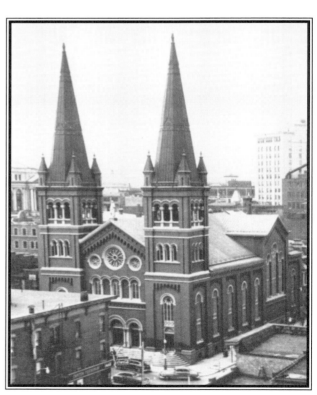

St. John's third and present church, first used on Christmas Day, 1869.

to walls in jails, poorhouses and even in their homes.

A growing, successful city fulfills the needs of its religious inhabitants, too, and Utica did just that.

Its Presbyterians attended services as early as 1793 in Whitestown and in 1807 built a church of their own in Utica at Washington and Liberty Streets.

An Episcopal church society was first organized in 1798 with services held in the homes of members. In 1803, a parish was formed and a church was erected on the corner of First and Broad Streets on land donated by John R. Bleecker. Trinity Church was born.

In 1838, Grace Episcopal Church was organized to accommodate the many Uticans who were moving from the village's first business and residential district at and near Bagg's Square and relocating several blocks south to the area of Genesee, Bleecker, Elizabeth, Columbia and Blandina Streets.

Later, Grace parishioners would build a stately structure that still exists today on the southeast corner of Genesee and Elizabeth Streets. The building was designed by Richard Upjohn, the leading church architect in the United States at the time.

The Baptists had the honor of having built the first church in the village. The Welsh Baptist Church was organized in 1801 and in 1806 parishioners built a church on Hotel Street.

Soon, church societies were being organized by Congregationalists, Methodists and members of the Dutch Reformed Church.

In 1815, there were only a handful of Roman Catholics in Utica. They had no church and belonged to St. Mary's Church in Albany. John Devereux, prominent Utica businessman, was a member of St. Mary's board of trustees.

By 1817, more and more Irish Catholics at work constructing the Erie Canal were settling in Utica so in 1819 Devereux and the Rev. Michael O'Gorman, rector of St. Mary's, convinced the diocese in Albany to build a church in Utica to serve all Catholics in Central and Western New York.

Judge Morris Miller, a prominent Utican – and a Protestant – donated land on the northwest corner of John and Bleecker Streets and Catholics and Protestants in the city raised enough money to build a Catholic church. The Rev. John Farnum became the first pastor of St. John's Church, today the mother church of Catholic churches in the Syracuse Diocese.

Later, the church was relocated across the street on the southwest corner – and that's where St. John's is located today.

Other exciting things were happening in the city at about the same time.

The Utica Waterworks began to operate with water from Starch Factory Creek at the city's eastern boundary being piped to a reservoir bounded by South, Linwood and Eagle streets. From the reservoir water was sent to all sections of the city and to 50 fire hydrants.

The Utica Gas Company was formed with a large storage house just below the intersection of Whitesboro and Washington streets. Although Uticans at first were afraid of gas lights and preferred what they thought were the safer candles and oil lamps, eventually they switched to gas lights for their homes and businesses.

It also was a time when political giants walked the city.

Horatio Seymour, who lived on Whitesboro Street (and also had a magnificent farm house in Deerfield) was elected governor of New York in 1852 and was one of the country's most influential Democrats. He was the party's candidate for president of the United States in 1868 and was narrowly defeated by Civil War hero, Republican, Ulysses S. Grant.

His brother-in-law was Roscoe Conkling, who had married Seymour's sister, Julia. Conkling, one of the top trial lawyers in the Northeast, was the boss of the Republican Party in the state and an outstanding congressman and, later, member of the U.S. Senate.

Political leaders from across the country and from Europe often visited Utica to obtain advice and counsel from either Seymour or Conkling or both.

The Civil War began in 1861 and found Uticans doing more than their share in support of President Abraham Lincoln and the Northern cause.

Two days after the war began, the Utica Citizens Corps – founded in 1837 as a military company to participate in parades and social and civic events – answered Lincoln's call for troops by wiring Washington that it would be ready to march fully-equipped in 48 hours. During the war, as part of the 14th Regiment, New York Volunteers (the First Oneida), members of the corps fought with distinction at places like Fredericksburg and Chancellorsville.

By the time the war ended in 1865, Utica had provided the Union Army with hundreds of troopers and 61 officers, including six major generals: Daniel Butterfield (who during the war had composed the mournful bugle call, "Taps"), H.S. Bradley, Charles A. Johnson, John W. Fuller, James McQuade (who was elected mayor of Utica in 1866), and J.J. Bartlett.

The city also gave the Army eight brigadier generals: Oscar F. Long, William H. Christian, Sylvester Dering, Rufus Dagget, George W. Ledlie, Walter Robbins, J.H. Oley and N.G. Williams.

Utica's medical profession did its share, too. A large number of doctors enlisted in the Union Army, including Doctors Theodore Dimon, William Morris, Alonzo Churchill, Walter Coventry, Edwin Hutchinson, J. Judson Hill, Samuel Wolcott, Joseph West and Matthias Cook.

Exciting things were happening on the home front during the war, too.

Utica's John Butterfield, in the 1850s, had formed the Overland Mail Company and was the first to deliver mail and passengers from the Mississippi River to California in fewer than 25 days. He returned to Utica and in 1862 headed a horse-drawn trolley company that installed tracks from Utica's Bagg's Square to New Hartford and then on to Clinton.

When trolley service began in 1863, Utica was only the fifth city in the country to have a regularly scheduled street-car line (the others being New York, Boston, Philadelphia and New Orleans).

As the city approached the 20th century, railroads and trolleys were its guarantee that it would continue to grow and prosper. Dozens of trains were rolling in and out of Utica daily with passengers, freight and foreign-born men and women to work in its mills and factories. Not only was there the giant New York Central, but also lines like the Delaware, Lackawanna & Western; the New York, Ontario & Western; the Utica, Clinton & Binghamton; the Chenango & Susquehanna Valley, and the West Shore.

The New York Central had ambitious plans for its facilities in Utica, including a new depot (Union Station) and enlarged freight yards.

The Civil War had helped to create new industries in the city that continued after the war had ended.

Soldiers needed shoes so several shoe manufacturers

opened factories in Utica, employing more than 2,000 people.

But it was the textile industry that continued to grow and expand.

In 1890, Quentin McAdam led a group who founded the Utica Knitting Company and in not-too-many years it had thousands of employees and more than a dozen mills in the vicinity.

There were other textile companies, too. The Oneita Knitting Mills was established on Broad Street at the foot of Kossuth Avenue and soon became nearly as busy as Utica Knitting.

It was Andrew Frey, a superintendent at the Oneita, who revolutionized the underwear industry when he sewed a top shirt to bottom drawers and gave the world its first union suit – complete with trap door at the bottom.

By the turn of the century, Utica was the knits goods capital of the world.

The year 1876 was a glorious one for Americans as they celebrated the country's centennial. Uticans celebrated by forming a historical society to preserve Oneida County's history forever. Horatio Seymour became the first president of the Oneida (County) Historical Society and its first major project was to purchase the site of the Battle of Oriskany and erect a monument there.

Other memorable events in the city's history during the second half of the 19th century included:

1867 – Dr. Edwin Van Deusen, rector of Grace Episcopal Church, gives an impassioned sermon about the need for a home for aged women in the city. Truman K.

City Hall – in Utica's Centennial year of 1932. Oneida Historical Society

West End Brewery Tour Center is an example of Victorian architecture. Founded in 1888, the brewery continues to produce beer using old world methods. The conducted tours have been attracting tourists for many years.

Milo V. Stewart photo

Butler not only listens to the rector's words, he decides to do something about them. So, he donates a house he owned on Columbia Street. In 1869, St. Luke's Home opens its doors. Three years later, a hospital department is added and later it evolves into St. Luke's Home and Hospital.

1870 – Chancellor Park, Steuben Park and Johnson Park are constructed.

1871 – Methodists in the city complete their first church building at Broadway and Court Streets – at a cost of $80,000 – under the leadership of their first pastor, the Rev. William Reddy. It's called First Methodist Episcopal Church of Utica.

1872 – The House of Good Shepherd is organized.

1873 – The growing German Catholic population in West Utica gets the church they have been asking for for years. St. Joseph's Church, on Columbia Street, is dedicated under the leadership of the Rev. Alphonse M. Zoller. Five years later, a convent is built for the Franciscan Sisters who teach in the parish school.

1874 – Faxton Hospital, a gift to the city and its people from industrialist Theodore Faxton, opens on Sunset Avenue. Dr. Alonzo Churchill is named surgeon-in-charge.

1874 – Westminster Presbyterian Church – first organized in 1844 – enlarges its chapel and connects it to its 17-year-old church on Washington Street.

1878 – The city's first professional baseball team is formed.

1881 – The Saturday Globe newspaper is founded by William and Thomas Baker. Its first edition was printed by Curtis and Childs, on Bleecker Street, and sold 2,000 copies. It became so popular, the Bakers moved to Charlotte Street and installed their own printing press. Within two years, it was one of the most-read publications in the world. It was the first illustrated newspaper in the country and its circulation reached more than 200,000. It had as many as 33 editions and each was sold in different sections of the United States – from Maine to California. Soon, the Bakers erected a large Saturday Globe building on the north side of Whitesboro Street, just west of Bagg's Square. (Later, when other newspapers began to use photos, the Globe's circulation began to drop. Other cities got their own illustrated papers and eventually the Globe went out of business.)

1883 – Plymouth Church is organized with 47 charter members and they promptly purchase land at Plant and State Streets on Oneida Square on which to build a church. The first pastor is Dr. Edward Taylor.

1885 – The Rev. Albert Brigham becomes pastor of Tabernacle Baptist Church and among his many accomplishments is the building of a chapel on King Street on land donated by Mrs. John Thorn.

1886 – Utica General Hospital, which opened in 1858 at South and Mohawk Streets in East Utica, is renovated and gets its first modern operating room with the latest equipment.

1887 – St. Elizabeth Hospital, the city's first private

Full-color cartoons and illustrations were a distinctive and popular feature of the Saturday Globe. *The Globe's artists gave especially vivid treatment to disasters such as the burning of the steamboat General Slocum on the East River, a 1904 tragedy that claimed over 1,000 lives. Photo by Douglas M. Preston.*

hospital which was begun 20 years earlier in a tenement house on Columbia Street, moves to new quarters next door. The first patient is Dr. Edwin Hutchinson, the man who had been the doctor-in-charge when the hospital first opened its doors.

The list of schools and churches erected in Utica during the years just before and after the arrival of the 20th century is a long one, many the result of the growing number of immigrants settling in the city.

During the city's early years, its immigrants had come from northern and western Europe. Late in the century, they began to migrate to Utica from southern and eastern Europe – especially from Italy and Poland.

In 1883, hundreds of Italian-born working on the building of the West Shore Railroad were attracted by what they saw and decided to settle in the city. At the same time, many Polish-born immigrants came to Utica to work in its mills. Churches like Holy Trinity – built by Polish Americans in West Utica – and St. Mary of Mount Carmel – built by Italian-Americans in East Utica – added much to the city's spirit and determination to improve its citizens' quality of life.

The last decade on the 19th century was a fabulous one for Utica.

Its trolleys converted from horsepower to electric power; more and more of its streets were being paved; the Masonic Home was built; its knitting mills continued to expand; a Chamber of Commerce was organized and new industries – like International Heater – were formed. In fact, when International Heater opened its offices and factory at Park Avenue and Broad Street in 1899, it was the result of the consolidation of five of the largest furnace-manufacturing companies in the Northeast and some began to call Utica "the furnace and heater capital of the world."

Utica's population had increased steadily through the 19th century – 17,556 in 1850; 32,496 in 1875; 44,007 in 1890 – so it's not surprising that when the 20th century arrived, the city had 56,383 inhabitants.

By 1902, there were 19 large knitting mills within the city limits employing more than 20,000 men and women. New industries continued to arrive every month, too.

In the 1890s, Utican, Arthur W. Savage had invented a superior sporting rifle – a hammerless, repeating, high-powered weapon – and opened a small factory on the southeast corner of Mohawk and Hubbell streets in East Utica. In 1900, he built a large factory on 35 acres off Turner Street along the city's eastern boundary. Soon, hundreds were at work there making rifles, pistols and shotguns. (Later, they would turn out washers, dryers, ice-cream cabinets, electrical appliances and, during the two world wars, tens of thousands of guns.)

On February 26, 1900, the Savings Bank of Utica moved into its new home – complete with a "gold dome" – on Genesee Street.

And in 1908, Maria and Thomas Proctor, the city's great benefactors, gave to the city the hundreds of acres of park land they had purchased through the years.

Francis P. Miller and Harry Mundy established Utica's first automobile dealership, the Miller-Mundy Motor Carriage Company, in 1901. They began by selling White Steamers and Piece-Stanhopes and later added other makes. This group of ladies posed in a 1903 Winton in front of the firm's second home on Oneida Square.

Overnight, Utica had one of the best park systems in the country.

The New York Central Railroad continued to expand in the city at the same time. A new channel for the Mohawk River was built, moving it from the Bagg's Square area north for about a mile. Then an overhead crossing was constructed, new freight yards built and, in 1914, its magnificent million-dollar Union Station was completed.

As did most Americans at the turn of the century, Uticans fell in love with that newfangled horseless carriage called the automobile.

In 1901, they formed the Utica Automobile Club, which at the time was one of the first such clubs in the United States. Later, it would join the country's other eight clubs and form the American Automobile Association.

One of Utica's proudest days was June 19, 1908 for on that day the Utica Observer telegraph machine received a message from Cleveland, where the Republican National Convention was being held. It said:

"Utica's Sherman nominated for vice president."

In November, Cincinnati's William Howard Taft and Utica's James Schoolcraft Sherman were elected 27th president and vice president of the United States.

Uticans were feeling good about themselves and their city as the years of the early 20th century passed by.

World War I did not change their minds.

The city's industry kicked into high gear to furnish the military with goods. Most of the underwear worn by U.S. soldiers were made in Utica. Savage Arms began to produce tens of thousands of Lewis machine guns and plants such as Bossert's were making war products by the thousands.

Thousands of Utica men and women enlisted and served on the seas, in military hospitals and on the battlefields of Europe. On the home front, organizations like the Oneida County Home Defense Committee contributed much to the war effort – planning food gardens, working on farms, raising money for the Red Cross, making surgical dressings and selling and buying Liberty Bonds.

The war ended in 1918 and the "roaring" 1920s began. But there was little roaring in Utica's knitting mills.

The military had cancelled most of its orders with the mills and all of a sudden thousands of women across the country stopped buying warm underwear in large quantities. After all, during the war many of them had gotten high-paying jobs for the first time and had proved that they were equal to men in the workplace. They had money and if they wanted to keep warm in winter they could afford to buy fur coats. So they did..

By 1922, the number of knitting mills in Utica decreased from 19 to six.

But it was not a time for industrial doldrums in the city. In fact, most businesses continued to expand and hire during the 1920s.

Radio Station WIBX was formed and in 1922, Frank E. Gannett, of Rochester, purchased the city's Sunday Tribune, Herald-Dispatch and Utica Observer and formed

Union Station built in 1914 on Main Street by Architects Stem and Fellheimer. It is designed in Italian Renaissance style. 1998 began a renovation to preserve the building's unique style and to adapt its space to County and municipal government functions as well as continuation of passenger and freight services.

Baggs Hotel as it looked in 1868, the year that Charles Dickens remained overnight, St. Patrick's Day, when his Albany bound train was delayed by floods. The hotel was founded in 1794 by Moses Bagg at the corner of John and Main Streets. In 1812 much of the original building was torn down and the central section of the brick hotel built. In 1869, following Dickens stay, Thomas R. Proctor became proprietor.

Oneida Historical Society

Oneida Historical Society

the Utica Observer Dispatch. (In 1935, he bought the Utica Daily Press.)

Then, in October 1929, came the Great Depression.

It affected Utica the same as it did other cities: building construction stopped almost overnight, factories cut production or went out of business and people by the hundreds lost their jobs.

Unemployment was such a problem that when Maria Proctor decided to raze her Bagg's Hotel – which had fallen into disrepair – she insisted that the building be torn down by hand instead of with bulldozers. That, she said, would give more men work.

The Depression came to an abrupt end on December 7, 1941 when the United States entered World War 2.

Overnight, Utica's knitting mills began once again to receive orders from the military for underwear and other knit goods.

Savage Arms began to hire hundreds to keep up with its multimillion dollar contracts from the U.S. and British military for Thompson submachine guns and Browning automatic rifles.

The Bossert Company made cartridge cases by the millions; Divine Brothers turned out fuses for artillery shells and bomb-loading devices; Utica Cutlery made bayonets and Brunner Manufacturing made pumps and freezing units for the military.

And thousands of Utica men and women were in the armed forces.

On the home front, civilians young and old not only

bought millions of dollars of war bonds, they worked with the Red Cross, collected scrap paper and iron and worked at the Army's new and huge convalescent and rehabilitation hospital on Burrstone Road called Rhoads General Hospital. By the time the hospital was no longer needed (in 1946), it had cared for more than 25,000 soldier patients.

When Utica's veterans came home from war, they quickly were aware that the city was one of the few cities in the Northeast without a college. They had not cared that much before the war, but now they had some money in their pockets, with the G.I. Bill, and they wanted an education. Their message to their political and civic leaders was a simple one: "Get us a college and get it now!"

The city's leaders – including civic leaders like attorney Moses Hubbard, industrialist Richard Balch and labor leaders like Rocco F. DePerno, of the Teamsters, and Samuel Talarico, of the meatcutter's union – answered the call. They worked with officials at Syracuse University – which was overflowing with freshmen students, especially veterans – to establish a college in Utica. In the fall of 1946, Utica College was born in classrooms in the Plymouth Church facilities at Oneida Square. It remained at the Oneida Square site until 1962 when it moved to its new campus on Burrstone Road.

Utica College was joined by the New York State Institute of Applied Arts and Sciences – which evolved into Mohawk Valley Technical Institute and then Mohawk Valley Community College. The institute at first was

Oneida Historical Society

Utica formally entered the Air Age on September 28, 1929, when the Municipal Airport on the old River Road in Marcy was dedicated. Regular service was provided by Colonial Airlines' eight-passenger Stinsons and American Airlines' Ford trimotors. Larger planes made the Municipal Airport obsolete. Scheduled air service returned to the Utica area in 1959 when Robinson Airways inaugurated flights to the new Oneida County Airport.

A new Wal-Mart Distribution Center now occupies the former muni-airport site where memorial plaques mark Utica's first air service in ceremonies on September 1998.

located in an old building on State Street and at the former Utica Country Day School in New Hartford. Later, it moved into a new campus on Sherman Drive in the southeastern section of the city.

The city celebrated its sesquicentennial in 1948 – the 150th anniversary of its incorporation as a village – with a grand "Pageant of Progress."

Eugene M. Hanson was chairman of the event with John L. Knower as secretary and Charles J. Lamb as treasurer. It was a huge success with tours of the city, sports events, parades, concerts, a soap box derby and, at Murnane Field, re-enactments of events in Utica's early history.

Helen Ann Witte reigned as the pageant's "Miss Utica." Her court included Anne Feeney as "Miss Columbia" and Marie Elefante as "Princess Royal."

Gloomy days lay ahead, however. The city's textile mills found themselves at a crossroads. Management looked at the cheaper labor available in the South – and at the cotton fields nearby. In Utica their mills and the machinery in them were old. Maintenance costs continued to rise each year. Beginning in the late 1940s and early 1950s, the city's textile mills began to close their doors and head south.

Thousands of men and women – many in their 40s and 50s – lost their jobs. The population began to drop and workers left the city to seek work elsewhere. Utica entered its "loom to gloom" era.

Just as Uticans who in 1845 had met the challenge of losing business and jobs to New England's steam-powered looms by building their own steam-powered plants, so did Uticans in the late 1940s and 1950s meet the "loom to gloom" head-on and replace it with an era of "loom to boom."

The drive was led by leaders such as Mayor Boyd E. Golder; James Capps, president of the Chamber of Commerce; attorney Henry T. Dorrance; former mayor Vincent R. Corrou, head of the chamber's committee of industrial-business development, and Richard Balch, president of Horrocks-Ibbotson. There were others, too, labor leaders and bankers who joined the struggle to revitalize the city's economy.

A spirit of cooperation pervaded the city and vicinity as state, county and town leaders joined the fight. Battle plans were drawn up as the region prepared to compete with other regions for new business and industry.

In 1946, for example, the Chicago Pneumatic Tool Company told the state that it was interested in building a new plant somewhere in the Northeast. When word reached leaders in Utica and vicinity, they were ready. Within 48 hours they were at the company's headquarters in New York City with a proposal that included land, tax incentives and information about available skilled and unskilled labor and the area's reputation of having good labor-management relations.

On March 24, 1948, ground was broken for the new Chicago Pneumatic plant.

It was followed by companies such as General

One of only a handful of professional symphony orchestras in Upstate New York, the Utica Symphony Orchestra has been bringing quality programs of classical music to area residents for 65 years. Today, the Symphony comprises more than 70 musicians under the baton of award-winning music director Charles Schneider.

The Stanley Performing Arts Center's upper foyer

Electric, Continental Can, Sperry-Rand UNIVAC, Bendix and Mohawk Airlines.

Companies that had been part of Utica for many years – Utica Cutlery, Divine Brothers and West End Brewery, for example – provided a link to Utica's past that was needed at the time and they continue to do so today.

The textile industry had collapsed, but in its place had emerged an economy based on electronics and service jobs in government, insurance, banking and other non-manufacturing positions.

It was a time, too, when more and more Uticans were beginning to move to the suburbs. The city's population began to drop and the number of people in Oneida County increased.

The city's black population grew steadily, however.

After the war ended in 1945, many blacks from the South began to migrate to Oneida County to pick beans, peas and potatoes. Some remained and moved to Utica.

At first, most of the blacks lived in the Liberty Street area of the city, but as their numbers grew, many moved south to the the city's Cornhill section. Churches like St. Paul Baptist Church moved to the section, too, and organizations like Cornhill People United were formed to improve their prospects.

In the late 1950s, the state began to investigate vice and crime and Utica would never be the same.

Instead of basking in the praise many were giving Utica because of its tremendous effort in successfully revitalizing its economy, many of its citizens were, instead, embarrassed by revelations of gambling, prostitution and other illegal activities.

They not only were embarrassed, they were angry – angry enough to elect Republican Frank M. Dulan in 1959 as their mayor and oust Old Guard Democrats who had controlled the city for years. The Reform Democrats then elected Tom Gilroy as their Oneida County chairman.

The city would undergo other changes, too, in the 1960s and 1970s.

Probably the most significant change occurred in Downtown Utica.

As more and more shopping centers appeared on the scene – usually in the suburbs – more and more downtown mainstays moved away from the city's business district. The Whitestown and North Utica shopping centers were the first to open followed by the Grand Union, New Hartford, Riverside Mall and Sangertown Square.

Soon, Downtown Utica no longer had a Wicks & Greenman, Neisner's, Kresge's, Doyle-Knower, Webb's and similar businesses that had been downtown for years.

A major blow occurred when, in the late 1970s, the Boston Store closed its doors. It was the city's largest department store and one that attracted hundreds of shoppers daily to the downtown district. Its closing meant fewer customers for other businesses in the area and also resulted in a reduction of bus service downtown.

Little by little, professional people – doctors, lawyers, dentists, accountants, etc. – began to move out of their downtown offices and into offices uptown or in the sub-

D. F. White

Hanna Park entrance leading to City Hall.

Hanna Park's Wooden Whorl Sculpture.

D. F. White

urbs. They were joined by car dealers, who once had showrooms in every section of the downtown area.

Restaurants began to disappear, too. They either closed or moved, including once-popular eating spots like Donalty's & Callahan, Lincoln Farms, the Home Dairy, Lubbert's Hof Brau, St. Mark's Inn and OK Lunch.

But while downtown was continually reeling from blows struck by shopping centers and the lack of parking spaces, it did occasionally connect with a few haymakers of its own.

The 115-year-old City Hall at Genesee and Pearl Streets was razed and a new one was built several hundred yards to the west.

Downtown also found itself with a new State Office Building and County Office Building. The old Stanley Theater, erected in 1927 as a movie house and about to be razed, was narrowly saved from the wrecker's ball and transformed into a magnificent performing arts center.

The Bagg's Square area got a new multimillion dollar overhead crossing bridge and work began on renovation and sprucing up Union Station.

In 1979, the Sheraton Inn opened its doors with spacious facilities for banquets and conventions and a large parking garage.

Exciting things were happening in other sections of the city, too.

A new post office was built on Pitcher Street on the eastern boundary of the city and a new Central Fire Station was erected on Bleecker Street to replace the old one on Elizabeth and Burnet Streets.

Meanwhile, many of the nearly 5,000 blacks in the city were demanding better jobs and housing. Many whites supported them.

On March 14, 1965, more than 4,000 people gathered at Oneida Square in response to an appeal by the Rev. Dr. Martin Luther King Jr. for "sympathy meetings," to support a civil rights march in Alabama, from Selma to Montgomery.

The rally in Utica was organized by the Inter-Religious Commission on Religion and Race of Greater Utica. The Rev. H. Robert Gemmer, speaking for the commission, told the crowd: "In Selma, many Americans have become involved. In Utica today, we are standing up to be counted and demonstrating that we, too, want to become involved in the battle for civil rights."

At the same time, the number of Hispanics was rapidly growing in the city – to more than 1,200 in 1970.

It was a time of church mergers, too, as congregations tried to cope with the city's declining population.

Church mergers resulted in new congregations with names that included: Plymouth Bethesda United Church of Christ, on Oneida Square; All Saints Episcopal, on Faxton Street, and Our Saviour Lutheran, on Genesee Street.

Utica added a jewel to its crown in 1960 when the new Munson-Williams-Proctor Institute's Museum of Art was opened to the public. The three-story building was designed by famous architect, Philip Johnson.

The observation floor of the New York State Office Building – at 16 stories, the tallest building in Utica – provides interesting vistas of the city and surrounding country. This view looks southwest over the Savings Bank's famous gold dome and the corner of Genesee and Washington Streets. Photo by John Caruso.

Hanna Park's Clocktower.

At the same time, the Utica Memorial Auditorium was built to honor the city war veterans.

One thing that did not change during all this time, though, was politics in the city. It remained as tumultuous as ever.

Dominick Assaro, who had co-written a book called "What Utica Needs," got the opportunity to turn his words into action when, in 1967, he was elected Utica's first Italian-American mayor. He was followed by Michael Caruso and, in 1973, by the colorful and controversial Edward Hanna, a former assemblyman and a successful international businessman.

Hanna's policies and statements soon were attracting national attention; the national media; and national figures – like comedian Bob Hope – to the city. People magazine ran a feature on the mayor, focusing on his battles with local media and politicians and his plans to beautify the city.

In 1975, his Democrat Party refused to renominate him, so he formed an independent Rainbow Party and won re-election.

Hanna accomplished one of his major goals and that was the building of Terrace Park (later renamed Hanna Park, in his honor) next to City Hall. Its beautiful waterfalls, performances and low-priced food soon was attracting hundreds during lunchtime and thousands at night.

One goal he could not achieve, though, was the building of "La Promenade."

"La Promenade" was a Hanna plan to enhance Downtown Utica and would have occupied a site consisting of four blocks bordered by Columbia Street on the north, Genesee Street on the east, Pearl Street on the south and Broadway on the west.

A hotel and convention center would have been built atop the Kennedy Garage near City Hall and a fountain and pedestrian covered walk bridge would have led to a building containing dozens of small shops and sidewalk cafes – many with a European flavor – and professional offices and "stylish" apartments.

It proposed an outdoor skating rink, landscaped gardens, kiosks and benches for downtown shoppers, workers and visitors.

Opponents, however, contended that it would cause traffic jams and that it would be better to build a hotel on the site. The debate continued for months until it was finally abandoned.

Hanna was followed as mayor by Democrat Stephen Pawlinga, whose victory marked a comeback for Old Guard Democrats and their East Utica leader, Rufus P. Elefante.

In 1983, Republican Louis LaPolla, who had lost to Pawlinga in 1979 and 1981, won City Hall. He was re-elected in 1985 and in November 1987 won not only his third consecutive term, but also the first four-year mayoral

term in the city's history.

In 1991, he won his fourth consecutive term.

During all those years, Utica continued to have its ups and its downs. The population continued to drop and some people could or would not pay their city taxes and decided to abandon their homes. The amount of taxable property in the city continued to decrease which meant a larger burden for the property owners who remained behind.

The LaPolla administration's record of accomplishments included the institution of a "blue bag fee" system to help pay for garbage collection in the city and the creation of the Utica Business Park on land that once was a tax-exempt golf course run by Utica College. The business park has not only meant jobs of the area, but also tax dollars for the city.

The administration also helped the downtown area when it joined the project to convert the abandoned Woolworth's building, on Genesee Street, to house Stetson-Harza.

But despite attempts to reverse downtown's decline, more and more vacant stores were appearing in the downtown district..

One major plus for downtown was the emergence of "The Good Old Summer Time" festival as a major event and attraction.

Summer Time – promoted by such downtown merchants as Syd Oberman – started as a small event in the early 1980s and grew rapidly with sections of Genesee Street closed to make room for events such as a Miss Greater Utica contest, a race for waiters and waitresses, bed races, food booths featuring ethnic dishes and games and rides. Also part of the festival was the Boilermaker Road Race and the arts festival at Munson-Williams-Proctor Institute.

The Memorial Auditorium continued to show top performers at times during the 1980s and 1990s, but at the end of each year usually showed a deficit.

In fact, the auditorium has been a problem for the city from its very beginning and a constant drain on the city treasury. For years, Utica's civic and political leaders have attempted to have Oneida County take over the operation of the auditorium

It has been part of a push to promote regionalization and that push has been successful in some areas.

The former Utica Water Board has become a regional authority governed by individuals from city and county.

Oneida County has assumed the city's share of aid to the Utica Zoo and control of the auditorium has been transferred from the city to an independent authority.

In 1995, Edward Hanna returned as mayor and focused on accomplishing four goals: improve the city's fiscal future and financial standing; make the city beautiful and clean again; regionalization many of the city's operations; and restore Hanna Park.

An early fiscal crisis was avoided, with the assistance of state money, and a citizen fiscal advisory panel report showed the way to improve the city's financial rating with minimum additional tax burden.

The looks of the downtown area did improve. A water fountain and mini-park was built to greet motorists coming from the New York Thruway and crossing the East-West arterial (Oriskany Street).

Hanna Park was restored and began to attract many events. A Utica Symphony Orchestra performance, in the "Monday Nite" entertainment series, attracted more than 2,500 people.

And as the 21st century neared, the mayor of Utica (Hanna), the mayor of Rome (Joseph Griffo) and the Oneida County Executive (Ralph Eannace) were emphasizing that all communities in the region must work together as a team to attract new businesses and to ensure a return of growth and prosperity.

In 1997-1998, revival of downtown Utica got much encouragement as local investors purchased major landmark buildings and began renovations. Harold "Tom" Clark purchased the old Bankers Trust Building, on the northeast corner of Genesee and Elizabeth streets. After major rework he moved in his Mac-Clark Restaurants office – which operate McDonald's restaurants in the Utica-Rome area – and the Adirondack Bank operations. In August, 1998, a group of local investors – Hotel Utica LLC – announced plans to return the Hotel Utica to its former splendor and reputation for food and lodging. They will spend more than $5 million to rehabilitate the hotel.

Mayor Hanna said, "This is a very bright day for downtown. We're bringing two buildings back to life that were dead and ready to be buried."

Despite the fact that most of the "loom-to-boom" industries that settled in the city during the 1950s were gone by the 1990s, there is much evidence that Utica has begun to reverse the effects of those losses. Utica Business Park is attracting new companies; existing firms like Con-Med and Fleet Financial Group continue to grow; hospitals have formed cooperative agreements such as the Mohawk Valley Heart Institute to expand local services while controlling costs; national retailers continue to look to this area in locating new stores and shopping areas; major events like the annual Heart-Run-Walk lead the nation in raising funds for heart research and treatment; The Boilermaker road race, and Distance Running Hall of Fame, have created a major sports event in July to attract visitor dollars and introduce newcomers to the historical heritage of the Mohawk Valley. Evidence of a new spirit abounds in a regular Observer-Dispatch feature called "Talking Proud," conceived by Editor Rick Jensen. Opinion Page Editor Dave Dudajek describes it as… "a feature that moves the city forward by emphasizing the positive things happening in Utica and vicinity as we reach the 21st century."

Growth of Utica by Annexations

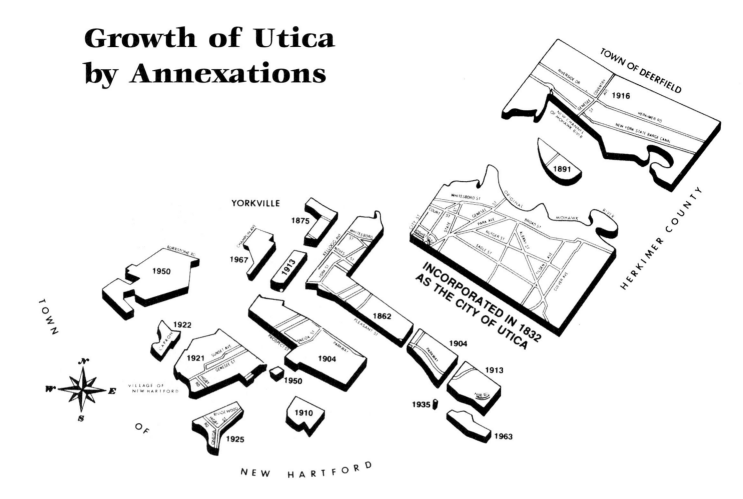

Growth of Utica by Annexations – The territory of Utica has grown by bits and pieces since it was incorporated as a city in 1832. At that time its boundaries were the Mohawk River (north), the Herkimer County line (east), a line just south of Oswego Street (south), and the line of present City Street (west). The city first expanded in 1962, south to Pleasant Street and west beyond the State Lunatic Asylum to Kellogg Avenue, with another westward extension toward Yorkville in 1875. A crescent north of the Mohawk River was transferred from the Town of Deerfield in 1891 in anticipation of the straightening of the river. The years 1904-1913 saw the city line moved south to take in the growing residential areas to Prospect Street, together with Forest Hill and New Forest cemeteries and the park lands given by Thomas R. Proctor. Another large piece of Deerfield was annexed in 1916, later known as North Utica. Most of the area between Prospect Street and the Village of New Hartford – known as "no man's land" after World War I – was taken over in 1921, followed in 1922 by the area called Capron around Richardson Avenue and Lomond Place, and the eastern portion of Ridgewood around Oneida Street and Higby Road in 1925. A small area near the bend of the Parkway was added 10 years later. Two more pieces were carved from the Town of New Hartford in 1950, the peninsular Rhoads Hospital site on the southwest for the General Electric French Road plant and a tract on Oneida Street, the site of Hillcrest Manor Apartments. In 1963, an area just south of Nob Road was added. The city reached its present limits in 1967 with the addition of a major portion of Utica College's Burrstone Road campus west to Champlin Avenue. Adapted from Utica: A City Worth Saving.

Utica Public Schools

By Richard L. Williams

A seven-member board of education today oversees the Utica School District through superintendent Daniel C. Lowengard and deputy superintendent Bernadette Eichler.

The schools offer a full range of programs such as special education, music, art, athletics (a new swimming pool at Proctor), an evening program at Proctor, a bridge program for seniors to take free courses at Mohawk Valley Community College, guidance, computer labs, advanced placement courses, a TV studio, and a school-to-work program.

Vocational education students attend classes at the Oneida B.O.C.E.S. Educational Center on Middle-settlement Road in New Hartford.

In the fall of 1998, about 8000 Utica children entered the city's nine kindergarten through six grade elementary schools, two middle schools, and the one senior high school. This compares with nearly 15,500 students housed in 23 public school buildings in 1986.

Utica currently has Proctor Senior High School with grades 10-12. In 1980 Utica had three high schools…Utica Free Academy (now Loretto Utica Center at 1445 Kemble Street), T.R. Proctor, and J.F. Kennedy in North Utica (now a middle school).

While Utica had 18 elementary schools in 1977, the nine remaining ones are magnet schools which emphasize a special curriculum such as technology, literature and writing, performing arts, careers, multi-media and communications, cultural awareness, computers, and science.

Utica Public Schools for 1998-1999

Opened	Name	Grades	Address
1936	T.R. Proctor H.S.	10-12	1203 Hilton Avenue
1990	James H. Donovan M.S.	7-9	1701 Noyes Street
1965	John F. Kennedy M.S.	7-9	500 Deerfield Drive East
1959	Albany Magnet School	K-6	1151 Albany Street
1958	Columbus Magnet School	K-6	930 Armory Drive
1960	Gen. Herkimer Magnet School	K-6	Keyes Road
1925	John F. Hughes Magnet School	K-6	24 Prospect Street
1958	Thomas Jefferson Magnet School	K-6	190 Booth Street
1935	Hugh R. Jones Magnet School	K-6	2630 Remington Road
1955	Martin Luther King, Jr. Magnet School	K-6	211 Square Street
1990	Watson Williams Magnet School	K-6	107 Elmwood Place
1916	Kernan Magnet School	K-6	929 York Street

Private Schools in Utica and Oneida County

By Richard L. Williams

Long a part of the area education scene individuals, churches, and companies have maintained private schools.

As early as 1829, 31 small schools were housed in private homes, church basements, and above stores where teachers rented space in Utica.

In 1998 Holy Trinity, Our Lady of Lourdes, St. Peter's, and Sacred Heart Elementary School and Notre Dame Junior/Senior High School exist in Utica. Elsewhere, Rome has Catholic High School and St. Peter's and Transfiguration elementary schools, and Clinton has St. Mary's School.

Catholic schools have recently opened full time classes for three and four-year olds) pre-kindergarten) to accommodate children of working parents. Also the use of technology has been given a major emphasis by the Catholic schools, according to Kathleen Coye, superintendent of the Eastern Region of Catholic Schools whose office is at 17 Herkimer Road in Utica.

As student population has decreased several Catholic schools have closed, and the system has been reorganized.

In 1980, 11 parochial elementary schools were in Utica alone along with Notre Dame junior/senior high school.

The Maranatha Christian Academy on Middle-settlement Road in New Hartford and the Marcy Pilgrim Academy at 9400 Kennedy Road in Marcy are two other church-related private schools.

Many other private schools such as the American Driving School, American Martial Arts Academy, Gigliotti's Driving School, Miss Delia's School of Dance, Valley Gymnastic Company, and the Tae Kwon Do School are operating to meet specialized needs of youngsters and adults.

Beyond the secondary level Utica and the County can boast of several institutions that have degree and certificate programs: Hamilton College, Utica College of Syracuse University, State University of New York Institute of Technology, Mohawk Valley Community College, Munson-Williams-Proctor Institute School of Art, St. Elizabeth's Hospital College of Nursing and School of Radiology, St. Luke's Memorial Hospital School of Radiography, and the Utica School of Commerce.

A New Era in Health Care

By Robert G. Stronach

Since 1975, there has been a major shift in the delivery of health care, to greater emphasis on preventative care, and to more economical access to care, outside of the hospital environment. The pressure to contain costs, emanating from public and private sectors, went hand in hand with the spread of primary care centers to advance preventative care. Other factors affecting costs are advances in technology; the trend to reduce hospital stays; and the growth of innovative health plans sporting names like health maintenance organization, prepaid health plan, and managed care.

Hospital competition has become a major focus as employers, insurance companies and the government reacted to spiraling health care costs and what they perceived as unnecessary duplication of services. The *Observer-Dispatch* referred to it as "hospital wars". While there was cooperation on several fronts, there continued to be fierce competition, especially for new services (such as heart catheterizations) and new technology (such as laser surgery).

Hospitals were looking to contain costs as well. Free care and bad debt write-offs, spiraling overhead expenses, reduction in insurance and government reimbursements, and a complete shift in how payments for services are determined, all were burdening hospitals with a greater share of the cost of health care. Furthermore, a growing emphasis on shorter hospital stays and broader outpatient care meant reduced income.

New York State Department of Health officials began criticizing regions where they perceived a lack of cooperation among health care providers and even rejected or delayed proposed expansions and new programs.

Thus, the stage was set for health care facilities to network, cooperate, consolidate, and share services.

In July 1992, Faxton and St. Luke's-Memorial hospitals formed the Mohawk Valley Network, agreeing to plan together, share services and operate under one parent umbrella. The Mohawk Valley Network, or MVN, grew to include a number of health care facilities and services, including Little Falls Hospital, nursing homes, lab, X-ray and other services.

With a high incidence of heart disease in upstate New York, and nearly 1,000 people each year leaving the area to obtain advanced cardiac care, hospital officials recognized a significant community need - and opportunity. Both St. Luke's and St. Elizabeth wanted to meet that need. Each had a staff of cardiologists and cardiac catheterizations labs for diagnosing heart disease. And each recognized that the area could not support two separate cardiac surgery programs.

During the summer of 1993, Sr. Rose Vincent, president and CEO of St. Elizabeth, launched the Cardiac Services Task Force. With an initial group of some 30 community and hospital people, led by James R. Pyne, president of Remet Corp., the task force conducted a community-wide campaign to establish cardiac surgery and angioplasty programs in Utica. It involved all three hospitals, recognizing, as Pyne put it, that "a cooperative effort would have a better chance of gaining widespread community support

and an eventual go-ahead from the Department of Health."

The task force timed a press conference for Aug. 4 to coincide with a tentative pact, and the headline across the front page of the next day's *Observer-Dispatch* read: "Hospitals unite for cardiac care."

Two months later, the hospitals announced an agreement to form the Mohawk Valley Heart Institute and realign services.

In just three and a half months, the task force, now numbering 66, collected more than 60,000 signatures on petitions in support of a local cardiac surgery program. Members of the task force, including hospital administrators, traveled to Albany on April 4, 1994, to meet with Health Commissioner Mark Chassin and personally deliver the stack of petitions. A duplicate set was delivered to Governor Mario Cuomo's office.

Despite overwhelming community support, and what the task force regarded as compelling evidence of need, approval for a local cardiac program did not come easily. Even after passing muster at several state review panels, the program was rejected on April 7 - just three days after the delegation's trip to Albany. During George Patacki's first year as governor, the Health Department reviewed the case again. Finally, on Feb. 1, 1996, it not only won approval, but praise from Health Commissioner Barbara DeBuono who said the cooperative arrangement in Utica was a model for the state.

After renovations and construction at St. Elizabeth, the Mohawk Valley Heart Institute welcomed its first heart patient on Oct. 17, 1997, when East Utica chef Joseph Prestia underwent six-vessel bypass surgery. During its first eight months of operation, the Heart Institute, with Dr. Paul Hatton as chief surgeon, performed more than 200 open heart surgeries - all successful.

Other hospital milestones and trends:

• Burgeoning of a coordinated emergency medical services (EMS) system in conjunction with the designation of St. Elizabeth as the Area Trauma Center and St. Luke's-Memorial as the EMS Resource Hospital.

• Shift toward "centers of excellence", with Faxton as the cancer and rehab center; St. Elizabeth as the trauma and cardiac center; and St. Luke's as the childbirth, pediatric, geriatric and dialysis center.

• Opening of Cooperative Magnetic Imaging in the Utica Business Park - a truly cooperative venture involving area radiologists and the three hospitals which brought MRI diagnostic technology to Utica.

• St. Elizabeth Hospital changes its name to St. Elizabeth Medical Center to reflect its growing critical care and cardiac services, along with an expanding network of health centers in Oneida and Herkimer counties.

• The boards of Faxton and St. Luke's merge into one governing board, with St. Luke's CEO Andrew Peterson becoming CEO of both facilities and Faxton CEO Keith Fenstemacher becoming president of the umbrella corporation, the Mohawk Valley Network.

Annsville

By
Flora Wattenbe

Annsville is located in the Fish Creek drainage basin in the north west part of the county. The east branch of Fish Creek drains most of the town and forms part of the eastern boundary. The west branch of Fish Creek forms most of the southern boundary. The town contains 36,316 acres and was formed from Scriba's Patent.

There is evidence of the glacier that helped to shape the land. Mack Pond is located in a kettle basin which was formed when a block of ice broke off from the glacier and was then covered by debris. After the ice melted, the resulting depression in the land provided the basin for the pond, which is of undetermined depth.

In April 1793 John Bloomfield came from Burlington, New Jersey. He and some others paid two shillings an acre. To induce his wife, Ann, to leave her home, he built a mansion, which is still in excellent condition on Route 285 north of Taberg. The town was named Annsville in her honor. Among other early landowners were Richard Bacon, J. Howard Kalk, Charles W. Nolan, and Lester Garvin.

Taberg was established at the junction of Furnace Creek and the east branch of Fish Creek in order to take advantage of the water power potential there. A blast furnace was constructed there in 1811 to smelt Clinton iron ore. Iron foundries, blacksmith shops, tanneries, wagon shops, sawmills, shingle mills, lath mills, a planing mill, a gristmill, a wool carding mill, and a butter tub factory all were operated at various times in the town. Several cheese factories made American and limburger cheese. The town was also the site of two canning factories, a cheese box factory, a cider mill, fishing tackle factories, a cotton mill, a harness shop, a tin smithery, a shoe fac-

tory, and millinery shops. It once had eight hotels and a stage and livery business.

The first two houses in Taberg were constructed by Benjamin Hyde and John Bloomfield. The third was a boarding house for men working at the Taberg furnace. The Taberg Post Office was established about 1815. The first Annsville town meeting was held March 2, 1824, and the first supervisor was Benjamin Hyde.

The first school in Annsville was established in 1812. Eventually 17 schools were located in the town. In 1956, a modern eight-teacher school with two aides and a cafeteria staff of three, was built. This serves most of Annsville's children and absorbed the remaining schools which had become part of the Camden Central School District.

A Baptist Church was organized in Annsville in 1831, with Samuel Bloss as pastor. It passed out of existence in 1920. The first Methodist Church was built in 1839. The first Catholic Church in Taberg was built about 1845. The present Blossvale Union Chapel was once a church in Delta, prior to the flooding of Delta village by the construction of Delta Reservoir. Interested persons raised $1,000 and bought it. It was dismantled by Joseph Kalk and hauled by horses to Blossvale, where it was erected in 1901. It is served by the Taberg Methodist pastor.

In the 1880s fire protection was initiated by a fire company which owned a hand pump. A disastrous fire Easter Sunday 1905 destroyed several business establishments in Taberg. In 1908 the Taberg Volunteer Fire Company was organized. The town is now served by the Taberg Fire Company and the Blossvale Fire Company, both of which have firehouses completed in 1974. Taberg has 125 members and Blossvale 31 members.

Rail service to Annsville was provided by the Rome, Watertown & Ogdensburg Railroad, which later became part of the New York Central and is now part of Conrail. This line passed through the southern part of the town with stations at Blossvale and McConnellsville, serving Annsville.

Blossvale, once known as Taberg Station, was closed in 1957. Freight traffic on the line included shipments of sand from McConnellsville and receipt of feed, groceries, and wood products at Camden. On April 1, 1976, the rail line from Rome to McConnellsville became part of Conrail. Freight service on the branch from McConnellsville to Camden will be maintained under a temporary federal-state subsidy program. A Blossvale station agent, Howard Lillybridge, was grandson of Ira Lillybridge, a settler who arrived in Annsville in 1824. The McConnellsville station was moved to the Erie Canal Village in Rome in 1974.

From the 1860s to 1888 Taberg had a fair known for miles around. The last ten years it was held by the Annsville and Lee Agricultural Society. The grounds and racetrack were on the property now owned by Carl Seiple and son and were considered among the best kept in the state.

Soon after 1880 a small orchestra was organized that finally became the Taberg Cornet Band in 1909. In 1927 the Taberg Community Band was organized. This was discontinued in the 1940s.

Annsville water no longer powers local industry, but during the 20th century it has become important as public water supply. The City of Rome diverts water from the east branch of Fish Creek in the town. The City of Oneida Glenmore Reservoir is located in the town and its Florence Creek watershed is located in Annsville and Florence. The Oneida City aqueduct runs south from Glenmore, passing to the east of Taberg. Taberg obtains its local water supply from the Oneida aqueduct.

Improved highway transportation has had a particularly important influence upon Annsville because rail service touched only the southern fringe of the town. In the mid-19th century the town benefited from the construction of the Rome and Taberg plank road, which helped lift the community out of the mud. This road suffered the fate of others of its era. Deterioration of planks occurred faster than funds could be generated from tolls to repair the road, and it was abandoned in 1872. With the advent of the auto, many residents gave up farming and became commuters to jobs in Rome, Camden, and other communities. Many acres in Annsville are now abandoned to wild growth as the number of farms diminished. During the 1930s many farms in Annsville were acquired by the state as reforestation land. Most of these are located in the northern third of

Virginia Kelly photo

Green Brook Manor – Ann's Mansion.
Route 285, north of Taberg village.

District 8 school at Taberg, before 1890.

C. Harrison Ward

the town, north of Sheehan Road. Smaller industries and stores have fallen victims to larger operations.

Agriculture remains an important part of Annsville's economy. In 1968 the town had 58 dairy farm, one poultry farm and 12 other farms. In 1975 two agricultural districts were formed, encompassing 27 farms and 7104 acres. In 1976 Annsville has two sawmills, a pizza factory, (formed in 1965, formerly a milk plant), and a fuel oil distributing company. The latter two are in Blossvale. One hotel, a recently built tavern, a general store, a garage with gas station, and two small auto repair shops remain. The post offices at Blossvale and Taberg continue in operation. The Glenmore Post Office was discontinued in 1926.

The town has produced many outstanding citizens who have left their mark. A Methodist bishop, Calvin Kingsley, was from Annsville. Thomas B. Allanson was supervisor of Annsville for 12 years and was elected to the state assembly when Grover Cleveland was Governor. Born in England in 1817, he came to the United States in 1831. His great-granddaughter, Mill Blanche Seifert, lives in Blossvale.

Annsville still has residents bearing names of well known early settlers. Among them are Lappin, MacFarland, Ward, Armstrong, Houston, Kilbourne, Taft, Sullivan, Nelson, Fox, Ferguson, Waterman, Link and others.

The oldest person to have been reported to live in Annsville, a black, William Smith, known as Uncle Bill, lived to be over 112 years old. The voting record for the town and perhaps for the county, may have been held by Aaron Waterman, born in a log cabin in north Annsville March 15, 1875. He voted for 76 consecutive years, including 19 presidential elections. He died at the age of 99.

Certain events have highlighted the history of Annsville. One is the passing of the pigeons in the fall of 1881. Thousands flew over the town, darkening the sky for four hours when lamps had to be lit. They had flown over other years, but not in such vast numbers. The next year not a pigeon was seen. This was recounted by G. Frank Barden to Florence Simon, postmistress for many years, who wrote a history of Annsville.

Another memorable occasion was on June 22, 1972 when Furnace Creek flooded Taberg as a result of Hurricane Agnes. Over a foot of water swirled down Main Street, causing much damage. About 60 families were evacuated in the fear that Glenmore Dam might give way. This did not occur and the people returned to their homes. Nearly $60,000 in flood relief was allotted to the town, with $18,000 spent to construct a dike along Fish Creek in the Blossvale area to control future floods.

In 1973 the town celebrated its 150th birthday from August 19 to 26. There were many activities, including parades, speeches, a beard contest, a beauty pageant, and

Taberg Coronet Band, circa. 1909. Front row: Harold White (director), Edgar Ballard, Harry Ward, Philip Smith, Rowland Wilson, Arthur Ward, Robert Mullen. Second row: Lawrence Converse, Robert Walker, John Brower, William Walker, Henry Morse, Christopher Ritter. Third row: Howard Ward, Roy MacFarland, Glen Ward, John Dean, Charles Light (drum major), George White, H. D. Kilbourn, and James Thorn.

C. Harrison Ward

A view prior to 1890 of the Wilson Factory, Taberg, where corn and peas were processed.

even a frog race. There were field days with booths, riding attractions, and other features. All organizations of the town, of which there are many, cooperated in the enterprise.

In 1968 the State Division for Youth established a camp near Taberg for delinquent boys aged 15 to 17 sentenced to probation. The camp accommodates 60 boys. It assigns the boys to conservation work in the state's forests and gives them classroom teaching, focusing on remedial work and mathematics and reading. They generally remain at the camp nine months to a year.

Advertisement for the Annsville and Lee Agricultural Society Fair, 1887.

C. Harrison Ward

Main Street, Taberg, looking north, about 1920. United States Hotel at left.

C. Harrison Ward

Augusta

By
Helen L. Alberding
and
Mildred Miner

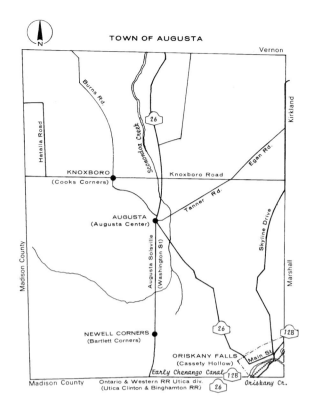

The Town of Augusta, named for Augustus VanHorn, was formed in 1798 as the 11th township in Oneida County. It is located on the southwest portion of the county. The township has been reduced in size twice since it was formed.

The villages in the township are Knoxboro, Augusta Center and Oriskany Falls. A few of the early settlements that were at one time active no longer exist today.

Each of the villages in the township developed to meet the needs of the people who lived there and changed as their needs changed. The continuous growth of Oriskany Falls may have been because the Chenango Canal and the railroad passed through the village. Both the canal and the railroad have been gone for many years. All that remains of the canal are some stone walls and locks located outside the village. There is no longer anything left that shows a railroad passed through the village. Of the three villages, Oriskany Falls today is still the most productive.

The early settlers coming from Connecticut and Massachusetts found the area excellent for farming. Today there are many farms in the township. Some of the smaller farms have been bought and added to larger farms. Descendants of the settlers who came here 200 years ago still run a few of the area farms. In the last few years, Mennonites have come to the area and have purchased some of the farms. The main farming products today are grain, hay, corn, milk and some farmers grow beans. Farming techniques have changed since the early settlers. Today the modern equipment available for milking and working the fields enables more efficient operation.

Farmers who find dairy farming no longer profitable have gone into raising beef cattle.

Local limestone found by early settlers to be useful for constructing buildings, and later improving roads, is still quarried in the same location. Today the quarry is known as Benchmark, NY and employs many area residents. It has changed ownership through the years, but still produces the products needed for road building. The quarry has increased in size and extends into the Town of Augusta. Operations at the facility have been improved bringing it up to present standards.

The largest employer in the township is the Sherwood-Davis and Geck Corp. The plant located on South Main Street in Oriskany Falls manufactures hospital products. It began with a knitting mill, built in 1897, which grew to the present facility with improvements and additions. The company was sold in 1998 to the Kendall Corporation.

The day of the one room school is a part of the past and many of these structures are gone. The few remaining ones have been renovated and are private homes. The only other school in Augusta Center is the Augusta Academy that closed in the late 1800's.

In Knoxboro, the early schools were no longer used when they became a part of the Madison Central School District. The new elementary school built there was closed in 1981 and in 1984 the Oneida County ARC took over the building and still maintains it today.

Private schools were located in Oriskany Falls until 1892 when a public school was built on the hill overlooking the village. The first school building burned and another was built in its place. This facility had two additions that replaced the early wood structure. The school closed in 1983 when it was annexed by the Waterville Central School System. These changes resulted in the children in the Town of Augusta attending either Madison School or Waterville School. The Oriskany Falls School building was sold and for a while was used as an apartment complex. Today, it is empty and has been taken over by the village. With the closing of the Oriskany Falls High School, for the first time in over 200 years, the Town of Augusta is without a school.

Several churches constructed by the early settlers are still active. The Methodist Church in Knoxboro is 126 years old. The Presbyterian Church in Augusta Center is over 200 years old. The Oriskany Falls United Methodist Church is 126 years old and the present St. Joseph's Church is 75 years old. The School of Religion building, constructed next to St. Joseph's Church, was renovated in 1996 and now contains a rectory and a parish center.

Many of the roads that pass through the township follow the trails used by the Indians, such as the east-west Knoxboro Road that is marked by one of the state historic markers put there in 1935. Over the years other historic roadway markers were lost. In 1998, therefore, the Town Board decided to replace seventeen markers as a part of the Town of Augusta Bicentennial Celebration.

Many of the country roads and state highways that crisscross the township have been rebuilt in recent years. In Oriskany Falls changes were made that included major construction and three bridge replacements. Main Street and South main Street were changed to one way streets; parking in the center of the village was changed; trees that had been removed during construction were replaced; sidewalks and new curbs were added on many streets. In addition, construction of a new bridge on Route 26 is proceeding outside of Augusta Center.

Post offices are located in Knoxboro and Oriskany Falls in the township. The post office located in Augusta Center closed many years ago.

The businesses that once served each village have changed. Today Knoxboro has an auto garage and an antique repair shop. In Augusta Center there is an antique shop. Oriskany Falls maintains businesses such as; a grocery store, hardware store, laundromat, antique shops, beauty shops, insurance agency, financial office, appliance store, hotel, three restaurants, doctor's office, funeral home, telephone office and a bank. Many of these businesses are located in historic buildings that have been renovated in the last few years. The National Bank of Vernon, for example, occupies a building that has been used as a

Stone Church, erected 1833, Oriskany Falls.

Oneida Historical Society

Augusta Presbyterian Church in Augusta Center 1909

bank since 1907. The Cassety Hollow Feed Company, a historic building in the village of Oriskany Falls was destroyed by a fire in 1996 and had to be demolished. In addition there are many privately owned businesses located outside each of these villages.

Many improvements have been made in the township phone system. The early hand crank phones were replaced by rotary dial, and now by push button phones. The phone company, located in a former auto garage, has also been improved and modernized to meet the people's needs. Today the company is known as TDS Telecom.

The first television reception in the township came from individually owned antennas. Now the residents of the township receive their television reception from commercial cable or privately owned satellite dishes.

The Village of Oriskany Falls updated its water system and installed meters on homes and businesses. All the main water lines were replaced when roads were being rebuilt. In 1989, the wastewater treatment plant project began and resulted in cleaning up Oriskany Creek. Residents of Knoxboro and Augusta Center rely on wells for water and have their own septic systems.

The sanitary landfill, which opened in 1975, is now closed and the refuse and recycled items are picked up by private sanitation companies.

The Village of Oriskany Falls is the only one in the township having a public library. It was located in the former C. W. Clark Home for over 40 years and in 1997 moved to a larger facility in the village. The new building provides more space, services, and programs and extended hours.

For many years the Augusta Town Board maintained offices at the town highway building in Augusta Center. In 1995 more room was needed, and town officials moved to rooms, upstairs, in the Oriskany Falls Village Hall. This building has been renovated and made handicap accessible.

Established in the early 1800's, the Oriskany Falls Fire Department has been located in different sections of the village. Today, a large building on Madison Street houses the trucks and a new ambulance that was purchased in 1998. A large field next to the firehouse and the pavilion behind it are used for many activities. In 1983 the fire company constructed a building in Knoxboro and a tank truck is kept there. Both the fire department and ambulance corps provides excellent service to the township.

The town offers residents a variety of recreational facilities. A basketball court is located in Knoxboro. Oriskany Falls has a bowling center, a ballfield on Maple Avenue, a basketball court and a new modern playground in Douglass Park and located just outside the village is an

Fowler's Country Store about 1900, Oriskany Falls.

Oriskany Falls, looking north. New York, Ontario & Western southbound train pulling loaded milk cars at Broad St. crossing.

18-hole golf course. Also located in Douglass Park is a gazebo built in 1993, which is used for weddings and special programs. In 1997 a fountain was added to the park. New benches are located near the fountain and in other areas of the park.

The local organizations continue to thrive with the Garden Club celebrating its 70th anniversary this year. Other organizations that have been active for many years are the Neighborhood Club, Masons and Eastern Star, Oriska Valley Senior Citizens, Cassety Hollow Rod and Gun Club, Rotary Club, Limestone Ridge Historical Society, Oriskany Falls Development Corporation, Kelly Phillips American Legion, Auxiliary and Sons of the Legion, Oriskany Falls Fire Department, Ambulance Corps, and Auxiliary and various church organizations.

Among the new organizations are the Cassety Hollow Crafters, a chapter of the Independent Homemakers, Pride in the Park Committee and Friends of the Library. All of these organizations are active; meet regularly, and are a benefit to the township.

The Kelly Phillips American Legion Post, located on Madison Street, have redone their facility and enlarged the dining room. This building and most of the buildings in Oriskany Falls are handicap accessible. Improvements of this kind in the township have occurred because of the dedication and generosity of individual citizens, which began with the early settlers and continues today.

Selected Reference

Limestone Ridge Historical Society Archives

Keys and Smith Stores and Fountain in Knoxboro C-1920

Falls in Oriskany Falls 1930

Ava

By Alson Castle,
Marietta M. Wright
and
William Belewich,
Town Historian

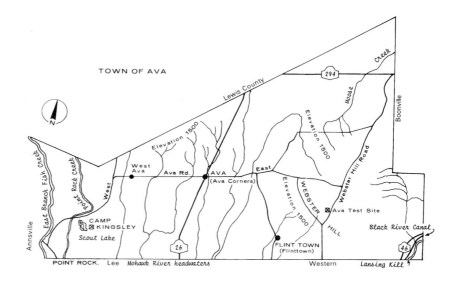

Ava is situated on the northern boundary of the county and includes portions of Matchin's and Adgate's Patents as well as others. The town was formed from the Town of Boonville on May 12, 1846, and was the second to last town formed in the county. The town was named for the Asian capital of Burma.

The headwaters of the Mohawk River and tributaries of the Black River flow through the town. The east branch of Fish Creek forms the western boundary of Ava. The streams provided the early settlers with an abundant supply of brook trout. Early settler Isaac Knight used to boast of catching a washtub full of trout in one day from the Moose Creek, a tributary of the Black River. Today the fish are still plentiful and the modern day fisherman can still catch his limit of brook trout. A few of the more popular streams these days are stocked by the state.

The land is high and rolling and is located in the central area of the Tug Hill Plateau. The Lansing Kill cuts across the southeastern corner of the town. The Black River Canal followed closely the path of the Lansing Kill through the town.

The town was settled early despite its distance from the main transportation routes. In 1797 Ebenezer Harger came to Whitestown from Connecticut and then in 1798 located less than a mile west of the present Ava or Ava Corners. Zephania and Abner Wood, Philo Harger, Benjamin Jones, Lemuel Wood, and Justus Beardsley settled in the town about 1800. By 1870, the population of the town had grown to 1,160, but in the 1880s, it began to decline. In 1970, 541 people lived in the town.

In early times large stands of timber provided the settlers with a livelihood. By the latter part of the 19th century, the supply of timber had dwindled and most of the lumber mills were abandoned. Today, however, areas in the southeastern and southwestern parts of the town have been reforested by the state.

Now the largest industry is a sawmill opened about 35 years ago by Wendell Still. This mill is situated about two miles south of the northern boundary of the Town of Ava on Route 26. When the business began there were only two or three employees, and tractors were used to move the logs. Gasoline-powered saws were used for sawing the logs into lumber. Later the saws were powered by diesel and now are all electrically driven. All machinery, trucks and trailers are owned by the Stills.

Now the business has grown and employs 25 to 30 men. It is still owned by the founder who has taken his son into the business with him. Most of the timber sawed is hardwood, although a small amount of softwood is sawed in a smaller mill on the premises in the summer to supply building material for local markets.

In the past this timber has been cut from lots in Oneida and Lewis Counties, but the present cutting is being done in Herkimer County. The Stills and their crew do their own logging operations and trucking to the mill, as well as sawing and building pallets. These pallets are shipped primarily to Massachusetts. About five to seven trailer loads are shipped each week, and when the demand is greater, as many as nine trailer loads are shipped. This business constitutes about 95 percent of the production of this mill, the other five percent being used for furniture.

Dairy farming is one of the chief occupations in the town today, as it was in the past. A number of cheese factories were located in the town including the one known as Ohm's Factory. This was operated for many years in the southern part of the town on the Webster Hill Road. The last cheese maker to operate before it closed in the 1930s was David Mani. Another cheese factory was operated in the western part of the town on the former Henry Hurlburt farm, West Ava Road, now owned by Walter Belevick. Just south of Ava Corners on Route 26, the Castle's operated a cheese factory for many years.

Since the earliest settlement of the town and even today, Ava (Ava Corners) has been the principal community in the town. The post office for the town is located here. In 1988 a new post office facility was erected for better service. Route 26, one of the primary north-south routes through the county, intersects East-West Ava Road creating the corners. From the time of early settlement, this route has been well traveled. A stage used to run daily to Rome and Boonville along the route.

One hundred years ago a hotel, harness shop, two blacksmith and wagon shops, two stores and a doctor were located here. The harness shop, a wagon shop, doctor's office and general store were destroyed by a fire about 1890. The general store was rebuilt near the corners by Frank E. Castle and operated by him until 1920. This same store is still in operation today. Another store, operated by H. C. Pohl, was converted to a house.

At the northeast corner of the intersection, a large frame hotel was located. For a time, a telephone switchboard for the community was located in the hotel. The hotel fell into disrepair and was demolished about 1923 and a milk plant was erected in its place. The milk plant was discontinued some years later and a sawmill, owned and operated by Willard Backer & Son, was in operation until Mr. Backer's death.

The Ava Methodist Hilltop Church was organized as the Methodist Episcopal Church in 1868 and a frame church was erected in 1869 on Route 26 south of the intersection of Ava Corners.

The church was built by Dewitt Grosjean, grandfather of William D. Pohl and his brother, Andrew Grosjean, grandfather of Arthur Grosjean. The interior was of plaster. There were two wood stoves, one in each corner of the back, connected to a long pipe running the full length of the church. The seating arrangement was of the day, the men on one side, the women on the other.

The town hall was built on Route 26 just south of Ava Corners for $600. The town barn was erected at Ava Corners in recent years to house the town's highway equipment.

By 1878 there were 10 school districts for the 371 schoolchildren in the town. Teacher's wages were $944.63 for 1877-78. The former school districts were gradually consolidated with the Adirondack and West Leyden Central School systems.

In the eastern part of the town is a settlement still known as Flinttown. This area was settled by the Flint Family from Montgomery County. John R. Flint and his sons, Peter, Adam and Robert, cleared the land and built a log house in 1840 on the farm later owned by William Fazekas on Flint Town Road. The first frame house in the settlement was erected by the same family in 1848 and is

Chester Williams

Looking north of Route 26 at Ava Corners, about 1910. A horse-drawn carriage is passing the hotel.

Castle's Store, Ava Corners. Standing today.

still standing on the south side of the road across from the site of the log house.

A few years later, in 1858, another family came from Montgomery County and settled in Flinttown. This was the Soloman Seeber family. They also built a log house first and a cheese factory where cheese was made from the milk from their own dairy. The frame house now standing on this farm and occupied by the Mondrick family was built by Mr. Seeber in 1867. He cut the timber from which the lumber was sawed on his own farm. The entire cost of the house was $500.

Ava Test Annex, commonly known as the Ava Site, was constructed in 1957 on Webster Hill Road by Research and Development at Griffiss Air Force Base. It is fundamentally an experimental transmitter site for tests for "over-the-horizon" radar. Hours of operation vary depending on experiments being undertaken.

Plans for a regional land fill site north-east of Ava have been in various stages of review in the 1990s. Township inhabitants continue strong resistance.

In the western section of the town we find one of the finest Boy Scout camps in America known as Camp Kingsley. The camp was given to the scout council in 1920 and dedicated in 1921 to the memory of Dr. W. J. P. Kingsley of Rome. At that time it consisted of 180 acres, including a spring-fed lake covering 30 acres and known as Point Rock Lake or Bullhead Lake, which has been renamed Scout Lake. The camp area now encompasses 430 acres and is operated by the Iroquois Council of Boy Scouts of America. It is located 15 miles north of Rome, west of Route 26 between Point Rock and Ava. The camp now serves most of Oneida County, except the greater Utica area, all of Madison County, and parts of Herkimer, Lewis and Hamilton Counties.

The camp cooperates with the Forestry Service, the Agriculture Service and the Fish and Wildlife Service and is a registered tree farm. A full-time ranger is employed there.

Presently the camp season consists of a six-week residence camp in summer plus a Cub Scout day camp and is open the year round for holidays and winter camping activities. It is estimated that between 1,000 and 1,500 scouts are accommodated during summer and winter months.

Hilltop Methodist Church, Ava, in 1909.

A steam roller crushing stone during construction of paved roads in Ava, 1916. Many stone fences were broken up to provide these road beds.

*Post Street between Schuyler and Erwin Streets on the Village Square,
taken in 1860s. Gothic house, left, still stands.*

Boonville

By
Laura Warren
and
James Pitcher

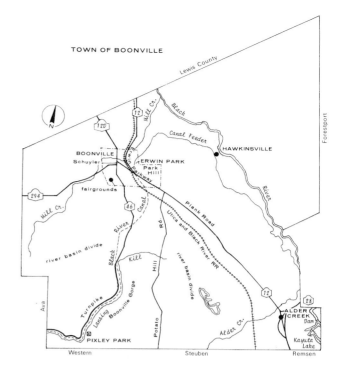

The town of Boonville lies in the northernmost part of Oneida County, bordering Lewis County on the north and west. The town's largest settlement, the Village of Boonville, rests on the divide between the Black River System (including its tributaries Mill Creek and Alder Creek) flowing northerly to the St. Lawrence, and the Lansing Kill, flowing southerly to the Mohawk. To the west lie the high Tug Hill Plateau and Lake Ontario, where are spawned the heavy snowstorms which blanket the area each winter. The soil is largely loamy and suitable for farming.

1796-1815

In the spring of 1795 the Holland Land Company sent Gerritt Boon to settle its northern holdings. Boon, accompanied by Andrew Edmunds and his family, found a favorable site on the Mill Creek and erected a sawmill on this large stream. The building burned, but the next spring the settlers returned, rebuilt the sawmill, and thus in 1796 founded the settlement. Edmunds built a house and tavern at a point that is the center of the present village, on the southeast corner of the village square. Other settlers arrived, including the tanner Jacob Rogers; Jacob Springer, whose daughter's birth was the first recorded in the village; and Aaron Willard, whose descendants gave their name to the Willard Press. Andrew Edmund's daughter Elizabeth and Henry Evans contracted the first marriage in the settlement. In 1799 there was a smallpox epidemic and Dr. Samuel Snow inoculated most of the families.

Only tenuous trails connected the early hamlet to the rest of the world: Barneveld, Fort Stanwix, the site of Lyons Falls, and Talcott's sawmill on the Sugar River.

The area comprising the Town of Boonville has been in five counties (Albany, Tryon, Montgomery, Herkimer and Oneida) and three townships (Steuben, Leyden and Boonville). When Lewis County was created in 1805, the hamlet of Kortenaer (later Boonville) remained in Oneida County and on March 28, 1805, the Town of Boonville was formed. Officers included many of the original settlers: Supervisor Jacob Rogers, Clerk Aaron Willard, and Postmaster Luke Fisher.

By this time the forest was transformed into a rude community. Here were schools, the first being Mill Lydia Bulkley's, opened in 1802; churches too, were evident, beginning with a Congregational Church formed in 1805, followed by the Baptists in 1810. The Presbyterians, Universalists and Methodists shared a small building on Post Street about 1820. Industry in the form of a sawmill, a gristmill and a tannery was progressing. There was a store and a tavern. Wilderness farms surrounded the little community. Seven miles to the south John Platt built a home, in 1805, on Alder Creek.

The War of 1812 filled the settlers with fear, for they situated on a possible route between Canada and the Mohawk River. The town officers appointed a committee to ask the Governor for arms and ammunition, and appropriated the treasury's surplus, all of $17.68, for the expense of transporting it.

1815-1900

Following the war, progress took place at a steady pace. The abundant forests gave raw materials to the various wood industries. As more and more arable land was wrenched from the wilderness, dairy farms, which are now a trademark of the area, began to evolve. Cheese factories appeared at many crossroads to handle surplus milk. A toll turnpike opened in 1817; a plank road in 1847-49.

The first two-story building in town was a hotel of

Trenton limestone erected in 1819 by Ephraim Owen. This building, now the Hulbert House, purchased and altered by Hulbert in 1839, still holds a prominent place in the center of the village.

The 1845 census tells of 25 sawmills, two gristmills, two carding machines, two iron works, three asheries and three tanneries. Of these businesses, two have survived to the present. Near the Holland Land Company's original sawmill, Livvin Jillson, in 1817, built a section of the Boonville Mills still standing today. About the same year, master-builder Ephraim Owen built a saw and gristmill that later became the N.M. Sargent & Sons chair and stool factory.

The Black River Canal, an offshoot of the Erie, was completed to Boonville in 1848. The next year it was completed to Lyons Falls, a waterway 36.62 miles long, costing three million dollars (at a time when laborers were paid $1 a day). It rose 693 feet from Rome to Boonville's Summit Lock 71, descending from there 386 feet to High Falls on the Black River at Lyons Falls. There were 109 locks and 33 lock houses. A feeder ran to Boonville from the Black River. Boats of 70 tons carried lumber, sand and produce south, returning with weighty manufactured goods from the cities. One of the canal's last duties, before abandonment in 1915, was transporting stone from the Sugar River quarries to the site of a new dam at Delta.

By 1851, Boonville's population was 1,000. There were seven dry goods stores and a school with 90 pupils and two teachers. In 1855, just 50 years after the town was formed, the Village of Boonville was incorporated and became a full-fledged municipality.

For years there had been talk of rail lines from Utica and Rome into the North Country. In 1853 the Black River and Utica Railroad Company was formed and work was begun the same year. A rival company in Rome began blasting and grading its way up the Lansing Kill Gorge, but no track was laid. In 1855 a line was completed from Utica to Boonville. The depot and terminus were located north of the Schuyler-Post Street intersection. On December 13, 1855 the first official train arrived, carrying notables from Utica, and several bands. Two thousand people greeted the train at the terminal; there was a parade, a feast, and many toasts.

Regular scheduling of trains began within a month, and 68,000 passengers enjoyed the railroad while Boonville was its terminus. Sportsmen and travelers heading for the famous Brown's Tract in the Adirondacks picked up supplies and refreshed themselves in Boonville. But there were no freight trains; the canal did the heavy work.

Prior to the Civil War, the underground railway also passed through the town. In 1862 Boonville's own regi-

Boonville Village, from business center, in 1910.

ment, the Conklin Rifles, the 97th, New York Volunteers, mustered under Colonel Charles Wheelock. The regiment served valiantly at the battles of Cedar Mountain, Manassas, Antietam, Fredericksburg and Gettysburg, to mention only a few.

By 1900 the appearance of Boonville had changed. The railroad tracks had been extended north and the tracks relocated to their present beds. This necessitated moving the cemetery to its present location on the slope of Park Hill. Half of the station house was moved to the new tracks, and the other half was used by the Baptist congregation as an addition to their new (1866) brick building nearby.

The Presbyterians in 1855 constructed a steepled frame church that is still in use.

The Methodists moved to their present location on Main Street in 1873, when the site became available after fire destroyed the Empire House. This hotel, a large three-story building, was a favorite stopping place for the circus troupes who performed in the town. The register, still in existence, records their names in proud, flowing script. On April 26, 1869, the record ends abruptly with a penciled scrawl: "Empire House caught fire about 11:30 p.m. and at 1:30 a.m. it was all in ashes."

The Catholic Society laid the cornerstone of St. Joseph's Church in 1878; the Episcopal Church erected the brick church on Schuyler Street in 1857. Hawkinsville

at this time had four churches, one of which is still in use, and Alder Creek had two.

The Union Free School, in the frame building built in 1855 at the corner of Academy and Charles Streets, was renamed Boonville High School and Academy in 1897.

The Boonville Driving Park Association, formed in 1872, evolved into the Boonville Fair Association, and since has been a feature of the village. The Boonville Cemetery Association was incorporated in 1857, and benefited from the generosity of Cornelius Erwin under his will. This successful native son, at his passing in 1885, left bequests also for the purchase and development of a park which now ornaments the village along Route 12, and funds for a library which bears his name.

The *Black River Herald* (formerly *Boonville Ledger*) was sold in 1862 to Harvey Willard. Its name was changed to the *Boonville Herald*, and it remained in the Willard family for 98 years.

The township's boundary lines were changed twice: the Town of Ava was created on Boonville's western border in 1846, and in 1890 the line running through the center of the growing Village of Forestport was moved eastward.

Industry changed and developed during this period. In addition to sawmills and gristmills and several tanneries, businesses included a foundry and machine shop, a tub, churn and barrel factory, sash and blind factory, glove fac-

The circus comes to town, 1910.

tory, canal boat builders, and a brick kiln and cooperage factory. Forest-related industries using the wealth of the Adirondacks and their foothills were a staple of the local economy, and remain so today. Several attempts were made to find oil and natural gas in commercial quantity.

Hawkinsville, meanwhile, welcomed William Anderson's Eureka Tannery in 1852, and until its failure in 1880, the community expanded. The manufacture of excelsior was instituted about 1885, using the power of the dam from the old Sterry Hawkins sawmill, and continued until 1966, when the property was purchased for flood control purposed by the Black River Regulating District.

1900-1930

The turn of the century found the newfangled horse-less carriage arriving in Boonville. Samuel Karlen converted his bicycle shop into a kind of garage, which also became Boonville's first car agency. With the popularity of autos came an end to talk of a trolley line from Rome to Boonville, and a need for paved roads. Macadam roads were begun in 1913 from Alder Creek to Boonville, and from Boonville to Talcottville. The pavement was continued into the village to the center of town where a brick road was laid. All major streets were paved with concrete by 1929.

The blacksmith and harness shops were gradually replaced with garages and filling stations.

The telephone came to town with the new century; the first chain store appeared in 1916. Various sand pits were developed. The high school moved, around 1911, to a much-needed structure located at the corner of Post and Ford Streets. The vacated building was remodeled into the Union Specialty Works. A knitting mill, textile mill and fox farm entered the economic picture.

In 1900 there were six hotels in the Village of Boonville, two in Hawkinsville and one in Alder Creek. The Hulbert House, American, Boonville and Park Hotels survive. In 1974 the Headwaters Motel was added.

Electric street lights came about 1898 in the form of a private contract to operate 25 or more 1200-candlepower lights in the village at an annual cost of $47.50 per light. The lights were not to be used on an estimated 110 moon-lit nights of the year, and of course they were usually turned off at midnight, when all "decent citizens" were home in bed. Soon more power was needed and a generating station was built at Denely.

The Cataract Hose Company and the Rescue Hook and Ladder Company served the community well and faithfully, and in 1956 reorganized into the Boonville Fire Company, Inc.

1930-1976

During the great depression of the '30s the price of fluid milk, the backbone of the town's economy, reached a

Key to panorama

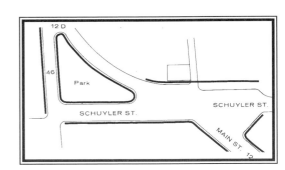

point below the cost of production. In August of 1933 a milk strike was called. The resulting altercation created unhappy headlines and bitter memories. Gradually the economy improved and milk production again became a profitable, if rigorous, means of livelihood.

In 1934 a camp of the Civilian Conservation Corps was established just east of Hawkinsville, projects included: The town's only state park, Pixley Falls in the Boonville Gorge, opened in 1932. In the same year, the turning basin for the unused canal was converted into a swimming pool as a major addition to the facilities of Erwin Park. Seven county forests, a total of 3,604 acres, were reforested in the township. Ski slopes were built in neighboring towns and a grid of snowmobile trails. Sanctioned state championship snowmobile races made winter tourism an important industry.

New businesses started after the depression. Among those in operation today are: Boontex Company, Carlcraft Company, Pulaski Wood Company, Boonville Graphics, Boonville Quarries, Radio Station WBRV (where weather reports are a specialty), Eastern Rock Products, and the Boonville division of Ethan Allen, Inc., the largest industry in the town.

Centralization of the school district became a reality in 1949. The district one-room schoolhouse, which had numbered 18 in 1896, were now closed. In 1966 the Boonville

district combined with the West Leyden and Forestport districts to form Adirondack Central School District, incorporating the largest land area of any district in the state, and a new high school was built.

A memorial block in Erwin Park commemorates the dead of World Wars I and II, as the mounted cannon in the little village park honors the Civil War casualties. The Victorian gingerbread bandstand still presides over the little village park, where weekly band concerts are given during the summer.

A spectacular fire on a bitter cold January night in 1958 destroyed the Comstock Opera House, that home to travelling theatricals, concerts, local meetings, high school graduations, movies and grad balls. Only the combined efforts of six fire companies saved the nearby buildings as the old landmark made its spectacular exit. Another landmark was destroyed in 1963 when the entire 95-year-old Union Block was consumed in a blaze that threatened the whole business section. Heroic work by area fire companies saved the adjacent Hulbert House, but downwind of the blaze the Franjo Theater, which had brought the best of Hollywood to Boonville since 1937, was destroyed.

Since the days of Dr. Samuel Snow's smallpox inoculations, Boonville has been attractive to professional men. As transportation became faster, ambulance service to area hospitals was instituted under the able auspices of the vol-

unteer fire company. An abortive attempt to erect a hospital in the village was thwarted during the depression, and the building was taken over in the 1950s by the General Telephone Company for regional offices. The Sunset Nursing Home, opened in 1964, is one of the largest and best in northern New York. In 1969, a Health Building was erected.

1976-1998

The two decades since America's birthday in 1976 have brought about many changes in the Boonville landscape. Construction of a huge cattle barn on the Mansur farm south of Boonville stirred curiosity, and even caused a bit of international intrigue when it was falsely rumored that the barn was somehow connected to the Shah of Iran's secret police. Eventually, the famed barn burned down, but not before another of almost equal proportion was built next to it. Unwanted fires also did much to change the face of Boonville's Main Street during the 1970's including the loss of: Holcomb's Bakery and Coffee Shop, Hill's Department Store, Hess' Pharmacy, and the Dellerba Block. Today modern buildings and a Memorial Park occupy the sites. The original location of the First National Bank, the Dodge Building, was also a victim to fire, but was given a second chance at life by area businessmen who undertook a careful restoration of the three-story brick structure.

By 1980, the Methodists chose to replace their one hundred year old building with a modern house of worship. Likewise, the Boonville Fire Department razed the old brick fire hall as well as a neighboring residence to make room for a modern facility. Concurrently, Victory Markets expanded by building an expansive Great American Store on land purchased from the Hughes family. While many of Boonville's old buildings were being torn down, a group of local citizens worked together to form the Boonville Historical District which includes eighty commercial and residential buildings. More recently, a campaign spearheaded by BAMA (Boonville Area Merchant's Association) established a down town revitalization program, which includes governments grants for the expressed purpose of preserving Boonville's unique Victorian architecture and pumping up economic opportunities. The project is currently ongoing and entering into phase II. In a further effort to capitalize on the area's rich history, BAMA is working jointly with the Village and town of Boonville Boards for the creation of a Black River Canal museum in the former Civil War barracks adjacent to the canal on lower Main Street.

In May 1983, Boonville was hit by a tornado that caused millions of dollars worth of destruction to the southeastern portion of the village. Many residences were heavily damaged, as well as Erwin Park and the Ethan

Black River Canal Lock #71, and State Shops, 1928.

Allen furniture plant, Boonville's largest employer. Miraculously, no one was seriously injured or killed and the local folks banded together to help the victims through the catastrophe.

Health care for the residents of Boonville and the surrounding area has always been a primary concern. The Adirondack Health Center on Route 12, built through a community effort, was eventually privatized and taken over by St. Luke's Hospital of Utica. The facility was expanded at about the same time that another medical center, The Rome Medical Group, located on Post Street in the former Brooks building was expanded. Sunset Nursing Home has undergone two major expansions to increase the number of people it can serve. The decentralization of mental health facilities led to the construction of a DDSO-ICF facility on South Post Street in 1987. This was followed by the building of three sites to serve United Cerebral Palsy, including a Day Treatment Center on Potato Hill Road and two ICF units, one on Post Street and the other on Pines Road.

Government backed housing for senior citizens also became a reality with the completion of Kortenaer Village in 1979. Within ten years the demand for more units led to an addition that doubled the size of the complex.

Economic progress for Boonville has followed a moderate but steady path. The completion of the Boonville Industrial Park on Potato Hill in the 70s resulted in the relocation of one of Boonville's oldest continuous businesses, Sargent's Chair Factory, CJ Logging and 3 B Saw Mill also took up sites in the park. The logging industry has long been an economic staple for the area and has supported numerous wood related industries: the most recent being the Beal Brothers Custom Wood Works. Boonville's storefronts remain occupied, indicating strong support for retail business. The completion of the Headwaters Plaza shifted some of the business to Boonville's south side and resulted in the appearance of Boonville's first fast food chain.

Progress for Boonville has also produced some controversial projects. The creation of the 765KV power line from Marcy to Massena evoked much public concern and protest. A plan to build a large dam across the Black River produced another public outcry especially in and near the hamlet of Hawkinsville. By 1986 the plan was scraped. The Iroquois Gas Pipeline project that parallels the path of the 765KV power line resulted in numerous fines and financial settlements to communities along the way that experienced damage as a result of its construction.

By 1993, Boonville was embroiled in another controversy which to date remains unresolved. The proposal of the Oneida-Herkimer Solid Waste Authority to build a 104 year landfill in neighboring Ava brought swift and immediate opposition from local citizens. In response to the negative

Black River Canal barge loading sand for Delta Dam Project, 1910 south of village near Rt. 46.

economic and environmental impact such a facility would have on the Ava-Boonville area, an opposition group, Adirondack Communities Advisory League, was formed.

Less controversial projects include the upgrading of the water supply, which now comes from wells located just south of the village along Route 12. The Village of Boonville is currently in the middle of a project to upgrade its sanitary and storm sewers. Along the way many new sidewalks have been completed and municipal parking behind Main Street has been expanded.

Private entities and individual volunteerism have done much to improve the quality of life in Boonville. The creation of Matthew's Place by the cooperation of local churches provides a place for low-income people to obtain necessities at a reasonable rate. The organization also conducts a food bank for those in need. The local Scout Troops annually conduct a food drive in the fall. The two baseball diamonds that comprise the Boonville Sports Complex, have been upgraded and expanded through the efforts of the BAA. Hiking and cross country ski trails that follow the historic Black River Canal were made possible through BREIA.

In 1996, Boonville residents held a dinner to honor the 85th birthday of one of its most famous native sons, author, Walter D. Edmonds. His death in 1998 at the age ninety-five brought to a close an important chapter in Boonville's history. Through his unique and simplistic writing style Edmonds was able to capture the essence of the area's rich heritage in his numerous historical novels.

In 1997, the Woodsmen's Field Days observed their Golden Anniversary. The establishment of their permanent headquarters on Main Street has insured the yearly presence of the hardy woodsmen every August.

A clean environment, low crime rates, inexpensive power, and friendly people are among Boonville's major assets. The number of new roads and streets appearing almost daily and a recent voter approved project to expand buildings in the Adirondack School District provide evidence of the growth that is taking place. Just further proof that Boonville provides the quintessential small town atmosphere ideal for raising a family.

Special thanks to Ron and Jean Ryder, James D. Warren, Roy and Barbara Bird, Carlene Wilbert and Mary G. Blade.

Selected References

Best, Tharatt G., *Boonville and Its Neighbors*, (Willard Press, 1960).

Edmunds, Walter D., *Rome Haul*, (Grossett and Dunlap, 1929).

O'Donnell, Thomas G., *The Sapbush Run,* (Black River Books, 1948).

Ryder, Ron, *The Way It Was,* (Country Books, 1975).

1976-1998 by James S. Pitcher.

Additional References

Boonville Herald.

Bridgewater

By
Janice Jaquish
Town Historian

The Town of Bridgewater is the southernmost one in Oneida County. It is rather small, having an area of 24.4 square miles. The western portion of the town is largely a rugged plateau, rising in places to 1800 feet above sea level. A considerable area of the eastern portion of the town is comprised of a range of hills running north and south, which are about 1500 feet high.

Situated between these two higher areas is an attractive valley, varying in width from over a mile at the north to about one-half mile in the south. This region comprises an area of level, very productive land. It has always been known as Bridgewater Flats.

Geologically the town has a variety of formations. Areas of shale are most evident. Limestone is plentiful, particularly near Babcock Hill. Gravel is common in the north area particularly. Also sandy loam is common, as well as regions mostly of clay soil.

Portions of the town were visited by a Captain Oliver Babcock, in charge of a scouting party during the Revolution. His accounts related after the war in his native Connecticut led to the beginnings of settlements in the town in 1789. About that time a Major James Farwell came to the southern part of what is now the village. Others followed, creating a settlement known as Farwell Hill. The Ives family cleared a farm one mile southwest of the Village of Bridgewater the same year. Others soon took up areas in North Bridgewater and Babcock Hill.

The town began as part of the Township of Sangerfield in what was then Herkimer County. The Town of Bridgewater was taken from Sangerfield in 1797. Community life had begun, as the Masonic Lodge was in being by that time and in 1798 the Congregational Church was organized.

Settlers came rapidly, so that by 1830 the township was divided into holdings of various sizes, mostly farms. It was a trying time with several epidemics of disease and the occasional periods of bad weather.

Schools appeared early here, including before 1830 a Female Seminary and an Academy. The government surveyed the route of the Cherry Valley Turnpike (Route 20) in 1809. This was soon followed by the opening of the road. The effect of this event was the growth of the village in its present location and the passing of the Farwell Hill settlement.

The construction of the Utica to New Berlin plank road soon after made a four-way point at the center of the village where today's Route 20 intersects Route 8. It became a stage coach station with several inns, blacksmith shops, sawmills, stores, and small industries. The roads permitted the shipment of grain, hides, pork, and whiskey. Large droves of cattle and hogs passed through on their way to Utica and Albany.

The high water mark of the town was in the 1830s, with a population of more than 1600. A decline set in with the opening of the Erie and other canals. This decline was increased later by the building of railroads. The spread of manufacturing in factories gradually led to the disappearance of many craft shops. By the outbreak of the Civil War the area's population was down to 1258.

The townspeople were involved in the national issues, particularly slavery. There was a station on the "underground railroad" run by Dr. Trowbridge in the village. He also trained young men as doctors. There were two lawyers here who often had young men reading law in their offices. Debates by local partisans on slavery were frequent, occurring in the Academy and in the Congregational and Universalist Churches.

The generation following 1830 saw the forming of several religious groups here: the Quakers, Baptists, Universalists, Welsh Congregationalists, and Episcopalians.

The Civil War period was a trying one, as the township furnished at least 100 men for the Union forces, of whom 13 or more lost their lives while in service. The town raised money for enlistment bounties and had to pay part of the county funds also used for this purpose. It was a period of wartime prosperity.

Soon thereafter the town had a railroad built through it to Richfield Springs. To facilitate the project the locality sold $50,000 worth of bonds. This railroad became part of the Delaware, Lackawanna and Western system. Another railroad was completed from here to New Berlin in 1893, known as the Unadilla Valley Railroad.

Agriculture has always been the life of the town and has taken several overlapping forms. In the early years some grain was converted into whiskey and some into food for hogs and cattle. Sheep raising soon was quite prevalent. Beginning in the early 1800s and steadily growing was the hop-raising industry. Dairy stock became more numerous by 1850, with butter and cheese for market. This led to cheese factories. One of these in the village was made by converting major Absalom Groves' tannery for that purpose.

Cheese factories operated during spring and summer seasons and were generally shut down in late fall and winter. Later the appearance of the fluid milk market led to pasteurizing plants.

The town celebrated its centennial on July 4, 1889, at the village four corners. The program was typical of the day – speeches, music, and stories by the town's elder. In politics the town stayed close to the Whig-Republican tradition. There have been a few breaks when conditions have allowed a Democrat to get into office, but not often. In pre-Civil War days several men rose to become members of the New York State Legislature. In 1964 Lyndon Johnson carried the town by 100 votes – the only time a Democratic presidential candidate ever did.

The social life of the town was lively, with plenty of music, dancing, and sports. For many years the town fielded good baseball teams, beginning in early 1880. There was a band also. The ladies began a study club in the 1880s, still in existence and known as the Women's Art Club.

In 1897 the Masons celebrated the centennial of the lodge. The next year the Congregational Church did likewise. Soon after 1900 the Masonic order was joined by the Kismet Chapter, O.E.S. A few years later local farmers and their wives founded the Unadilla Valley Grange. It prospered well and erected a building in the village. However, conditions changed and it disappeared in the 1930s. The same fate overtook the Universalist and Episcopal Churches in the same decade.

World War I failed to change the town much. A Homecoming Day was observed on September 1, 1919, with parades, speeches, a ball game, athletic events, topped off with a dance. The 1920s saw changes as the use of electricity became general, the auto became common, and the radio provided entertainment and information. The Florida boom burned some and the stock market crash, others.

The depression period was featured by misery for

many. There was a woodcutting project, a stonecrushing project, and there were a few men in the Civilian Conservation Corps. World War II followed, with approximately 125 area persons seeing military service. Three young men did not return. Quite a few were in service in Korea, one of whom was killed in action.

Over the years the numerous district schools consolidated. In the 1890s the Bridgewater Union School, later known as the high school, came into being. In 1929 a central school district was established and a new school built. It was dedicated in 1932. It was taken into the Mount Markham District in 1969. The building is now a grade school in the larger district.

Local people talk about Bridgewater's most famous son. He was Professor Stephen Moulton Babcock (1743-1931), whose early life was spent in the town. He went on to Tufts, Cornell, and Gottinger, Germany to be educated in chemistry. He spent several years with the New York State Agricultural Experiment Station at Geneva, New York. In 1887 he affiliated with the University of Wisconsin, where he did pioneer experiments in the then developing knowledge of vitamins. More important, in 1890 he discovered a method to determine the butter fat content of milk: the Babcock Test, used since then in all dairy countries. He refused to patent his invention and made no profit from it.

The need for fire protection led in 1914 to the formation of a local fire company. This organization, beginning with little equipment, has steadily grown to become a well equipped force, capable of protecting the town. To better finance it, a tax-supported fire district was established in 1950.

Late in the last century a separate village government was set up for limited purposes: sidewalks, street lighting, and maintaining matter peculiar to the village area. It has separate officers and taxes. The former Grange Hall is now a village property. There have been a number of mayors, with Herbert Palmer and R.J. Wilkinson serving for long periods. The voters have been progressive, electing two women, Lucy Robinson and Mrs. Charles Woodworth trustees, soon after women received the vote. In March 1973, voters elected Everett Holmes their mayor. So far as is known, he was the first black mayor in this state.

Within the last 25 years considerable but not generally recognized changes have come upon the townspeople. The widespread practice in the past of many family-sized dairy farms has largely disappeared. A small number of larger farms operate instead. Large areas of former dairy farms have gone into comparatively few enterprises devoted to crop farming such as grains, beans and potatoes on a large scale.

Beginning about 1965 the generally stable population of the area began to increase. From a figure of roughly 800, which it had been for many years, by 1973 the population increased to about 1260.

The reason for this was the appearance of mobile

Bridgewater Union School

*Congregational Church,
Bridgewater, NY*

homes here in the early 1960s. The town has no zoning regulations as have many nearby towns. Hence, in addition to three local trailer parks, any person with access to a lot can place a trailer on it. Because of a concentration of people in a comparatively small area, sanitation and water supply problems are apt to develop. The existence of considerable amounts of shale and clay under the areas involved can create sanitation problems, as these two substances do not absorb wastes readily.

Also the increased population has come in the area where there is no established water system. It is quite likely that in the not too distant future, outside government agencies will insist upon the creation here of both a water system and sewage disposal plants. The creation of these two projects in a town of this size can bring a very heavy tax burden upon the comparatively small value of local real estate.

Most employment locally has to be obtained in other places, which entails long journeys. The area is more and more a suburb of nearby cities.

This, plus the disappearance of the local school, creates a problem of keeping up local identity. This can be detrimental to the continuance of all voluntary agencies such as the fire company, churches, and the library.

Near the end of the year 1975 the town acquired a building in which to house its offices for officials, town records, a court chamber, and an auditorium to hold elections and public meetings for the citizens.

Bridgewater today remains mostly agricultural. It has some of the most fertile flat lands around. The village has raised many of the old abandoned and fire damaged buildings and they are now being replace with profitable business. The town population is at a slow but steady growth. Codes and zoning were implanted in 1995 with an active Planning Board and Zoning Board of Appeals. The Bridgewater Historical Society was formed in 1992 with the interest centered on gathering and preserving the towns history.

Selected Reference

Owens, Stanley R., editor *Bi-Centennial History, Town of Bridgewater, New York,* (Bridgewater Town Board, 1976).

Cobblestone Hop Kiln on Route 8 north of Bridgewater. During the late 19th century when hops were an important cash crop growers built kilns to dry the hops prior to shipment. Most were frame buildings and this cobblestone version is extremely rare.

Camden

By
Ona Schoville
Town Historian

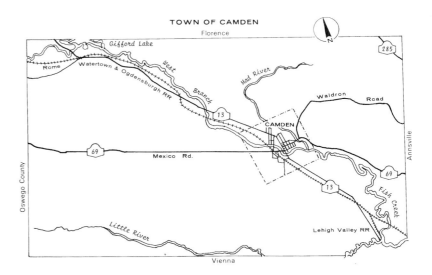

TOWN OF CAMDEN

Camden is often called the "Queen Village" because of its beauty, surrounded by rolling hills, its well-kept streets, lovely homes and progressive industries. It is located near the northwest corner of Oneida County, and is bordered on the south by Little River. The west branch of Fish Creek flows through the town, and unites with Mad River at Camden village.

Camden had its beginning after the Revolutionary War, when plans were made to settle the land west of the Hudson River. In 1791 a company headed by Nicholas and John Roosevelt purchased 500,000 acres of land in central New York, which included most of Oneida and Oswego Counties and part of Herkimer County. Later the Roosevelts sold the land to George Scriba, who was a member of their company, and it became known as Scriba's Patent. Part of Scriba's Patent became the Town of Camden on March 5, 1799. The first town meeting was held in a rough log hut built by Samuel Royce, one of the town's first settlers. The town was briefly known as "Linley," but was given the name of Camden by the Oneida Indian tribe.

Connecticut soldiers who traveled through, or were stationed near this area during the war, observed the possibilities offered by acres of level land, an abundance of rushing streams for water power, and the availability of many kinds of wood for building. Many of the first settlers were those same soldiers returning with their families to establish homes.

Among the first to buy land in Camden was Jesse Curtiss. He built a sawmill on Fish Creek at the Mexico Street Bridge in 1794 or 1795, but did not make a home here until later. The site of his sawmill later housed the Penfield and Stone Gristmill, and most recently, the Case Farm Machinery Dealership operated by Willard Rood. A few years ago, the building was razed and the area is now the jointly owned town and village municipal parking lot.

Judge Henry Williams, for whom Williamstown was named, was Camden's first permanent settler. He and his wife settled at Cook's Crossing, which is now known as Harden Boulevard, around 1797.

Other early settlers were Elihu Curtiss, Benjamin Barnes, Sr., Benjamin Barnes, Jr., Daniel Parke, Seth and Joel Dunbar (for whom Dunbar Road is named), Aaron Mathews, Judge Israel Stoddard, Samuel Royce, Noah Tuttle, Levi Mathews, Thomas Comstock, Philip Barnes, Levi Munson, John Caine, Oliver Cook, Bartholomew Pond, Noah Preston, Amos Mix and Theophilus Whaley.

The first pioneers who settled in Camden chose the strip of land between the west branch of Fish Creek and Mad River to establish the village. It was level yet high enough to prevent flooding. The village was incorporated in 1834.

The first Camden school began in 1800 and was located in what is now the village park. In 1823 a school called the New Academy was held on the south side of the village park. This was followed in 1824 by a school for young ladies and little girls. Next came the Old Academy, which operated at the site of Stoddard's store. The town hall was the site of a private school in 1842 – 1843. In 1844 the town hall provided a place for a normal school. The first high school started operation in 1847 on Union Street and was rebuilt after a fire. The school was expanded in the 1930s to house elementary, junior and senior high schools.

The growing school population and the centralization of outlying school districts into the Camden Central School System (July 1, 1943) soon created the necessity for expanding the school facilities. In 1956 the elementary school, kindergarten through fifth grade, was built at the head of Main Street on the site of the E.H. Conant residence. A large, modern high school, designed by Mr. Lorimer Rich, was built on Oswego Street in 1967. All rural schools have now been abandoned, and most of those which remain standing have become private homes.

The First Church of Christ founded in 1798, was Camden's first church. In 1807 this organization built a log meetinghouse in West Camden. The First Congregational Church of Camden was also organized in 1798. The first meetinghouse was a rough log structure 56 by 44 feet, enclosed but unheated, with rough benches and a temporary pulpit. In 1836, improvements were made in the building; however in 1867, it burned to the ground. At this time several members left the church and formed the Presbyterian Society and built their church where the Mystic Stamp Company is now located. The Congregationalists reconstructed their church, "a new brick edifice costing over $20,000," starting in 1867, on the original site at the corner of Church and Main Streets. The Presbyterians and Congregationalists reunited in 1931, later voted to make the Congregational Church their permanent church home, and continue services there today as the United Church of Camden, Presbyterian.

Camden has had many newspapers over the years, the first being the Camden *Gazette*, published in 1842. This was followed by the Oneida *Mirror* in 1849, the Camden *Freeman* in 1860, the *Monitor* in 1861, the Camden *Journal* in 1864, the Camden *News* in 1866, and the Camden *Advance* in 1873. In 1885 the *Journal* and the *Advance* were consolidated under the name of the *Advance-Journal*. The *Advance-Journal* is still in publication, having been sold in 1973 by the Stone family who

were the original founders. It is now co-owned by the publishers of the *Queen Central News*, which began operation in 1974.

The Camden Library Association was founded in 1891, the library first occupying a room in the B.A. Curtiss block and then in the Opera House block. In 1895 the Association was given the use of a large room in the town hall, which it occupied until 1938. At that time, the present Camden Public Library was built on the corner of Second and Union Streets. In 1963, the Association joined the Mid-York Library System.

Camden's first factories began at the lower part of Third Street, where Fish Creek provided excellent water-power. Among these factories in 1832 was a foundry run by Horace McIntyre and James Barger. Another factory to make use of waterpower of this area was Dana's Sash and Blind Factory, which operated from 1891-1941. Mr. Dana also manufactured china closets and Early American maple bedroom furniture. Waterpower was used in his factory for many years before conversion to electricity.

The Conant Chair Factory began operation in 1851 in the north part of town. The original building still stands and is occupied by Rochester Shoe Tree Company. This company, with its Camden and New Hampshire branches, is the only shoe tree company in the United States and employs approximately 200 people.

The making of wagons and sleighs was always important in Camden. In 1864, C. A. Boehm, a wagon wood-worker, and James Stark, a blacksmith, came from

Old Town Hall built about 1810.

Boonville and purchased a carriage shop on Church Street, next to the town hall. In 1871 Mr. Stark started a shop of his own on Main Street at the present location of Farnsworth Printing. The Boehms carried on their business, making all kinds of horse-drawn vehicles, specializing in travois bobs and cutters until the advent of the automobile gradually put an end to their business. Boehm bobs and cutters were unique in that the runners were so constructed that they did not sink into the snow.

Canning factories were an important part of Camden's early history. McCall Brothers Canning Factory was formed in 1872 on the corner of Waldron and Taberg Roads. L. P. Haviland's canning business was developed from a small business which began in 1866. This plant was located on Westdale Road, and changed hands many times.

In 1883, the Camden Knitting Mill was the parent of a cordon of knitting goods factories that stretched across central New York. The founders and principal owners were W. J. Frisbie and W. H. Stansfield.

J. M. Young & Sons Furniture Factory began operation in 1890. It is now owned and operated by Neil Wright, and is still located in the original building on Masonic Avenue. There is no conveyor production line and the furniture is made in the old-fashioned way from fine, northern hardwoods cut in small farmer-owned sawmills.

Lingenfelder's Moccasin Factory, which began operation in 1916 on Fourth Street, was one of several moccasin factories of this era. It is now a private residence. The Turbine Water Works began operation in 1894 where the

Laribee Machine Shop is now located. The Camden Woodworking Company was organized in 1910 for the purpose of manufacturing turnings, Indian clubs, dowels, tool handles, and a host of other novelty items.

The Camden Wire Company was formed in 1929 to fabricate copper wire and wire products. With four plants in the Camden area it is the principal employer. In the early 1930s the company installed and began use of fine wire drawing equipment. Following a program of specializing in fine wire drawing, the company is able to produce copper wire finer than a human hair – starting from a 5/16" rod. In January 1977, Camden Wire assets were sold to Oneida Limited and growth continued in plant locations and product diversity. Then, in 1997, International Wire Inc. purchased Camden Wire along with similar businesses in Williamstown, NY, and Spargo Wire in Rome, NY. In addition to the Camden Wire Company, the Laribee Wire Company has been engaged in the fabrication of cable and wire products since 1947.

Williams' Stationery Company began operation in 1933 and continues business at its original location on Railroad Street.

The Farnsworth family has owned and operated a printing business in Camden since 1886. At that time, they specialized in the printing of milk tickets. These were coupons bought from a dairy and used as a means of ordering and at the same time paying for home-delivered dairy products. The business has grown over the years, now specializing in the printing of church offering envelopes and

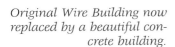
Original Wire Building now replaced by a beautiful concrete building.

Camden Town Hall as completed in 1896 – the building looks the same today without the steeple over the clock. The woodwork and chimneys on the side were removed as they caused serious leaks in the roof.

calendars. In 1947 an offshoot of the printing business was started and named the Farnsworth Envelope Company. It occupies the building on lower Main Street, which was once the Odd Fellows Temple.

The Mystic Stamp Company was begun by Lawrence Shaver when he was a very young man. This company has served stamp collectors all over the world. It had small beginnings in a few rooms over the old post office building. With its growth it has expanded to larger headquarters in the old Presbyterian Church building on Main Street.

Since 1856 nearly all of the business section of Main Street has been burned, some parts more than once. In 1866 a fire on South Park Street consumed a wagon shop, a paint shop and a blacksmith shop. In 1867 fire starting in the Whitney house barns, then located opposite the village park, burned the buildings south and north and east, consuming the Episcopal Church, the Congregational Church and a private residence. In 1876, a fire burned all of the stores from the south corner of Main and Mexico Streets to the present Farnsworth Envelope Company. Later fires consumed the Whitney house east to Second Street and south nearly to Farnsworth's Printing Company. The Penfield Block where Kirch's Hardware now is; the west side of Main Street from the *Advance-Journal* office to the Episcopal Church; the Presbyterian Church; Conant's Chair Factory; a tannery; a knitting mill, were also burned. On a windless 3rd of July night, the Boehm Shop located right next to the firehouse burned. Terrible as these fires were, the end result was that Camden's business district was built and rebuilt and is now more modern than those of many similar towns.

Unique to our area is the Camden Continental Fife and Drum Corps, which began in Taberg as the Taberg Drum Corps. There it was active in Civil War drills and also helped train united for the army. The corps was founded by Alanson White, succeeded as manager by his son, Romain White and grandson Ray A. White, who headed the corps from 1910 until his death in 1973. Under Ray White's leadership the corps was moved to Camden in 1942 and adopted its distinctive American Revolutionary-style uniform. Harold Willson and Jeffrey Waterman became co-owners of the corps in 1973, and in 1975 Waterman became the sole owner. It is the third oldest such group in the United States and is active in many local parades and functions, as well as statewide activities.

Another feature unique to Camden is Forest Park, a tract of woodland covering more than 100 acres, with well-kept roads, footpaths and picnic pavilions established and maintained for the pleasure of area residents. Here full use has been made of nature's resources, rippling streams, tall timber, shady bowers, flowers and ferns, to provide a lovely recreational facility.

The Queen Village Historical Society, incorporated in 1970, is dedicated to stimulating interest in a preserving the heritage of Camden and area landmarks. In the summer of 1975, the first president of the society, Laurence Barker, was instrumental in obtaining a building for the society's use as a public museum. Constructed in the 1860s as a carriage house for the Thomas Stone residence, the structure was moved in 1950 to the present site on North Park Street.

In 1996, three energetic citizens developed a unique recreational facility on Oswego Street, across from the high school, known as Camden Yards. It was the idea of Daniel Yerson, David Gardner, and Daniel Bowman. With the help of community organizations and individuals, a five to six acre space was landscaped and equipped for a variety of outdoor athletic and recreational purposes for young and old. Under the continuing direction of President, Kenneth W. Ferris and Vice President, Kenneth Seymore, the Yards activities include baseball farm teams, tennis, basketball, and league teams form seniors to Little League.

Selected References

Camden *Advance-Journal*, 100th Historical Edition, (May 9, 1974); also issues 1873-1975.

Frisbie, Mrs. W.J. et al., *Camden Pioneer History*, (1896).

Grips, *Historical Souvenir of Camden*, (1903).

Deerfield

Virginia Loin
Town Historian

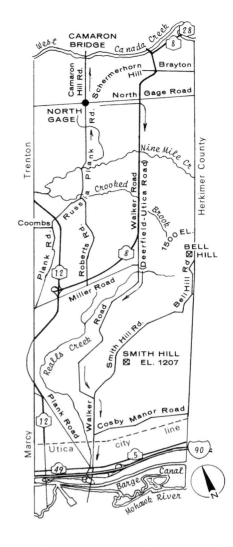

The Town of Deerfield formed in 1798 from land of two Royal grants. The first, known as Cosby's Manor, amounted to 43,000 acres of land acquired by New York Governor William Cosby. It extended three miles on each side of the Mohawk River from present day Frankfort on the east to Yorkville and Maynard Road, Marcy on the west. The second grant occurred in 1769 when King George awarded 18,000 acres to General Thomas Gage, His Majesty's Commander of troops in North America. This grant had frontage of four miles along the west Canada Creek and extended south west approximately eight miles to the northern boundary of Cosby's Manor. Thus land from the Mohawk River to the West Canada Creek joined to become the town of Deerfield. It lies mostly in a high plateau, rising from the Mohawk River to 1500 feet above sea level at Bell Hill. The 1990 Census recorded the Town population of 3,942.

In the spring of 1773 three adventuresome pioneers came from the valley near Herkimer and settled along the north bank of the Mohawk River opposite the fording place. Mark Damuth, Christian Reall and George J. Weaver built log homes and cleared the wilderness land to make a home for their families. The annual spring flood-ing of the Mohawk drove them further north to the area of Deerfield corners where they started rebuilding their settlement. They remained here until the summer of 1776 when the settlement was broken up by a raid of Tories and Indians.

The settlers were warned of this raid by a friendly Oneida Indian named Blue Back who was hunting in the northern end of town. He was approached by the war party and asked questions about the settlement at the Corners. Blue Back was very evasive in his answers and after the hunting party left, he ran through the woods to warn settlers of upcoming danger. The settlers had just enough time to hide their possessions and escape with their families to Stone Arabia, a small fort in what is now Schuyler. The houses and crops were destroyed and the earliest settlement of Deerfield was left in ruins – thus these pioneer's lives were interrupted by one of the great political upheavals of that century – the American Revolution.

After seven long years, peace came to the beautiful and fertile valley and the first settlers returned to their lands with their families and others began to rebuild. About 1785 another group of settlers came to Deerfield from the Mohawk River Valley – Peter Weaver, Nicholas

Weaver, George Damuth, and Nicholas and Philip Harter who all settled in the same "neighborhood."

The first white male child, the son of George M. Weaver, was born in Deerfield on January 15, 1787. The Weavers played important roles in the development of Deerfield and Oneida County. Christian Reall who had his cabin on the bank of Reall's Creek did not stay long and migrated west. Mark Damuth ventured west also to join the Realls.

One of the most important undertakings of these early settlers was the construction of a bridge across the Mohawk in 1792. This bridge was built on a Sunday to get as much help as possible, and was the first official bridge across the Mohawk River anywhere. It was not well engineered, however, and washed away with the first big flood and had to be rebuilt.

Under an Act of the State Legislature, dated March 15, 1798, Oneida County was established and the Town of Deerfield was organized. The first town meeting took place on April 3, 1798 at the home of Ezra Payne. Dr. Francis Guiteau was the first Supervisor and Isaac Breyton, the first Town Clerk. The function and make-up of the town government, today, remains much the same as the Town Boards of earlier years.

In 1803 Timothy Smith, after first settling at Deerfield Corner, moved with his family and settled on Jeam's Hill, later renamed Smith Hill. Pratt Smith, one of the sons of Timothy, stayed in Deerfield and became one of the most prominent and successful farmers in the county.

As more families settled in Deerfield, more roads were needed. Local roads were constructed by the town government. Private companies developed plank roads and turnpikes, such as the Northern Plank Road to Remsen and the Schenectady Turnpike (Herkimer Road), making travel throughout the town much easier.

One of the first turnpike tollgates was located in the area that today is McDonalds on North Genesee Street. It was built about 1840, about the same time that the road commission was created. Other tollgates in Deerfield were located on Crooked Brook Road, the Russia Plank Road and the Trenton Road.

The tollgate was put up as a means of paying for the improvement of the highway. For example, from Deerfield Corners to Utica, history declares this road to have been one of the worst stretches of highway between Albany and the west. The average receipts were over $5 per day which would bring its income close to $2,000 per year. From this came the gate keeper's pay, the interest on the loan, the cost of maintaining the road and making improvements from time to time, and incidental expenses. One of the curious features of the tollgate was the sign at the top, across the road. It notified drivers that any attempt to pass without paying was cause to be fined $25.

The toll rates were well known to those who passed constantly. They were fixed by law, as follows: for every vehicle drawn by two horses, mules, oxen or cattle, 3

Accessor reviewing all property in Deerfield, 1898.

Oneida Historical Society

House on Cosby Manor Road in 1898, that was a stop on the Underground Railroad.

cents: for an additional horse, mule or cattle, 6 cents, etc. The gate was torn down in 1910 after the county bought the road and the little tollhouse was carted away to serve out its old age as somebody's chicken coop.

Vegetable farming was a very profitable industry in the southern part of Deerfield, providing fresh produce to customers in the city. Most of this farming was done on the farms of Weaver, Clapp, Smith, Burton, Marsh, Coventry and Wells located in the area of Herkimer Road, Trenton Road, Walker Road and Cosby Manor Road.

While the southern part of town was being settled, there was much activity in the "northern" part along the West Canada Creek and at North Gage. Early settlers in this area might have come up the West Canada Creek or traveled the Steuben Road. Jacob Schermerhorn built the first frame house in Deerfield on what is now Schermerhorn Hill. There was a tannery-shoe shop (Schermerhorn), a sawmill on Nine Mile Creek (Hetherington) and witch hazel production at North Gate Corners. Agriculture was a mainstay of the early settlers in this area with cheesemaking becoming a profitable way of preserving milk for marketing. Many cheese factories existed in the area but unfortunately none were preserved. A post office was established at North Gage in 1831 and continued until 1903.

The Camaron Hill Bridge, a covered bridge which spanned the West Canada Creek, was constructed in 1803 at the foot of Camaron Hill on land donated by the Camaron family. Troops serving in the War of 1812 tramped over this bridge to Military Road and then on to Sackett's Harbor. The bridge was deemed unsafe in 1937 and was burned by agreement of officials from Oneida and Herkimer County. Old timbers can still be seen near the unpaved extension of Camaron Hill Road.

In the early to mid-1800's a settlement existed in the Deerfield ravine known as Brown's Gulf or Mechanicsville. The village was situated on a shelf several hundred feet above Realls Creek which provided the water for about a dozen industries, a grist mill, distillery, tavern, sawmill, and cooper shop among others. The village had disappeared by the turn of the century. Nothing was left and the question is still asked, "what happened to this settlement?" Could it have been the typhoid or cholera epidemic? Was there a flood that washed everything away?

In 1838 land was donated for a Catholic church on Bell Hill. People came on foot, horseback and carriages from as far away as Fairfield and Norway, Schuyler, Newport and Marcy to worship here. This church, The Church of the Holy Cross, served its congregation of about 500 people until 1868 when the Mass was said for the last time. St. Peter's Roman Catholic Church was organized and built in 1872, at Deerfield Corners, shortly after the closing of the church on Bell Hill.

In 1798 the Second Baptist Society was formed and the Baptist Church was later erected, which is now the

Camaron Bridge spanned the West Canada Creek from Deerfield to Russia from about 1803 to 1937.

Town of Deerfield Municipal Building.

New York State Register of Historic Place. The Episcopal Church was organized as a Union Sabbath School and services begun in 1874 with the congregation meeting just north of the Corners.

Early North Gage residents maintained religious practices by meeting in nearby homes or outdoors before the Presbyterian and Baptist Society of Deerfield was organized. Under the direction of Presbyterian officials from Utica, a Union Church was established with Deacon Duncan Blue as the first elder. In 1859 the church was razed and a larger building was built. The North Gage Excelsior Literary Society purchased as bell from the church in 1878. The bell which weighed 393 pounds was shipped to Trenton and then brought by wagon to the church. The Old Home Day Society was officially founded in 1927 with mention in the minutes that the celebration of Old Home Days went back to 1916. Each year on the third Sunday of August the Society hosts the Annual Meeting with a service and covered dish luncheon.

Gravestones in the cemetery adjacent to the church bear the names identified with the northern area of Deerfield – names such as Blue, Schermerhorn, Cox, Donnafield, Cameron, McKay, Fishbech, Dewey, Coffin, Johnson, Brayton, Walker, among others. Washington Payne, born a slave, is buried on the Matteson plot. Legend tells us that he saved the life of Rev. Matteson in the Civil War.

The first school in Deerfield was a log cabin erected in 1807 at North Gage on Schermerhorn property. Aaron Reed was the first teacher. By 1865 there were eleven school districts employing eleven teacher. These one-room schools served 745 pupils and the total budget was about $2,693. Today all schools are centralized with the Whitesboro and Poland Central School System. Deerfield Elementary School is currently the only operating school in the Town.

The settlement at Deerfield Corners was prospering when the Deerfield Post Office was established in 1855. Many businesses existed in the area from the Corners to the north side of the Mohawk River. Brick manufacturing thrived with as many as seven brick yards operating at one time. Jesse Auert had a general store and operated the Union Hotel at the Corners. There was a varnish factory, slaughterhouse, florist, wagon shop, a freight company and numerous other small businesses and professional offices.

In 1891 Utica annexed from Deerfield a small section on both sides of North Genesee Street to the new site of the Mohawk River which had been moved about a mile northward to provide for the location of the New York Central Railroad tracks. On May 9, 1916 Utica annexed the southern portion of Deerfield, including all of what is now North Utica. Deerfield lost its four-corners as well as its business district and lost a combined population of

Snowbanks in the Deerfield Hills in the 1930's.

North Gage Post Office and General Store, 1898.

1700 people in the two annexations. Residents thought they would be better off, receiving police protection, electric lights and school support from the city. The Deerfield Town Board opposed the annexation.

The first volunteer fire company was organized about 1890. Peter Schilz, a volunteer, built a firehouse to serve both the fire company and to serve as a Town Hall. This building and the volunteer organization, was included in the later annexation. In 1949, the present Deerfield Volunteer Fire Company was established. The Deerfield Fire District #1 was established in 1952. The Fire Company currently operates out of two firehouses; on Roberts Road and on Trenton Road.

Prominent residents of Deerfield included Dr. Alexander Coventry, a Scottish immigrant who owned a farm on Walker Road in Deerfield. The brick house has remained in the Coventry family of the Hughes family since its construction. Dr. Coventry was instrumental in the establishment of the Oneida County Medial Society and the Agricultural Society and was a prominent leader in the community. Pratt Smith was a prosperous farmer and landowner on Cosby Manor Road and his residence is now a bed and breakfast.

Horatio Seymour, "The Sage of Deerfield," lived on his farm estate called "Marysland" on a hill overlooking Utica, now part of the site of the SUNY Institute of Technology. He was Mayor of Utica, twice governor of New York State, ran for President of the United States and lost to Ulysses S. Grant in 1860. He was a gentle man as well as a prominent politician.

Today, Deerfield is a quiet "bedroom" community with many housing developments, many civic and social organizations, and several park and recreation facilities (Wilderness Park being the largest.) WKTV and WUTR television stations are located on top of Smith Hill and the Fleet Bank Operations Center is located along the west side of Horatio Corridor along with numerous businesses along the east side of the corridor. Businesses are also located along the West Canada Creek and Trenton Road.

Deerfield is a town that is special to its residents, encompassing the energy of its suburban community and the serenity of its countryside.

Source

Loin, Virginia C., *Deerfield, NY: A Glimpse into the Past,* Utica, 1998.

Historic North Gage Church.

Photo by Vennaro

"Raising the Flag" at a back road school, 1916.

Courtesy Alan Keyes

*Methodist Church, Florence, about 1900.
The bell was moved from the Baptist
Church about 1885. Still active.*

Florence Historical Society

*St. Mary's Roman Catholic Church, Florence,
about 1900, originally the Baptist seminary.*

Florence Historical Society

Florence

By
Gertrude Dillon

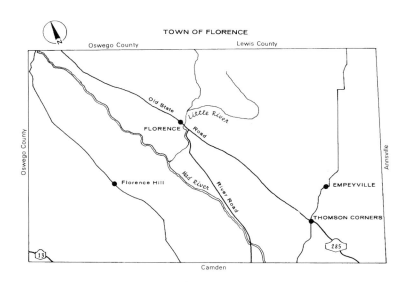

TOWN OF FLORENCE

The Town of Florence covers 33,473 acres in the northwest corner of Oneida County. By legislative act on February 16, 1805, the political town was formed from a part of Camden. The boundaries coincided with those of the survey town of Florence, which included the fourth and part of the third townships of Scriba's Patent. It was the only town in Oneida County which retained the name of the original survey town.

In 1819 Gerrit Smith of Peterboro, New York, purchased 17,560.50 acres in the Town of Florence from William Henderson. To promote the development of the Town of Florence, Smith hired land agents, who sold the land for him at $4.50 an acre. Gerrit Smith was known for his advocacy of the abolition of slavery. He was a close friend of John Brown of Harper's Ferry fame. With Cornelius Vanderbilt and Horace Greeley, he signed the bail bond for Jefferson Davis after his arrest at the end of the Civil War. In 1852 he was elected to Congress on an Independent ticket. He was a candidate for President in 1848.

The earliest settlers were people of English ancestry who came from the New England states. In the 1830s there was an influx of Irish who had heard of the sale of land at a low price, or had friends or relatives who had settled there. Some of them had worked on the Erie Canal, and some continued to work on the canal during the summer to earn enough to pay for their land. A log cabin was usually built in which the family lived until the land could be cleared, crops planted, and until they could afford to build a house.

Four settlements developed: Florence, Florence Hill, Thomson Corners and Empeyville. Roads were built as the need arose and as land in remote sections was settled.

Churches and schools were among the primary concerns of these people. Rural schools were built throughout the town. The school district number ranged to 20.

In 1943 the Florence schools were centralized in the Camden Central School District. The village school was operated under the centralized district until 1967. The building was purchased by the Florence Methodist Church in 1974.

Two churches remain active in the town, both in the village of Florence, and use the original buildings. The Florence Methodist Church was organized sometime before 1833. In 1833-34 a building was constructed on the River Road a short distance from the Old State Road. The land was sold to the society by Mrs. Polly Storms for $1. It is believed from tradition that construction was done by the members of the congregation with lumber from local wood lots. The bell on the Methodist Church, which still summons the congregation to worship service on Sunday, was moved from the Baptist Church building about 1885.

St. Mary's Catholic Church was founded as a parish in September 1845, by Bishop Hughes of New York City. The parish boundaries included the towns of Annsville, Camden, Taberg, Osceola, Redfield, Williamstown, North Bay, Black Creek (Cleveland), and Constantia. Father Kelliher, the first pastor, organized them into mission units, celebrated mass and instructed them in their homes as he traveled among them. The parish now consists of residents of the Towns of Florence and Osceola.

The Catholic Church building was built in 1833-34 by the Rev. Daniel Hascall, a Baptist minister. Hascall was one of the leaders in the founding of the Baptist Educational Society of New York and the Hamilton Literary and Theological Seminary, which later became Colgate University. Hascall planned a seminary in Florence for young men interested in the Baptist ministry, and others of good character. He planned to have a farm in conjunction with the school, which would afford students an opportunity to work to earn part of their expenses.

The building was built of native stone from a quarry

153

on Little River near the site. Land for the school was purchased from Gerrit Smith for $1075. Smith agreed to give a financial donation toward the construction of the school.

The Baptist Society agreed to help finance the school, but later changed their minds. Hascall attempted to continue by himself but in 1838 he admitted failure and the building reverted to Smith. In 1845 the seminary building and grounds were purchased by the Catholics of Florence.

Other church organizations were formed which have been discontinued. In 1823, a Baptist church building was constructed in the center of the village of Florence. This was built by the members of the congregation from local stone and lumber. This was also built with assistance from Gerrit Smith. In a letter of March 8, 1824 Smith wrote from Peterboro:

"I will contribute in cost, two hundred dollars and fifty acres of land, in one of my lots adjoining the Village Reserve. You may further take from my quarry and from my forests all the stone and timber, excepting spruce and pine, that will be needed for the building. Your house in this case is to have a steeple, and it is to be as large and as good, in all respects, as the Baptist meeting house in this village… I will also add to my donation a proper site for the building."

In 1839 the town began to use the basement of the Baptist Church to conduct town business. In 1888 the town purchased the building. It is still used as the town hall. In June 1976 the town authorized the Town of Florence Historical Society to establish a local historical museum on the main floor for a trial period of one year.

The population increased in the Town of Florence to a peak of 2,802 in 1860, then began to decline.

Industries which developed were those which served the needs of the residents, such as blacksmith shops, asheries, tanneries, sawmills, harness shops, cobblers shops, gristmills, cheese factories, etc. There were also several hotels, general stores, a drugstore, and a box and casket factory. As the need for these services diminished, the businesses went out of existence. During a period of time in the 19th century professional services were offered by two doctors, a dentist, and a lawyer.

A post office was located at Thomson Corners until April 1863, when it was moved to Empeyville where it was still located in 1878. There is no available record of the date this office was discontinued.

A post office in the village of Florence was closed in 1953 and mail service since that time has been by the post office in Camden.

During the last several years many farms have been sold to the State of New York. In 1973 tax records showed over 11,000 acres had reverted to state ownership.

A large stone arch bridge built of local stone without

Florence-Osceola stage in front of Orr's store about 1900.   Florence Historical Society

mortar crosses Little River at the edge of the village of Florence on the River Road. No records are available on the date of construction or by whom it was built. The road over the bridge leads to the Graves Cemetery at the top of the hill across Little River. Stones in the cemetery bear dates from the late 1800s and early 1900s.

Florence is one of the core towns of the Tug Hill area. The Tug Hill area is approximately 40 miles wide by 50 miles long and contains some 1,285,000 acres. The region includes 39 towns in parts of Jefferson, Lewis, Oneida and Oswego Counties, and a population of about 81,500. Forests cover much of the area.

Florence is one of nine towns which got together in June 1974 to organize a joint planning program to try and protect this area.

A commission called the Temporary State Commission on Tug Hill was formed to recommend ways to preserve this area. Their recommendations were in part: prepare a land use capability and development plan, including implementing programs and controls, for the Tug Hill region; design the planning program to consider resources of regional and state interest, such as the watershed, forests, agricultural lands and unique gorges; and be consistent across town and county boundaries. At the same time, use a process that will make it possible to build the plans from the town level up rather than the state level down.

Further the commission's report mentions a proposed reservoir in the Town of Florence.

The City of Oneida diverts approximately 3.5 million gallons of water per day from the Florence Creek tributary of Fish Creek and is planning an additional reservoir in the Town of Florence.

The proposed impounding reservoir will be on Florence Creek four miles upstream from the present reservoir located in the Town of Annsville. The water is carried from this reservoir through 24-miles of 20-inch pipe to the City of Oneida.

Selected References

Franklin, David, *From The Cradle to the Grave*, unpublished recollections about Florence.

Riley, The Rev. Thomas M., *Florence in History*, unpublished.

The Tug Hill Region: Preparing for the Future, Report of the Temporary State Commission on Tug Hill, 1976.

Florence Historical Society

Little River stone arch bridge leads from the River Road to Graves Cemetery.

Originally built as a Baptist Church in 1819, this structure has been the town hall since 1880. Photo about 1900.

*Floyd Fire Department
harvesting ice about 1960
to use during the
summer field days.*

The Camroden School which was kitty corner from the church.

Floyd

By
Edwin C. Evans
Town Historian

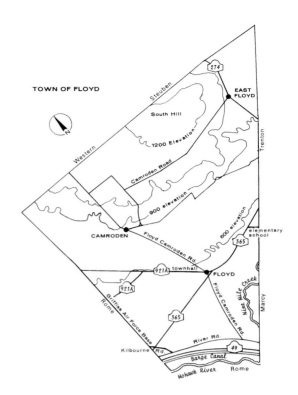

The Nine Mile Creek and the Mohawk River, two known Indian waterways, were probably major contributing factors to the early settlement of the Town of Floyd. Veterans of the Revolutionary War and their families were the original settlers in the area, Captain Benjamin Pike of Massachusetts being the first. Having made his way up the "Te-ya-nun-soke," the Indian name for the Nine Mile Creek meaning a beech tree standing, he settled on the bank of the creek in an area called the Punch Bowl in the year 1790.

Shortly after, from Connecticut, came the famous Moulton boys, a rugged family of revolutionists headed by Stephan Moulton Jr. and including Major Salmon Moulton, Joseph, Benjamin, Linus, Ebenezer and Colonel Stephan Moulton Sr. Colonel Stephan Moulton Sr. had distinguished himself by equipping a Continental regiment at his own expense and contributing heavily towards the cost of the new American government.

The early settlers formed a village in the Punch Bowl where the first sawmill was erected. During these early days, the pioneers in the Punch Bowl faced many hardships. The forests were infested with panthers, wildcat, bear and huge packs of timber wolves. Legends have been passed down of the howling packs of wolves as pioneers trod the moonlit Indian trails along the Te-ya-nun-soke. At this time, the Indians were still fishing and traveling the creek and hunting the hills, and it was not unusual for the residents of the Punch Bowl village to observe their canoes.

In a short time, the frontier spread to the Corners, now Floyd village. Soon afterward, a man named Thomas Bacon was the first to settle on the higher plateaus, and for

some time the hilly area was known as Bacon's Hill. Another portion of the town, the southwest section, was pioneered by the early settlers near Kilbourne Road, and was called Red Hook.

The Town of Floyd, comprising 20,650 acres , was the sixth town in the county to organize. The first town meeting on March 4, 1796, at the home of Samuel J. Curtis, elected Colonel Stephan Moulton Sr. as supervisor, and Moses Coffeen, town clerk. The name Floyd was chosen to honor the statesman and signer of the Declaration of Independence, Major General William Floyd. This seems to have been the result of his interests in the town, its citizens and his warm relationship with the veterans.

Several town officers rose to prominent positions in the state. Mr. Abel French, supervisor 1798-99, was elected to New York State's first assembly, serving from 1798 through 1803. Jarvis Pike, son of Captain Pike, and supervisor from 1800 until 1811, became Judge of the Court of Common Pleas in 1808. Another veteran and early settler, Captain Nathan Townsend, following three terms as supervisor, served a term in the state assembly in 1813. As further evidence of its participation in early government affairs. Floyd contributed heavily in manpower during the War of 1812.

Perhaps the most colorful of all early town legislators was Colonel David Moulton, grandson of Stephan, who served 22 terms as supervisor, was county sheriff, state assemblyman, and a delegate to the Democratic National Convention. He was instrumental in the nomination of Franklin Pierce, who subsequently became President. Being a wealthy gentleman, Moulton took a firm hand in Democratic politics and soon became known throughout

Upstate New York as King David. His adamant adherence to his party led to a Democratic monopoly in Floyd for some 50 years. Being a huge, powerful man, he did not hesitate to resolve any dispute through the decisiveness of a wrestling match.

By 1845 Floyd had become an affluent, society-minded, prestigious community with a population of 1592, ranking third in the county in the number of students attending colleges and universities. Shortly thereafter, however, during the development of plank roads, canals, and railroads, Floyd's importance declined. All means of heavy travel and transport circumvented the township and the population shifted to areas of industry where work was obtainable. Floyd became a victim of progress, where only agriculture and very small industry survived. By 1865, the population dropped to 1227.

In the period from 1810-1830, the original townsfolk were of "Yankee" stock. The first "wave" of foreign settlers all came from Wales. They spoke a strange, complex language, Cymrag – or Welsh.

Geographically, Floyd is divided into the lowlands, and the hill. Since the Yankee population was concentrated in the lowlands, the barren, sparsely populated hill area was selected by the Welsh, in that it resembled their native Wales, and at the same time afforded them the opportunity to clan together. As a result, a peculiar situation, politically and population-wise emerged, playing a significant part in town history and growth. The hill, consisting almost entirely of Welsh-speaking citizenry, developed into an industrious, clannish, conservative and Republican community, the heart of which was located at Camroden Corners. This area in the early days was called by the Welsh "Cymmrodorion" which translated means Welsh comrades. Through the years the name was anglicized and shortened to Camroden. By 1872 Camroden was a village with a post office and tannery employing over 40 people. The hill became a powerful factor in town elections and its characteristic Republicanism proved a match for Democratic lowlands. To this day, no longer Welsh nor clannish nor Republican, it is still keenly observed by the aspiring politician.

In times preceding the Civil War, Floyd was selected by many abolitionist organizations in Oneida County as a center for anti-slavery teachings. Meetings were held in some of the churches, as well as in the form of outdoor rallies to promote the movement. In response, there were several pro-slavery gangs and organizations in the county that would journey to Floyd to confront the abolitionists, resulting in bloody fights and verbal confrontations.

The anti-slavery people won out and when the Civil War finally broke out, many men from Floyd answered the call, at least 10 of them dying in the line of duty.

By the 1900-1930 period, practically all forms of industry, save agriculture and cheesemaking, ceased to exist. The cooper and wagon shop at Floyd Corners, the tannery at Camroden, the sawmill and the old hotel at Floyd were in their last days. The decline in population also led to the decline in active churches. The Union Church of Floyd Corners, the Baptist Society on the hill, the Welsh Congregational Church at Camroden, and the

Floyd Corners about 1900; left to right: blacksmith shop, store, residence, Floyd Hotel.

Edwin C. Evans

Methodist Church at Floyd Corners and the Camroden Presbyterian Church.

This period saw the telephone lines coming to the town, the first being constructed at Floyd Corners in 1905. Inasmuch as the line did not serve Camroden and the hill, Griff W. Jones, Charles Evans, Hugh Roberts, Ellis D. Jones and others, built a private line using hemlock poles. This enthusiastic enterprise thus became known as "the hemlock line."

The town board had not yet found itself a permanent meeting place, the common practice being to meet at the town clerk's home. The first proposal for a town hall was made at the March meeting of 1898. J. Barker's store was rented for one year. Subsequently, for several years various halls or stores were rented on a yearly basis. From 1935 until 1940, most meeting were at the Grange Hall and in 1940 the present hall was constructed as a combination town hall and garage.

Since the early days, there were mostly one-room type of schoolhouses in the town, and by mid-1930 there were only seven of these in session. These were all closed in the late 1930s as a result of centralization with Holland Patent and Oriskany districts. The last to close was the large two-room school at Floyd Corners in December of 1945. Following that there were no school buildings within the township until 1960, when the Holland Patent District constructed a new elementary building at the corner of Route 365 and Mill Street, naming it Stittville Elementary School. In the spring of 1975, the Floyd town board and other civic organizations petitioned to rename the building

in honor of General Floyd. A compromise name was agreed upon: the General William Floyd Elementary School at Stittville.

The construction of Griffiss Air Force Base caused further isolation of the township, eliminating the direct state highway route from Rome through Floyd to points north. In 1949, a new gateway to the north through Floyd was constructed in the form of Route 365 north. The new highway opened the town for development, contributing heavily to a new surge in population.

In 1934 the town board created a fire district. By 1960, meetings and hearings for the contemplation of a town fire department generated enthusiasm and controversy. Several of the citizens spoke for consolidation with the Stittville Department, while many others favored a single Floyd Fire Department. The latter group won out and the opposition joined forces with them. In a short time a new building was constructed and equipment was purchased, almost exclusively through the efforts of volunteer labor. The Floyd Fire Department went into active service in 1962.

Churches in town again became active in the 1960s. The Camroden Presbyterian Church added a parish room. The Floyd Methodist Church outgrew the old building (which still stands) and constructed a beautiful new church in 1969. In 1968, the Grace Baptist Church of Rome established a mission in Floyd, which rapidly evolved to full church status by 1969. The congregation undertook the construction of a church in 1972, and under the able guidance of the Rev. Darrell Coble, a volunteer work force completed the project in 1973. The Floyd Baptist Church

Edwin C. Evans

General store, Floyd Corners.

Blacksmith shop.

parish house located across the road from Colonel Stephan Moulton's homestead.

In 1965 the town purchased several acres of land from the Frank Sampson farm, across Camroden Road from the town hall. In 1969 a new town highway garage was constructed on that site, and in 1970 and 1974 the present town hall was remodeled and expanded.

In 1975 funds were provided for a new town park, located on the hill overlooking the highway garage on Camroden Road. The park, some 12 acres was completed following the hauling of some 3000-odd loads of fill dirt which was needed to bring the site to proper grade. A picnic area, recreation area, and ball fields were added for the completion of the project.

In the early 1950's, the United States Air Force purchased some 47 acres of land located on lower Koenig Road for the construction of a test site for various radar and related experimentation. The site was officially named A F Floyd Annex. On August 12, 1960, the historic first intercontinental voice message by satellite, originating in Trinidad, was received by Air Force scientists at the site. In 1982, the Air Force deeded the property over the U.S. Army at Fort Drum.

Due to declining attendance in the early 1990's, the historic old Camroden Presbyterian Church was teetering on the edge of oblivion. Town historian Edwin Evans and Mr. Robert Henry, suggested that the Town of Floyd might be interested in the building. The Floyd Town Board met with the small congregation and it was agreed that the building should be preserved for historical purposes – resulting in the formation of the Floyd Historical Society. The land and buildings were sold to the town of Floyd for one dollar. The church donated $5000.00 to the Historical Society. The church proper and the adjoining parish hall were in excellent repair and are used for exhibits, meetings and for storing town records.

In 1984 it was discovered that some water wells in Floyd, located near Griffiss Air Force Base were contaminated. Following positive proof that the contamination was caused by certain operations at Griffiss, the Air Force agreed to fund public water to a portion of the Town of Floyd. The City of Rome supplied the water extensions and "city water" first flowed to a total of 672 taps in Floyd, along with several hydrants in 1991. The residents of Charles and Davis Roads (referred to as "Area B") agreed to pay all expenses for expanding the water lines into their area, and this was also completed in 1991.

For years there had been discussions about the erection of a memorial to the Revolutionary War veterans who

Major Salmon Moulton, son of Lt. Col. Stephen Moulton Sr., had been captured by the British during the Revolutionary War and imprisoned.

came to settle in Floyd as well as to all of Floyd's sons and daughters who served in the many wars of the past. In 1991, historian Edwin C. Evans formed a committee to explore the concept. The bulk of the funds needed were provided by New York State Department of Parks, Recreation and Historical Preservation. The balance required was approved by the Town Board and subscribed by private donation and the Floyd Volunteer Fire Department. The monument became known as the "Lieutenant Colonel Stephan Moulton Memorial", honoring Floyd's first supervisor and Revolutionary War leader.

The project was completed in 1996 – the bicentennial year of Floyd's formation. It was decided to use the memorial as a focal point for the bicentennial celebration. Elaborate ceremonies included a parade, the presence of Moulton family descendants, several state and county governmental dignitaries and veteran organization and firefighter organization representatives. Among the some 500 people in attendance were members of families of those veterans who gave their lives in WW2 and the Vietnam War, as well as other veteran's families.

From the beginning, Floyd always seemed to have more than its share of romantic legends. One of these is a true tale of a very famous "dance hall" which existed at Floyd Corners. Known far and wide for its rowdiness, Saturday night fist-fights and strip dancers, the owner would at times pull a $50 dollar bill from the bar room cash register and offer it to any man in the house who could lick him. The dance hall soon became not only a topic of area conversation, but was very irritating to the towns people who viewed the situation as disgraceful.

Town officials tried to persuade the owner to change things. Petitions were circulated and signed. Then in 1937 the first town ordnance of any significance was written into law. Known as the "Dance Hall Ordnance" it passed on February 15, 1937. It generally outlawed prostitution, gambling, marathon dancing, or any "suggestive, immoral, unrefined, or vulgar dancing in any public place in Floyd". (This law is still on the books today.) Even this failed to slow the action at the dance hall.

Soon an event transpired that caught the proprietor's attention. On an evening when the dance hall was in full swing; on a hill some few hundred feet behind the hall, a fiery 20 foot cross was burned to the quiet dismay of all the patrons. Although there was no known Ku Klux Klan operation in Floyd, it was a warning that such behavior would not be tolerated. Soon after, the dance hall closed, the owners moved away, and the old hall building is long gone.

Steuben: Depicts Baron Von Steuben's log home and his grave monument located on the land that he was given as payment for his invaluable training of Washington's troops during the Revolution.

Trenton: Depicts the magnificent falls that were, at one time, on the visiting schedule of all foreign tourists to America in the late 1800's, and rivaled Niagara in attendance.

Vienna: Depicts the quaint little settlements along the north shore of beautiful Oneida Lake, and some of the early watercraft that plied these waters.

Whitestown: Depicts the historic town hall, which was used as the first courthouse in upstate New York. It was the seat of government for all the area of "wilderness" west of Albany.

Paris: Depicts the restored Episcopal Church at Paris Green that sits at the edge of the commons.

Bridgewater: Depicts the four corners on the Great Western Turnpike with its hotels, stores and one of the first Masonic Lodges in the early settlements.

Sangerfield: Depicts the hop business, which dominated farm production of this area for about 40 years. The world price of hops was set every morning at the hop market in Waterville.

Augusta: Depicts the restored Historical Society building facing the village park, which was formerly the location of the Chenango Canal and its towpath.

Marshall: Depicts the home of the Deans who were among the first settlers to the township. This still stands near the four corners of Deansboro.

Fort Stanwix (Rome): Depicts the siege of the fort by St. Leger's army of British and Canadian Regulars; Joseph Brant's Mohawk Indians, and Walter Butler's Greens. This siege led to the Battle of Oriskany as General Herkimer and the local militia tried to relieve the Fort.

Sherrill: Depicts an early Oneida community factory and the community members. Note the pantaloons worn by the women.

Vernon: Depicts the "stone store", a landmark on Main Street.

Verona: Depicts an Erie Canal packet boat and mules on the towpath. All the small communities in the township were heavily involved with service to the canal and its activities.

Westmoreland: Depicts the four corners and early water mill activity. The bell from the original town hall and firehouse is on display in the park next to the present town hall.

Kirkland: Depicts the restored library for the township located on College Street in Clinton.

Ava: Depicts the hardworking snowplows and crews that keep the roads open through unusually deep snow that the township receives annually.

Lee: Depicts the new town hall built in a very tasteful traditional style of architecture.

Florence: Depicts the town hall, built in 1824. It has been restored and is in use today.

Camden: Depicts the village hall and the commons in the center of town. Also shown are the gazebo and Christmas lights of the season.

Annsville: Depicts the original fife and drum corps that is now the celebrated Camden Fife and Drum Corps. Behind the corps is the original town hall.

The Canal Lock "Combines": Depicts the multiple lift locks found on the Black River Canal, the Erie, the Inland Navigation and Chenango Canals.

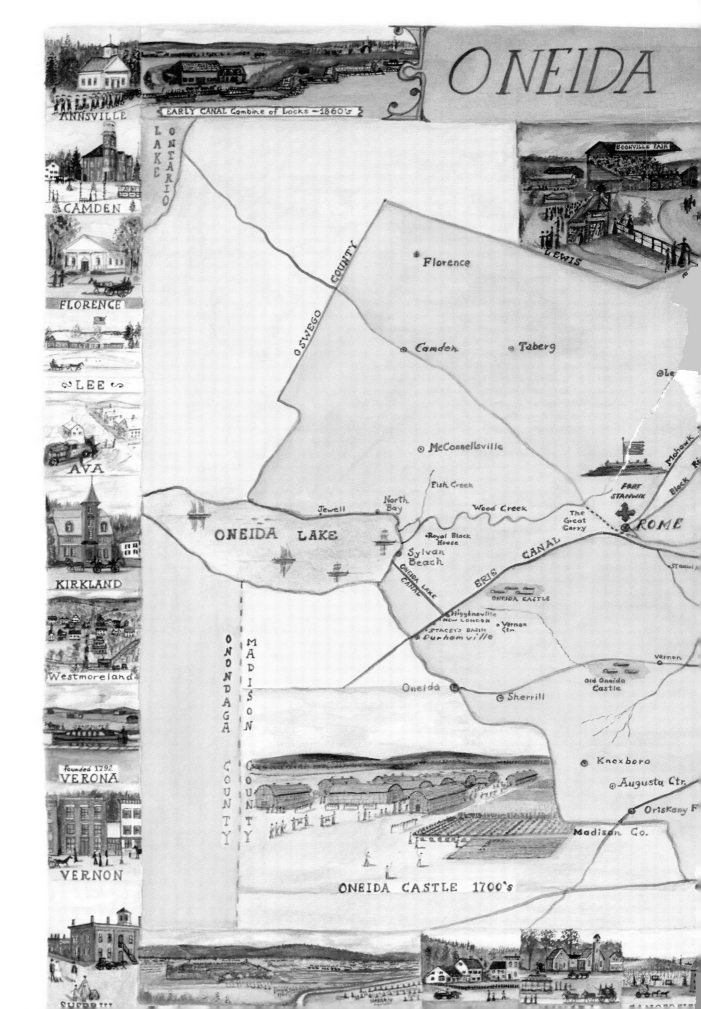

ONEIDA

ANNSVILLE

CAMDEN

FLORENCE

LEE

AVA

KIRKLAND

Westmoreland

Founded 1792
VERONA

VERNON

EARLY CANAL Combine of Locks – 1860's

BOONVILLE FAIR

LEWIS

LAKE ONTARIO

OSWEGO COUNTY

Florence

Camden   Taberg

@Le

McConnellsville

Fish Creek

Jewell   North Bay   Wood Creek   The Great Carry

ONEIDA LAKE   ERIE CANAL   ROME

Royal Black House

Sylvan Beach

ONEIDA LAKE CANAL

ONEIDA CASTLE

FORT STANWIX   Mohawk   Black Ri

St Stan

Higginsville
NEW LONDON
STACEY'S BASIN   Vernon Ctr.
Durhamville   Vernon

ONONDAGA COUNTY

MADISON COUNTY

Oneida   Sherrill

Old Oneida Castle

Knoxboro

Augusta Ctr.

Oriskany F

Madison Co.

ONEIDA CASTLE 1700's

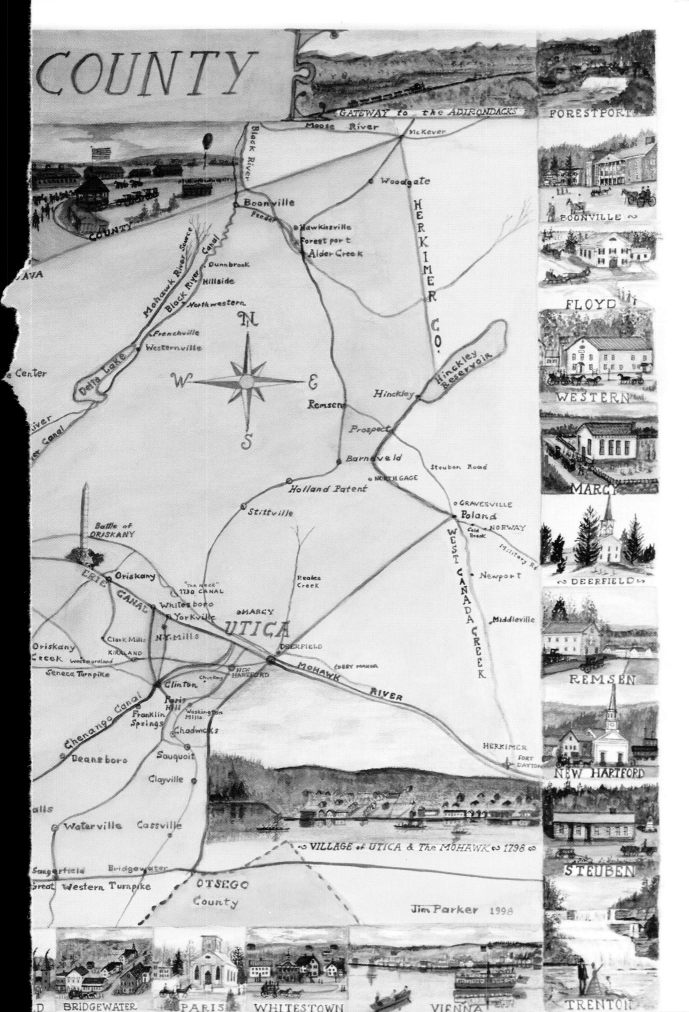

COUNTY

GATEWAY to the ADIRONDACKS

FORESTPORT

BOONVILLE

FLOYD

WESTERN

MARCY

DEERFIELD

REMSEN

NEW HARTFORD

STEUBEN

TRENTON

Moose River
McKever
Black River
Woodgate
HERKIMER CO.
Boonville
Feeder
Hawkinsville
Forest port
Alder Creek
Mohawk River Source
Canal
Dunnbrook
Black River
Hillside
Northwestern
Frenchville
Westernville
Delta Lake
Hinckley Reservoir
River Canal
Hinckley
Remsen
Prospect
Barneveld
Steuben Road
NORTH GAGE
Holland Patent
Stittville
GRAVESVILLE
Poland
NORWAY
Cold Brook
Military Rd.
Battle of ORISKANY
ERIE CANAL
Oriskany
"The Neck" 1730 CANAL
Whitesboro
Yorkville
MARCY
Reales Creek
WEST CANADA CREEK
Newport
Middleville
Oriskany Creek
Clark Mills
KIRKLAND
Westmoreland
Seneca Turnpike
N.Y. Mills
UTICA
DEERFIELD
EBBY MANOR
MOHAWK
RIVER
HERKIMER
FORT DAYTON
Clinton
Chuckey
NEW HARTFORD
Paris Hill
Washington Mills
Franklin Springs
Chadwicks
Chenango Canal
Deansboro
Sauquoit
Clayville
Waterville
Cassville
Saugerfield
Bridgewater
Great Western Turnpike
OTSEGO County

VILLAGE of UTICA & The MOHAWK 1798

Jim Parker 1998

BRIDGEWATER   PARIS   WHITESTOWN   VIENNA   TRENTON

About the Oneida County Bicentennial Painting

The idea of a painting to depict the historic wealth of Oneida County was developed by the Oneida County Bicentennial Committee as one of its first projects. As the painting progressed it also involved each of the historians who represent the twenty-six towns and three cities of the county.

The painting focuses on the pathways of history laid out over a map of Oneida County. These are the early canal developments, the Erie, the Chenango and the Black River Canals, the early turnpikes – toll roads, railroads, and Indian trails. The map portion also includes several early history scenes placed in areas where Oneida County abuts its neighboring counties. Utica is shown, as seen from the Mohawk River, during the early bateau and Durham boat era of river transportation. The Boonville Fair is depicted where harness racing and a balloon ascension delighted crowds. And a typical Oneida Indian settlement is recreated showing various social activities.

Around the map are some twenty-six small paintings of significant buildings or scenes that highlight each of the towns of the county. Also, in this colorful border, is an illustration of a three-lock "combine" – used on two of the early canals. A recreation of the siege of Fort Stanwix by St. Leger's forces is shown. And, to bring our paths of history up-to-date, the border includes a view of the Adirondack Railroad carrying tourists to the largest "forever wild" park in America with its thousands of lakes and majestic mountains.

It is the Bicentennial Committee's hope that the prints from this painting will encourage residents and tourists to visit and enjoy all of our unique towns and cities; visit our historic sites; travel our canals, railroads and highways which truly are pathways to history. As the artist commissioned to create this painting, I want to convey my special thanks to all the historians, volunteers and elected officials for their invaluable input to help create this representation of the variety and wealth of our past 200 years.

Jim Parker
Folk Artist

Description of The Border Paintings
Clockwise from the Upper Middle Right.

The Gateway to the Adirondacks: Depicts an Adirondack Railroad train heading north towards Remsen, Thendara, Old Forge and beyond.

Forestport: Depicts the powerful Black River flowing over the mill dam, with the quaint village main Street in the background.

Boonville: Depicts the historic Hulbert House, the gazebo and the village park and square.

Floyd: Depicts the beautiful church at Camroden, north of the village.

Western: Depicts the restored and rebuilt town hall that was salvaged from the adjoining village of Delta before it was submerged under what is now Delta Lake.

Marcy: Depicts an early Welch Church, still standing, on Church Road in the Township.

Deerfield: Depicts the beautifully maintained and restored North Gage Church.

Remsen: Depicts the Welch "Stone Church" that is a repository of much of the Welch settlement and church history for the surrounding towns and villages. It is beautifully restored.

New Hartford: Depicts the "town centerpiece" the impressive and historic Presbyterian Church, the early Sanger Grist Mill and later mills that were developed along the Sauquoit Creek.

Forestport

By
Hilda Avery

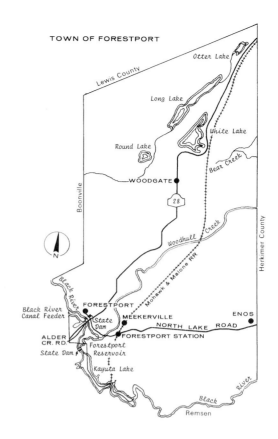

TOWN OF FORESTPORT

Forestport is the youngest town in Oneida County and one of the largest in area. Located in the northeastern corner in the foothills of the Adirondacks, it is also the fastest growing town, according to Livingston Lansing, of the *Boonville Herald.*

It is almost impossible to visualize the wilderness of 200 years ago which greeted the few hardy pioneers who came into the area at the close of the Revolutionary War. Parts of three early land patents are included in Forestport.

In 1761 Matthew Adgate, a member of the first Constitutional Convention and the New York State Assembly, purchased by contract 45,000 acres of land for two shillings sixpence an acre. His patent, to what is known as Adgate's Western Tract, was issued January 30, 1778, and was later broken up into the Picquet, Gouverneur, Miller and Swanton, and Devereaux tracts. It embraces White Lake and Otter Lake as well as Forestport.

The Remsenburgh Patent of 48,000 acres was granted in 1787 to Henry Remsen, J. G. Klock, George Klock and John Van Sice after they petitioned the legislature that this area had been conveyed to them by deed in 1766. This acreage is in the general area of Enos Road and Kayuta Lake.

Thomas Machin was granted a patent in 1788 of 31,360 acres. He emigrated from England in 1772. He was a skilled engineer and surveyor and assisted in placing the chain across the Hudson River to protect West Point from British ships during the Revolution. The Woodhull Tract of eight miles square, or a full township, was apparently a later grant. This comprises the land in the village and east of the village.

In its early days the town had several names. The first was Smith's Mill, from a sawmill on the west side of the Black River. Truman Yale started a chair factory nearby and also built the first frame house on the east side of the river. Then Dr. Platt Williams moved in, built an impressive home on the Alder Creek Road, and a sawmill a mile and a half down the river. The settlement became known as Williamsville. It was also known derisively as Punkeyville for the tiny biting insects that staged an annual spring invasion.

The building of the Black River Canal Feeder, which was completed in 1848, brought both work and transportation to the area. Besides the feeder itself, two dams were built to provide storage reservoirs for the canal. One was made across the outlet of North Lake and the second replaced a sawmill dam in what is now Forestport village.

With adequate transportation and shipping assured, more sawmills began to spring up. People who lived in the outlying settlements of Grantville and Meekerville moved to the village. At one time lumber was hauled from the mill at Grantville for shipment on the canal by means of a wooden railroad. There is nothing left of either Grantville or the railroad now. Meekerville, on picturesque Woodhull Creek, is a ghost town except for a few summer homes.

With the increase in population, schools and churches were needed. A two-room schoolhouse was built with a room for smaller children on the ground floor and one for the older pupils upstairs. Long counters circled each room where the children sat with their backs to the teachers, whose desks were in the center.

Four churches were organized: Methodist, Episcopal, Presbyterian, and Roman Catholic. The Methodist Church closed nearly 50 years ago and later the Episcopalians bought the building, remodeled it, and tore down their own beautiful church that stood near Beechwood Cemetery.

The first minister in the Presbyterian Church was the Rev. William Cleveland, brother of President Grover Cleveland. The President brought his bride here to visit and for a short time Forestport was much in the limelight as reporters overcrowded the hotels and filed daily news stories by means of Horace Dayton's telegraph. A parade led by the town band was staged in the President's honor.

In the early days while the town was still a part of Remsen, its neighbor to the south, voting became a problem. The residents alternated voting one year in Remsen and the next in Williamsville. However many of the Williamsville men worked in the woods and it took real effort to reach the polls before closing time. This seemed an injustice and the resentment grew until one year a small group of men persuaded Frank Tracy, who always had the fastest horse in town, to drive them to Remsen. Before the astonished Remsenites realized what was happening the men snatched the ballot box and took it to Williamsville where their co-workers would be in time to vote.

That clinched the matter. In 1860 a committee was named to divide Remsen and Williamsville into two separate towns. James Mitchell and Charles Thomas of Remsen with William B. Jackson and Alfred Hough were paid $1.50 per day to serve on the committee. It was not until November 24, 1869, that the new town was formed and the first town meeting held in March 1870 made it official. Robert Crandall, postmaster, suggested that the name be changed to Forestport and everyone, including the United States Post Office Department, agreed. It is the only post office with that name in the United States. The old records spell it as two words Forest Port, but in a short time it was changed to one word.

In 1870 the population was 1,276. Records listed 25 log dwellings, the largest number in the county. Some years after the division from Remsen, the land on the west side of River Street was annexed from Boonville.

Anson Blake had acquired much of Dr. Platt Williams' holdings by marrying his daughter and he decided to clear the land and grow corn. He brought crews from Canada to help cut the virgin timber, which was eagerly converted, into lumber by the sawmills. Piles of hemlock bark accumulated and a large tannery owned by Proctor and Hill at Woodhull took advantage of this to become the largest in the state, with 480 vats which used 6,000 cords of bark each year to process 25,000 hides. All this aided industry in the area but the farming venture failed. The soil was too

Ron Ryder

An outing on the Black River Canal Feeder at Forestport with the sawmill in the background.

Sam Utley's harness shop, Forestport.

Hilda Avery

sandy and the growing season too short.

Among the early mill owners were T. R. Stanburgh, Seifert and Harrig, James Gallagher, Hough and Hurlburt, Forestport Lumber Company, Phillip McGuire, Charles Hayes, Francis LaFountain, Denton and Waterbury. All this lumber business generated a thirst and saloons sprang up as fast as the mills. The husky bartenders aided by a baseball bat had no trouble keeping order, for "there was no law north of Remsen."

For the superstitious, Forestport history bears out the old adage that things happen in threes. Three times the village was destroyed by fire and rebuilt. There were three breaks in the canal feeder. After the second fire, which took 14 buildings, the village incorporated with John H. Neejer as its first president. A water system was installed but before it could be turned on a third fire burned seven buildings. For a time the village owned its own electric light plant but this was sold many years ago and in 1937 the village voted to disincorporate.

The turn of the century saw the land being stripped of timber and the mills began to close. Jobs were less easy to find. Before this, in 1897, a few men put their heads together and decided that a break in the canal feeder would solve that problem. At one point the canal parallels the Black River and is 70 feet higher. Holes dug surreptitiously during the night became larger in a few hours and morning found a vast opening in the canal bank, with water

pouring into the river. Seventeen hundred men and teams worked around the clock for a month before the damage was repaired. The men were paid $1.65 a day and the teams 35 cents an hour.

The first break brought such prosperity that another occurred the following May. Again everything boomed but the state began to be a little suspicious. When a third break occurred in September 1889, the state sent Pinkerton detectives to investigate and 13 men were arrested. Five were sent to prison, three fined, and five freed, two for turning state's evidence.

Forestport once had two supervisors at the same time. After the death of John Coughlin the town board could not agree on a successor and by a fluke both Fred S. Liddle and Mrs. Laura LaFountain were appointed. Neither would withdraw, and the matter was finally settled by the courts with Mrs. LaFountain the winner.

Forestport had the first central school in Oneida County built in 1927 after the existing schoolhouse burned. A few years ago the district consolidated with Adirondack Central in Boonville. A new elementary school replaced the old one, which is now used for town offices, meetings and community activities. Otter Lake and Woodgate have discontinued their one-room schools and have joined with the Town of Webb school at Old Forge.

At present the Rome Specialty Company which man-

Hilda Avery

Employees at the Denton and Waterbury sawmill about 1885.

Forestport's rotary snowplow known as the "White Elephant."

Hilda Avery

ufactures fishing tackle is the only industry in Forestport. The Village Boat Shop has an active business through out the summer months and restaurants, such as the Buffalohead, provide year-round employment. The Mid-York Bookmobile serves the village while local interest in starting a Forestport Library has had limited success.

In the pre-electric refrigeration days Woodgate supplied ice to the City of Utica. Each winter the huge blocks were cut packed in sawdust and stored in a large icehouse for the hot summer days ahead. The icehouse burned one night with flames that could be seen for miles. The Oneida Pink Granite Company operated a quarry at one time about a mile or so from White Lake and shipped carloads of the beautiful stone for building purposes.

Otter Lake never had an industry except logging. It did have one of the early hotels where guests were introduced to Adirondack vacations. Roscoe G. Norton did a great deal to develop Otter Lake into the thriving summer community it is today.

The volunteer fire company, organized after the big fires, was reorganized as the Forestport Fire Fighters. In 1998 the Fire Fighters operate from one station on River Street, Forestport, and serve approximately 245 square miles in 3 districts. It is the largest protection area for a single-station volunteer company in the State of New York. The Fire Fighter's 43 active members, plus an Explorer Scout unit and social members are also an impor-

tant unifying organization in a community that sprawls along more than 70 miles of town roads. The trend of developing the center of the community reversed many years ago in Forestport.

Community donations are the principle source for equipping the Fire Fighters. Today, there are 6 well-equipped trucks, tankers and emergency vehicles that respond to over 170 calls per year.

The forest has reclaimed the land again and the few farms have disappeared. White Lake and Otter Lake are ringed with summer camps and pleasure boats ply their waters in summer. Little Long Lake boasts Camp Nazareth, a Catholic summer camp for boys and girls. Round Lake is owned by the Masonic Home in Utica whose residents spend the summer there. Camps nestle on the shores of Kayuta Lake and sit beside Woodhull and Bear Creeks. Houses now line the North Lake Road and Enos Road and the people socialize in many little communities scattered throughout the area.

In this bicentennial year we look back on a wilderness, a sawmill town, a summer resort. These are the three phases of Forestport.

Selected Reference

O'Donnell, Thomas G., *Snubbing Posts: An Informal History of the Black River Canal,* (Black River Books, Boonville, 1949).

Kirkland

By Philip E. Munson, Village Historian
and
Edward W. Stanley

1998 Revisions by

Mary Elizabeth Kimball, Town Historian and
Esther Delaney, Clinton Historical Society.

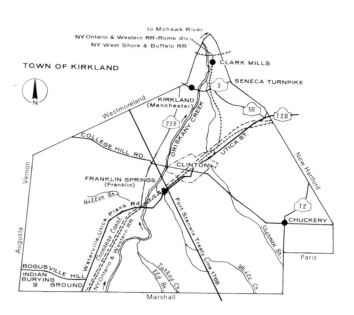

Over two hundred years ago the area which comprises the Town of Kirkland was a wilderness sparsely inhabited by Oneida and Brothertown Indians. Crisscrossed by Indian trails, it was occasionally visited by the Rev. Samuel Kirkland in his missionary duties and conferences with the Oneida Chief, Skenandoa.

The Line of Property, established by the 1768 Treaty of Fort Stanwix, separating the lands of the Indians from the territory of the white man, bisected this area beginning at Wood Creek at Fort Stanwix (Rome) and continuing south to the headwaters of the Unadilla River.

Crossing the town from south to north is the Oriskany Creek on its way to the Mohawk River. Early a source of water power, the Oriskany is fed by many small streams, including Turkey Creek, Ely Brook, White Creek, Miller Brook, and Sherman Brook, which drain the rolling hills to the east and west.

In 1787 New England settlers led by Moses Foot chose a spot not far from the Oriskany Creek for a new home, naming it Clinton after George Clinton, the first governor of New York. Part of Coxe's patent, it was the third settlement of consequence, after Whitestown and Westmoreland, in what later became Oneida County.

The new settlement was within the boundaries of Whitestown, which then comprised all the western part of New York State. In 1792 a large portion of it, including Clinton, became the Town of Paris. It was named for Isaac Paris of Fort Plain, who supplied grain for the hungry settlers at Clinton when food became scarce during the second season in their new home. The northern portion of the Town of Paris became the Town of Kirkland in 1827. Part of the township was at one time jointly owned by George Washington and George Clinton.

Family names prominent among the early settlers were Foot, Bronson, Pond, Bristol, Curtiss, Carpenter, Marsh, Stebbins, Hastings, Hart, Hopkins, Barker, Williams, Kellogg, and Gridley.

Though Clinton was the original settlement in the Town of Kirkland, and the only one to become an incorporated village, others shortly followed. One of the earliest was Franklin, a mile south of Clinton. Dating from 1790, in 1867 after the erection of the blast furnaces, it officially became Franklin Iron Works. With the discovery of mineral springs in the 1890s, the name was again changed to Franklin Springs.

East of Clinton is the crossroads settlement of Chuckery. It briefly had its own post office in the late 19th century. Another early hamlet was Manchester, a stage stop on the Seneca Turnpike. Re-named Kirkland in 1829, it had a post office as early as 1815.

In the northernmost part of the township lies Clark Mills. It derives its name from the Clark family, who established cotton mills here on the banks of the Oriskany Creek in 1846. The first post office was opened in 1858 as Clark's Mills. Changed to Clark Mills in 1893, it continues to serve this lively community to this day.

Setting the moral tone for the budding settlement of Clinton was the establishment of a Congregational Church in 1791, the first in the present Town of Kirkland. Later changed to Presbyterian, a fine building of native stone at the south end of the village green now serves an active congregation.

In 1821, the Universalists erected a brick church on Utica Street. Replaced by a new one on Williams Street in 1870, this congregation disbanded in 1897. Their Williams Street structure, now a private residence, was afterward used for a time by St. Mary's Roman Catholic Church until their new church edifice was finished in 1912, and later as a home of the Clinton Masonic Lodge #169.

The Baptist Church, erected in 1832, now the home of the Clinton Historical Society remains the oldest church building still standing in the town. The Methodists built a church on the eastern side of the village green in 1842. In 1965, this building was transformed into the Kirkland Art Center, when a new Methodist Church was completed on Utica Street.

St. Mary's Roman Catholic Church was organized in 1850. Their first church, of wooden construction, was completed in 1852-54 and replaced by the present handsome stone structure in 1912. St. James' Episcopal Church was organized in 1862 and construction was started the same year.

In Clark Mills, St. Mark's Episcopal Church dates from 1863, while the Roman Catholic Church of the Annunciation, constructed in part of lumber from the former female department building of the Clinton Liberal Institute, was completed in 1908. This community also has an active Methodist congregation.

The town's educational heritage was begun in 1793 with the opening of Hamilton-Oneida Academy on the hill west of Clinton. Envisioned by Samuel Kirkland as a school for the education of whites and Indians, in 1812 it became Hamilton College.

During the next century a profusion of private secondary schools sprang up about Clinton, earning it the sobriquet "School-town." Dedicated to the education of both males and females, the more widely known were the Clinton Grammar School, Clinton Liberal Institute, Royce Seminary, Kellogg's Young Ladies Domestic Seminary, Home Cottage Seminary, Dwight's Rural High School, Houghton Seminary, and Cottage Seminary. There were at least a score of various sizes. All have now disappeared, though a few of the buildings, like Royce Seminary, Florence Seminary, and Kellogg Seminary, still exist as private homes.

Some of these schools had a marked influence upon the direction and actual founding of several colleges. Among these patterned upon their foundations were Mount Holyoke, Knox, Oberlin, Tufts, Elmira, Howard and St. Lawrence. Among the thousands of students who were educated in part in these same Clinton schools were Leland Stanford of California fame, Clara Barton, founder of the American Red Cross, and President Grover Cleveland.

The largest of the private schools was the Universalist-sponsored Clinton Liberal Institute. Its buildings were once the pride of the community. The male department was housed in a four-story stone structure built in 1832, and the female section in a spacious, pillared building erected in 1851, both striking architectural examples of the period. Like the school itself, the buildings have long gone. The main campus of the Clinton Central School system today occupies the land once used by the Cottage Seminary (girls) and the Clinton Preparatory School (boys).

The most recent addition to the town's educational scene was Kirkland College for women founded in 1965. Hamilton College became co-educational in 1978, when it absorbed Kirkland College, which had been established on a spacious campus across the street on College Hill.

Clinton Historical Society

Leland Stanford attended the Male Dept. of the Clinton Liberal Institute, a stone building once located at the corner of Utica and Mulberry Streets, Clinton. Photo about 1870.

Clinton Historical Society

Clara Barton attended the Female Dept. of the Clinton Liberal Institute when it was located at the head of William St., Clinton, Photo about 1875.

Iron ore was discovered early on the low hills east and west of the Oriskany Valley. Named Clinton hematite, this designation is still used throughout the mineral world wherever this type of ore is found. Mining was extensively pursued at various times during the 19th and part of the 20th century, resulting in the erection of sizable blast furnaces, since demolished, at both Franklin and Kirkland, as well as a factory for the manufacture of metallic paint, which made use of the ore's red pigment. The last mine closed in 1963.

Though dairy and truck farming are still important facets of the local economy, hop raising was once a flourishing agricultural pursuit. Light manufacturing has also occupied many of the town's residents. Woven cloth, furniture polish, push carts, plastics, tools, paint, grinding compounds, and a variety of knit goods are among the articles produced in the past. One of the largest manufacturers was the Hind and Harrison Plush Company at Clark Mills, which, from the 1890s to the 1940s, produced vast quantities of cloth for women's coats, draperies, and upholstery material for automobiles, much of it for the Ford Motor Company. A clubhouse for employees of this company, known as the Arthur Hind Club, is now the home of the Clark Mills American Legion Post.

Today a network of paved highways, serves most of the immediate area's transportation needs. It wasn't always thus. The stage coaches came early which crossed the township at Kirkland on the Seneca Turnpike on their way west, and those north and south which used the Waterville and Utica Plank Road (1848-1877). The Chenango Canal (1836-1878) furnished the first economical freight movement, bringing coal from Pennsylvania and carrying iron ore in return. The first railroad, the Utica, Clinton and Binghamton, arrived in 1866, followed in 1871 by the Rome and Clinton, both to become a part of the New York, Ontario and Western Railway, which ceased operation in 1957. In 1884 the New York, West Shore and Buffalo Railroad crossed the town's northern section through Clark Mills, eventually bringing that section rapid electric trolley service, popularly known as the "third rail." Trolley service between Clinton and Utica was inaugurated in 1901 and was replaced by buses in 1936.

Highlighted by the nationally recognized Hamilton College Chapel, designed by Philip Hooker, the Town of Kirkland has many excellent specimens of early architectural, as well as local historical, significance, running the gamut from the early Federal period to the late Victorian. A few examples are the restored, original home of the Rev. Samuel Kirkland, early settler Barnabas Pond's homestead (circa 1793), the Alexander Hamilton Inn, formerly the Othniel Williams home (circa 1830), and the Victorian style Kirkland Town Library, a former college fraternity house. The library was founded in 1901 and in 1996 a major addition was completed and the original building renovated to provide the community with modern library facility. The project was possible because of a

At the Franklin Iron Works, Franklin Springs, this pond, created by a dike, provided the power supply as well as recreation, as suggested by the diving board in the foreground.

View about 1890 of Augustus Fake's store, located on the present site of the firehouse, Clinton.

successful "Once Every 90 Years" capital fund drive which was supported by the generosity of individuals and the local government. The Clark Mills branch library found a permanent home in 1992 when space was provided for it in the Town of Kirkland Senior Citizen's Building. This building was erected in 1978 to accommodate an active Senior Citizen group and is located on New Street in Clark Mills.

A small Brothertown Indian burying ground is located in the southwest corner of the town near Bogusville Hill. It is here, tradition has it, that the Rev. Samson Occum, the famed Indian preacher and Dartmouth College benefactor, is buried.

Most commercial activity within the township is concentrated on West, North, and East Park Rows and adjacent College Street in Clinton. The oldest business enterprise is the *Clinton Courier*, which provides local and area news on a weekly basis to the residents of Kirkland and surrounding towns. Begun in 1846 as the *Clinton Signal*, it has been in continuous publication since that time. A rival paper, the *Clinton Advertiser*, appeared for about a decade at the turn of the century.

Providing valuable services to the community at large are the volunteer fire departments at Clinton and Clark Mills. The Clinton Fire Department, established in 1866 is located in its own firehouses: one, built in 1921, on North Park Row, Clinton, the other near Franklin Springs, built in 1967. The Clark Mills Fire Department was organized in 1855. Supplying another valuable contribution to the area, is the Volunteer Ambulance Corps, which is headquartered in Clark Mills. It was inaugurated in 1970.

The main buildings of the Lutheran Home complex, which provide adult care and nursing home care, are located on Clinton's Utica Street. The original Lutheran Home was established in 1920. Services were greatly expanded with the erection of the Martin Luther Nursing Home in 1975, with 160 beds. With the completion of the Katherine Luther Home in 1992, another 120 residents can be accommodated.

The town's interest in sports, particularly ice skating, hockey and figure skating, resulted in the erection of the Clinton Arena in 1948 and its rebuilding in 1953 after fire destroyed the original structure. Clinton's hockey teams have carried its name with distinction throughout this country and Canada.

In recent years various areas have witnessed new housing developments attesting to Clinton's continuing growth as a fine residential community. Several apartment complexes, some of which accommodate the elderly, have also been built.

Kirkland has had its share of prominent men. Some of the more notable were Elihu Root, former Secretary of State and international statesman, Clinton Scollard, author and poet, and Thomas Hastings, prominent 19th century composer of religious music, including the hymn "Rock of Ages."

The Clinton Hermatite Mines, Brimfield Street.

Clinton Historical Society

The Hind and Harrison Plush Co., Clark Mills, operated from 1890 to 1943.

Clinton Historical Society

In 1925 Elisabeth Scollard, daughter of Clinton Scollard, published the following tribute to the Town of Kirkland.

The Hills of Kirkland

The emerald hills of Kirkland
Climb up to greet the spring.
And lift their laughing heads aloft
Beneath her blossoming:
The golden hills of Kirkland
Climb up to touch the blue
When summer veils the valleys in
Her sunlight and her dew;
The purpling hills of Kirkland
Climb up to reach the sun
When autumn lights the lanterns of
The maples one by one
Come rain or shine in Kirkland.
Green-or-white-mantled ground.
A beauty bides in Kirkland
That nowhere else is found.
And yet the sons of Kirkland –
How far afield they roam!
They search the world for that which hides
Amid the hills of home!

Selected References

Clinton American Revolution Bicentennial Committee Booklet, 1976

Dever, Mary Bell, *The History of Clinton Square*, (Clinton, 1961).

Glancing Back at Clinton and Neighboring Communities, Philip Munson et al; published for the Clinton Central School District Foundation, (Vestal, NY, 1993).

Gridley , the Rev. A.D., *History of the Town of Kirkland, New York*, (New York, 1874).

Pillington, Walter, *Hamilton College 1810-1963*, (Clinton, 1962).

Rudd, Helen Neilson. *A Century of Schools in Clinton*, (Clinton, 1964).

Stanley, Edward W., *A Half Century Life of Clinton, New York, 1915-1965*, compiled and edited form the files of the Courier (Clinton, 1966).

Clinton Historical Society

The New York, Ontario and Western depot at Clinton; this view about 1900.

New York, Ontario and Western railway depot and post office at Clark Mills, about 1900.

Clinton Historical Society

The Clinton Village Green by Guy Danella, a Utica artist, is reminiscent of the birdseye view that were at the height of popularity in the 1880's. From a pamplet sponsored by the Clinton Chamber of Commerce.

1. Village Green: Site of a marker commemorating the founding of the Village in 1787 by Moses Foote and seven other settlers from Connecticut.
2. Fountain and Statue: Donated to the community in 1936 by the alumnae of Houghton Seminary, one of Clinton's more than thirty former private schools, whose rosters once included such well-remembered names as Clara Barton, Grover Cleveland, and Leland Stanford.
3. Stone Presbyterian Church: Built in 1878, this is the home of Clinton's earliest religious denomination, whose first sanctuary, completed in 1801, once sat on the Village Green opposite.
4. Baptist Church: The oldest existing church structure in the village, now the home of the Clinton Historical Society, was built in 1832.

8. Former home of Clinton Female (Royce) Seminary, 1814-1856.

9. Railroad Historical Marker: Site of the right-of-way of the Utica, Clinton and Binghamton Railroad which arrived in Clinton in 1866, and was abandoned as part of the New York, Ontario, Western Railroad in 1957.

10. Burns Agency Building: Original location of the Clinton Grammar School, 1813-1892, another of the many schools that earned for Clinton the sobriquet, "Schooltown".

11. Alexander Hamilton Inn: Built about 1830, the Othnell Williams family homestead for more than one hundred years, it was here that President and Mrs. Grover Cleveland were entertained at the Clinton Centennial in 1887.

12. Gorton's: Now the Park Row Bookseller, was the site of Clinton House, from 1805 to 1920, the Village's most well-known hostelry.

14. Ginko tree: Located in the grocery store parking lot on Chenango Ave., this unusual Oriental specimen is one of the many unusual varieties found in and around the community, many planted by the 19th Century Clinton Rural Art Society, one of the first garden clubs in the United States.

15. Clinton Central Schools: Built on the beautiful campus another of Clinton's many former private schools, the Cottage Seminary, 1862-1898.

16. Kirkland Town Library: Erected in 1872 as the Sigma Phi house, the first Greek letter fraternity at Hamilton College.

17. Bristol Road: Location of several early homes dating back to the late 18th century.

18. Harding House: Homestead of the Rev. Samuel Kirkland, missionary to the Oneida Indians, and father of Hamilton College, built in 1793.

19. Sycamore Tree: Another of Clinton's many interesting old trees, this huge sycamore was planted as a seedling in 1811.

20. Hamilton College: Men's liberal arts college founded in 1793 as Hamilton-Oneida Academy, and chartered as a college in 1812. It became co-educational with the adsorption of Kirkland College.

21. Kirkland College: Women's liberal arts college, named for Samuel Kirkland. Chartered in 1968, it was absorbed by Hamilton College in 1978.

22. "Line of Property" Marker: Marker erected in 1884 to mark the spot where the historic treaty line, negotiated between the British Colonies and the Iroquois Nations at Fort Stanwix in 1768, crosses the foot of College Hill.

23. Post Office: Site of new building erected in 1989.

5. Kirkland Art Center: Former Methodist Church, built 1842.

6. Lumbard Memorial Hall: Built in 1926, this building houses Clinton village offices and the town clerk of the Town of Kirkland, a town formed from Paris in 1827. This building housed the Post Office until 1989.

7. Old Burying Ground: Site of Clinton's first burial in 1788, and final resting place of 48 Revolutionary War Soldiers.

Bertha Ruchti

*The first post office in Lee Center was in Jay
Hitchcock's store; photographed about 1910.*

Beatrice Paine Smith

*Harold Paine's Point Rock-Rome stage on July 4, 1913,
in front of the Lee Center post office.
William R. Paine (Harold's father) built the stage.*

Lee

By
Maryellen S. Urtz
and
Virginia Lee Ackerman,
Town Historian

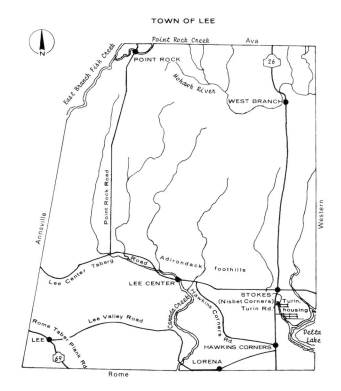

In 1790 Esek Sheldon and his sons Stephen, Reuben and Amasa came from Adams, Massachusetts to be the first settlers in what was to become Lee. They came up the Mohawk River from Fort Stanwix to settle in the village of Delta. There were no settlements between them and the Fort. Reuben Sheldon had married Jane Fennor while still in Massachusetts. Jane gave birth to the first child born in Lee in 1790; a son named Fennor Sheldon.

In 1811, a legislative act was passed authorizing the separation of Lee from the Town of Western. James Young Jr. and Joshua Northrup formed the committee accomplishing this and requested the new town be called Lee after their home town of Lee, Massachusetts. The new boundary lines were surveyed by Benjamin Wright. March 3, 1812, the first town meeting was held at the old West schoolhouse (the only frame one in town). The same schoolhouse is the one-story portion of the present Walter and Alfred Tuthill farmhouse on Hawkins Corners Road. In 1823 a portion of Lee was given to Annsville decreasing its acreage to the present 27,771 acres.

Jelles Fonda was granted a 40,000-acre patent in 1786, which became a large part of Lee. Terms required a settler to be on each 500-acre section within three years. The land was considered a wilderness at that time, and he promptly sold most of the land to large land dealers for 10 cents an acre. Most of these owners leased their parcels to settlers. Rental terms in one situation required 18 bushels of wheat delivered to Albany for a 100-acre tract. This lease land was considered a curse to the town. Other large landowners were often willing to sell their land to settlers for a dollar an acre.

The northern part of the town is hilly, rising sharply north of Stokes and Lee Center along the Fonda Patent northern boundary. Springfed streams have cut into this section of the Tug Hill foothills providing dependable waterpower. The east branch of Fish Creek borders on the northwest. The west branch of the Mohawk cuts into the northeast corner, and a section of the Mohawk cuts into the southeast corner at the former Delta village. West Creek provided waterpower for the Lee settlement on the State Road, now Route 69, and Canada Creek in the center of town is well supplied by small streams. The southeast portion of the town is quite level and has the best farmland in Lee.

In 1823 a turnpike road (unplanked) was completed commencing at Stokes, going through West Branch, Ava and on to Turin. In 1826 this road was extended south to Rome. The Rome and Turin Plank Road was completed in 1848. One tollgate was located at Nisbet hill (now Stokes hill). The toll was 10 cents for two horses and five cents single. In 1826 daily mail service began between Rome and Turin. Later a stage followed this route.

A daily stage providing transportation and mail service served Point Rock, Lee Center, Stokes, Delta, Ridge Mills and Rome. Another stage went from Lee Center to Rome via Lorena.

About 200 men from Lee fought in the Civil War. Most of them saw a lot of action in the 97th, 117th and 146th Infantry. A few years after the war an active Grand Army of the Republic (G.A.R.) Post of about 30 members was organized at Lee Center.

In 1864 Rome was the largest cheese market in the world. Jesse Williams had established the first cheese factory in the United States in 1851 at Rome. American cheese was much in demand in Europe. Swiss farmers were attracted to this area and many started cheese factories. Dairy farming was a profitable business and land value increased in Lee. Some of the town's cheesemakers were Jacob Karlen, John Reinhardt, John Ritter, Samuel Kappler and John Anken.

Many of these cheese factories closed down by the mid-20th century. Transportation of fluid milk had become more efficient and the local farmers received a better price for the fluid milk than the cheese factories could offer. Dairy farming is still the town's largest industry but now only the larger dairy farms continue to operate.

In the early 1900s the Rome and Osceola Railroad Company was working on a railroad that would go through Point Rock and Lee Center. Some track was laid and other work done, but the railroad was never completed.

The Town of Lee had 17 public schools in 1845. Most of these were still in use in 1957 when consolidation closed them down. School No. 5 on the Lee-Point Rock Road (now Skinner Road) was built of stone in 1833 and still stands. Lee Center Union School was built in 1872. The town barn is located on its former site.

For many years high school education was not available in this town. Often students would board in Rome from Monday to Friday to attend Rome Free Academy. Harold "Hi" Paine became the Point Rock to Rome stage operator in 1913 and later in the 1930s began transporting schoolchildren. The town now has two schools, Stokes Elementary and Rome Community Christian School on Lorena Road. Schoolchildren in the northern section of town attend Adirondack Central and Camden schools and those in the southern part attend schools in the Rome City District.

The Town of Lee is a prosperous town but it was dependent on the Rome area for employment. In the early 1950s the growth of Griffiss Air Force Base created a need for housing, resulting in the building of three developments on upper Turin Road.

DELTA

The story of the old village of Delta is a sad one. Delta was the first area settled in the town because it could be reached by following the Mohawk north from Fort Stanwix. Most of the business district was in Lee, but a complete history would include the Town of Western as well. Delta was named by Gates Peck after the Greek letter Delta that resembled the outline of the valley in which the village was located. Unfortunately for Delta, this valley also was well suited for the creation of a new lake to provide water for the Barge Canal. The new dam was completed in January 1912. The cemetery was relocated, all the buildings were moved, and residents relocated in the surrounding area. (See Town of Western for more information on Delta.)

HAWKINS CORNERS

Hawkins Corners derives its name from Marinus Hawkins who kept an attractive inn at Turin Road and Hawkins Corners Road. A gas station now occupies its former site. Bartell's Machine Shop is located here also.

STOKES

Stokes is located on Turin Road north of Hawkins Corners. It was previously called Nisbets Corners after Robert Nisbet, a progressive dairy farmer in the early 1800s. It has more recently been called Lee Corners, and later, Stokes, after Charles Stokes, the first postmaster here and at Lee Center. Stokes has a good location for trade. LeFeber Arms, J.F. Pepper Company and Lee Mobile Home Sales are located here.

Pupils at the Lee Center Union Free School in 1921.

Bertha Ruchti

LEE CENTER

Lee Center was a prosperous village due to the reliable waterpower of Canada Creek. Hills rose to the north but did not impede the building of mills in the village.

James Young Sr. settled one-half mile south of Lee Center at South Street and Marsh Road in the 1790s and Deacon John Hall settled nearby. Former residents of Brookfield, Massachusetts settled at Brookfield Settlement southwest of the village. General William Floyd built the first much-needed gristmill in Lee south of Lee Center on Canada Creek near the Rome border in 1796.

The Olney and Floyd canning factory that operated in Delta moved here in 1912. It provided a market for local produce and seasonal employment until its closing in the late 1960s. Dr. Truman Cox operated a sanatorium in Lee Center. Later this building was used as a mission church for the Roman Catholic residents. The beautiful St. Joseph's church on the Stokes-Lee Center Road was built in 1952. In March 1935 fire destroyed the Methodist church and parsonage in the village. A new church was built on the site within a short time. The Masonic Lodge was originally built as an ecclesiastical church and town hall in 1819.

LEE

Lee is located on the old State Road (now Route 69) that crosses the southwest corner of town. This village had the first post office in the Town of Lee. West Creek provided waterpower, and four sawmills were active here in 1851. David Bryan built a gristmill previous to 1812 to serve this section of town. As settlement progressed a large canning factory and a sash and blind factory located here. An old-fashioned grange hall is still used by Lee Grange 707. Because of the busy highway many businesses still flourish here.

LORENA

For a time a post office was located on the Lee-Rome boundary line at Lorena. This hamlet contained a tannery, a school and a Methodist church. Sleepy Hollow Golf Course is now located here.

WEST BRANCH

This village is located where the west branch of the Mohawk crosses the former Rome to Turin turnpike (now Route 26).

This was a Quaker settlement. Some of the early Quaker burials were only marked by a natural stone at the head and foot of the grave. The original Friends Meeting House burned in the 1870s, and a new one was built in 1878. This building is presently used by the grange. Sawmills have continued to prosper in this small village.

POINT ROCK

Point Rock is in the northwest corner of the town. It is named after the point of rocks where Fish Creek and Point Rock Creek merge. The Indians recognized this point and called Point Rock Creek "A-on-tagillon," creek at the point of rocks. Point Rock was a lumber town, and dairy farms appeared as more land was cleared. The Methodist church here is served by the Lee Center pastor. It was built in the 1870s and is a beautiful example of an old country church. Bruce Kelly, formerly of the Point Rock area, occasionally shows his slides with accompanying tape recording called "The Point Rock Story."

Selected Reference

Harriet Trombley has made a collection of slides of Delta village and the construction of Delta dam.

Canning factory in Lee Center

Stittville Methodist Church.

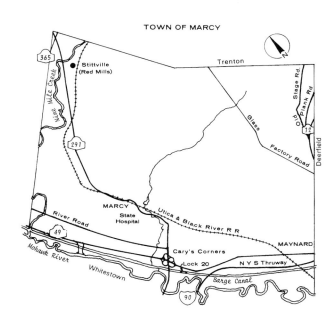

TOWN OF MARCY

Marcy

By
Raymond Ball

The Mohawk River lies along the southern boundary of the Town of Marcy and brought travelers who left their mark at several historic sites. Native American campsites, between today's Lock 20 and the Marcy Marina, have been the source for a collection of arrowheads, spear points, rubbing stones and pottery that is to be seen at the Village of Oriskany Museum. In 1730 a neck of land formed by a loop of the meandering Mohawk River was cut through to improve the river route. Located a mile or so east of the Marcy Marina, it became New York State's first canal. This site, although an "unofficial" improvement, was placed on both the New York State Register of Historic Sites and, in 1995, the National Register of Historic Sites.

The first settler in what is now the Town of Marcy was John Wilson, who came from Windsor, Vermont in 1793, with a large family of children. He settled on a river farm one-half mile east of Nine Mile Creek, in the south western corner of the township. He built a small log house and cleared several acres of land. He was taken ill of a bilious fever and died in the same year he settled; this was the first death in the town. The homestead was taken over by the elder children.

Eight of his nine sons joined the Continental Army and took part in the long struggle for independence. Early in the year 1794, James Wilson, brother of John, came to Marcy and settled in a large log house, 18-feet square, on the Nine Mile Creek near its junction at the Mohawk River. In the following spring Wilson purchased an unimproved lot about a mile north of Oriskany Village, where he became a successful farmer. The same year two brothers, Isaac and Jacob Wilson, moved to Marcy. None of their descendants now remain in the town, all having died or moved away.

While there were no Indians residing in the township when it was first settled, there was a place known as

Indian Castle on the north bank of the Mohawk River about a half-mile east of the Oriskany Creek merger with the Mohawk. As early as 1796 it was mostly covered with second growth timber, but a small mound about 18 inches high and from eight to ten feet across the top could be seen. In the area could be found 20 to 30 "hopper" holes, holding about 10 bushels, used to hide corn on the approach of an enemy. Several of these were also found on the farm purchased by James Wilson along with iron hatchets whose design suggested Spanish manufacture.

The early settlements in Marcy were mostly made along the river and near each other. Among the early settlers were the Camp and Carey families. William Mayhew, Anthon and Jonathan Wood settled in 1820 on the River Road which is now occupied by the Walmart Distribution Center and Central NY Psychiatric Center.

Early in the history of the town, Welsh settlers found their way into the central and northern parts. Their numbers increased until they constituted the largest part of the population in that district.

The early settlers were plain people, manufacturing in their homes almost every article of wearing apparel. Industry of any scale was not known until 1812 when a window glass company, later known as Utica Glass Company, located on what is now called Glass Factory Road. This factory is credited as the first industry in Oneida County to have a production line system. Despite its ups and downs, it lasted for 27 years before moving to the town of Oneida and merging with the Oneida Glass Factory.

By the census in 1850, the town contained 1,769 inhabitants. It then contained one gristmill, seven sawmills, one trip hammer and two tanneries.

In 1853, a group of investors from Boonville obtained a state charter and proceeded to build the Boonville-Utica Railroad. Early studies convinced the investors that it was

177

impossible for any locomotive to pull a train up over the Deerfield hills. A route was selected to go through Marcy, following the least slope, through the Crane Creek lowlands and on into Stittville. In just three years the line was open to Remsen and shortly thereafter, to Boonville. The railroad was later renamed the Utica-Black River R.R. and the trackage forms the present day route for much of the Adirondack Rail Road.

A cheese factory was built in 1862 by Levi Tanner, A.W. Wood and Charles Ashby on the Tanner farm. The same year another was built by David Wilcox and Amos Potter. A corn mill was located on the north side of the Rome-Utica State Road on Snaker Hill. At this mill corn was hulled. A few sawmills were built in the early years. Nearly all of these factories and mills have gone. Gradually the farmers turned more of their energies to dairying and cheesemaking.

In the list of principal taverns, Rice's Nine-Mile Creek is mentioned. This tavern was patronized by pioneers who drove to salt springs, near Onondaga Lake for their yearly supply of salt. Not every householder went but a few in the settlement were selected or offered to go for salt. These were yearly trips for supplies. This was also the stopping place for the stage coach and mail. This site was a short distance west of the Nine Mile Creek on the State Road.

By a law passed on March 30, 1832, the Town of Marcy was formed from the Town of Deerfield and named in honor of William L. Marcy, then Governor of New York State. He later served as Secretary of War during the administration of President Polk and as Secretary of State in the administration of President Pierce. A few months after the formation of the town, Governor Marcy visited it, and was the guest of Samuel C. Baldwin, who was then the first supervisor of the town.

The first town meeting in Marcy was held at the schoolhouse near Samuel Camp's farm. One of the first jobs of the early town was to repair roads. In 1836, $14 out of $15 raised was spent on roads. In 1838, it was resolved that $190 be spent if necessary on Camp Bridge over the Mohawk River.

Down through the years bridges were the largest expenditure. In 1843, the Overseer of the Poor was instructed to hand all money in his hands over to the Road Overseer in charge. In 1858, $1000 was raised for road work. With high waters in 1865, the bridges were carried away. In 1868, it was resolved "that we do not accept any additional territory to the Town, that includes expensive bridges."

About 1892 the township boundary line on the north was changed and the hamlet of Stittville moved from the Town of Trenton to Marcy. The number of acres ceded by the Town of Trenton to the Town of Marcy included not only all the present hamlet of Stittville but many acres of farmland especially to the north and the east of it.

Olin's store, located next to the Methodist Church in Stittville, burned in 1910.

Elizabeth Humphrey

In 1911 the state legislature authorized the purchase of 1000 acres in Marcy initially to move the entire population of Utica State Hospital out of Utica. This never happened however and both hospitals continued to grow. In 1931 Marcy State Hospital became a separate hospital from Utica State. Marcy Psychiatric Center's geographical district includes Oswego, Onondaga, Madison, Warren, Oneida and Herkimer Counties.

The Township population in 1920 was 1,191 and in 1930 it was 2,602 including the state hospital. The reason for the population decline in 1920 was the movement of the people from rural areas to the cities due to the manufacturing boom of wartime and the early '20s.

In 1928 the City of Utica purchased a large tract of land for an airport, on the River Road where the Walmart Distribution Center now stands.

It opened with great fanfare in 1929 and for many years was a hub for private aviation and commercial aviation. Airmail was flown in and out and American Airlines conducted regular passenger flights. In the mid-1940s however, it became clear that commercial aircraft needed longer runways than the site along River Road could provide and a new County airport was located southwest of the Village of Oriskany.

In the early '30s Marcy came to a turning point in its history. Instead of declining, it started to grow. By 1957, there were 3,550 people excluding the state hospital. Due to this growth many needs arose such as highways, education, and other activities which required financial assistance from outside sources to become a reality. The Marcy State Hospital patient population was 3,100.

During the 1960s the town continued to grow as more and more people turned to suburban living. The present population of the town (excluding the hospital) is estimated at over 5,000. During the '60s much change took place as farming continued to decline and home building increased.

The New York State Thruway was built through the Town of Marcy in 1955. It is located parallel to the Mohawk River for a distance of three miles. Although the Thruway goes through Marcy, there is no direct exit; the nearest available exit is in the City of Utica. In 1957 the modern cloverleaf was built at Cary's Corners. Its main purpose was to do away with the dangerous intersection and obsolete canal bridge.

Three main churches are located in Marcy. The first church was the Stittville Methodist Church organized in 1836. There are also Marcy Community Church organized in 1842 and Maynard United Methodist Church organized in 1839. There are two fire departments, the Stittville and Maynard Fire Departments.

Schools and education have always been important in Marcy. The first school was erected on the old River Road about one half mile east of Nine Mile Creek. As the Town

The Maynard Methodist Church, built in 1839, has been moved to the Erie Canal Village, Rome.

grew it necessitated ten school districts, each with its own school, and one district in Stittville to serve all the families. Teachers were paid $50.86 for teaching up to seventy pupils for six and one half months. By 1891 the rate of pay was up to $5.50 per week and sometimes included room and board. These one-room schoolhouses continued in use, in some cases, until the 1940s when consolidation of public schools began. Marcy students became a part of the Whitesboro School District serving the southern portion of the Township. The Whitesboro District located their new modern high school adjacent to Route 291 in the Township. The students in the Stittville area were consolidated with the Holland Patent School District.

In 1966 New York State purchased 840 acres on the eastern Marcy Townline, between Mulaney Road and Route 49, to locate the SUNY Institute of Technology of Utica/Rome. The Institute is an upper division college for transfer and graduate students in professional, technical or liberal arts programs.

Stittville

About the year 1778 a sawmill and dwelling were built on the south side of the Nine Mile Creek about six miles north of the Mohawk river. Pioneers at once began to cluster about the place; the sawmill was enlarged and a gristmill added. For a number of years this spot was known as Red Mills. In 1828 Robert Stitts, who married Eliza Haskin, came from Pittstown, New York. He built

the first store and hotel, and so in time the Red Mills came to be called Stittville after Robert Stitts.

The original settlers were mostly from Rensselaer County, New York, and from New England. The Nine Mile Creek was about three times as large as at the present time and furnished good water power. The forest stretched from either bank and was composed of beech, maple, elm, ash, birch, hemlock, and bass wood, all splendid wood and lumber. When once cleared away the soil was excellent.

About 1833 a quarry of the Trenton limestone was opened near the present railroad. This was operated a number of years by Thomas Powell. The tiers ran to the unusual thickness of from one to three feet; and it was a clear, bright and beautiful stone, well adapted for building purposes as well as lime. When the Black River Canal was built, there were between two and three hundred men employed there. The stone for 10 locks was taken from this quarry. The immense pillars in front of the Utica State Hospital were also taken from this quarry. The contractors who built the Black River Railroad used a great deal of this stone. For many years the stone was used for miscellaneous building purposes and burned into lime, but the strata now dips in such shape that it does not pay to quarry it for building purposes.

Several years after the original saw-and gristmill was destroyed by fire, a carding mill was erected which was afterwards used for the manufacture of bleached cotton

Marcy Grange Hall

and sheeting. It was operated by William Grant and John Draper, and the hoods they made ranked with the best in the country. They afterwards manufactured clotheslines. After the death of Mr. Grant and Mr. Draper, the plant was sold to Hayes and Valley of Cohoes and changed into a two-set knitting mill.

In 1833 Ezra Shattuck built a sawmill the south side of the Nine Mile Creek and two miles south of Stittville, and Calvin Shattuck built a wagon shop which was later made into a flaxmill and run by a Mr. Sherman on the north side. Both have passed out of existence, and the farm in 1932 was owned by Ernest Roscup.

The first skim milk cheese made in this country was made by A. S. Bagg in the Stittville cheese factory.

The post office was established in 1849, William Grant becoming the first postmaster. About 1875 Edwin Fox edited a weekly paper known as the Temperance Zealot, which had a large circulation and was much enjoyed by local readers. This printing establishment was located on the farm owned by Richard Thomas in 1932.

Plank roads began to be constructed about 1846. Northern Plank Road company authorized and built a road in 1847-48. Holland Patent and Marcy organized and built a road in 1850. However, these roads soon proved costly. They lost favor and disappeared as rapidly as they had come and gravel roads followed. In 1913 a macadam road was built, and in 1924 it was resurfaced with concrete.

About 1890 Ellis D. Jones established a private telephone line between his store and residence, and a few years later founded and was manager of the Oneida County Rural Telephone Company.

About 1893 The Stittville Canning Company was organized, and became one of the largest canneries in the world. The company no longer exists. The buildings were used for a time by the Town of Marcy for highway equipment.

In 1910, the hamlet of Stittville had its greatest fire which burned the largest part of the community right to the ground. There had been fires before in several mills, but this one was so disastrous that it made newspapers all over the country. There were no water lines in town, no fire department and only a millpond as a source of water. The disaster led to the forming of the Stittville Fire Department in 1925 which continues today.

Selected References

History of the Town of Marcy, 1832-1970, (Marcy Town Board, 1969).

SUNY College at Utica/Rome, located in Marcy.

Main Street, Deansboro in late 1800's. Note horses with wagons of milk cans on way home from Condensory at the Osborne's store.

Forge Hollow was the site of an early hamlet of Marshall on State Rte 315. There are caves on the right and Big Creek is on the left going southeast toward Waterville.

The 1st Forge in 1801 was run by Sherman Daniels & Son, a sawmill and furniture factory were once run by water power.

Marshall

By
Kenneth G. McConnell

Revised by
Dorothy McConnell,
Town Historian

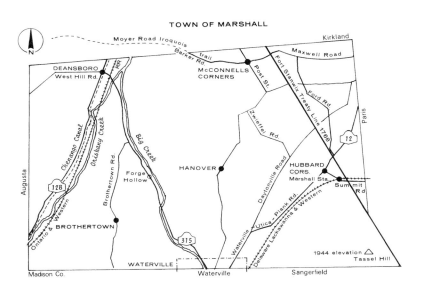

The Town of Marshall is situated in the south central part of Oneida County, which was once part of Albany, Tryon, Montgomery and Herkimer Counties, Marshall was once part of the Town of Whitestown, the Town of Paris in 1798, of Kirkland in 1827, and finally became the township as we know it on February 21, 1829. It is composed of the Brothertown Tract and Coxe's Patent, Marshall was named in honor of the U.S. Supreme Court Chief Justice, John Marshall. Marshall has an area of 19,322 acres. Tassel Hill, in the southeast corner of the town (a state forest preserve), has an elevation of 1944 feet and is the highest point in Oneida County. There are 42 miles of town roads, 24 miles of state roads and 15 miles of county roads.

Marshall has a population of about 2100, primarily centered around Deansboro and that portion of Waterville that is in Marshall. There are about 35 full time farmers. Dairy farms are most prominent, but Marshall's rich soil also produces potatoes, cabbage, Brussell sprouts, sweet corn, pumpkins and other cash crops. In comparison, the census of 1880 showed 280 farms raising chiefly hops: 810,030 pounds. The Benchmark-New York (formerly Eastern Rock stone quarry), Agway Petroleum & Gale Feed Mill are some of the larger businesses other than agriculture.

In 1774, the Rev. Joseph Johnson, a Mohegan Indian and Baptist preacher, along with Indians James Shattuck, Johen Scheesuch and Samuel Tallman came to the Oneida Indian Nation along with the Rev. Samuel Kirkland to plead for land. Johnson had a dream of a place of refuge for all the remnants of these once proud tribes from New Jersey and Long Island that had been decimated by war, disease, alcohol, and indifference. Johnson envisioned a united nation of Indians called Brothertown (also called Brotherton), with a culture patterned after the Christian religion. In October 1774 the Oneidas granted him 10

square miles (24,000 acres) situated mostly in present-day Marshall with a portion in Kirkland. In 1775 five families came, only to find they had settled in a no-mans-land between the warring colonists and the Iroquois and Tories. The founders of Brothertown were forced to wait out the war at Fort Stanwix and some fled to Stockbridge, Massachusetts.

Upon their return in 1781, they found that the potatoes they had planted were still growing. The Brothertown Indians eventually grew to about 450. English became the language of necessity, because they had no common language: they were composed of so many diverse tribes from New England, Long Island and New Jersey. In 1785, they set up a government patterned after New England which lasted until 1843. Three whites, one of whom was an attorney, were appointed by the State Legislature to oversee the Indian affairs. Every April the Indians met to elect a clerk, two overseers of the poor, two marshals, three fence viewers (assessors), one-pound master (tax Collector) and one overseer of highways. A peacemaker (justice) and tithing men were appointed. Tithing-men were responsible for enforcing puritanical religious rules. Breaking the Sabbath, card playing or "frolicking" brought a 75-cent fine or two hours in the stocks. By 1795 the Brothertown Tract by legislative decrees had been reduced to 9000 acres.

One Brothertown of note was the Rev. Samson Occum, who arrived in 1785 and was an ordained Presbyterian minister. The Rev. Occum, a full-blooded Mohegan, won an audience with King George III while on a fund-raising trip to England. The trip enabled him to put up the then huge sum of $50,000 to help establish Dartmouth College. A prolific writer of popular hymns, he also delivered a temperance sermon at the hanging of an alcoholic murderer which was published and went through 19 editions over a period of 50 years. Occum organized the first Christian

Indian Church without white assistance. Well-respected, he preached before whites and married and buried them. He was remembered as a paunchy man who wore somber black dress, befitting a reverend of the times, and carried a gold-headed cane given him by King George.

In 1795 the Society of Friends (Quakers) sent a Westchester County Missionary named John Dean to work among the Brothertowns. He was succeeded by his son Thomas who was very prominent and respected and for whom Deansboro (originally Deansville) was named. The Dean Homestead still stands in a state of excellent preservation now owned by Eloise Beerhalter. The older wing contains a fascinating beehive oven, probably built between 1798-99, and was the Indian Agent's office. The main portion was built about 1824. Thomas was responsible for removing the Brothertowns to Green Bay, Wisconsin, the last great exodus taking place in 1848. The Brothertowns were paid $14,249 for their land by New York State.

The Brothertowns were a highly successful group, building sawmills, gristmills, a church, a school and many beautiful frame homes that are in use to this day. At Green Bay they became very respected citizens; some became state senators and judges and all assimilated completely into American society.

The earliest white settlers came in on the Moyer Road, as they settled along it and in the immediate vicinity. The Moyer Road was an Iroquois Indian trail and ran from the Mohawk river near the present day Frankfort to Sauquoit, to Paris, along Maxwell Road to McConnell's Corners, across Post Street, down Barker Road to Whitney's Corners, across Lombard Road, through the field to Bogusville Hill Road and on to Stockbridge and Oneida Castle.

The earliest known white settler is Joseph Eastman who settled in Marshall in 1784; the next being David Barton in 1792. Two farms in the town, Barker's and McConnell's, are still in operation by the descendants of the original settlers. Malecki and Wardwell Barker arrived at the present location of the Barker farm in 1795 and Thaddeus McConnell settled on Maxwell Road near the intersection of Post Street in 1796. Other early families were the Melvins, Millers, Harts, Williams, Hubbards, Pecks, Gridleys and Rouse families, most coming around 1793 and 1797. Many settled at Hanover Green which now has only a few farms but which once boasted a tavern, store, gristmill, sawmill, post office, stage stop, school, church, cobbler and carpenter shop.

Forge Hollow was another early settlement, so named because of the iron forge there. Gun barrels for Frederick Remington, founder of Remington Arms, were made there. A blacksmith, cobbler, cooper, hotel and tavern, sawmill, clothing shop, tanner, church, and school were once there also.

By 1819 a stage run was established between Utica and Waterville with a stop at Hanover where the Marshall Post Office was located. After the coming of the Chenango Canal in 1836, Deansville (changed to Deansboro in 1894) became the center of the town. Deansboro has seen many businesses come and go, chiefly due to the decreasing importance of water power from the two branches of the Oriskany Creek. These once powered several gristmills, three feed mills, three distilleries (one later converted to a cider mill), and three saw mills. The Oriskany generated electric power for the town. However about 1900, eels and

Thomas Dean Homestead, Deansboro. The main house was built about 1824. The adjacent, original homestead was built in 1799. The Deans were a Quaker family and an agent for the Brothertown Indians. The homestead has a well-preserved brick fireplace, with a beehive oven and a smaller auxiliary unit for heating a large pan of water.

their tough skins wound around the generator turbine and slowly brought it (and the power) to a halt.

The Chenango Canal was abandoned in 1876. In 1849 a stock company was formed and a toll road, the Waterville and Utica Plank Road, was constructed by way of Deansboro. This road was paved in 1915. Between 1871 and 1957 the Ontario and Western Railroad operated in the Oriskany Valley stopping in Deansboro. The Delaware, Lackawanna and Western served the eastern portion of the town from Waterville to Utica starting in 1866. It once stopped at Marshall Station, on Summit Road, just down from Lincoln Davies General Store. A Clinton-Deansboro-Waterville Bus Company was operated as early as 1913.

The town once had 11 school districts, the oldest school built sometime prior to 1800 and the earliest known schoolmaster being Seely McConnell, who taught in the old Lapham District I, at the intersection of Ford and Maxwell Roads. Marshall is now in the Waterville School System. The Deansboro School is now the Town of Marshall Town Hall and Community Center. It houses the Deansboro Branch of the Waterville Public Library, the Justice Court & Town offices (lately remodeled) and provides a meeting place for various organizations and summer day camp.

The earliest churches were the Hanover Society Congregational (formed in 1797); the first Baptist Church of Paris (1797) at McConnell's Corners; The Universalist Church of Forge Hollow, (about 1800); the Deansboro Congregational Society (1835); and the Deansboro Methodist Episcopal Church (1837).

Deansboro clubs and organizations include the Marshall Historical Society; OJS (Order of Joyous Service); Deansboro Garden &Nature Study Club; Deansboro Doers Independent Homemakers; Boy and Girl Scouts; The Friendly Club; and Deansboro-Waterville Lions Club.

The Deansboro Fire Company was formed in 1896 and reorganized and incorporated in 1906 as the Barton Hose Company. The fire house was built in 1957, with a second floor addition in 1994.

The Deansboro Water Company was established August 26, 1896 with chlorination in 1946. All assets of the Deansboro Water District is run by an advisory Board with Morrie Sturdevant as Supt. In 1997 a Sand Filtration system was installed with more capacity for future needs.

Deansboro now has Gazzal's Superette, Koren's Hotel, Benedict's Antique Shop, Joan's Country Café, post office, locksmith, Chet's Excavating, Dwyer's Concrete Figurine Castings, Schwartz's Metal Work Forge and Blunts Produce as well as Sturdevant Forge and Curio Shop. Outside of Deansboro, in the township, there is a furniture shop, and auto body shop, a feed mill, a bookstore, a stone quarry, a petroleum plant, a sewer plant, for the Village of Waterville, a glass blower and many small home businesses.

The Deansboro Musical Museum became well known in 1948 when it housed the Sanders family collection of restored musical instruments that dated back to the 1500s. This fascinating and unique museum was known to collectors all over the country and was finally closed through an auction sale in 1998.

The Town of Marshall has not grown much in population or industry over the years but it combines old-fashioned charm with modern conveniences and diversity, featuring some of the friendliest people in the state.

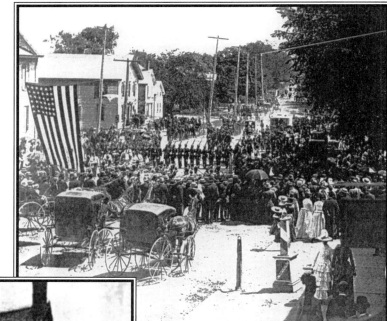

New Hartford Centennial 1888.

May 14, 1890, was a festive day in New Hartford, for, on that occasion, Butler Memorial Hall (left) was formally presented to the Village. The community put on its brightest spring appearance. Morgan Butler, one of New Hartford's oldest, most respected and generous citizens, presented this wonderful gift to the Village. An article in the Utica Morning Herald *reads: "This hall contains a post office, with 360 glass boxes and 139 locked boxes, a justice office, a public library, a reading room, a room for ladies' gatherings, a gymnasium and bowling alleys, a kitchen, and large hall, finely furnished which will seat 450 persons. Upon the stage is a Chickering Grand Piano." It now houses the village and town offices.*

Special Metals Corporation

Utica National Insurance Company

New Hartford

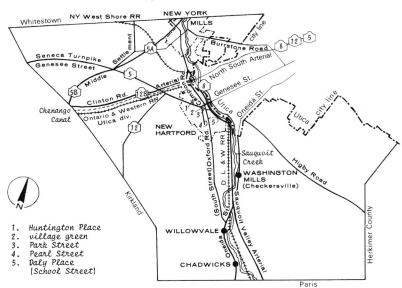

1. Huntington Place
2. village green
3. Park Street
4. Pearl Street
5. Daly Place (School Street)

The Town of New Hartford was settled in 1788 when Jedediah Sanger bought 1000 acres of the Coxe Patent from George Washington and George Clinton. This land, separated into two equal parts by the Sauquoit Creek, was part of the Town of Whitestown until 1827 when the Town of New Hartford was formed. An 1827 map shows the boundary of the Town of New Hartford running two or three blocks north of the Parkway and Burrstone Road. At that time, New Hartford included South Utica. As the City of Utica developed south and southwesterly, many plots were annexed to the city. Consequently, the existing boundary has many angles and jogs.

In 1871, a year after the Village of New Hartford incorporated, the Sauquoit Creek was established as the eastern boundary of the village. Today the town is bounded on the north by the Town of Whitestown; the northeast by the City of Utica; the southeast by the Town of Frankfort, Herkimer County; the south by the Town of Paris; and the west by the Town of Kirkland.

The town includes the Village of New Hartford, part of the Village of New York Mills, and communities of Washington Mills and Chadwicks, both having post offices. The settlements of Checkerville, Willowvale, and Middle Settlement have figured in the history of New Hartford. The present population of the town is 21,430.

Many of the early settlers came from Connecticut, near Hartford, which is probably how the town got its name. The settlers were primarily of Dutch and German descent. Many were relatives. There were several families each of Kelloggs, Risley, and Higbys. Others had been friends and neighbors in Connecticut. Sanger sold several hundred acres north of the Sauquoit Creek to Joseph Higby. This land covered the hill on which Higby Road is located. Sanger deeded much of his land for churches, cemeteries, and manufacturing purposes. The early settlers were largely self-sufficient, using logs for their first hous-

es and growing their own foodstuffs. Farming developed on the rolling hills.

The presence of the Sauquoit Creek proved to be a great asset for community development. A gristmill (1789) and a sawmill (1790). Erected by Sanger utilizing water power, served as a nucleus. Thereafter, manufacturing development progressed along the banks of the creek. Cording mills, a cap factory, and knitting mills were established within the present Village of New Hartford.

At New York Mills, the Upper Mills of the New York Mills Manufacturing Company included an old wooden building know as the Buhr Stone Mill that had been converted from an early gristmill. The Upper Mills manufactured some of the first fine shirting in this country. The Utica Cotton Mill was established about 1814 on the creek between the Villages of New York Mills and New Hartford, and it was known as the Capron Factory. A woolen factory was established in Checkerville, now Washington Mills. A tannery was converted to a bleachery by George W. Chadwick in Willowvale. Sawmills, a cider mill, and a plaster mill are among the other industries that located on the banks of the creek.

The development of the Seneca Turnpike by the Seneca Road Company in 1800 added to New Hartford's commercial importance. Sanger invested in that company to assure that it would include the existing settlement. As it was one of the earliest east-west routes through the state, it provided opportunities for the establishment of many inns and hostelries. The hamlet of Middle Settlement was the site of Palmer's Inn, one of the earliest local landmarks, which was razed in the 1960s to make way for a shopping center.

The Chenango Canal cut through the town roughly along the path that the Horatio Arterial follows today. Horsecars were operated from Utica to New Hartford in 1863 by the Utica, Clinton and Binghamton Railroad

Company until the introduction of electric cars in 1889. The trolley tracks were removed from Genesee Street in the early 1940s.

Although the early manufacturing facilities of the town have disappeared, some prominent buildings still exist. The Presbyterian Church is a village landmark and has the distinction of being the oldest public building in Oneida County. On the corner of Huntington Place and Genesee Street, the home of the first Mayor of Utica, Joseph Kirkland, still stands. It was later owned by the Sherrills and their descendants, the Butlers.

Throughout its history, New Hartford has had many schools. The first teacher in the area was Samuel Dakin. He was a young lawyer who arrived here from New England about 1815. He was unable to establish a practice until he had been a resident for three years. He made his living preparing young men for college.

In the early 1800s, Joshua Palmer, proprietor of Palmer's Inn on Seneca Turnpike, gave several acres for a school. The Middle Settlement School was built. It was moved and replaced in 1922. That school was torn down in 1973 to make way for Sambo's Restaurant.

Another school, erected in the early 1800s, was located on South Street (now Oxford Road) and Park Street across from the village green. It had two stories, the lower housing boys and the upper, girls.

In 1876 Miss Eunice Toll and Mrs. Theodosia Toll Foster, sisters from Verona, established The Home School for Young Ladies in a large home on the point of Paris Road and Genesee Street. The school eventually was moved to the Toll Homestead in the Town of Verona. In 1901, Judge Sanger's house on the point was torn down to make space for the Union Grade School, which became known as the Point School. In the 1930s a new junior-senior high school was built on Oxford Road, which is the present grade school.

School expansion was necessary after World War II with the development of New Hartford as a fast-growing suburb. The various district schools – Sherman Hills, Roberts-Sessions Road, Middle Settlement, Benton Hills and Washington Mills – were combined to form the New Hartford Central School in 1946. In 1952, a large junior-senior high school was constructed as an addition to one already on Oxford Road and Daly Place. The remains of

Utica Mutual Insurance Building, top center, The Horatio Arterial, also known as the north-south arterial, swings across top right corner. Beyond the arterial, top right, is the Yahnundasis Country Club Golf Course. To the left of the insurance building, nestled in the trees, is the Wedgewood Apartments. The Utica Country Day School and later the Utica Technical College were located there.

Sangertown Square Mall, pictured above, is bordered by Genesee Street and Commercial Drive. Extensive expansion of the Mall is presently being proposed. The open area above the Mall in the picture is the Yahnundasis Country Club and Golf Course.

the New Hartford Cotton Manufacturing Company, as well as the long unused village cemetery, were part of the parcel of land used for the school. A monument placed in front of the school commemorates the site of the cemetery. The Myles Elementary School was erected on Clinton Road in 1956, and two years later the Hughes Elementary School was built on Higby Road. Ralph Perry Junior High was constructed in 1966.

The Utica Country Day School was established in 1921 as a private school for grades 1 through 12 where the Wedgewood Apartments now stand. It was discontinued in 1941. A small trolley shelter built in the architectural style of the school for the joint use of students and Sherrill Brook residents still stands. After World War II, the building was used for the Utica Technical College, which eventually became Mohawk Valley Community College.

The plot of land which was occupied by Rhoads Hospital and now is Notre Dame High School was formerly in the Town of New Hartford, but was annexed to the City of Utica in the early 1940s for construction of the hospital. This provided the hospital with city sewer and water facilities, as well as city fire protection. It is surrounded by the Town of New Hartford.

New Hartford has known many churches. Some still exist; many have disappeared. It is known that the first church meeting were held in Sanger's barn on Mill Street in 1790. It was decided that a church should be built. In 1791, the First Religious Society of Whitestown was founded as a Congregational Society. In 1802, it became the First Presbyterian Church. Sanger gave the land on the corner of Genesee and Pearl Streets for the location of the church.

In the 1820s a Quaker Meetinghouse existed on Oxford Road. No mention of it can be found after 1885. In 1825, St. Stephen's Episcopal Church was built on Oxford Road on land donated by Sanger. In 1842, the Methodist Episcopal Church was built on Oxford Road, having held services in various locations since 1826. In 1869, a larger church was built nearby. This is now the Players Theatre. A modern, larger Methodist Church was built in 1961 on Genesee Street. The Baptist Society built a church in 1856.

St John the Evangelist Catholic Church was built on Oxford Road and Sherman Street in 1885. A new church was built in 1966. A convent and Catholic school are locat-

New Hartford High School

Ralph Perry Junior High School

E.R. Hughes Elementary School

Myles Elementary School

ed on Sherman Street and Pearl Street. About 1890, the Welsh Church was established and housed on Pearl Street. It was defunct by 1941, and the building was given to the Amicable Lodge. Later churches were the Moravian Church, the Messiah United Church, the Bible Baptist Church, and the Clinton Road Baptist Church.

The construction of the Horatio Arterial and the Sauquoit Valley Arterial has diluted the main flow of traffic from the original Seneca Turnpike. Increased population, most of whom work outside of New Hartford, has established this as a suburban community.

The town park, consisting of 240 acres between Route 12 and Route 12B near Route 5, was established by the town board in 1960 and has been developing since. The site possesses many natural scenic features, including a ravine. Much is wooded with hardwood and hemlock clumps. The entrance is a large open field area. It presently includes a large playing area, a playground, picnic area, and foot trails through the woods.

First United Methodist Church of New Hartford

First Baptist Church 1855

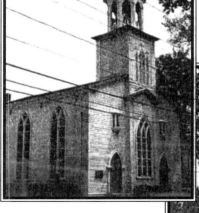

(above) St. John the Evangelist Roman Catholic Church

(right) St. Stephen's Episcopal Church

(inset) New Hartford Presbyterian Church, Today
Presbyterian Church in 1880

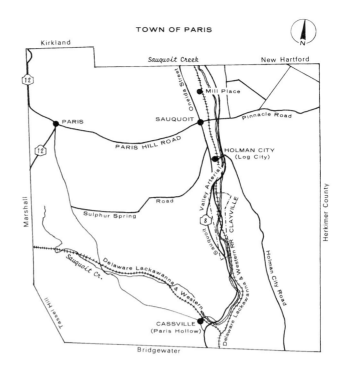

TOWN OF PARIS

Paris

By Mae Listovitch,
Town Historian.

Thanks to
Gertrude Jones, Leonard Grubel,
Ruth Shupe and Polly Blunk,
Landmark Art Studio.

The Town of Paris was once a part of Whitestown and was much larger than its current size. When organized in 1792, it was a part of Herkimer County. In 1798 Herkimer County was divided, and Paris has been a part of Oneida County since that time. The last change was made in 1839 when a portion of Kirkland was added to Paris.

The name Paris was given the town in appreciation for help given in time of need by a Fort Plain farmer and miller named Isaac Paris. There was a famine in 1789 in the area where the village of Paris is now located. Paris sent food by way of flatboats up the Mohawk to the mouth of the Oriskany where the cargo was transferred to a log canoe built by the settlers. The grain was taken up the creek to Clinton from whence it was taken by cart to the village.

According to Rogers, who wrote a history of the town, the first settler was a black man who had escaped from a British army officer. After his garden was raided by passing Indians, he left the area. The first permanent settler was Major Royce of Hartford, Connecticut, who settled in the Paris Hill area in 1789. Shortly after his arrival John and Sylvester Butler and Asa Shepherd came to the area. Phineas Kellogg was the first to settle in Sauquoit.

Five main villages existed in the early history of the town. They were Paris, Sauquoit, Cassville, Clayville and Holman City. All except Holman City and Paris remain with post offices. In 1820 the post office was named Sauquoit from an Indian word Sagh-da-que-da. Clayville was so named in honor of Henry Clay in 1849, after being previously called Paris Furnace. Cassville was known as Frog Hill or Toad Holler until 1830 when it was called Paris Hollow. The current name was given in 1835. Log

City was the name of the Holman City area until 1840.

The villages of Paris, Clayville, Cassville and Sauquoit have their own volunteer fire companies. The first fire engine in Sauquoit was Fulton No. 3 which was purchased in 1835 from the City of Utica when it became inadequate in size for the city's needs. Fulton No. 3 is now the property of the Oneida Historical Society and appeared in the 1998 Bicentennial exhibit at the society.

Although some portions of the early roads have been abandoned, for the most part the main early ones are still being used under other names. A corduroy road ran on the present Pinnacle Road between east and west Sauquoit. A completely new road following no previous routes in the Sauquoit Valley Arterial completed in 1970. The Delaware, Lackawanna and Western Railroad from Utica to Binghamton was constructed in the 1850s and is still in use.

The geographic feature which most influenced the development of the town is the Sauquoit Creek which rises on Tassel Hill and flows 17 miles to the Mohawk. It has a drop of 90 feet per mile and supplied power for 144 industries which were located at various times along its length. Not all of these were in the Town of Paris.

Another feature which provided a source of interest for a time was a "burning spring", of sulphurated hydrogen gas. This spring was located at the point where Sulphur Springs Road and Oneida Street join, and where the park is now located. The Gilberts once ran a hotel there that was lighted by natural gas.

On Holman City Road east and north of the former Isaac Walton League building, now a private home, is a geographical formation known as "the basin". It is a hole about 100 feet deep, perfectly round and 850 or more feet in diameter. Geologists claim it was caused by a meteorite as evidenced by the pure iron in the depression.

From 1789 to 1812 the earliest form of livelihood after land clearing was the establishment of family farms and small industrial concerns which used the Sauquoit Creek as a source of waterpower. The first cotton mill in the valley was set up in 1812. Gere's oil (linseed oil) was marketed locally and in valley towns. Factories in Clayville included a shovel factory (1814), a scythe factory (1818) and a blast furnace from 1801-1832.

From 1830-1880 dairy farming increased with the advent of railroads and cheese factories. Hollister's woolen mills began in 1847 but failed in 1850. David Millard began an implement factory which later went out of business. Sterling Millard's scythe factory opened, and the Empire Woolen Company began to operate in 1861. This woolen mill stimulated the economy and was the largest industry in the township in 1880. In 1847 a silk mill was built on Griffith Place in Sauquoit by Abner Brownell. This later operated as a knife factory owned by J. Pope. This was a four-story building, and, as is true of most of these mills, is now demolished. However, the stone mill known as Farmer's Factory (1853) is now operated by Hillman for poultry raising.

After 1880 there was a gradual elimination of the older mills. For example, about 1900 Ladd Lewis operated a silk mill on Mill Place in Sauquoit, which is now gone. Also on Mill Place there was a canning factory owned by Johnson and Murray, wholesale grocers of Utica. From 1904-1940, this plant was owned and operated by Albert Hatfield.

During World War II and the Korean War, there was a reawakening as old textile mills were converted to other uses. The Empire Woolen Mill was used for the making of jet blades. Today none of the mills is in operation. The town has become a bedroom community for the Utica-Rome area. In addition to private homes, there are three trailer parks.

The number of farms and persons employed in agriculture has declined. The number of acres farmed has not decreased greatly, but the farms are larger and more mechanized, therefore needing fewer workers. Many are part-time farmers with acreage in cash crops such as beans or beef cattle. Commercial enterprises include small retail stores, taverns, garages and filling stations, a feed store and similar small operations. Lincoln Davies, Inc. is a large retail store where one can purchase everything from a pound of coffee to all the material to build a house or barn. The store has been known in the valley since the 1870s.

A number of churches were established early in the township. St. Paul's Episcopal Church in the hamlet of Paris is one of the earliest parishes in the county. The church was founded in 1797, and the early building burned. The present architecturally significant structure dates from 1818 and is now used only for summer ser-

Lewis Knitting Mill, a silk mill of the early 1900s.

Fire drill at Sauquoit Academy about 1905. This building, constructed about 1801, housed the Methodist Church until 1942.

vices. The Paris Religious Society was founded in 1791, later became Congregational, and had the first church bell in the township. The United Methodist Church of Sauquoit, organized in 1801, is the oldest Methodist congregation west of Albany. The current building, the second on the site, was erected in 1842.

The Sauquoit Valley Central School came into being when 15 districts combined in 1930. Most of the earlier, original schoolhouses are gone or are now homes. The Doolittle schoolhouse has been restored and is now open for programs, tours for students and the public.

The Sauquoit Valley Central School was built on Oneida Street in 1932. In 1953, a new elementary school was erected on Sulphur Springs Road and in 1990 a new middle school was also built on Sulphur Springs Road. In order to accommodate the growing enrollment of students in the school district, additions and renovations were made, in 1996, to both the elementary school and the high school.

There was a newspaper in Sauquoit called the Sauquoit Valley *News* published in the 1930s.

Several well-known people lived and/or were born in the town. Perhaps the most famous beyond our own area is Asa Gray, the world-known naturalist, who was born at the foot of Pinnacle Road, Sauquoit, in 1810. He spent his boyhood in Clayville where his father had a mill. Tunis LeRoy, a mechanic living in Holman City, invented the power drill press. B. T. Babbitt, born in Holman City, start-ed a soap company and became a millionaire. Dr. Gerrit Parmalee Judd was a missionary to the Sandwich Islands. His efforts helped to make Hawaii American. Kirkland Griffin was incarcerated in Mill Prison, England, as a traitor during the American Revolution. He was released and served under John Paul Jones on the *Bonhomme Richard* during the battle with the *Serapis*. William Babcock was a son of Nathan Babcock who was a member of the Boston Tea Party.

The Town of Paris will continue to be a bedroom for the Utica-Rome area. Population growth will probably continue to be slow although industrial sites are available for new businesses. The town has a rather homogeneous population with no one national or ethnic group dominating its life. The location on good roads, with a good sewer system, sufficient utilities and availability to the shopping and entertainment centers of Utica make citizens of the Town of Paris happy to live here.

Selected References

Kelly, Virginia, Merrilyn R. O'Connell, Stephen S. Olney, Johanna R. Reig, *Wood and Stone*, (Central New York Community Arts Council, 1972).

Rogers, Henry C., *History of the Town of Paris and the Valley of the Sauquoit*, (Utica, NY 1881, reprinted 1976).

See Clayville Library and Town Museum in Sauquoit Valley Elementary School.

Falls in the Sauquoit Creek near the Sauquoit arterial; photo 1918.

Wheelman's Fountain, Cassville, June 18, 1897. A popular stopping place on the bicycle path from Utica to Cassville. People used to stop here for spring water although the marble fountain is now gone.

Roland Anthony's carriage shop, probably located on the Cincinnati Creek, Remsen.

Six Remsen citizens pose with the tools of their trades, left to right: Wm. E. Davies, printer; Roscoe E. Roberts, blacksmith; Edwin S. Pirnie; Hugh Hughes, printer; James V. Reed and Elmer Thomas, blacksmiths.

TOWN OF REMSEN

Remsen

By
Margaret P. Davis
and
Pat Hill
Town Historian

It is difficult to believe that Remsen was not in existence at the time of the American Revolutionary War, 200 years ago, but it is true. After the war the land to the west was open for occupancy and people from Connecticut and the Hudson Valley were among the first settlers. Shubael Cross and his family were early residents but Barnabas Mitchell from Meriden, Connecticut claims to have been the first permanent settler. This was in 1792. In September of 1795 five families from Wales located in this vicinity, being the first of that nationality to stake their prosperity in these towns against what the forest wilderness might have in store for them. Thus two distinct strains made up our pioneer element, each with its own traits and desires. It is amazing what they found for food, for today the corner store and public market are a necessity. However, these people brought with them certain qualities of perseverance, courage, self-reliance and industry which their descendants have every right to be proud of and to emulate with affection.

By an act of the New York State Legislature passed March 15, 1978, forming the County of Oneida from the County of Herkimer, it was also decreed that all of the Town of Norway lying in the new County of Oneida should be organized into the new Town of Remsen. The town was named after an early patentee of the area, Henry Remsen. So we find that, unlike most other townships. Remsen was organized by the legislature without petition, action or movement on the part of its inhabitants to advance such organization.

It was necessary at this time to clear the land in order to till it for food. The implements were very crude. Wooden plows were used. Wheat and rye were harvested with a sickle and threshed with flails or tramped out by horses and cattle. The soil in general differed little from that of other high sections of the county and was better adapted for grazing than for agriculture. In those days the Cincinnati was a far more pretentious stream than it is now and probably furnished food and transportation, and later, water power, as well as a source of direction for travelers.

Prior to the Revolution emigration to the United States was slow, but as soon as peace was restored the flow of people to America continued, prompted solely by the desire to improve and develop their station in life beyond what was possible for them at home. The people of Wales at this time were in a state of extreme poverty. So it was to improve their distressful situation that these people were willing to encounter the unknown dangers of a new country. For half a century the Welsh people poured into Steuben and Remsen to join friends and relatives. Steuben Corners, Sixty Acres, Fairchild and Bardwell became settlements of some character when Remsen village could boast of but three log dwellings. The home of Robert Thomas, on the road to Steuben, was the temporary stopping place for Welsh people who had no kindred or friends who preceded them to these parts – his home being their home until they could determine a location to suit them.

In 1813 the population of the township was 4891. At this time Forestport was included in Remsen.

In 1812 the turnpike from Utica to Sacketts Harbor was completed and for two or three years afterward it was a busy thoroughfare. Supplies and stores for the 1812 war were hauled through by day and by night and many soldiers and sailors passed over it on their way to Sacketts Harbor.

The same year Colonel Mather Beecher purchased the Noble and Blue Tannery and established a shoe factory. This was one of the first establishments of it kind in the United States and the work was carried on in the stone house on Main Street in the village, just north of the present Baptist Church. Boots and shoes of his own tanning effort were shipped to Chicago by the Great Lakes when that city was little more than a military post, Fort Dearborn.

195

What is known as the State Road was so called because it was constructed by the state from the proceeds of a lottery authorized in 1803 to raise $41,500 for the purpose. It extended from Johnstown to Sacketts Harbor, crossed the West Canada Creek at Prospect, and traversed the township of Remsen diagonally. There were several inns on this road that are attractive homes today. Witherell house, Sheldon house (1809) and Higby's Tavern. Portions of this road are still in use today.

The completion of the Plank Road in the fall of 1848 added to the facilities for transportation of merchandise, diminished the time of transit and lessened the exertion of both men and teams. It brought to travel in general a degree of comfort before unknown. The road was graded the width of two lanes but only one track was planked. It was a toll road with gates at intervals of four miles. The State Highway 12 was constructed about 1912 and in 1948 and 1949 was relocated as a four-lane superhighway on the westerly outskirts of the Village of Remsen.

The first settler within the Village of Remsen was Peter A. Becker, who took 110 acres of land at the southern line of the present village limits. This he sold to Deacon William Platt, a man of activity and enterprise, who built a sawmill and gristmill and later added a blacksmith shop to the lower end of the village. Here in the wall of one of the oldest buildings of Remsen was placed a bench mark. (A bench mark is a surveyor's mark on a permanent landmark that has a known position of altitude.) Strange as it may seem that bench mark is now missing from that old wall and the space left empty. It had meaning only where it had stood for years.

Broughton White and Lemuel Hough came to Remsen from Steuben and built an ashery on what is Steuben Street now, and opened up a small grocery store. In a few years they sold the store to Jacob Betticher, better known as Jake (pronounced Jock). He sold grog as well as groceries and it was a popular place. The Welshmen gave the a short sound and the village was called Jäck in all languages long after Jacob Betticher had passed away and been forgotten.

The history of Remsen and Steuben is not complete without the story of the Welsh chutes. Whatever else our ancestors included in their luggage as they embarked for their new homes, they always carried their Bibles. While I can no longer read the Welsh language, I cherish the possession of these Bibles. The first Welsh settlers came to this area about 1795, but the first church was built in the Steuben area in 1804. However, prayer groups, called seiats were held in the homes twice on Sundays and once during the week. The first church building erected in this area was of logs and built during the pastorate of the Rev. John Pierce. It was to be used for school purposes as well. It was completed in November. It burned to the ground on Christmas night that same year. During the year 1805 a frame structure was built and in this they worshiped until it became too small.

In 1819 the frame building was removed to give way for a commodious stone edifice. This stood for 83 years

Covered bridge over Cincinnati Creek, north of Remsen village.

Bristol House, Main Street. Pictured: the Gainsway family, John Brant family, Ernest Worden, Ray Gainsway and Ingham Griffith.

and would have done service for many more years had it not been for a spring under the northwest corner of the foundation, which, with its alternate freezing and thawing, slowly but surely undermined the corner and racked the structure. A new chapel was built and dedicated June 23, 1904, called Capel Ucha. The Everett Memorial window faced the highway as a reminder of 100 years of service faithfully given and received by Welsh immigrants from Wales. The church was sold at auction because of disuse in 1948.

Many churches were built following this to meet the needs of a neighborhood, one within walking distance of homes. The Welsh brought with them fierce denominational loyalties and strong theological convictions and so each small group that came established his own church.

The Welsh have a passion for singing and oftentimes familiar tunes were heard as farmers tilled the soil on their farms. The Gymanfa Ganu (song festival) remains as the most popular expression of Welsh life today. Once each year the Fortnightly Club of Remsen sponsors a Welsh Sing in the Methodist church to sing the old familiar hymns. In 1998, the Gymanfa Ganu is held on the last Sunday in September during the Remsen Barn Festival of the Arts. There are two sessions. One takes place in the afternoon at the Stone Meetinghouse and another is held at the Methodist Church that evening.

The first organized school in Remsen was founded in 1813. On September 4 of that year it was voted to divide the area into two districts. The first building was at Fairchild just east of the old part of the cemetery. The village school was a log building on the northeast side of the turnpike about where a brick house is in 1976. A building for older children, the Academy, was built on the site of Stanley Shufelt's house. In 1852 in order to be more centrally located, a Union school was built on Prospect Street near where the Mohawk and Malone Railroad was later constructed. During that time A. J. MacElroy taught there and through his efforts the school became a high school in 1899. A new building was built on Steuben Street about 1912 which served until the consolidation of the districts, to become Remsen Central School in 1935. With the trend of families moving to the country the school was greatly overcrowded. As a result, the elementary school for grades K-5 was completed in the spring of 1979 and in 1990 an addition to this school enabled the 6th grades to be moved from the high school. In 1998, construction began on an addition to the high school. It will include a new gymnasium with stage, science rooms, classrooms and a music room.

Remsen was a busy industrial place in the early days. Each pioneer household was a workshop and long after the pioneer period was past, the manufacture of linen and woolen cloth was continued by the family. In nearly every farmhouse preparation for the supply of winter clothing began with summer or as early in the season as the wool from the sheep's back could be picked over, oiled, and carded. The spinning of the wool for bed blankets, hosiery, underwear, and winter clothing was no light task. All day long, throughout the summer, the sound of the spinning

W. C. White

1914, grading the Prospect road in Remsen.

Main Street, Remsen, September 16, 1908. Left to right: bank, tailor shop, pharmacy and Didymus Thomas Library, and meat market.

Margaret P. Davis

wheel was incessant. In large families extra help was usually needed during the spinning season and there would be much rivalry among the spinners, lending added zest to the work. The number of knots a young woman managed to run off in a day established her standing in the community: 40 threads on the reel made a knot, 10 knots a skein, two skeins a run and two runs a day's work. The price paid for spinning was six shillings or 75 cents a week and board.

After spinning came the dying process, then the weaving and finally the cloth was sent to the fulling mill to be made into fulled cloth. When it was ready for men's clothing, the coats and jackets were cut by a tailor who did little else regarding the work, for tailoress was then employed by the family who with her "goose" (a flatiron used for tailoring) occupied a prominent position during her sojourn with the family. Day after day she stitched away until finally the finishing touches were put on her garments. Then she and her goose, in a jumper or wooden sleigh, were conveyed to the home of the next family awaiting her services. In mid-winter preparation for summer clothes began. The flax was spun and finally woven into cloth for table use, bed linen, towels, and for summer wear generally. The hides of cattle slaughtered on the farm were tanned on shares and an itinerant shoemaker came in to make and mend the boots and shoes.

Capel Ucha-Congregational served Steuben and Remsen. Here is a brief summary of the churches of the township of Remsen. C.M. mean Calvinistic Methodist.

Cong. means Congregational:

Pen-Y-Caerau 1824-1907 First Calvinistic Church of America. Only a marker.

Capel Cerrig 1831-1998 Presbyterian Federated with Baptist 1965. Acquired by Remsen-Steuben Historical Society 1989.

Pen-Y-Graig 1828-1930's C.M. Only a marker.

Historic Bethel 1928-1930's Cong. Christmas in July Service (July 25). Acquired by Remsen-Steuben Historical Society.

Peniel 1839-1937 Cong. St. Ann's Catholic Church School.

Enlli 1837-1998 C.M. Spring and fall services. Acquired by Remsen-Steuben Historical Society.

Ninety-Six 1841-1900 C.M. Removed

Bardwell 1809-1917 Baptist. Only a marker.

Remsen United Methodist 1852-1998 Rev. Wade Jarrett, Minister.

Remsen Baptist 1892-1998 Federated with Stone Church 1965. Acquired by Remsen Lodge #677 F&AM 1997.

As the woods were cleared another industry of much importance was the manufacture of potash or pearl ash. As trees throughout the vicinity were burned, ashes were collected. The lye was extracted and sent to New York where it was made into saleratus (a leavening agent consisting of potassium or sodium bicarbonate) and kindred compounds.

On July 21, 1907, this boulder was moved from the Pirnie farm, south of Remsen, to the village park in Herkimer where it became the base for a statue of General Nicholas Herkimer.

Margaret P. Davis

Brick manufacture was carried on at the Mitchell farm. The production of quick-lime was an early and important industry. There was limestone just south of the village. This limestone was cut and used for building purposes. Then, too, wherever there was waterpower, a gristmill or a sawmill was the best asset. Manufacture of butter tubs and cheese boxes was needed also. Blacksmiths usually took care of the iron craft for the community. Shingle weavers provided shingles for building.

In the early 1800s John R. Ellis established a foundry and machine shop. He manufactured steam boilers, cheese presses, and treadwheels for churning by dog power. All of these were his own inventions. Probably many of our door latches, hinges, bolts, rivets, and nails were made by John R. Ellis.

At the present time many of the former industries have been outmoded. Farms have changed in size; butter is no longer made by each household; fluid milk is produced by large groups. The little farms have disappeared along with the cheese factories and now bulk tanks are in. A cold storage plant was owned and operated by B. K. Brown in the early 1900s. Products were stored and shipped to the summer resorts in the Adirondacks. In 1927 it was sold to the Dairyman's League for $95,000. Milk was shipped here from surrounding communities and big business was carried on. And again there were changes, and the Dairyman's League no longer functions.

There have been many merchants in Remsen village through the years. Remsen for a time was sufficient unto itself, but with the coming of railroads, better roads, and automobile travel it has become a small part of a larger community, really a bedroom for Utica and Rome.

Forestport was set off and organized as a separate township in 1869, and the village of Remsen two years later obtained a new charter.

How proud we in Remsen are of our Didymus Thomas Library, incorporated in 1899, and how fortunate we have always been to have dedicated people to serve as librarians. Among books which we prize are the History of Remsen, written by Millard F. Roberts and published in 1914. Mrs. Edna Roberts also published a book in the 1920s, *Honey Out of Rocks,* describing life in Remsen. In 1998, a book we've treasured over the last twenty years is *Honey out of the Rafters* written by Margaret P. Davis in 1976. It contains early history and pictures of Remsen and Steuben. Mrs. Davis was a dedicated Remsen historian and school teacher who enriched the lives of many.

When railroads were in vogue Remsen was advantageously situated as a railroad center and for several years the service was exceptional. The resort areas of the Adirondacks and Thousand Islands were popular attractions which could be reached only by trains. But the railroads never brought to Remsen the commercial prosperity many had anticipated, for instead of bringing wealth into the community, people went to Utica to take advantage of a greater selection of goods. The merchants of Remsen were no longer needed.

School near Bardwell Mills.

Margaret P. Davis

Welsh Presbyterian Church, Remsen, built in 1831.

Margaret P. Davis

In 1976 Remsen, a residential village with a few businesses, carried on to make for good living. Some of these businesses were: Williams Oil Company, Inc., Walter Hardware Store, Blood's Remsen Mobil Service, Remsen Transit Mix, Inc., Technical Structures, Inc., Ltd., Evans Equipment Company, Inc., John Ackley Funeral Home, Oneida National Bank, and Daniels Poultry Laying House.

Radio Station WREM in Remsen first went on the air in February 1958. In those early days a good deal of the broadcast was devoted to programming which was of interest to local farmers. WREM received 10 national awards for farm broadcasting. For the past seven years WREM has been the only full-time country music station in the Central New York area. In 1968 the radio station changed hands and became WADR. At the present time, in 1998, there are 5 other radio stations affiliated with WADR. They include AM stations WRNY and WUTQ and FM stations WOUR, WSKS, and WRFM.

On January 28, 1977 Remsen suffered a terrible loss, a historic landmark, the Remsen Hotel constructed in 1814, and adjoining businesses were destroyed by fire. The closing of Walter's Hardware in 1995 was another loss felt by many residents. In 1996, after serving our area for 70 years, Williams Oil Co. discontinued deliveries of petroleum products and heating oil. Another change came in the early 90s with the installation of a new sewer system and treatment plant in the village.

Several new businesses have been welcomed into our community over the years including: NAPA, Northern Lights, Main Street Newz, Fleet Bank, Remsen Big M, Remsen Country Bakery, Taylor's Trackside, Back of the Barn Antiques, Café Nero, Express Repair, Metal Parts Concrete. The Remsen VFW Memorial Post #982 built a new home on Steuben Street. We also welcomed back Remsen Lodge #677 F&AM. The Masons purchased the Baptist Church in 1997 and returned home to Remsen after 115 years.

During the past 18 years our village has become a familiar place for craft enthusiasts. In September 1980 the first Remsen Barn Festival of the Arts was held. It was so successful that it has been held the 4th weekend in September every year since. It attracts thousands of people to our small rural community.

On January 20, 1989 the Remsen-Steuben Historical Society acquired Capel Cerrig, an early Welsh church, and began restoration of it. Today it is called Stone Meetinghouse and is located on Prospect Street in the village. It is one of Remsen's proudest landmarks and is listed on the National Register of Historic Places. Another project the Historical Society is in the process of planning is Heritage Park.

The population in 1990 was 1,737 in the town and 465 in the village. The school enrollment in 1998 is 359 in the elementary school and 350 in the high school.

In 1998, the sounds of construction will be heard throughout the town. The high school's addition will begin. The town board has plans to build a much needed new highway garage on Phelps Road. And in yet another part of town the Remsen Development Corp. will be rebuilding the railroad depot. Trains passed through Remsen for a brief time on their way to the 1980 Winter Olympics held in Lake Placid. In the summer of 1998, the Adirondack Scenic Railroad is scheduled to resume trips to the north passing through our community once again.

Remsen will celebrate its Bicentennial in 1998. During the past year the Remsen Bicentennial Committee has been planning many events and festivities for the upcoming year. Our small town has many reasons to celebrate and be proud. The past 200 years have given to our community a rich and enduring heritage. It's this heritage, along with our hard working citizens, that will build our future.

Selected References

Daves, Margaret P., *Honey out of the Rafters,* (Remsen, 1976).

Remsen-Steuben Historical Society, *Newyddion Tref Remsen-Steuben,* (published yearly).

Roberts, Millard F., *History of Remsen 1789-1898,* (1914).

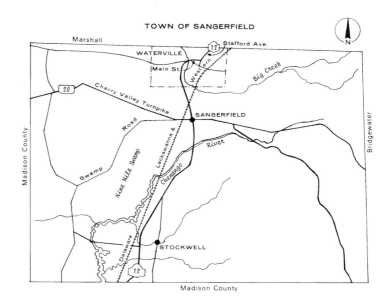

TOWN OF SANGERFIELD

Sangerfield

By

Mary C. Cleary, Town Historian
M. L. Peterson, Researcher
Hilda R. Barton
Martin F. Cleary
Sydney Erickson

The Town of Sangerfield, with the neighboring Town of Bridgewater, occupies the most southern portion of Oneida County. Its water supply attracted early settlers and its rich soil provided the basis for successful farming through the years.

U.S. Route 20 (east-west) intersects Route 12 (north-south) at the hamlet of Sangerfield, very near the site of the first dwelling built by Zerah Phelps in 1791 when he emigrated here from Massachusetts. The land then was owned by three land speculators, Michael Myers, John J. Morgan and Jedediah Sanger. Judge Sanger, anxious to have the area settled and named after him, promised a cask of rum for the first town meeting and 50 acres of land to the religious organization building the first church.

The Town of Sangerfield was officially established on March 5, 1795. The first town meeting was held on April 7, 1795, in Mr. Phelps' home. Records show that "after the meeting was opened, they voted to adjourn to the barn," no doubt to sample Judge Sanger's rum, which had been delivered as promised. The 50 acres were equally divided between the Congregationalists, who were the first to organize, and the Baptists, who had the first church building.

The year following the first town meeting the tax rolls showed 85 taxable inhabitants who paid a total of $108.56 in taxes. The highest tax of $5.04 was paid by Benjamin White.

Settlement was encouraged by the Cherry Valley Turnpike, built in 1811 as an extension of the Great Western Turnpike. Turnpike travel made the thriving community of Sangerfield Center the most important settlement in the township. Numerous taverns on the village green at the Center catered to the needs of the drovers who passed back and forth between Albany and Buffalo. When hay sold for $20 a ton, innkeepers charged $1 to keep a span of horses overnight, but when hay dropped to $10 a ton, the price dropped to 50 cents. These wagons progressed slowly up the hilly terrain, sometimes taking a week to haul freight from Sangerfield to Albany.

In those early days, the town also boasted its own newspaper, the *Civil and Religious Intelligencer*, founded in 1815. The name was later the *Sangerfield Intelligencer* and *Madison* and *Oneida Counties Gleaner* in 1830. The paper's editor-publisher, Joseph Tenney, prided himself on his firm's efficient delivery of papers over sometimes dusty and sometimes muddy roads by a boy on horseback who loudly announced his coming with a blast of a horn. In 1856 the *Waterville Times* was established and is still published weekly in Waterville.

By the late 1820s Waterville's expanding industries began to outstrip those of Sangerfield Center. Earlier established gristmills and sawmills were joined by taverns, stores, a distillery, a tannery, a brewery, a cotton mill and a foundry. Contributions to Waterville's early growth were made by many families who came here from New England, and were mainly of English stock. Prominent names include the Tower brothers; Jeduthan, Justus, John and Jotham; Benjamin White, Amos Osborn, Sylvanus Dyer, and Amos Muzzey. (Jeduthan Tower was the great-grandfather of Charlemagne Tower Jr., lawyer, industrialist and U.S. Ambassador to Russia, Austria-Hungary, and Germany in the late 1800s.)

With the land cleared, houses built, and industries started, the people began to turn their attention to the educational needs of their children. In 1815 the first public school was built on the corner of White Street and Academy (now Stafford Avenue South).

Waterville Central School District was organized in 1928. The curriculum of this new school was expanded to include agriculture, shop, music and home economics; and the commercial and physical education departments were enlarged. The school had a separate auditorium, the gift of George Eastman, founder of the Eastman Kodak

Company, who was born in Waterville. From 1930-1954 the student population doubled. A new open-space junior-senior high school was completed in June of 1974.

The Waterville school system annexed Oriskany Falls Union Free School in 1983. In 1985 renovation of the high school building, and a large addition to Memorial Park Elementary School were completed. Another renovation project of the school buildings took place in 1994.

By far the most important industry in the town has been farming. Farmers once raised their own grain for milling, fattened cattle and hogs for meat, and made their own butter and cheese. With the introduction of hops in 1830 these practices were largely abandoned. Hop growing reached its peak in the 1880s, although it continued well into the 1900s. Waterville became the main shipping point for hops, and the exchange center for hops in the United States. In 1882, when hops sold for the high price of $1 a pound, deposits in the National Bank of Waterville totaled three-quarters of a million dollars. Many people who did not grow hops made a living in related work, such as the manufacture of hop presses, buying and selling hops, transporting hop-pickers, drying or shipping hops.

In this time of prosperity, many farmers retired and built homes in Waterville. The village by this time had a thriving railroad, the Delaware, Lackawanna and Western; a new residential street, Putnam Street; a new Opera House built in 1880; a new firehouse built in 1872 on White Street, several hotels, and a new public water supply. A public library system was begun in 1874.

The hop industry began to decline around the turn of the century due to; the high risk involved in fluctuating hop prices, depletion of the soil, increase in hop diseases and pests, and most important of all, growing competition from the hop growers in Oregon and Washington. When this happened, farmers in this area began to return to dairy farming and added peas or beans as a cash crop. Peas were a major crop through the 1930s and 1940s, but declined after World War II, and practically disappeared in the late 1960s. Broccoli, asparagus, cabbage, Brussels sprouts, potatoes and snap beans are now raised, but on a smaller scale. Efforts were made to revive the hop industry in the late 1930s and 1940s, but proved unsuccessful. Many residents have a hop pole or two in their back yards to grow hops as ornamental vines.

Although the number of farms has declined in the past hundred years the dairy farms in the Town of Sangerfield contribute significantly to the rank Oneida County holds as the third largest milk producing county in the state.

Another interesting industry in the township was brick and tile manufacturing. A brickyard was built by John Haven of Connecticut in 1812. At the height of its production, 12 men worked year-round. Brick and tile were shipped to many parts of the country. Little mention can be found of this industry after World War I.

A business with a long history is the Buell Boot and Shoe Factory. At one time this company employed 100 people, about 80 in the factory and 20 at the tannery. One of the fastest-selling items was a lumberman's boot which

Hop harvest, Waterville, NY

Hop wagons from Zweifel-Hanover Farm enroute to D.L.&W. railroad station in Waterville c. 1920.

reached to the knee, and had two rows of wooden pegs in the sole, in between which the lumberjack could insert spikes to help him keep his footing on slippery logs. Most of the shoes and boots were shipped to the Midwest, which may or may not account for the story that the shoes worn by Abraham Lincoln at his inauguration as President in 1861 came from Waterville.

For many years the largest employer in Waterville was the Waterville Knitting Mills, established in 1922 by LeRoy Harding and Shelby Jarman in the former Buell Boot and Shoe Factory. It was last operated by Barclay Knitwear Corp. of New York City, which built a new building on Conger Avenue. The business, which had 200 employees at peak season, closed in January of 1971. The brick building is now the home of C&H Plastics, a plastic injection molding company, which moved its operations from Route 315 in May of 1995. The firm is headed by William Humphrey and his son William Humphrey III.

Stockwell was first settled in the 1790s. Early settlers included Enos Stockwell and his wife Mary, John Berry and his family, and the Stetson family. Benjamin Stetson was a veteran of the Revolutionary War, and the father of ten children. The oldest, Joel, built a lumber mill.

Smaller businesses were the cheese box factory and the soap factory in Stockwell, a hamlet located in the southern part of the town. The cheese box factory was operated by members of the Benjamin Stetson family for over 150 years. Shoe boxes for the Buell Boot and Shoe Factory were made there, as were hop boxes.

An enterprising businessman, Charles Marsh, made shoe pegs for the Buells. He also made a hard white soap that would float, which he called Ivory Soap. However, he failed to have the name patented, and was forced to change the name to Ivy Soap. Years ago, the stencils for Ivy Soap wrappers were displayed in the window of the *Waterville Times* in Waterville.

Throughout Sangerfield's history, its church organizations have been a vital force. Following the organization of the Lisbon Congregational Society in Sangerfield Center in 1796, a church was built on the green by 18 members. In 1823 the First Presbyterian Church was organized in Waterville.

The Baptist church was begun in 1808 on a site near the present church on Main Street. The steeple of the first structure was finished on the day word was received the War of 1812 had ended. The people placed lighted candles in their windows, and a sailor climbed the steeple and placed a candle at the top. There was no wind, and the candle burned to its base. The present brick church was erected in 1832.

Grace Episcopal Church had its beginnings in 1840. The first society of the Methodist Episcopal Church in Waterville dates back to 1835. Before 1850, when the first Catholic Church was built in Waterville, Catholics attended mass in private homes, the Berrill Foundry and the ballroom of the American Hotel.

No history of Sangerfield would be complete without mention of its most colorful and notorious family – the

This stately Federal style home dates to 1815. Originally the Tower homestead, it is now the residence of Mrs. Robert M. (Catherine) Harding.

Stockwell Church, built before 1830 was moved to Americana Village at Lake Moraine in 1969.

Loomis Gang of Nine Mile Swamp. The Loomis homestead overlooked the Nine Mile Swamp Road between Sangerfield Center and Heads Corners. Although this house has vanished, stories of the family' cunning and ruthless exploits are still remembered and rival the deeds of the legendary outlaws of the old West. Accused of arson, counterfeiting, horse stealing and other offenses, the Loomis brothers, Wash, Grove and Plumb, and other members of the family were always able to avoid the punishment of the law. Sheriff James L. Filkins proved to be their undoing when he led a raid on the Loomis home, accompanied by three young men, Cort Terry, Henry Bissell, and John Garvey. This raid on October 31, 1865, resulted in the death of Wash, and severe injuries to Grove. A second raid took place on June 16, 1866, in which the house was looted and burned and Plumb hanged almost to the point of death to get him to reveal information. Plumb, who had several brushes with the law after this, stayed in the Waterville area, and enjoyed cussing matches with men he knew in the Waterville taverns, although he was not a heavy drinker, Plumb died of a heart condition in 1903. The last member of the family, Wheeler Loomis, was a prosperous and respected farmer in Canada.

Since the 1970s the Town of Sangerfield has come full circle with a mini-boom of agricultural businesses. Agway Regional Feed Mill opened in 1970 to manufacture dairy and chicken feed, followed shortly by Agway Crop Center, supplying fertilizer, seed and chemicals. Allied Mills, built in 1973, has been owned and operated since 1991 by I.L. Richer of New Berlin.

In 1973, Titan Homes, a division of Champion Home Builders of Auburn, Mich., was opened in Sangerfield. Currently employing 185 workers in the manufacture of modular homes, it is the town's largest employer.

The New York State Potato Growers Association headquartered in Sangerfield, went bankrupt on Aug. 24, 1994. The following year the Town of Sangerfield purchased the building. It now serves as the Town Hall and the Sangerfield Post Office.

The newest business in Sangerfield is Pioneer Farm Credit, which erected a new building in 1995.

In Waterville, the Harding Nursing Home added four new rooms and a nursing station, expanding facilities for its residents in 1997. The 92 bedroom facility was built in 1971 behind the former Tower Homestead on Tower Street.

In June of 1998, Community Memorial Hospital of Hamilton was granted permission to add 75 feet to the rear of the building, to house the Barton Memorial Health Clinic established in 1995.

There are numerous social, religious and civic organizations in the township. Waterville Fire Department is probably the oldest organization in Waterville, dating back to 1829. The Waterville Area Volunteer Ambulance Corps was formed in 1971 to provide ambulance service to residents of southern Oneida and northern Madison Counties.

Today the Town of Sangerfield remains predominately rural, but is able to provide services generally found in more heavily populated areas. Its blend of diversified manufacturing, farming and farm-related industries provides the stability necessary for steady and continued growth.

Selected Reference

Waterville, New York, Centennial History 1871-1971, (Waterville Centennial, 1971.).

Town of Sangerfield-Bicentennial 1795-1995, Waterville Historical Society, Waterville Times files.

Main Street, Waterville, looking east, in the 1890s; cotton mill on the left and the spires of the First Presbyterian Church in the background.

Waterville Historical Society

Steuben

By
Leonard Wynne
Town Historian

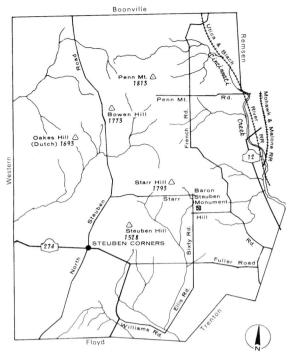

TOWN OF STEUBEN

The Town of Steuben first came into being on June 27, 1786, when the State of New York granted to Frederick William Augustus Henry Ferdinand von Steuben a quarter township of land (16,000 acres) before any public lands were offered for sale. Steuben was permitted to select a quarter township for his own use, without fee or reward, or paying any consideration for the land granted to him. He chose the land located in what is now the Town of Steuben. In 1787, surveyor James Cockburn and five assistants ran north-south and east-west lines through the trace, dividing it into 160 farm lots, averaging 100 acres each.

In 1787, Steuben's agent made a contract with Samuel Sizer, a carpenter from West Springfield, Massachusetts, to build a frame house. Sizer was to receive $175 for building the house. Mr. Sizer was the first permanent settler in the town. By late 1790, there were about 12 farms in Steuben.

In March 1796, the Towns of Rome and Floyd were taken from Steuben. In 1797, the Town of Steuben was again divided and the Towns of Western and Leyden were taken from it. Small parts of Western and Remsen were annexed in 1803, and a small section was set off to Remsen in 1809, leaving the Town of Steuben with an area of 26,126 acres.

The first town meeting, held in what is now Steuben, was at the house of Silas Fowler, formerly that of the late Baron von Steuben. Some of the early settlers were Captain Joseph Ingham, David Barnes, Noadiah Fairchild, Joel and Samuel Hubbard (from Middletown, Connecticut), Noadiah Hubbard and Elisha Crowel (from Connecticut).

The first Welsh immigrants arrived in Steuben in 1795. In the year 1796, the first Welsh child was born in Steuben – first in Oneida County, and first west of the Hudson. Some of the first Welsh settlers were Griffith Rowlands, William Williams, Evan Owens, Hugh Roberts, and Owen Griffiths. In 1798 or 1799, they were joined by several others: Deacon William C. Jones, William Griffiths, Robert Griffiths, John Parry, and William P. Jones, most of whom were professors. After this there was a large Welsh migration and Steuben was mostly occupied by the Welsh.

Steuben until recently was mostly an agricultural community. In the early period cattle and sheep were raised; sheep until 1915 and cattle after 1915. In 1927 there were 162 working farms in Steuben. In 1998 there are fourteen dairy farms and one horse farm in the town; four excavating firms, one leather shop, one iron works, one pick up firm, one architectural and engineering firm and one antique shop.

Steuben is mostly hilly. Penn Mountain is the highest hill, about 1813 feet, and Starr Hill is a few feet lower. Some of the other hills are Bowen Hill, Dutch Hill, named after the many Dutch settlers that settled in that area, and Steuben Hill, just north of Steuben Corners.

In earlier years there were several sawmills, cheese factories, and blacksmith shops; but they are all gone now.

The state and county have large tree plantations in the town. Almost one fourth of the land is owned by the state or county.

Steuben Corners is the only hamlet in the Town of Steuben. The Methodist Episcopal Church is located there. Also located in Steuben Corners are the Grange Hall, the town highway building, and nine homes. East Steuben at one time had a milk station, which was discontinued about 1932, and a railroad stop that included a grocery store in one part of it. All of these things are gone now.

The schools in the Town of Steuben, until 1931, included 13 districts. After 1931, they were centralized into the Remsen, Holland Patent, and Boonville Central School districts. Most of the school children are taken to school on school buses.

The Steuben Methodist Church in Steuben Corners is the only church in the Town of Steuben that holds regular services. It was established in 1855. There are two other churches still standing in the town: the North Steuben Methodist Church and the French Road Methodist Church. In earlier days there were seven churches in Steuben.

Most of the roads in the town are hard topped and passable all year-round. The first paved roads in town were built with town machinery: a tractor, stone crusher, stone bin – which had three different grades of stone, steam roller, and dump wagons. All the work was done by men and horses. The stone was donated by the landowners adjoining the road, broken up by dynamite and by hand with stone hammers, then loaded and hauled to the stone crusher to be crushed into suitable size for laying on the road. The stone crusher was last used in 1928 to build the road from Steuben Corners north to Boonville.

The first iron bridge was built in 1899 at the place of the late William O. Pierce. It included two abutments and cost $225.

In 1911, a special meeting was held at the Bristol house in Remsen, the objective of which was the purchase of five iron bridges. The town board of Steuben met the bridge men there and purchased the bridges to be erected at the following places: Clara Warvers, Fink Hollow, Henry Jones, Jefferson Thomas, Albert Humphry. The price of the bridges was $1065, including the services of the men to erect them. All of these bridges are gone now. Most were replaced with more modern bridges.

On September 12, 1931, Governor Franklin D. Roosevelt dedicated the Steuben Memorial Park. This 55 acre park includes a replica of Baron Steuben's cabin and the sacred grove where the Steuben monument marks the final burial site of the Baron. The park was rededicated May 14, 1998 by Bernadette Castro, NYS Commissioner of Parks.

The Federal Aviation Administration Radar Installation and the Oneida County Radio Transmitter, which occupy adjacent sites on Starr Hill will soon be fully automatic. The fire tower has been removed.

The Town of Steuben is serviced by three fire companies, the Remsen, Western, and Holland Patent Volunteer Fire Companies.

The social life in the town is provided by the Cultural Advisory Committee under the leadership of Hobart Kraeger. This committee was organized as a result of the Town of Steuben Bicentennial celebration in 1992. Helen Lewis serves as Director of the Steuben Seniors. The Steuben Grange #1471 and the Steuben United Methodist Church provide other social activities. There

North Steuben Methodist Church, 1864.

Steuben Corners Methodist Church.

are no taverns or hotels located in the town at present nor have there been any in the past. There are two Bed and Breakfasts: Bon Freer and Stor Felen. The only restaurant is Mondi's Bar-B-Q.

Notable residents of the town have included Baron Steuben, Major General and Inspector General of the American Army between 1778–1784. He died on November 28, 1794.

William Lewis was born in Utica in 1812. In 1860 he was elected to the State Assembly, where he was able to get the appropriation of $500 made by the state for a monument to perpetuate the memory of Baron Steuben. He was also active in gathering recruits during the Civil War and was commissioned by Governor Seymour to secure black recruits in Virginia in 1861.

The Rev. Robert Everett, D.D. was born in 1791, at Cronant, Flintshire, North Wales. He emigrated to America in 1823, where he was the pastor of Bethesda Welsh Congregational Church of Utica. He settled in Steuben in 1838, where he was the pastor of the Capel Ucha and Pen Y Mynydd chapels for 30 years. In 1840 he published the *Cenhadwr,* a monthly religious magazine, which he continued to publish, until his death in 1875. The *Cenhadwr* was more than a local magazine; it was circulated throughout the United States, Canada and Wales. The Rev. Everett was a reformer and as such was among the first to enter the ranks against slavery.

Augustus Loring Richards was born in Belmont, Massachusetts in 1879. He graduated from Harvard Law School, practiced law in New York City, and in 1941 retired from active practice. During the next ten years, he lived in Steuben. He and his wife were particularly interested in conservation and farming problems, including the restoration of abandoned farms and timberland. One project of theirs involved the planting of over two million pine tree seedlings, which forest they later gave to the state of New York. The Richards also helped many local boys and girls from the farming community around Steuben to continue on to college through scholarships that they established. For many years the identity of the founders of these scholarships was kept secret.

In June of 1983 planning for a Town Hall and Equipment storage facility was started. Land was purchased and a construction contract awarded. The building was dedicated to the citizens of Steuben on August 24, 1984. L. John Evans, Town Supervisor, led the effort to establish the first town hall in the history of the Town of Steuben.

Selected References

Memorial of Augustus Loring Richard from Memorial Book of the Association of the Bar of the City of New York, 1951.

Davis, Margaret, *Honey out of the Rafters,* (Remsen, 1976).

Parker, John McAuley, *General von Steuben,* (Yale University Press, 1937).

Roberts, Millard F., *History of Remsen 1789-1898,* (1914).

Steuben Monument at Memorial Park.

Baron Steuben cabin recreated.

Jerry Waskiewicz

Mappa Hall built 1813 by Holland Land Company for Adam Mappa.

Alger and Barker Hardware Store, Barneveld, 1910. Operated by them 1892-1972. Now Hinge Hardware on Route 12 North.

Trenton

By
The Trenton Town Historic Committee
Betsy Beil Mack, Chair

The Town of Trenton contains three villages and four hamlets, all rich with scenic and historic resources. Formed from parts of the Servis and Holland Patents, which had been granted early in 1769, it became the Town of Trenton on March 4, 1797 when it was separated from the Town of Schuyler in Herkimer County.

Located in the central portion of the eastern edge of Oneida County, it is bounded on the east by the waters of the West Canada Creek. The creeks many scenic cascades became famous for the Trenton Falls which reached a height of popularity during the middle 1800's. Also running through the Town are the Steuben, Cincinnati, and Nine Mile Creeks, all of which were important to the development of the Town as homesteads and businesses were established along them.

Barneveld *by* Elizabeth H. Collins

The Village of Barneveld had its beginnings in 1793 when Gerrit Boon, an agent of the Holland Land Company, marked a trail through the forest north from Fort Schuyler. Arriving at the junction of the Steuben and Cincinnati Creeks, he pitched his tent, and soon began the settlement. He named it Olden Barneveldt in honor of Dutch Patriot, John of Olden Barneveldt in Holland, a champion in both church and state.

Near his original campsite on the Cincinnati Creek Boon built a frame house which he occupied for the rest of his tenure there as agent for the Holland Land Company. He attempted some enterprises, such as year-round production of maple syrup and the construction of a grist mill, which proved unsuccessful. The costs were borne by the Land Company. He was later succeeded by Col. Adam Gerard

Mappa who planned a beautiful stone mansion on the same site. Therefore Boon's frame house was moved across the road while the new one was under construction. Because the cost and difficulty of turning it around proved insurmountable, the house was set down without turning, so that the rear of the house now faces the road. The large home of the Mappa family was constructed of Trenton limestone drawn from the nearby quarries. It was known then and today as Mappa Hall, although for a period from 1864 to 1920, when owned by the Wicks family, it was called Rubble Manor and appears as such on maps of that time.

The village of Olden Barneveldt was incorporated in 1819. However, in 1833, the name was changed to Trenton. Mail and freight were frequently missent to Trenton, New Jersey. As a result, a petition was sent to the U.S. Post Office requesting that post office and railroad station names be changed back to Barneveld. The request was granted in 1903. Finally, in 1975, by a village vote of 88 to 49 the village name was changed to Barneveld.

As the community grew, another grist mill, a sawmill, a foundry, and a fulling and carding mill were built in what is now known as Parker Hollow. Other industries which arose around the town during the 1800's included a cheese factory, a coopering shop, a grist mill, a woolen mill, a carriage and wagon shop, a tannery, a candle factory, a sash and blind factory and a large greenhouse.

Several new developments were brought by the extension of the railroad; the construction of dams and the hydroelectric facilities in the Trenton Falls Gorge. They resulted in changes in the economy of the village as well as in the surrounding areas. By the 20th century motor vehicles were in use and ultimately replaced the horse-drawn carriages, and the village businesses which supported them were either closed or bought out by new and different enterprises.

Although undergoing numerous changes in ownership, there are in the village some stores which have survived since Barneveld's early days. The grocery store on the corner of Mappa Ave. and Rte 365 was Daniel French's Meat Market in 1842. Since then it has been operated by Martin Chrestian, Bob Houck, Arnold Allen, and now is Wergin's. The hardware store started in 1878 remained in the family of Alger & Barker until 1972 when it became Hinge Hardware until 1985, at which time Bill Hinge moved his business to the present Rte 12 location near the junction with Rte 28. Rte 12 which bypasses the village has resulted additionally in the removal from the village of the gas stations, the drug store, and Jet Sew, maker of industrial sewing machines sold worldwide, which started in the village and expanded its operations to a new and larger location on Route 12.

Remaining in the village is the Square Stamping Company with newly expanded facilities on North Street; Sampo, Inc. manufacturer of fishing equipment; and Turner Lumber Company. Barneveld has two hotels, in operation many years, Hotel Moore and Van's Tavern.

The Barneveld Library originated in 1874 in a room supplied by Jacob Wicks who then owned Mappa Hall. In 1875 the library and several main stores in the block were destroyed by fire. The present library building was erected in 1877 and still serves the public today, now being equipped with computers enabling access to Mid-York Library services and the Internet.

The first schoolhouse, erected on a lot deeded to the school district in 1819, was a combined schoolhouse and town hall. It was a two story limestone building built by Thomas Tanner. It also served as a community center until the Unity Hall, dedicated in 1896, began to accommodate most of the meetings, plays and other forms of entertainment.

In 1906, the school district erected a larger and more modern school building to the south on Mappa Avenue. The new school was used until 1959 at which time all pupils were absorbed by the Holland Patent Central School system and the school building was bought for a private residence.

By 1912 the original stone school was used so little as to become unsafe. The school district sold its share in the lot and building to the Town. In 1924 the building was razed and a new Town Hall erected on the site. This was used as the center of the Town and Village meeting until the Town of Trenton Municipal Center was erected in 1995.

Due to the existence of several fresh water springs bubbling out of the ground, there were at one time as many as five water tubs in the village. The one in front of Van's Tavern is used as a planter now, while the only other still supplying water is located on Park Ave. It is still a popular

Howard Prevost

Prospect Falls, circa 1850, east view from Pleasant Point.

source of water for local people as well as many who come up from Utica to fill their containers. The Village installed a water system in 1940 which pipes water to each house within its confines as well as a few just outside the village, and also provides water hydrants for fire protection.

As to the churches within the village, the Unitarian was built in 1816 and claims the distinction of being the oldest Unitarian Church in the entire U.S. west of the Hudson River. The Methodist Church was founded in 1832. The worship services were conducted in a building upon the site which was used as a store, but in 1848 the present structure was erected at a cost of $1800 and was free of debt at the dedication. The present Episcopal Church was originally built in 1858 by a group of Welsh Congregationalists. It was purchased by the Episcopalians in 1904, and St. Andrews Episcopal Church was founded. In 1970 it merged with St. Paul's of Holland Patent and became St. David's. The Presbyterians in 1822 built a house of worship on Mappa Ave. This building was later used as the Grange Hall and later still was known as The Social Hall. The Word Bible Fellowship purchased the Masonic Temple in the 1980's.

The population of the village (around 400) has remained relatively constant since the late 1800's. The villagers are proud of their past history and take pride in maintaining many of the original buildings, most of which were identified by handsome signs erected at the time of the Village Bicentennial.

Prospect *by Barbara H. Cale*

The first settlers in the Prospect area probably came from Connecticut in 1794. The largest settlement was near the junction of State Street, James Road and Middle Road, north of the present village. This settlement included Matt Hoyt's tavern, a tannery, an ashery, several log houses, and a log building that served as a school house, church, and a gathering place. What is now the center of the village was a wilderness with a rough road running through it. This area was first known as Beech Flats and then New Jerusalem. On November 18, 1811 the settlement was named Prospect, possibly because of the words, "What a beautiful prospect", said to have been spoken by Colonel Mappa, a Holland Land Company agent, when he viewed the first of the series of the magnificent Trenton Falls.

After the war of 1812 the center of Prospect shifted to its present location. Around 1827 Matt Hoyt's grandson, Clark, built the Union Hall on State Street. Union Hall was later known as Toper's Inn, the Forest Lodge, and the Union Hotel. It was destroyed by fire on January 5, 1997. The Dodge House (later known as the Adirondack Inn) was built in 1880 on State Street. It burned down in 1926 and was replaced by the Prospect Hotel (now known as Yoo-Whoo's Bar and Grill).

The first school was built out of logs north of the village about 1813. It was replaced by a frame building about 1830 and later moved south to a site near the cemetery. The Little Red Schoolhouse served the community until

Recognition was given to Professor Herman D. Squire and his wife, Nellie for their early aeronautic exploits with this plaque mounted on a boulder adjacent to the United Methodist Church, September 1998. The Squires lived in Prospect much of their lives.

1870. Prospect Academy opened in 1850 and burned in 1869. The Prospect Union School was erected on the same site in 1871. On July 10, 1937 this was partially destroyed by fire. A new brick building, built on Church Street, was dedicated in 1940. It became part of the Holland Patent Central School district until 1965, when the school was closed. The building was sold in 1979 to the Bethel Baptist Church and a large addition was later added to it.

In 1825, in Prospect Basin below the falls on the village side of the creek, were a tannery, a saw mill, and a grist mill. Below Boon's Bridge were two stone quarries. The Prospect Lime Quarry opened up in 1852 and was operated by Howarth and Levart until Evan Thomas purchased it in 1869. Prospect stone was used for the Baron von Steuben Monument and many public buildings in Utica. Eastern Rock closed the limestone quarry in 1967.

In 1841 the Methodist Episcopal Church, forerunner of the Park United Methodist Church, was built. It is still in existence today. Among the architectural distinctions of the church are the slanting floor of the sanctuary, wood grained wainscot, pressed metal ceiling, stained glass windows, and fine acoustics afforded from the pulpit. The first Welsh church in Prospect was built by the Baptists in 1854 on State Street. In 1857 the Welsh Congregationalists built Capel Mariah on Hinckley Street. In 1878 the Free Will Baptist Church purchased a lot on Academy Street. This church closed in 1960 and is now an apartment building.

Prospect had three railroad stations. In 1853 the Black River and Utica Railroad opened. In 1892 the Mohawk and Malone was built, and in 1897 a branch line was built to Hinckley. Prospect was the jumping off place for the Adirondacks for wealthy sportsman, lumberjacks, trappers and travelers who usually spent the night at Union Hall before heading north.

The Prospect Old Home and Field Days were started in 1934 and are still held each Labor Day weekend. The Prospect Firemen's Softball League was organized in 1946. In those days almost all the neighboring villages had teams and developed ball fields with night lighting. In 1996 Prospect celebrated the 50th year of the Prospect Invitational Fast Pitch Tournament. This tournament, held Labor Day weekends, is well known throughout New York State and has had a team from Toronto, Canada participate every year since 1984, except for 1988.

In Prospect today there are two churches, a restaurant, village park, ball park, village fire house, fire hall, ambulance, village office building, library, museum, post office, computer service, three construction companies, hair shop, used car and auto repair shop, blacktopping business, sportsman magazine, and a glove sales business. The population of Prospect is approximately 390 persons.

In 1957-59 Niagara Mohawk Power Corporation built the Prospect Dam to direct the water to the new power house below Prospect. Now water flows over Prospect falls only a few weeks each spring.

Hinckley Sulphite Mill and Rossing Plant (Fiber Co.).

Howard Prevost

During the progress of the War of Rebellion in 1863, grave doubts began to arise in the minds of foreign statesmen as to the relative strength of the North and South. At that time the Confederate Army was having considerable success against the northern armies and some of the foreign nation were considering, if not on the verge of, recognizing the Confederacy.

At this junction the Secretary of State, William H. Seward, conceived the idea of taking as many foreign diplomats as possible on a tour of the northern states with the object of showing them the flourishing industrial condition of the North and convincing them that the North was by no means whipped.

In the course of the excursions this party was brought to Trenton Falls and a photograph, on the right, shows this distinguished group posing in the ravine on the flat rocks just below High Falls.

It is of interest to note that the object of this journey was completely accomplished, since none of the countries represented gave further thought to recognition of the South.

The Beautiful Prospect

"What a beautiful prospect!," the early settlers did
    exclaim.
And that, so goes the story is how Prospect got its name.
They were looking at the gorge and the falls in all
    their glory.
"We'll call it Prospect and settle here," at least that is
    the story.
They settled in the basin, millers and farmers from
    the hills.
They used the falls for power to run the big grist mills.
Prospect seemed to prosper and spread for many a mile.
Visiting Prospect to see the falls back then, was quite
    the style.
Dams have stilled the creek's loud roar.
The grandeur of the falls is seen no more.
Only the gorge stands like a sentry, the guardian
    of our past.
In the name of progress, "The Beautiful Prospect"
    couldn't last.

By Margaret F. Thomas, Prospect, NY   1989

Hinckley (Gang Mills) *by Betsy Beil Mack*

Early Hinckley was a sawmill built on the south side of the West Canada between 1810 and 1812. Up until this time there were only a few small farms. About 1840 Gardner Hinckley and partners built a large sawmill at the same place. The company manufactured boards, broom handles, laths and joists. Some time later a box factory was added. The original name of this growing community was Gang Mills.

In 1891, Gang Mills was changed to Hinckley to honor the man who started the mills and made his home in the village. He and his descendants lived in the Hinckley House for 100 years.

The first post office was opened in 1871. The village was on both sides of the creek and the first bridge was a wooden covered one soon replaced by a "pipe bridge." In 1992 this bridge was replaced at a cost of $700,000.

In 1892 a spur of the Mohawk and Malone railroad, from Poland, joined with the Black River railroad opened in Prospect and Hinckley. The trains backed in from Prospect since there was no way to turn around in

Dignitaries at Trenton Falls

1. *Wm. H Seward, Secretary of State*
2. *Baron De Stoeckel, Russian Minister*
3. *M. Molena, Nicarguan Minister*
4. *Lord Lyons, British Minister*
5. *M. Mercier, French Minister*
6. *M. Schleriden, Hanseatic Minister*
7. *M. Bertenatti, Italian Minister*
8. *Count Piper, Swedish Minister*
9. *M. Bodisco, Secretary Russian Legation*
10. *Mr. Sheffield, British Attaché*
11. *Mr. Donaldson, U.S. State Department*

Hinckley. The spur came right through the village and brought in machinery and supplies for businesses.

1900 to 1920 were very busy years in Hinckley. In 1911 the construction of a state dam was started just east of the Hinckley mills. The dam's purpose was to control the waters of the West Canada, act as a feeder to the Barge Canal, and impound drinking water for Utica. The resulting lake flooded 1700 acres of land including about one third of Hinckley, an area known as little Italy.

Downtown Hinckley had 7 hotels, 2 grocery stores, 3 general stores, a man's clothing store, a hardware store, 2 blacksmith shops, a shoe repair shop, 2 barber shops, 2 churches, a livery and an ice business. The Doctor had an office open 2 days a week and a community hall housed a championship basketball team. On Friday and Saturday movies were shown and behind the hotel was a bowling alley. The first school was built in the early 1900s and operated as a 4-year high school until 1924.

In 1920 The Consolidated Water Company of Utica bought all the Mill property and buildings. Company owned houses and the Hinckley Inn were demolished. The Niagara Mohawk Dam in Prospect flooded land back to Hinckley and wiped out one street. Hinckley, today, is a small hamlet with few people. The Catholic Church remains as does the Post Office. Everything else is a memory.

Trenton Falls *by* Betsy Beil Mack

The West Canada Creek flows through a two and a half mile long limestone gorge, descending in a series of cascades called Trenton Falls, between Prospect and the hamlet of Trenton Falls.

The hamlet was settled in the 1790s. It grew slowly until Rev. John Sherman, former minister of the Unitarian Church, in Olden Barneveldt, acquired 60 acres from the Holland Land Company along the West Canada. Here he established the "Rural Resort" hotel near the Falls. After his death in 1828, his son-in-law, Michael Moore built the world famous Moore's Hotel in the same area. Moore married the former Marie Sherman and together they made the hotel a welcoming resort to travelers from Utica and beyond. In 1868 The Trenton Falls illustrated, by N. Parker Willis noted as follows: "Mr. Moore has made very large additions to the building, and the hotel now has a front of one hundred and thirty-six feet, a piazza twelve feet wide, a dining-room sixty feet by thirty, large suites of apartments, sleeping rooms well ventilated, and in fact, all the luxuries of a first class hotel at a "Watering Place."

Most of the villagers in Trenton Falls were, in some way, connected to the hotel and its visitors. Michael Moore also served as Postmaster.

In 1899 the Utica Electric Light and Power Company acquired the Moore property and water rights to the creek.

South Trenton Community Hall and school built 1877.

Children in front of the school December 1920.

They built a power plant which began serving Utica in 1901. In 1917-18 a second power plant was constructed. Moore's Hotel was eventually demolished as travel into many areas of the Adirondacks became more popular. As a result of up-stream water impoundment and power plant operations, the waters of the West Canada no longer come tumbling over the High Falls except when the spring melts are temporarily released to the gorge. Today a bronze tablet marks the hotel site. Descendants of Michael and Marie Moore continue to live in the Trenton Falls area.

South Trenton *by* Barbara H. Cale

South Trenton is small hamlet located on the Nine Mile Creek in the southern part of the Town of Trenton. In the spring of 1794, Thomas Hicks, a pioneer employed by Gerrit Boon of Olden Barneveldt, hailed a party of four men as they came into Fort Schuyler (Utica) by boat on the Mohawk River. He was looking for carpenters to work in Olden Barneveldt for Mr. Boon. Luck was with him as the men, Cheney Garrett, his brothers, Peter and Samuel, and an apprentice, William Palmer, were all carpenters from Connecticut. About nine miles north they crossed Nine Mile Creek and built their log cabin in 1795, near a spring of abundant, clear water. The following year Cheney Garrett built a sawmill on the north side of the Nine Mile. In 1801 he erected a frame house which has been occupied by Garrett descendants until 1964. Both his log cabin and later frame house were well known as "taverns" or rest stops for travelers, because the distance from Fort Schuyler to Barneveld was so far and travel was so difficult. It is the oldest frame house in South Trenton today.

About 1800 a log cabin was erected near the present site of the Union Church and was used both as a school and a church. John Garrett, the father of the Garrett boys, was the first teacher. In 1812 a larger frame building was constructed across the road on the site of the South Trenton Community Hall. This also was used as a school and church until the Union church was built in 1840. In 1869 there were four churches: Union, Welsh Methodist, and two Baptist (Welsh and English).

South Trenton received its name about 1831 and the first post office was established about that time.

The Community Hall was built in 1876-77, replacing the school house which had been torn down. The first floor was used for a school until the early 1940s when the children were taken to the Holland Patent Central School. Many items from the old school have been preserved in the Hall and Holland Patent students tour it as part of their unit on one room school houses.

The second floor of the building, which was built by subscription, has been used to the present day as a community meeting place. The South Trenton Grange (organized April 7, 1938) used it for many years. Today the South Trenton Community Association (organized June 14, 1945) plans and provides programs and activities for the community such as the pitch game held the third

Moore's Hotel, Trenton Falls, 1862.

Saturday of each month. The hall is also used by the Town of Trenton for voting, collecting taxes, and for a youth winter recreation program.

At one time South Trenton hummed with industry. There were two sawmills, a grist mill, a flax dressing mill, a cider mill, a land plaster mill, and a clover mill. There were tanning, cloth dressing, shoe making, and hat making. There were wagon, cooper and blacksmith shops. There were peppermint oil and witch hazel distilleries. Two principal industries were the making of long clock cases by W.D. Rowley and Ebenezer Thomas and the manufacturing of South Trenton bricks by the Garrett brothers. The brickyard was in operation in 1888. A cheese factory was built in 1862.

In 1947 a new four lane highway was built through South Trenton. Buildings had to be razed, moved or turned including the South Trenton Union Church. In 1971 another new four lane divided highway was opened to the east. Once again South Trenton became a quiet, rural, peaceful hamlet. Today there is one church, three cemeteries, a trailer park, the community hall, a pub and a used auto parts business.

Mapledale Corridor

by Merwin Pritchard and Barbara H. Cale

Before 1947 a two lane concrete road known as Route 12 extended north from Utica over Deerfield Hill. At some point a passing lane was added on both sides of the hill. This road went through the communities of South Trenton,

Barneveld and Remsen. In 1948 the (Charlie) Law and (Al) Leaf Construction Company built the first four-lane concrete divided highway which started north of Coombs Road at the old stone barn, went through South Trenton and ended south of the railroad trestle near the barn of the Reba Frame farm where Hinge Hardware is located today. From there the road narrowed down again to two lanes that went under the old railroad trestle, and through the villages of Barneveld and Remsen to all points north.

In 1955 the Lane Construction Company from Connecticut rebuilt the railroad overpass; took down the old railroad station; removed Emma Sebastian's gas station and the hill on which it stood. A four-lane highway was extended from Utica to just south of Alder Creek, going east of the old Route 12 by-passing South Trenton and Barneveld and going west of the old Route 12, by-passing Remsen. Today its is the main route from Utica to all points north.

The construction of this road brought many changes particularly to that area now known as Mapledale/North Gage. Before the new Route 12 was built there were only a few businesses in existence such as the Mapledale Hotel, Ray and Bill's gas station, Emma Sebastian's gas station and cabins, the Frame farm, and the John Story farm. Today the section of Route 12 from the South Trenton turnoff to the Barneveld turnoff is known as the Mapledale Corridor. There is a traffic light at the intersection of Route 12 and Mapledale Road (on the west side) and

Old stone schoolhouse being restored by Wethersfield Historical Society.

North Gage Road (on the east side) made necessary because of the heavy travel and number of accidents. This once pleasant, quiet, rural section now has over sixty active businesses, making the Mapledale Corridor Trenton's fastest growing commercial area.

Wethersfield *by* Barbara H. Cale

Between the villages of Olden Barneveldt and Holland Patent, where Route 365 meets Mapledale Road, a little settlement of Wethersfield was established in 1796-97 when immigrants came westward from Wethersfield, Connecticut. The Simon Willard family was one of these first settlers.

Wethersfield was a farming community where typically large families were self-sufficient units. There were nineteen working farms which furnished milk, crops for canning factories, maple syrup from three large sugar bushes and cider from Tellin's Tallman Sweet Orchard on Posey Hill.

The wooden school house built in 1813, was replaced by a stone school house in 1819. The building was the community center, the meeting place, and the social center for this hamlet. The school was used as a real estate office in the 1970's. Today the Wethersfield Historical Preservation Society is trying to purchase it.

The quarrying of limestone was an important local industry. In the early 19th century a quarry was opened near the school house which furnished stone for local and public buildings in Rome and Utica. In 1922 a small quarry was opened by the town on the Teelin property to supply stone for roads. Stone quarried in Wethersfield was also used for riprapping the Barge Canal.

The quarries have been closed for many years. The large farms are gone. The stone schoolhouse, the stone house on Pierce Road, the stone house on Mapledale Road, and several old frame houses remain today along with remnants of fruit orchards, lilac bushes, and stone fences.

Holland Patent *by* Clarence Siffer

In 1769 King George III of England granted to Henry Fox, Lord Holland, of England, 20,000 acres of land principally in the Town of Trenton. Two generations later the patent was sold, surveyed and divided into lots of about 100 acres each. In 1797, 5000 acres were sold to Bezabel Fisk, Pascal C.J. DeAngelis, Hezekiah Hulbert and Issac Hubbard who settled on the land.

Another tract of land was given to the newly-formed community for a public square where settlers' livestock was protected from predatory animals. This central public square – considerably larger than it is now – gave the village its first name: Public Square. And so it was called, until a meeting of citizens in 1845 decided upon the name Holland Patent and the village was officially incorporated with that name.

Eliphalet Cotes built the first log house and constructed a sawmill on Willard's (Willow) Creek. In 1797 Capt. DeAngelis built a sawmill and gristmill on Nine Mile Creek; Hezekiah Hulbert opened a store and Isaac

Ralph Kessler

Holland Patent Coronet Band on the Village Green. At right, Welsh Congregational and St. Leo's Church at left; June 1889.

Gazebo in the park still very much in use.

Hubbard operated a distillery. In the same year a road was surveyed from Olden Barneveldt to the Floyd line, thus forming Holland Patent's present Main Street; and the first church of the village, the Presbyterian, was established.

There soon followed another gristmill and distillery on the flat below the Welsh Church, also a tannery, and a blacksmith shop. Shoemaking and the operation of limekilns were other early industries. Eliphalet Cotes planted the first orchard. Dairying became a prominent occupation, and the first of several cheese factories was started in 1861.

The DeAngelis Tavern, first in the village, was built in 1800 on the site of the present library. The DeAngelis homestead was erected the following year and occupied by DeAngelis descendants until 1961.

In 1815 Simeon Guthrie built a small tavern on the corner of Main Street opposite the park. About 1840 this building was remodeled and a large ballroom was added on the second floor. Twice destroyed by fires, in 1867 and 1906, the hotel emerged as the New Clarendon in 1907, and since 1938 it has been known as the Butterfield House.

As the settlement grew, more churches followed the Presbyterian. The Baptist Church was founded in 1812, the Episcopal (third oldest in Oneida County) in 1821. A Unitarian Church was founded in 1842. Its last service was held in 1866, and the building was taken over by St. Leo's Catholic Church in 1886. The Welsh Congregational Church was organized in 1842. These five church buildings, four of stone and one of wood, still stand facing the village park as enduring memories of Holland Patent's beginnings.

The first school was established in 1806 and various locations were used for classes until 1870 when a Union Free School District was formed. Holland Patent Academy was formed by public subscription in 1833. The building was transposed to the Episcopal Society in 1838, and named Hobart Hall in honor of Bishop Hobart. Hobart Hall Academy was a co-educational school in the village for 16 years. The Holland Patent Free Library was instituted in 1916.

President Grover Cleveland, though not a resident himself, often visited his family at their home on the corner of Main and Elm Streets, where his father had brought his family when he was called to the pastorate of the Presbyterian Church. Grover's remarkable sister, Rose Elizabeth, official White House hostess during President Cleveland's first term of office, did live there.

Although the country village atmosphere still lingers, business and industry are noticeably changed, being represented now by Steffen Publishing Company, the Oneida County Rural Telephone Co., Suburban Propane, the Holland Patent Pharmacy, Jweid's Market, Benny's Place and the Stewart's Shop. The old milk processing plant now houses the Holland Patent Farmer's Co-op (clothing store) and nearby is the newly refurbished Agway store. The whistle of the once busy train that ran from Utica to the north-country four times daily is now rarely heard, and a passenger train has not stopped at the railroad station since the late 1950's

The brick Clarendon Hotel faced the Holland Patent village green until it burned in 1906.

Holland Patent Memorial Library

Holland Patent Memorial Library

Holland Patent Union School in 1896. No longer standing, this stone school faced the village green.

Vernon

By
Sadie E. Namminga
Town Historian (1977)

Ellen Murphy
Village of Vernon Historian (1998)

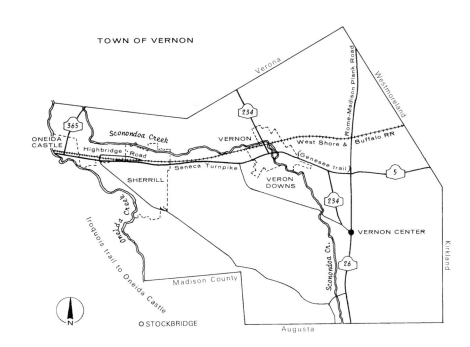

The Town of Vernon is located in the southwest border of Oneida County, and was formed from parts of Westmoreland and Augusta. Included in this town are the patents of Baschard, Bleecker, Sargeant, Wemple, and Van Eps. All of these were in the original Oneida Indian Reservation.

The Town of Vernon has an area of 41 3/16 square miles and contains 27,000 acres. The terrain is rolling and the soil is composed of clay, with scattered areas of gravel and limestone.

The following are minutes of the first town meeting which were thought for many years to have been lost:

"First town meeting of the Town of Vernon holden at the house of David Tuttle in said town on the first Tuesday of March 1802 for the purpose of electing town officers for the ensuing year."

The first permanent settler in the Town of Vernon was Josiah Bushnell, who located in 1794 on what was to be the Bleecker Patent, Richard Hubble located in 1795 on land which later became part of the Van Eps Patent. After the Oneida Reservation was sold at auction and the patents were granted, the settlements grew rapidly.

Early settlers in the town were mostly from Litchfield County, Connecticut, and Berkshire County, Massachusetts.

The Mt. Vernon Presbyterian Society was organized in June 1805, taking its name from the commonly used title for the village. The Baptist Society formed in 1807. The Methodists and Catholics came later.

The Sconondoa Creek flows northward across the town and because of its drop in elevation was a major factor in the town's early settlement. At one time, there were five sawmills, three gristmills, two tanneries, a carding and fulling mill, a distillery, and several other manufacturing sites which utilized power from this creek.

Three glass factories were in operation here for a number of years because of the abundance of trees for firewood. These were the Mt. Vernon Glass Company, 1810-1844; Oneida County Glass, 1809-1836; and Seneca Glass Company, which was incorporated in 1810. These businesses moved when the fuel supply dwindled. It was more economical to move than to transport fuel.

Probably the town's single largest developing factor was the Genesee trail, which ran from east to west through the town. This road was chartered in 1800 as the Seneca Turnpike toll road and was surfaced with planks later in the century. Today this highway is known as New York State Route 5. In 1960 the portion of this road within the easterly part of Vernon Village was straightened and widened to six-lane highway. In 1882 when the New York, West Shore and Buffalo Railroad Company made plans for the route of the railroad to be built on the right-of-way of the Seneca Turnpike, the citizens of the area objected. The railroad was laid out in a straight line and still disrupted the turnpike by crossing it four times in about two miles.

The Village of Vernon was incorporated on April 6, 1827. For many years Vernon was the home of the Vernon Fair. In the beginning, about 1848, it was held on the Mt. Vernon Presbyterian Church lawn. Later on it was held where Vernon Downs is now. The last fair held on the fair grounds was in 1952. One more was held after that in the new Vernon Downs buildings. In 1976 a Vernon mini-fair was begun and continued each year since.

Abram Van Eps opened a store in what is now Vernon

Village in 1798. Before this he operated the first stores in Oriskany and Westmoreland. Thus he was the first merchant in three townships within the limits of Oneida County. He also established a grist and flour mill which operated continuously until it closed in June 1952. Vernon Mills flour was famous throughout Central New York. Many housewives said they couldn't bake without Vernon Mills pastry flour.

Although many industries have been located within the town, dairy farming has been the largest continuous source of livelihood for its inhabitants. Today the southern and northern portion is primarily devoted to farming, the farms being fewer, but larger in size.

The Oneida Indians' chief village was called Oneida Castle and the present-day Oneida Castle Village is located near the site of the last castle of the tribe. A small boulder at the intersection of Route 5 and Highbridge Road, just east of the village of Oneida Castle, marks the approximate site of the home of the eminent Chief Sconondoa.

The present Oneida Castle Village was organized in 1815 (the Randel Survey map designates the village as Oneida Castleton). The public square (now Castle Park) was reserved by the state as a drill ground. In 1832 a section of the square was set aside for public buildings. The village purchased the park from the state for $2 in 1927. Located there today are the Cochran Memorial Presbyterian Church, the village hall (the old Presbyterian Church), the fire department and the grade school. Oneida Castle is the approximate geographical center of New York State and three attempts were made to have the state capitol located here.

Oneida Castle has been a quiet residential village through the years with few industries. However, it was here in 1823 that Mr. Sewall Newhouse discovered a way to make a greatly improved steel game trap. He joined the Oneida Community in 1849. The traps were then manufactured in Sherrill and distributed by Oneida Community Ltd. The business section of Oneida Castle is located on Route 5 near Oneida Creek.

The hamlet of Vernon Center is located in the southeast part of the town. State Route 26 passes through from south to north. This was originally known as the Rome-Madison Plank Road.

The following is copied, in part, from a deed of the Vernon Centre Green:

"Whereas Huet Hills, Levi Thrall, Horace Higley and Wait Hills, did in the year of our Lord One Thousand Seven Hundred and Ninety-eight – by the Agency of Huet Hills purchase of Thomas L. Witbeck a certain piece of land containing Six Acres called the Centre for the purpose of a public square in the new Town of Vernon, County of Oneida, and State of New York, to be and remain solely for public use forever (viz.) for the equal use of all denominations of Protestant Christians to erect building thereon for public worship and for education."

Grandstand at the evening harness races, Vernon Downs, Route 5.

Lots of one acre were surveyed around the green where many of the first settlers located; each proprietor was to chop and clear to the center of the green. In the last quarter of the 19th century, the Methodist and Presbyterian churches each elected a man to act as Park Commissioner. It was at this time that trees were again planted.

In 1900 the gazebo was constructed and was such a fine example of this type of structure that the American Management Association of Hamilton, New York copied it for their reconstructed village. Up to the time of World War II, the park was a social gathering place during the summer months.

On Thursday, the 8th day of July 1802, 17 persons gave their assent to the "Confession of Faith and Articles of Admission and Discipline" and thus the first church body in the Township of Vernon was organized. The society adopted the Congregational form of government, but later voted to adopt the Presbyterian mode. Today, after nearly a century and three-quarters, this church is still active and is known as the Vernon Center Presbyterian Church.

In 1826 the Methodist Church was founded. It was originally built on the green, but in 1852 was moved to its present location. It is now know as the Parkside Methodist Church.

In the early days of the hamlet it was necessary for the people of the Catholic faith to travel several miles to attend mass. In 1884 these people purchased Pettibone Hall to be used as a place of worship. This became St. Agnes Church. The first pastor was the Rev. S. J. Cannane, who was also in charge of the Oriskany Falls pastorate. He served at St. Agnes for 25 years. In 1974 St. Catherine's Catholic Church in Vernon burned. The parishes of St. Catherine's and St. Agnes were joined to form the Church of The Holy Family with a new edifice built in Vernon.

Maple Park Home for the Aged Ladies is located here. This home was founded in 1904 and incorporated in 1905. Over the 72 years of its service to the aged, it has been a pleasant abode for many ladies in the autumn of their lives.

The town's early schools were also used for church services, public meetings and social gatherings. The village schools became more like today's schools with separate classrooms, while the outside district schools kept the character of the classic one-room school until they were closed in the 1950s following centralization.

The town was also the home of several tuition schools. Within the Village of Vernon, the Mt. Vernon Academy for Young Men and the Vernon Female Seminary opened in 1833. The Seminary became the female department of the Mt. Vernon Academy when the Academy was incorporated in 1838. The Mt. Vernon Academy building was turned over to the Vernon School District in 1876. In 1918, the old structure was removed and a brick building erected. This building was used until 1971. It was demolished in 1973 to make room for an apartment complex.

In the 1850s there were also the Mt. Vernon Boarding School for Boys and the Van Eps Institute for Young

Vernon Historical Society

Vernon Mills on the Sconondoa Creek in Vernon, operated as a grist and flour mill from the early 19th century until June 1952.

Bronson's Academy in Castle Park at Oneida Castle was operated from the 1820s to 1863 as a private school. It became a public school but is no longer standing.

Mrs. Donald Bellinger

Ladies. In Oneida Castle, The Bronson Academy opened in the 1820s and was operated as a private school until 1863. The building was then turned over to the village for use as a public school.

The 31 district schools in Vernon, Verona, and Sherrill were centralized in 1950. A new junior-senior high school was built in 1953 midway between the villages. Each village now has a new elementary school: E. A. McAllister in Sherrill; William A. Wettel in Vernon; and John D. George in Verona. At present Oneida Castle is affiliated with the Oneida City School System. The small one-room district schools have been sold and have either fallen down or are now homes. The Vernon Center School is now the Vernon Center Post Office.

The first bank in Vernon was started by Salmon Case in 1839 in the stone store. Becoming the National Bank of Vernon, it later moved to its own building across the street which is the Banks present site. The National Bank of Vernon has expanded over the years, opening two branches – in Westmoreland and in Oriskany Falls. It is still the only independent bank in Oneida County.

Vernon is the location of a number of successful industries: Dairylea Milk Company; H.P. Hood Milk Company; Oneida Containers; Mid-State Raceway (Vernon Downs); Ferris Industries; Eastern Crown; Burton Livestock Exchange; Old Forge Metals; Kuhn Farm Machinery; and TDS Telecom.

Current estimates of the population of the Town of Vernon project over 6,000 with the City of Sherrill accounting for nearly one-half of the total.

Selected Reference

Vernon – Our Town, (Town of Vernon Bicentennial Committee, 1976).

Vernon High School (originally Mt. Vernon Academy) and Presbyterian Church, Seneca Turnpike, Vernon, prior to 1918. The school was moved in 1918 and in 1919 the church tower was removed.

Vernon Historical Society

The Welch block was erected in 1907 at the northwest corner of Seneca Avenue and Castle Street in Oneida Castle.

Vernon Historical Society

Verona

By
Dorothy Cmaylo
Town Historian

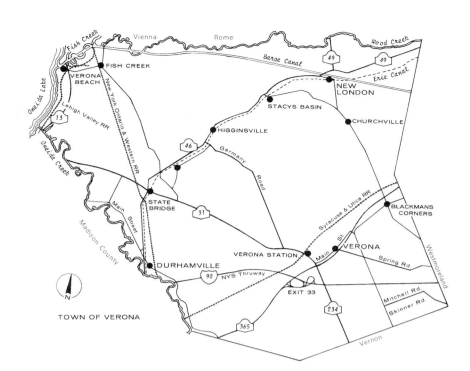

TOWN OF VERONA

Presently, there are no incorporated villages in the Town of Verona, although there are quite a number of communities. The largest are Verona, New London and Durhamville. Others are State Bridge, Verona Station, Higginsville, Dunbarton, Stacy's Basin, Churchville, Fish Creek, Blackman's Corners and Verona Beach. The town is within the former Oneida Reservation, the land of which were sold at auction in 1797. The southeast portion of Verona is generally undulating, while the northwest portion is very level, having been covered by the waters of ancient Lake Iroquois.

The first white settler, George A. Smith, left Dean's tavern at Westmoreland on Christmas Eve, 1791, arriving eight days later at the site of the Tamiami Hotel, where Oneida Creek empties into Oneida Lake. His daughter Eve was the first white child born in what became Verona Township in 1795.

Another early arrival was Asahel Jackson, from Berkshire County, Massachusetts, in 1796. Some of his relatives still reside in Verona township. He built a pub, trading post, and tavern near the Royal Block House, where Wood Creek empties into Oneida Lake. William Cottman's marina is located there now.

The Town of Verona was formed from the Town of Westmoreland in 1802. In March, the first town meeting was held at Martin Langdon's house one-half mile west of Verona Village. There were the 102 families, comprising 439 inhabitants. The first election was held April 30, 1802, when the Democrats got 31 votes, Federals 28. This was under the first state constitution, which enable a citizen to vote for governors and senators.

In August of 1805, a typhus epidemic broke out and lasted about a year. Miss Elizabeth Day had been residing with friends in Litchfield, in Herkimer County, and on returning complained of feeling ill; her sickness spread to others and about 100 persons died before it was over.

Agriculture has been a mainstay of the town's economy since early settlement. From the 1860s until the early 1900s, milk for cheese-making provided the predominant farm income. Sugar beet growing fizzled out in 1896; again in 1965. For a time Crown Brand canned goods were marketed by T.B. and C.W. Bishop of Verona, and John Wilhelm did a thriving business for some years. Mr. Wilhelm is remembered for saying, "I don't keep books much, 95% of der people are honest – and de other 5% are our very best citizens." The Oneida Canning Factory, formed 1892-3, was operated until 1958 by the Albert Dam Canning Company. The property is now owned by Donald Burch, Virdon Estates.

Beginning in the 1920s, the Empire State Canning Company, located at Stacy's Basin, processed thousands of cans of locally grown vegetables, giving employment to many until it burned in 1950. In Verona the Willow-Dell Canning Factory operated until 1958. Murphy's Custom Canning operated in the 1950s in Verona, with gardeners receiving cans containing the very same vegetables they brought in.

An early resident of the town invented a workable field mower. Abraham Randel settled in the town in 1813 upon the recommendation of his brother, who had surveyed the area for a proposed central capital of the state to replace Albany. The machine that Randel invented in 1810 and patented contained the shearing principle of all mowers since. It was drawn by two horses, and made of four, four foot by four foot hardwood scantlings, mounted on high wheels. He said he got the idea while watching his wife use her scissors. The Randel homestead until recently stood on Randel Road and it was here that Abraham's son Dr. Ogden Randel practiced for 40 years.

The original Erie Canal cut diagonally across the town on a path that today's Route 46 closely follows. The canal was opened through the town in 1820 and provided transportation for goods produced by local industrialists and farmers and for the shipment of lumber cut from the abundant local resources. This local supply of lumber and the canal combined to create one of the town's most vital early industries – boat building. Boats were constructed and repaired from the 1830s to the early 1900s in New London, Stacy's Basin, Higginsville and Durhamville.

The Erie Canal was enlarged and straightened in the 1860s in the area of Stacy's Basin. Then in 1918, the Barge Canal was completed across the northern part of the town and has been in use since. The Erie Canal was left intact through the town as a feeder for the Barge, but no longer did it bring traffic and commerce to the many communities that had grown up along its way.

The old Oneida Lake Canal (Side Cut Canal) was used from 1835 until 1863 to connect the Erie at Higginsville with Oneida Lake, since the original Erie bypassed the lake. The new Oneida Lake Canal operated from Durhamville to South Bay, Oneida Lake, from 1877 to 1878. Never a success, this waterway leaked excessively. Today, stonework from two of the locks still exists in a marina area along South Bay.

Glass factories thrived from the 1840s to 1890 in the town, because there was wood for fuel and a local supply of sand. Factories that manufactured window glass were located at Durhamville and Dunbarton. At Durhamville, a large glass works was operated by Fox, Gregory and Son. At peak times, the company employed as many as 125 people, and was one of the largest companies of its kind in the nation.

The Dunbarton Glass Works, located near Higginsville, also manufactured window glass. These companies purchased raw materials from England, Germany and New Jersey, and shipped their finished products primarily to New York City on the Erie Canal.

They say that at the Durhamville factory leftover glass in late afternoon was given to the employees to make items for their wives or sweethearts – glass canes, paperweights and small trinkets. Some of these pieces are in the Historical Association Collection. Also surviving are some company houses built for employees of the Dunbarton works, although the factory buildings no longer stand.

Another early industry was related to the town's natural resources. About one-half mile north of Verona

Town of Verona Historical Society

Empire State Canning Co., Stacy Basin on Rte 46 was destroyed by fire in 1950 and was rebuilt in approximately the same location.

Glass works in Durhamville were established in 1845 and operated until about 1900.

Town of Verona Historical Society

Hamlet, iron ore was discovered by Jebediah Phelps and was used by furnaces in Westmoreland and Taberg. While digging for ore, a spring was discovered which made a water hole that never went dry, even through the drought of the 1930s, and provided a much-needed supply of water for cattle and horses at that time.

For a time, Verona Springs was a noted local resort. Located at the corner of Mitchell and Skinner roads, the springs were known to the Indians who had lived in the area. About 1830, Havillo Eames from Massachusetts purchased the springs and erected a hotel. Other proprietors, several of whom were physicians, followed. Into the 20th century visitors enjoyed the waters which, it was claimed, would cure a wide variety of maladies.

On the shore of Oneida Lake, Verona Beach has been a recreation area for many years. It was settled about 1840 by four Roberts brothers, Valentine Morris and others. Sand from beds along the lake shore was shipped to other areas by the Ontario and Western and the Lehigh Valley Railroads. Until 1888 a hand-operated ferry ran from Verona Beach to Sylvan Beach. Some of the old hotels and boarding houses are now residences; others have been demolished. In 1947, New York State built the Verona Beach State Park along the shore of the lake.

The earliest schools in the town were at Blackman's Corners, Verona Depot and the Happy Valley District School, originally called the Jerusalem School. The Toll sisters, who set up the Home School for Young Ladies in New Hartford about 1876, moved back to the family homestead in Verona and set up a school there. The present Vernon-Verona-Sherrill High School is located on the site, on Route 234. In 1950, the 31 Verona districts merged into the Vernon-Verona-Sherrill Central School system.

The Board of Cooperative Educational Services (BOCES) established a center in the town in 1969 on Spring Road to provide career training for high school students.

Verona

Shubal Brooks cut the first tree at "Hand's Village" which became Verona, and he was probably the fourth settler in the township, coming in 1797. Captain Ichabod Hand Jr. kept a public house there, and B.J. Dodge, writing in 1932, said this was the same Verona Hotel then kept by John Kline, and around the turn of century, by Frank Phelps. It is now operated by George Eggan.

Captain Josiah Osgood was another Revolutionary veteran whose family remained on Spring Road until the 1920s. Later generations called them Hardshell Baptists, as they drove four or five miles in horse and buggy to Vernon Baptist Church.

Town of Verona Historical Society, Inc.

Whalen Farm, Higginsville along the Erie Canal.

Sgt. Samuel Whaley had a blacksmith shop north of the village. Charles Felts was a successful storekeeper in partnership with Clarence W. Arnott, who bought the store from Thomas Ray in 1945. Robert Arnott, son of C.W., now has it, the only grocery store in Verona Village.

The Brewster family were New Englanders claiming descent from the Mayflower preacher. Twins who were a carpenter and a blacksmith were known as Wood Brewster and Iron Brewster. The Brewster Insurance Agency in Oneida is operated by descendants. Verona's only Tory was Timothy Resseguie (note how all these families changed the spellings), who had lived most of his life near Saratoga before coming here with Timothy Jr. A nephew of Henry, Lyle Ressegue, at 90, wrote with wit and humor of the old days.

In 1806 the first religious society (Congregational) was formed, and in September 1807, the Rev. Israel Brainard became pastor-for 30 years.

The Revely Tailor Shop in Verona Village from 1840-1865 was in a building later owned by Ernest Eggan. The shop ledger now owned by great-grandson G. Allison Smith, shows "cutting a vest – 25 cents, coat – 50 cents, suit – 75 cents, making a suit with two pair of pants – $4.50." Much of the pay was in barter, like butter, apples, meat, potatoes, etc. There was wartime inflation when butter rose from 16cents a pound in 1847 to 50cents a pound in 1864.

Gardner Weeks started making cheese and sold out to Gottlieb Merry in 1869. Merry and William Nash Peckham formed the Oneida County Canning Company and the buildings of this are nearby. The Merry cheese factory at Verona was moved to Erie Canal Village.

Merle J. Davis writes that by 1913 there were 80 students in Grades 1-12 in Verona High School. In 1928 a brick high school was built at a cost of $50,000, and the old building was used for various purposes until it was demolished in the 1960s. The J.D. George Elementary School was built in 1961 at a cost of $567,680, and its 1966 addition cost $923,090. In 1967 Seward B. Dodge, first principal of the George School, was given the first honorary life membership in PTA ever awarded in Verona by the national PTA.

The Verona Fire Department originated after the Central Hotel burned in 1914, when bucket brigades were effective only for saving nearby buildings.

Our Lady of Good Counsel Church was built in 1914, when sufficient numbers of Catholics had started having Mass at Joseph Nunn's farm on Spring Road (now the Evanciew farm). The first garage in Verona was built by George H. Dann in 1915 on the site of Maltby and Armitage's brick store. H.E. McBain now stores his oil trucks there, and the old post office, built beside it in 1910, is Mrs. Betty McBain's County Art Gallery.

Town of Verona Historical Society, Inc.

Verona Springs Sanitarium,
destroyed by fire in 1905.

Gottlieb Merry Cheese Factory, Verona
moved and rebuilt at Erie Canal Village

Town of Verona Historical Society, Inc.

In the latter 19th century, there was Lyman Cady, a shoemaker, a Mr. Hicks, harnessmaker, E.T. Dena, whose tailor ship was Harry Kline's barber shop in the 1920s and 30s, now enlarged for a house. Charles E. Crandall's General Store became Verona Market, operated by Stanley and Frank Merrell, later by Fred Avard through the 1940s and 50s.

In 1932, three of the Presbyterian Church horse sheds built in 1848, had been removed to make room for the fire house. (All are gone now). The Catholic Church sheds had a much shorter existence, as the church itself was built just as autos were coming into general use.

The site of the Central Hotel, which burned in 1914, is now the Veterans Memorial Park. The World War I boulder monument, originally set up in front of the Presbyterian Church, was moved across the corner after World War II.

At the present time, local businesses include Freihofer's day-old baked goods store, Joel's Steak House, a new Super 8 Motel, Wesley Wendt, proprietor, Felts' Store and a Nice and Easy Convenience Store. On July 20, 1993, the Oneida Indian Nation opened its new, large casino, "The Turning Stone", located on property purchased from the Davis family. Later their Bingo enterprise, which had been located on the Oneida Reservation, was moved here. In 1997, a 286 room hotel/resort complex was added. Nearby are two golf courses, currently under construction. Other enterprises undertaken by the Nation are a truck stop at the intersection of routes 31 and 365, a SāvOn gas station, adjacent to the Casino/Resort, a car wash, also adjacent to the resort, and an RV Park, on Route 365, near Sconondoa. Several thousand acres of farm land have recently been purchased by the Oneida Nation in the towns of Verona, Vernon, and Canastota for future development.

They say history repeats, and LaVerne W. Davis points out that long before there was a Thruway interchange at Verona, there was a toll-gate near the site of the traffic light on the corner of Routes 365 and 31!

Durhamville

Durhamville was established before 1813 and then named for Eber Durham, who came from Manlius in 1826. Durham leased surplus water from the Erie Canal and applied it extensively for running various mills and factories. Later, steam and water from the Oneida Creek replaced the canal water. Durhamville prospered during the 19th century with boat yards, the glass industry and many small businesses that provided supplies and services for the canal traffic.

Just north of Durhamville, the Irish Ridge area of the town was settled by Thomas Ennis and his former neighbors from Ireland. He was an assistant surveyor on the

Durhamville Dry Dock

Erie Canal and, taking part of his pay in land, settled here about 1826. He gave the settlers each 40 acres and $100. These settlers built St. Mary's of the Irish Ridge Catholic Church in 1831, and when no priest was available, James Hyland, a settler, read from a book of sermons he had brought from Ireland.

Today Durhamville is a residential community with active community groups and churches.

New London

Ambrose Jones is listed as erecting the first frame building on the site of the present village. He called it the Eagle Hotel. He was instrumental in having the post office opened in 1825, naming the new settlement after his hometown, New London, Connecticut.

The first industries used the raw materials at hand, lumber and fuel wood. The virgin forest trees grew to 30 feet in diameter. Lumber was shipped out by the millions of board feet. Five boat building yards hummed with one of the largest industries in the state. The story circulated that New Londoners built their boats each a mile long then sawed them into barge-length sections and boarded up the ends, thereby turning out an "instant" fleet.

New London, incorporated in 1848, was a commercial center of 800 permanent residents. Three hotels cared for the hundreds of transients passing through on there way westward. Cheese from three cheese factories, grain, vegetables, and in spring arbutus flowers for perfumers were shipped to New York City. The westbound barges unloaded sugar and manufactured goods at New London to go by wagon train northward to the settlements in Jefferson and Oswego counties.

The opening of the Black River Canal and the new network of railroads drained commerce from the Erie. The industrialization of nearby Rome and Utica drew families to those towns. A serious fire in 1856, another in December 1900, and again nine years later, wiped out the docks and warehouses, hotels, stores, and classic mansions, never to be rebuilt. The wild rough days of the canallers have become part of Central New York folklore.

The New London of today, straddling the old Erie Canal at the junction of state routes 46 and 49, is entirely residential. A dozen homes of the early canal period remain, clustered around the United Methodist Church, Masonic Lodge, and firehouse. Only the church keeps its original identity.

Life in the '20s and '30s centered around a Dramatic Society, Merry Makers Orchestra, Masonic Lodge and Eastern Star meetings, sleigh rides, and Saturday night dances at Grosjeans Hall. The canal was still a factor, with accidents and drownings. The 1937 great freeze caught barges end to end from New London to Lock 21.

In August 1947 a charter was granted the New London Volunteer Fire Department. A 1931 Chevrolet truck was purchased, on which was mounted a U. S. Government-loaned 500 gallon skid-type pumper, two ladders, and 600 feet of hose, The rig was kept in a former bicycle shop, and later in nearby barns, In 1949, when the weight of the equipment dropped the truck through the barn floor, the campaign to raise funds for a firehouse was accelerated. In 1950 the first firehouse was built on the corner of Main and Cornell Streets.

In 1966 and 1967 there was much talk of the Erie Canal Park, with recreational development at its extremes of New London and DeWitt. The Canal Park is on the record, but is as yet one of the many undeveloped areas belonging to the New York State Park System.

Selected Reference

Ernenwein, Raymond P., *Verona Town History,* (Verona Town Board, 1970).

Durham boat on the Mohawk River.

Vienna

By
William D. Evans

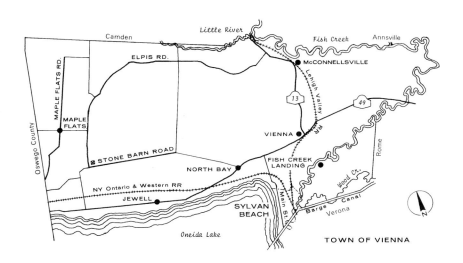

The Town of Vienna lies on the western border of Oneida County. It was formed from the Town of Camden on April 3, 1807. At that time it was called Orange. In 1808, it changed its name to Bengal and in 1816 to Vienna. It has remained Vienna ever since.

The town consists of a land area of approximately 38,102 acres. It comprises townships nine and ten of Scriba's Patent, and is part of the original grant to Nicholas Roosevelt of New York. The latter not complying with the terms of sale, a large share of his purchase was resold to George Scriba, a merchant in New York. The remainder, including this town, was subsequently sold and General Alexander Hamilton, John Lawrence and John B. Church became the purchasers.

The southern boundary is Oneida Lake. Little River and the west branch of Fish Creek lie on its north. This stream joins the east branch of Fish Creek at Blossvale and forms the eastern boundary of the town. On the west, Vienna butts into a part of Oswego County.

The surface configuration of the southern part of the town is relatively level and in places quite marshy. In the north, the land is hilly and broken. The soil is generally sandy. In the northwestern part of the town lies a section that early came to be known as Maple Flats because of the rock maple trees that grew in abundance there. The rest of the town is predominately covered with hemlock, white, yellow and pitch pine.

During the early years, the lumber interests were quite large. Numerous ponds and small streams made it possible for 37 sawmills to operate in the area; but few are in existence today.

Early Settlement

Ephraim Church was the first settler in the Town of Vienna. He probably came in 1797. He later sold out to a Mr. Jarvis. Coming with Mr. Church was Isaac Cook. Timothy Halstead is credited with being the third settler, arriving in 1798 or 1799. Halstead built the first frame house. He bought his land from Mr. Cook, who had urged him to leave the Town of Trenton where he had first settled.

Mr. Halstead had a son Henry, who, with the exception of the time he spent with 35 members of the 68th Regiment at Sacketts Harbor around 1814, lived here all of his life. Others who came to the town between 1800 and 1803 were Eliphalet Pierce, Alexander and Jonathan Graves, John Tully, Luther Fisher, Peter Gibbons, a Mr. Kilbourne and a Mr. Smith.

Two children of the Fishers were the first deaths recorded in the town. They were buried on the farm. Part of the farm is the McConnellsville cemetery. Alexander Graves was killed in an early sawmill accident at McConnellsville, Eliakim Stoddard, who settled in Camden in 1799, came to the South Corners (which later became Vienna) in 1803. He became the first supervisor of the Town of Vienna.

Schools

The first school in Vienna was taught by Lyman Mathers in 1803 or 1804. School was held in a small log house owned by Isaac Cook and located a short distance below McConnellsville. By 1815 there were a number of schools in the town. All of the buildings were small, made of logs, with the exception of the one at South Corners, which was built of brick.

Early records of the town were lost in 1871 and it is now impossible to know how many schools were built, moved, burned down, transformed or abandoned. It is known that 19 school districts came into existence. Today Vienna is part of the Camden Central School District.

Protestant Church

In 1804, William Keith from Baltimore came through the country preaching in small towns. Soon church meetings began to be held in barns and later in schoolhouses. In June 1811, the first camp meeting was held on what was the Bailey farm, now the home of Glen Teelin.

The Methodist Society built a church building in McConnellsville in 1832. The Baptists built in North Bay in 1842.

During the early years, the Vienna, McConnellsville and North Bay churches were combined as one charge. They were served by circuit preachers. From local church records we learn that the circuit preacher, if a single man, received $80 a year and would furnish his own horse. "For a man with a family a small sum would be allowed for each child and if they received $250 they would be satisfied."

In 1841 the Rev. George Gary was the youngest man at 15 years old ever licensed to preach in the Methodist Episcopal Church.

Catholic Church

Although Jesuits had been in the area for a long time conducting missions to the Indians, it wasn't until 1835, when a Mass was celebrated by Father Quarter in the home of Major Daniel Mulholland at North Bay, that the Catholic Church was established here. Major Mulholland donated land about a mile north of the village and St. Peter and Paul Church was dedicated in 1843.

Vienna

The way the village of Vienna came into being is that two roads crossed; one went north and south, the other went east and west. First it was known as Parker's Corners, then South Corners, later, the people settled for Vienna.

Before 1815 a public house (hotel) was built, a stage stopped, a shop and store came, a school and church were established and a blacksmith was needed and a post office developed. This brought a sawmill, a gristmill, a cheese factory, a wagon and sleigh shop, a tannery, a shoe shop and a carding mill.

A Mr. Parker carried the mail from Utica for a long time. At first he rode on horseback, then he used a team and wagon. The Corners always had a sawmill or two.

Today it has one. There is also a firehouse, a hotel, a store, a church-related elementary school and two churches.

North Bay

North Bay in the 1800s was the largest and most prosperous village in the Town of Vienna. Having a commanding view of Oneida Lake it soon became a noted summer resort. Its fishing facilities were superb; the lake was teeming with fish; boats were available for hire, and the area was easily accessible. Picnic parties in great numbers came, many on the New York, Ontario and Western Railroad. Also, in one season it is recorded that 35 canal boats were built here.

At one time there were seven hotels, three churches, a school, a post office with Hiram Higby its first postmaster, two sawmills, three stores, a planing mill, a shingle mill, two potteries, a blacksmith shop, a harness shop, a wagon and sleigh shop, a semi-monthly newspaper the *Vienna News*, (50 cents for a year's subscription), and two physicians, Dr. Nicholas and Dr. Broga.

It was Ed Montross who had the last blacksmith shop in the village. He used an old horse treadmill for working the bellows of the forge. Ed's blacksmith shop was

Harden Furniture Company in 1974. Note piles of lumber in background. Now makes over 300 designs of Early American furniture and employs 250 people. Fish Creek in foreground

1865 photograph of Harden's Dam and gristmill on the west branch of Fish Creek in McConnellsville where Frank Harden began manufacturing furniture.

Clarence Harden

changed into a gas station by his son Clayton to service the new horseless carriages. Clayton was one of the first automobile mechanics in the area.

H. J. Myer was one of the most active founders of North Bay. He came to the area in 1832 and built the first building, a hotel. He fixed up the grove overlooking the lake and built the Lake View House and 10 or 12 houses, which he sold, and 20 Durham boats.

Harley Phelps started a canning factory in the valley around 1906. During World War II, the factory packed as many as 16,000 cases of beans and corn a year. Harley Phelps also started the village water system and hydro-electric plant. He started a privately owned water system serving 175 customers. This was sold by his son Russell to the village water board in 1972, when a water district was formed. The hydroelectric plant furnished electricity to the village between 1922 and 1927, when it was sold to Niagara-Lockport (presently Niagara Mohawk) Power Company.

Although it is no longer a summer resort, North Bay is a thriving community today. There is a church, a town hall, an elementary school building, and a modern fire barn.

Jewell

Jewell is in the southwest corner of Vienna on the shore of Oneida Lake. For 100 years it had been known as West Vienna, but in 1921 it was changed to Jewell to honor the memory of its first settler, Eliphalet Jewell. He came to the area and had a gristmill prior to 1817. The first

store was built in 1838. A post office was started the same year. J. Newell Conant became postmaster in 1845. He used to put all of the mail on a table and everyone picked out his own. The mail was brought in on horseback from South Corners, later by stage, then on the New York, Ontario and Western Railroad. In 1866 the postmaster's salary was $52 a year. The post office was discontinued in 1963. The people in the area are now served by the Cleveland post office.

McConnellsville

McConnellsville is located in the northern part of the town, on Fish Creek. It took its name from Joseph McConnell, an early settler. A church, a school, a store, a post office, and a factory may not sound like much, but McConnellsville is a thriving community. The post office was established in 1812.

A sawmill was built in 1801, owned by a company composed of Timothy Halstead, the third settler, William Smith and others. The sawyer was a Mr. Hammill. Mr. Smith built a gristmill near the same place in 1804. Besides the above, the settlement contained a school-house, a church, a blacksmith shop and a wintergreen distillery.

Although two railroads ran through the village, McConnellsville grew slowly. Tuttle and Christian had their canning factory completed by the end of 1880; Charles Harden was building a new house for Nelson Powell; Central New York Mill, owned by Babcock and

William D. Evans

Stone Barn on Stone Barn Road, Town of Vienna.

Foot, was paying cash for buckwheat, rye and oats, doing custom grinding, also buying spruce logs.

In a few months Harden's son Frank would be buying the Babcock and Foot mill, and in 1902 he founded the Frank S. Harden Company. The Harden Company manufactured a solid kitchen chair. The company struggled along with a work force of about eight or ten employees. Today, it is the town's biggest employer, with about 250 employees, manufacturing over 300 designs of furniture and selling it all over the United States.

Fish Creek Landing

Located in the southwest corner of Vienna is the hamlet of Fish Creek Landing. In the year 1807, George Covell and his brother William left the town of Lanesboro, Massachusetts and came here. They purchased a lot together and then divided it. Fish Creek Landing during these early days contained a store, a blacksmith shop a short distance up the creek, and a two-story building erected to serve as a schoolhouse, a church and a public hall combined.

Before the construction of the Rome, Watertown and Ogdensburg Railroad in 1850-51, the landing was the depot from which most of the lumber manufactured in this area was shipped. It was transported from as far as Williamstown in Oswego County and Osceola in Lewis County. As much as two million feet was sent from here in a single year by Durham boats. Pine lumber was the principal product shipped and this was produced by the mills at South Corners and North Bay.

The first bridge built in Vienna was of solid oak. It was on the direct road to Rome. The bridge was built on trestles, the posts of which were 22 feet long and 18 inches square; the cap-pieces were 18 feet long and 18 inches square.

Historical Landmarks of Vienna

The Stone Barn, as it was called by its owner Charles W. Knight of Rome, a prominent civil engineer, was started in 1899. It was completed at a cost of $140,000 seven years later. The barn, patterned after an English castle, was 120 feet long by 42 feet wide when it was finished.

Knight used the barn for his dairy farm for 11 years. During the early 1940s the barn and 513 acres of land were sold. In 1946 the barn was swept by a mysterious fire. The castle-like ruins that remained were the subject for painters and photographers. The barn is now being restored.

Like most towns, Vienna has silent markers memorializing soldiers who have served their country. Some of these are in cemeteries while others stand off by themselves in some farmer's field or alongside a road. One of these markers is located on Elpis Road. It marks the graves of Jonathan Harvey and his family. He was born in 1760, and fought in the Revolutionary War. Another marker, for Lt. Marsden, who was Gen. Washington's aide, is located on Route 49, halfway between Jewell and North Bay in Eckel Cemetery.

From the Lehigh Valley Railroad depot, this bridge crossed Wood Creek to Sylvan Beach.

William D. Evans

Sylvan Beach

By
Jack Henke
Author of
Sylvan Beach–A History
and
John Clements
Village Historian

1917 view of the Sylvan Beach roller coaster,
dismantled about 1960.

Sylvan Beach has been called the Coney Island of Central New York. It has, throughout its history, entertained and pleased thousands of pleasure-seekers. It vibrates to the tunes of honky-tonks, carousels, dance bands, rock bands, and breaking waves. The Beach, as affectionados know it, is a product of Oneida Lake and its tributary waters. The lake gives this village its vast recreational assets – boating, fishing and bathing. The Fish and Oneida Creeks, the lake's two east shore tributaries, carry among their sediments the sand that, when mixed and distributed by lake currents and Oneida's ever-present, ever-powerful west wind, produce a beach that slopes gradually, producing optimum bathing conditions.

Sylvan Beach's development came about through a combination of two factors. First, the Beach was blessed by resort potential resources, recognized by observers as early as 1790. In their writings, such noted New Yorkers as Francis Adrian Van der Kemp, Elkanah Watson and DeWitt Clinton recorded observations about the beauty and potential of Oneida Lake and its unique east shore.

The Lake's location made recognition of its resources inevitable. In colonial times Oneida Lake occupied a key position in the significant water route from New York to Oswego and then, via the Great Lakes, to the west. In the colonial and early national eras (to 1825, the Erie Canal's advent), this route was the most convenient waterway across New York. Many travelers had to journey through it and thus witnessed the rich regions through which it flowed.

James D. Spencer can rightfully be considered Sylvan Beach's founder. A man known for his industry and frugality, Spencer brought his large family to the hamlet of Fish Creek, Town of Verona, in the 1840s. He engaged in

the sand business, ran a small tavern, farmed a bit and even attempted drilling for oil on his property. Spencer began a series of real estate investments in 1847 in Verona and Vienna Townships. The bulk of his land was located in the prime development areas bordering Oneida Lake. It was through Spencer's real estate manipulation that resort settlement on Oneida Lake's east shore began.

Sylvan Beach's first commercial resort facility was the Forest Home, established by Spencer's son, Lyman, in 1879. In the years 1881-1886 the hotels, cottages, and a small amusement area first appeared.

In the beginning Sylvan Beach was a largely quiet place, often referred to as a retreat from civilization's woes. It had one large hotel, the Algonquin, which held over 100 guests, and its cottages and boarding houses were usually booked well through the summer season. It had far from reached its peak, however. In 1891, Dr. Martin Cavana, a physician from Oneida, moved to Sylvan Beach and established the Cavana Sanitarium for the treatment of chronic diseases. Martin Cavana became Sylvan Beach's leader, boss man and dedicated promoter. It was through his work that the village emerged from its retreat status to become the Coney Island of Central New York.

Cavana lived at the Beach from 1891 until his death in 1924. These were the resort's golden years. During this era Sylvan Beach played host to hundreds of mass picnics, and gatherings of groups and organizations who found the village a prime watering spot. Sunday School groups, industrial workers, veterans' organizations, and political parties met at the Beach each summer for galas beyond compare. The largest picnic of Cavana's day was that of hop growers. Every July some 20,000 to 40,000 hop people, growers, workers, and even sympathizing hangers-on, converged on the Beach via scores of New York, Ontario and Western, and Lehigh Valley Railroad cars.

In Cavana's time, the Beach's hotels and cottages could accommodate over 1,000 guests at a time. Old-time beach people fondly recall the summer boarders descending from trains on Railroad Avenue (now Main Street), laden with heavy trunks for a lengthy beach stay. The greatest of beach hotels was the Saint Charles, founded in 1899. This hotel, owned by Louis B. Chesebrough (of Vaseline fame), was considered a high class place, rivaling the best lodges of the St. Lawrence or the Adirondacks. The Saint Charles operated private carriages to transport its patrons from the railroad station to the hotel. It held balls while other beach establishments celebrated with dancing parties. Until its destruction by fire in 1914 the hotel remained a symbol of Sylvan Beach's prosperity in the Cavana years.

During the Cavana Era Sylvan Beach's identity as a workingman's middle-class resort emerged. Throughout its history the Beach opened its doors to all people. The black man, indigent farm workers, proper schoolmarms and churchmen, factory laborers, businessmen, the unemployed and the prosperous have all been welcomed at the Beach.

From Cavana's death until the early 1930s Sylvan Beach underwent a period of great transition. The Beach, from 1924 onward, never fully or permanently regained the prosperous magic of its golden years. The Great Depression undermined the resort's financing; many businesses suffered from the hard times. More importantly, however, replacement of passenger trains by automobiles hurt the Beach economically. From 1920 to 1930 the number of autos in New York quadrupled to approximately two million. No longer did Sylvan Beach occupy the role of "most convenient, reasonably priced resort in Central New York." Autos brought the Adirondack, the Catskills, and every corner of New York within driving range. Sylvan Beach's "trounced-in two-week tourist" became a hard-driving, two-hour stay motorist. Hotels, dependent on the boarding vacationer, were crippled. The village fortunes since the '30s transition period have been irregular and often lean.

The various decades at Sylvan Beach since Cavana's death have had their highlights. The '30s and '40s witnessed the heydays of Russell's Hotel and Danceland, a melodic nightclub catering to the big band sound. Russell's played host to such famed thousand-dollar bands as Glenn Miller, Harry James, the Dorsey Brothers, Duke

William D. Evans

A track inspection car at the New York, Ontario and Western Railroad depot, Sylvan Beach.

Cavana's sanitarium, facing Oneida Lake, opened in 1891.

William D. Evans

Ellington and his Harlem Aristocrats, and the Latin sounds of Desi Arnaz. Crowds of upstate lovers of dancing consistently filled Russell's Hall. For the Glenn Miller concert the beach crowd was so large that traffic was backed up three miles south of the village on Route 13, the Beach's main highway.

The '50s at Sylvan Beach were prosperous years, characterized by large beach crowds, hundreds of patrons jamming the vivacious Midway, a nightlife extending into morning's early hours, and above all, a good feeling within the village.

Since the '50s Sylvan Beach has, in general, experienced years of decadence. Its once famed Midway deteriorated into an artifactual state; its waters were rumored to be polluted (a myth that has since been thoroughly refuted); and its people lost the secret of working together that propelled them in the past. In the '60s the Beach's famed fishing pier was closed as being unsafe and the many popular commercial bingo halls were forced, by law, to shut their doors. These were bad years for the village.

In 1971 a group of beach residents banded together in an attempt to solve village problems. Entitled the Committee for Incorporation, the group succeeded in having the village formally incorporated and governmentally separated from its surrounding Town of Vienna.

Moving Into The Next Century

The incorporation of the Village in 1971 gave this lake shore community what it so desperately needed. Home rule – that capability of controlling its own destiny and control it, it did!

From the reopened fishing pier to the million dollar federal grant that created the Beachfront Park and Bathhouse, the Pedestrian Mall through the Amusement Park, the Bandstand in the Village Park, the Brick sidewalks and the gas lights on the streets.

This grant was the spring board for the private sector to come forward and invest in their own future. New reassurance, night clubs and new rides in the amusement park, new camp grounds, upgraded marinas and a merchants association that would make Sylvan Beach a household word synonymous with good clean family recreation.

Village government prospered under local leadership that sought and found grants and loans to finance sewers and domestic water. These improvements in the infastrutures led to further residential and commercial development. Now Sylvan Beach is on solid ground to move into the next century.

Selected Reference

Henke, Jack, *Sylvan Beach – A History,* (Boonville, NY, 1975).

William D. Evans

The St. Charles Hotel (1899-1914) provided elegant accommodations for its guests.

Canal at Western.

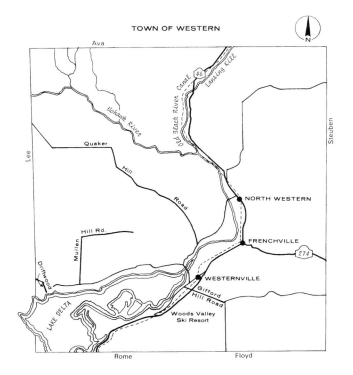

Western

By
Marion DiCarlo
and
Russell Marriott
Town Historian

The wilderness area about eight miles north of Fort Stanwix which became the Town of Western was largely included in grants by the crown of England to two men, Jelles Fonda, who received 40,000 acres and Thomas Matchin receiving 24,000 acres.

Jelles Fonda was formerly a Major in Colonel Guy Johnson's regiment of Tyron County Militia. He sold parcels from his 40,000 acre patent for 10 cents an acre to John Lansing Jr., George Clinton, William Floyd and Stephen Lush. This property now constitutes parts of the Towns of Rome, Floyd, Lee, Western and Steuben.

The very first bridge ever built across the Mohawk River was built in the Town of Western in the fall of 1789 by some of the inhabitants of this town.

In 1789 Asa Beckwith Sr. and his son Asa Jr. purchased 550 acres on the east and west sides of the Mohawk River in what is now the Town of Western. The Beckwiths, apparently the first white settlers, built a log house on their property which was the first dwelling in the town. The location was on a well-known Indian trail leading from Oneida Lake to the Adirondacks. Eight years later a brick house was completed about one-half mile south of the log house, still on the western side of the Mohawk River. The bricks were made by hand, from a strata of clay found along the river. This was mixed with the necessary amount of sand. The two kinds of soil were properly joined by driving cattle back and forth over the mixture. The house was completed in 1798 and remained an occupied dwelling until it was taken down in the early 1970s. In 1851 the Beckwiths sold their holdings to

Robert Warcup, whose descendants still own the original 550 acres.

The boundaries of the Town of Western were established in 1797 from the original Town of Steuben which encompassed a very large area. The name Western came from the fact that this town was the western portion of the original township. It then included what is now the Town of Lee, which was set off in 1811. The first town meeting was held at the house of Ezekiel Sheldon on April 4, 1797.

During the pioneer days there were no roads as such from Rome to Western. There were only Indian trails which followed the Mohawk River and Lansing Kill Creek. This trail was made into a road which could be traveled by horse and wagon. It was the first real road in town. It was probably about 16 feet wide in the country but 12 feet wide in the villages. This road, with rerouting in places, is about where Route 46 is now.

As more land was cleared and more residents arrived, farmers raised and produced more than they needed for the family consumption. Cheesemaking was the answer for surplus milk. It is not clear who started the first cheese factory in Western but David Brill built the second one in 1830 in North Western.

Farmers took the milk to the factory where it was weighed and made into Limburger and Cheddar Cheese. Each spring the farmer was given a choice of major cheese centers for pricing. Watertown and Governeur were two. Whatever the selling price for cheese in the center chosen, that would be the price farmers received during the summer months.

Jacob Karlen came from Switzerland in the mid-1850s. He established cheese factories in all areas where enough milk was available to make cheesemaking practical. At one time there were 36 cheese factories in the town. With the advent of refrigerated trucks, cheesemaking in the town disappeared by mid-1950.

Most of the settlers of Western were of English, Irish, Welsh, German or Swiss descent.

The early schools of the town were among the best, for the period, in the country. Probably the first school in the town was on the top of the hill bordering on the river by what was then the William Piper property. Parents of the first students assisted in the construction of the 25-foot square frame building. It was dedicated in 1802. Tuition was paid for in grain and labor. The last school in Westernville was a brick building of colonial design built in 1941 on the corner of Route 46 and Gifford Hill Road. The land was formerly the property of General William Floyd.

The first school in North Western was built in 1824 and 1825. It too was replaced and relocated twice. The building still stands and is a private home. The schools were built in every neighborhood; children usually not having to walk more than a mile or a mile and a half from any direction.

July 1, 1957 the school in Westernville and the affiliated districts bordering it consolidated with the Rome School District. The children are bused to the appointed school for each grade. For the next few years only kindergarten, first and second grade were held in the brick school. The brick building in Westernville now belongs to the Town of Western. It serves as the town library and recreation center for youth.

School districts both east and west of Westernville including Gifford Hill, Frenchville, North Western, Mullen and Quaker Hill Schools, centralized with Holland Patent School in 1936. The school districts north of North Western centralized with Boonville. The final chapter for school in the Town of Western is finished. It is regrettable but there are no schools in session in the Town of Western. They lasted from 1802 to 1936, a period of 134 years.

Since the nearest shopping center in 1790 was Fort Stanwix or Rome, the shopping trips were few and far between. George Brayton and Jonathan Swan ran the first store. Since it was the only store at the time, the settlers were dependent on him to supply the basic raw materials like sugar, molasses, and salt. No doubt many of the transactions did not involve money. The settlers would exchange eggs, butter, or whatever they had, for the merchandise they needed. Mr. Brayton sold the farm products in the city. He did a large business with Indians because they were numerous around this area then.

As time went on stores sprang up in many areas of the town. Thomas R. Reese's store in Westernville was one of the largest ones. It was a general store, selling almost any-

In the Village, North Western, NY.

Gladys Evans

thing needed from groceries and notions to cloth, shoes, dishes and hardware. It burned in 1918. Country stores have long been part of the Towns heritage. Unfortunately, the doors of the Capron Store, in Westernville, and the Davis Store in North Western are now closed.

The people of central and northern New York repeatedly petitioned the state to construct a waterway that would connect their area with the Erie Canal. After many delays the canal was finally finished. On June 23, 1849 water was first turned into the Black River Canal. It served the area for almost 80 years. Wood for fuel, lumber, potatoes, and dairy products, among other things, were loaded on canal boats at various dry docks during the canal season from April to November. Many of the products went on to New York City. The busiest year for the canal was 1910 when all the sand and rocks for the construction of Delta Dam were shipped over it. After that the tonnage dropped. The agricultural picture was changing; coal was replacing wood. The canal had served its usefulness; it was officially closed at the end of the season in 1924.

Before 1908 there was a thriving village in the southwestern part of the town. This village was Delta, a lovely community consisting of over 100 homes on very fertile land. The State of New York was building the Barge Canal, a deeper and wider successor to the Erie. To help maintain the water level in the canal reservoir needed to be created. Delta Dam was constructed across the Mohawk River at its narrowest point in the valley which was the southern point of the palisades of the Mohawk.

So it was that the Delta village and the fertile farms were doomed for extinction. The buildings were dismantled. Many of the residents relocated in Rome and other nearby towns. The graves in the cemetery, some of which dated back to 1805, were removed to a high point on the northwest shore of the lake. The dam was completed January 28, 1912. Water began to cover the condemned land later that year.

There began talk of turning this wasteland into a park in 1950. The Lake Delta State Park was finally opened in 1968. The facilities include a boat launch site, a large sandy beach with bathhouses, parking for 300 cars, large picnic areas, and a campground.

About 1880 Charles Pillmore, a very enterprising young man, built the first gristmill as a local source of livestock feed. In the early 1900s Mr. Pillmore was searching for a cheaper power source to run his mill. He purchased the feed mill in North Western on the Mohawk River, and rebuilt the dam on the site. With this water power he began the manufacture of electricity which became the town's first source of electrical power about 1918 or 1919. He intended to use it solely for his mill in Westernville, but the clamor for electricity was so great by residents that it was made available for those who wished it. It was available during the day and evening but turned off at 10:30 PM. Within a few years Mr. Pillmore sold this phase of his operations to a public utility company.

Marian DiCarlo

The watering trough at River and Main Streets, Westernville, about 1910.

Necessity was the motivation of Charles Decker when he built a telephone line in 1908, from his home to Davis's Store to connect with the Old Home Telephone Company that had one line from Rome to North Western. His business was fur buying in the north country and selling the fur in New York City. Almost immediately other people wanted phones so his telephone business grew until he had about 24 lines. It remained in the family until 1953 when his wife sold to Oneida County Rural Telephone Company.

There were several small businesses during the 19th century that were active for a while but have since completely disappeared. There was a shoe peg factory and a limestone quarry at Frenchville. There were sawmills, tanneries, and woodworking shops in various parts of the town.

Other industries were the Olney & Floyd Canning Factories at Delta and Westernville. They provided a market for the farmers who raised cash crops such as: peas, beans, corn and pumpkin. The canning factory provided work for all ages of the labor force the year around. Another canning factory located below the William F. Pillmore farm was operated by Mr. Pillmore.

The Town of Western changed as time went on. In the beginning the dairy farms were small, occupying practically all the land of the town outside of the villages and forest slopes. Now the dairy farms are larger and fewer. The small dairy farm has all but disappeared.

Some farm land have been abandoned entirely, some rented to the larger farmers. Other farmers raise beef cattle and cash crops of hay or grain. Horse farms are getting popular too. A large percentage of the residents are now employed elsewhere in Rome or Utica.

Recreation is becoming increasingly important. Woods Valley Ski Resort, just off Route 46, is very popular. Lake Delta State Park has miles of snowmobile trails. Future plans in the town include horseback riding trails, hiking trails and bicycle paths.

The only industry outside of farming is the George J. Olney, Inc. Machine Shop which presently employs about 30 workers. George J. Olney Sr. started this shop as a young inventor of food processing machines in 1909. During the years his machines have been sold all over the United States and to countries abroad. The company continues to be operated by his three sons George J. Jr., John B., and William Floyd.

An expanding business in Western is the Farmers Fire & Lighting Insurance Company started in 1877 by L. G. Van Wagenen and Israel White. The company serves the counties of Oneida, Lewis, Madison, Oswego and Herkimer.

The social side of life in Western includes three churches, a Boy Scout Troop, 4-H Club, Senior Citizens Club, American Legion, Fireman's Auxiliary, Home Demonstration Unit and Home Bureau. A very active Volunteer Fire Company was founded in 1945.

John Ellis

Gaylord Jones drove the stage that carried passengers and mail from Rome to North Western about 1900.

In order to plan for the orderly growth of the town, a planning board was created in the 1960s. A master plan is in force and the town is now officially zoned.

The last twenty years have brought about a renewed interest and pride in the historic and architectural heritage of the Town of Western. When our country celebrated the Bicentennial of the United States Constitution, the Town joined other municipalities in becoming a "Bicentennial Town". And, with that celebration came the birth of the Town of Western Historical Society, which celebrates its 10th anniversary in 1998. The Society is engaged in the Landmark Program which researches and recognizes sites and structures of historic and architectural significance, such as Western Town Hall. It was recently placed on the National Register of Historic Places. Heritage Green, former site of the Westernville Hotel which burned in July 1993, was purchased by the Society and is being developed into a Village Green. And, in 1997, the Society was proud to organize the Town of Western's year-long Bicentennial celebration.

Other milestones during the past two decades have been the 175th anniversary of the Westernville Presbyterian Church in 1993. The Town of Western Volunteer Fire Company consolidated two smaller fire houses into a new fire house on State Route 46. In 1989 the Highway Department also moved into new facilities on Route 46. American Legion Post 1840 completely remodeled its facility near Frenchville. In 1994 the Library was extensively remodeled and made handicapped accessible.

The youth of Western continue to be supported through the Town's summer recreation program. A recreation park, including a new ball diamond is presently under construction just north of Westernville on State Route 46.

Prominent among the Town's milestones are the accomplishments of Alberta and Art Schallenberg. Alberta became the Director of 4-H in 1936. She remains in that role in 1998 compiling 62 years of dedication to the town's youth. Her husband, Art, is presently the longest serving Justice of the Peace in New York State, having served for 61 years. Together they will celebrate 60 years of marriage.

The General William Floyd House celebrated its 195th anniversary in 1998. This National Landmark was visited by an organization known as the Descendants of the Signers of the Declaration of Independence, in 1985. Among the guests were descendants of such notables as Benjamin Franklin, Samuel Adams, Robert Morris, and of course, General William Floyd.

The Town of Western remains a town of traditions… of people proud to be who they are and where they live.

Selected Reference

Moccasin Tracks to Ski Trails: The Story of the Town of Western, (Western Bicentennial Committee, 1976).

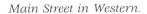
Main Street in Western.

Early view of General William Floyd House in Westernville. General Floyd settled in Western in 1803 and died there in 1821 at age 87.

Chester Williams

*Bridge over Deans Creek – now Route 234
with Hotel Barn in background.*

*An early invitation from 1892 to a Musical
Entertainment give by Neptune Engine Co. #1 &
Metcalf Hose Co. before being called Westmoreland
Fire Department.*

*Westmoreland
Malleable Iron Co.*

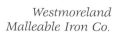

Westmoreland

By
Nancy Pritchard
Historian
Westmoreland Historical Association

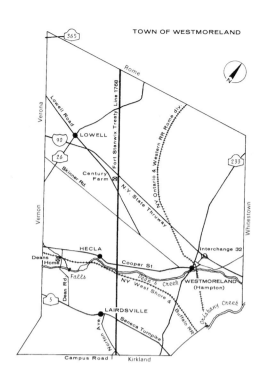

The 26,674 acres comprising the existing Town of Westmoreland were originally part of Coxe's Patent and the Oneida Indian Reservation under the Treaty of 1788. The dividing line between Coxe's Patent and the Oneida Indian Reservation was the 1768 Fort Stanwix Treaty line, which extended from the junction of Canada Creek and Wood Creek in Rome to the headwaters of the Unadilla River in Bridgewater.

The first settlement in the town took place in 1786 on Dean's Patent, a 15,000 acre tract of land granted to James Dean by the Oneida Indians in recognition of his many years of service as a missionary to them. James Dean was a central figure in keeping the Oneida Indians sympathetic to the Revolutionary cause. He initially chose a tract of land on the north side of Wood Creek in the present Town of Vienna and settled there in 1784. In 1785 he and his companions were flooded out and had to live in the garret of their log cabin for three weeks.

After the experience Dean concluded that he had chosen a bad place to settle and requested that the Oneida Indians give him a different tract. They let him choose a new site and he picked the land surrounding a waterfall on Kanaghtarageara (now known as Deans Creek). Dean settled there in February 1786 before the legislature ratified his patent. In the fall of 1786 he visited Connecticut, was married to Lydia Camp, and returned with his bride to the patent.

James Dean was accompanied by his brother, Jonathan Dean. Other early settlers were Captain Stephen Brigham from Shrewsberry, Massachusetts; Joseph Blackmer from Kent, Connecticut; and Robert Morrison from Hebran, Connecticut. Early landowners include George Washington, who owned much of Coxe Patent

lying north of the hamlet of Westmoreland, Silas Phelps, Nehemiah Jones, the Blackmers, the Townsends, and Samuel Laird.

In 1789 the rate of settlement accelerated and settlers began locating on other patents. In 1792 the Town of Whitestown was divided, one part being organized as the Town of Westmoreland with the first meeting at James Dean's home.

In the settlement of any wild land, the waterways in the area played a large part in determining the location chosen. This was also true of Westmoreland. There is Deans Creek, which runs from the western end of the town to merge with the Oriskany Creek and Sucker Brook, just east of the hamlet of Westmoreland. Oriskany Creek forms a portion of the eastern boundary of the town.

As the town was settled and communities established, a principal source of livelihood to small industries and businesses, was agriculture. The town contains some of the best agricultural land in the county. For many years agriculture in the town was dominated by dairy farming and the raising of corn for grain. For a time, hops were raised and several cheese factories prospered before it was possible to refrigerate and ship fluid milk. In 1976 the bicentennial committee wrote that in recent decades, farming has declined and some former farmland has been given over to residential use. In 1998 agriculture continues to be important, but with fewer farmers cultivating larger tracts of the town's productive land. Along the road frontages that used to be farm land, there are many more one family dwellings.

About 1805 the Westmoreland Furnace was established in the settlement now called Hecla. The furnace used Clinton ores of which there were two beds within less than a mile. After being run about 30 years, the blast furnace was converted into a cupola furnace – one which remelted old iron and scrap into castings for gate hinges, window fastenings, coffee mills, etc. It was then known as Hecla Works and was a sizable company village. After it discontinued operations, F.J. Olney converted the foundry to a sawmill and gristmill. About 1906, the Merritt brothers operated a chair factory here, producing rackers and table stands under the name Willowick. Today there is little to be found of this foundry.

Westmoreland Malleable Iron Company began in 1850 when Erastus W. Clark and Abel B. Buell started an iron foundry. In the 1850's, the company manufactured a wide variety of metal products, including bed casters, footboard handles for carriages, carriage steps and whiffle tree pins for attaching horses to wagons. In 1976 the company was still being operated by descendants of Erastus Clark. The company has since closed its doors. The building lay vacant for several years and Oneida County had it razed because of the concern for contamination. The bell that was on top of the building is now on display in front of the Town Hall.

The town contains a number of hamlets and communities of which Westmoreland, Lowell and Lairdsville are the largest. The community of Westmoreland, originally named Hampton, was settled by Daniel Seely in 1789. Here small industries, shops and stores were established to serve the village and surrounding community. The seat of town government is located here. A new Town Hall was built in 1985 and a new Fire Hall was constructed in 1993. In 1998 numerous small manufacturing, service related businesses, and a bank have located along the Rt. 233 corridor north and south of the village.

There are a number of old buildings still in existence. The house next to the Nice 'N Easy Gas Station on the south side of West Main Street was at one time a hotel.

The Clark-Lyman-VanBenschoten house on East Main Street was a hotel named W.C. Champlin's Temperance House. The owner has the old sign. The brick building on the northeast corner of Rt. 233 and East Main Street used to be a grocery store and is now known as the Westmoreland Diner.

Lowell, in McKesson's Patent, was settled by Stephen Stilson in 1802. The post office was originally called Republican and the hamlet called Andover before the names were changed to Lowell. People in the mid to late 1800's used to come to Lowell for its mineral springs. The hotel resort and mineral springs were located on Springhouse Road west of Rt. 26. In the 1950's when the Thruway was under construction, a gravel pit near Lowell provided much of the gravel used to complete the Thruway in this area. In 1998, Lowell is a small community of homes with a church and fire station.

Lairdsville was settled in 1788 by Samuel Laird. His log tavern became a well-known hostelry along Seneca Turnpike. Lairdsville flourished when the Seneca Turnpike was a major route west, but declined when travel was diverted to the Erie Canal and railroads. It presently contains a fire station, church and homes.

As early as 1792, school was taught in a log building, which stood near the burying ground a short distance west of Lairdsville. The town was later organized into 17 common school districts, each with a schoolhouse. In 1932 these were consolidated into Westmoreland Central School and a new building was constructed at Westmoreland. Many of the district schoolhouses still stand, having been converted to dwellings. A grade school, located on the green at Westmoreland, was dismantled in 1952. There have been several additions added to the Westmoreland Central School as Westmoreland continues to grow.

In the mid 1800's a boarding school was operated on Graves Road near Westmoreland. It was known first as the

*The Dean Homestead
as it appeared in 1874.*

DeLancey Institute and later the Williams Collegiate Institute. The empty building was demolished during construction of the Thruway.

Near the DeLancey Institute was Halleck springs discovered by Samuel Halleck before 1837. Halleck developed these sulphur springs into a summer resort, which was active during the mid 19th century.

One of the earliest churches was the First Congregational Church of Westmoreland, organized in 1792. A building was erected by its members on the green in Westmoreland in 1798. The Congregational Church, later sold to the Hampton Lodge Masons, was destroyed by fire in 1960. The new Masonic Temple stands on the original church property.

An independent Congregational Society was organized in Lowell about 1820 and a church built about 1824. Two successive buildings of the society burned and were rebuilt. A Methodist Church erected in Westmoreland in 1835 still stands. An Episcopal congregation was formed in 1842 in Westmoreland hamlet and a church erected in 1858. This building was dismantled in 1922 and moved to Sherrill, where it serves as the Church of the Gethsemane. The Bartlett Baptist church was founded in 1818 and a church erected in 1819 still stands. The Lairdsville Methodist Church was built after 1831 but before 1866 when it was moved to Rt. 5. It was moved again in 1978 to its present site. The church in Hecla and the church in Clark Mills were built in the early 1900's and are both still standing today.

Pomroy Jones, who compiled the early history of the county, *"Annals and Recollections of Oneida County,"* lived his life in Westmoreland. He was born in the town on December 30, 1789, and experienced the early development of the region, as it grew from a frontier to a commercial and transportation center.

In 1985, the Town of Westmoreland celebrated its 200th Birthday of its founding. The town had a two-day celebration that culminated in a community dance and fireworks. The townspeople enjoyed it so much "Founder's Day" is celebrated yearly in July.

Many organizations are working together to better our town resulting in good community spirit. The Questers and Westmoreland Historical Association are interested in preserving the town's history. The Westmoreland Area Chamber of Commerce promotes the benefits of doing business in the town. The Westmoreland Grange promotes the farming community. The Westlanders meet weekly at the Town Hall so that senior citizens can enjoy each others company. A school organization that has a large following is the Pride Pack. They are supporters of the Westmoreland School Marching Band. The Westmoreland Kiwanis promotes community-minded activities and the Mason are a charitable and fraternal organization. The Westmoreland Methodist Church has added a large fellowship hall with the members doing the construction themselves. There are sports, scouts, 4-H and a community pool. All organizations would welcome new members.

The Town of Westmoreland is looking forward to the future. The State of New York and the County of Oneida are planning major improvements on the roads and sidewalks in the hamlet of Westmoreland. The project is scheduled for 1998. The Town of Westmoreland is also planning a Town Park. There will be ball fields, basketball courts, foot paths, etc. for the community to use. The New York Thruway Authority is planning a tandem truck parking facility at the Westmoreland interchange.

After 200 plus years, the Town of Westmoreland is still a quiet, pleasant rural community in which to live. We are proud and happy to live here.

Westmoreland Elementary School built about 1922
and the Congregational Church, picture taken in 1950s.

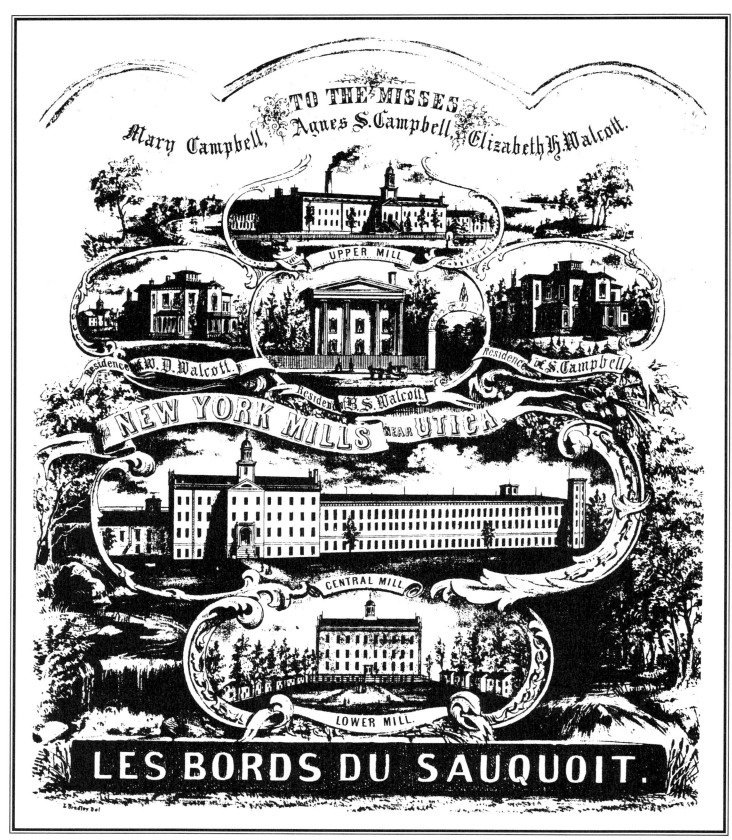

Cover of sheet music depicting New York Mills, probably about 1855,
translated, the title is "The Banks of Sauquoit."

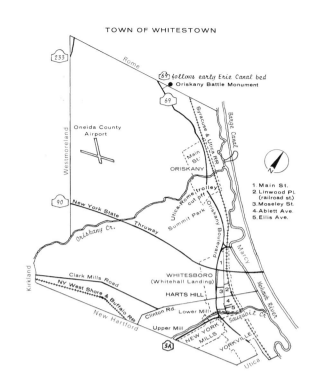

Whitestown

By

Shirley Burtch, Oriskany

Judy Dimbleby, Whitesboro

Mary Jane Kohlbrenner, Yorkville

Paula Killian, New York Mills

From original history by
Clarence J. Webster (deceased)

When Whitestown was created in March 1788, its boundaries extended westward through the wilderness to Lake Erie, and north and south, from Pennsylvania to Canada. Whitestown was half of New York State. From this 12-million-acre expanse of land, 28 counties and more than 400 towns ultimately were formed. Little wonder, then, that Whitestown has been called the "mother of towns."

In August 1777, before settlement of the Whitestown area had begun, the Battle of Oriskany placed the area west of Oriskany Creek in the history books as one of the key points in colonial resistance to a three pronged offensive by British forces in that year. Under attack by British General Barry St. Leger was Fort Stanwix, controlling access to the Mohawk Valley from the West. To relieve the Fort, General Nicholas Herkimer brought a force of 800 Tryon County militia recruited from Schenectady to Deerfield. They were ambushed on August 7th by a much larger force of Mohawk and Seneca Indians, Tory and Royal Yorker colonists, and British regulars in a ravine west of Oriskany Creek. The battle lasted throughout the day and was one of the bloodiest of the Revolution. Over half of the Tryon Militia were killed, including General Herkimer and Colonel Coxe. And at the end of the day the Mohawk and Seneca Indians had lost five of their chiefs, and the desire to continue to fight. During the course of the battle the men at Fort Stanwix were able to capture large quantities of supplies from the unprotected camps of the British, including valuable records and maps describing St. Leger's plans. But to the families of the Mohawk Valley it looked like a disaster in loss of life and exposure to a threatening British force. In the following days a relief column headed by General Benedict Arnold reached Fort

Stanwix, initiating a complete rout of St. Leger's command. This prong of the British plan was broken and in full retreat. During the ensuing months Tryon County families began to realize the significance of the bravery shown by husbands and sons at Oriskany. The western approach to the Mohawk Valley had been secured. Confidence and the will to resist returned. Morale was an especially important factor because the American commanders of Continental troops depended on the militia. During the battles of Bennington, Vermont, and Saratoga, later in 1777 militiamen again left their homes in the Mohawk Valley to assist in defeating the British. (The Battle of Oriskany is described and illustrated in more detail on the color plate, following page 16).

On August 6, 1884, a monument overlooking the Oriskany battlefield was dedicated with an address by Horatio Seymour, to those who lost their lives in that conflict.

Whitestown has made history in many ways. The cotton cloth manufactured in New York Mills, beginning in 1808, was the first in New York State. The woolen mill, built in Oriskany, in 1811, was also a New York State first. The first power loom in the United States was installed in 1818. The *Whitestown Gazette,* founded in 1793, was short-lived, but it probably was the earliest newspaper west of Albany. Oneida Institute (later Whitestown Seminary), established in 1827, was one of the earliest centers of the reform movement from which sprang the temperance and anti-slavery crusades that had deep impact on American history in the 19th century.

The pioneer traveler and trader, Elkanah Watson, called Whitestown in 1788 "truly a center of civilization." In his journal he reported a settlement with "seven houses, a gristmill and a sawmill."

Whitestown was founded by Hugh White, veteran of the Revolution and a resident of Middletown, Connecticut. He was 51 when he journeyed up the Mohawk in the spring of 1784 with five of his eight children and a daughter-in-law. They cleared land, planted corn, and built a log cabin on the bank of the Sauquoit Creek. In early autumn, they returned to Middletown. The following spring, 1785, White brought back with him all of his large family to begin his remarkable 27-year leadership in town and county.

White was a partner in the ownership of 3000 acres in both the Sadequada and Oriskany Patents. Associated with him were three prominent New Yorkers and fellow Revolutionary War veterans – Zephaniah Platt, Melancthon Smith and Ezra L'Hommedieu. Like many soldiers, they knew the richness of Mohawk Valley land, and in the middle 1780s the price was right for buying – six to ten cents per acre.

For Platt, Smith and L'Hommedieu, this venture in upstate real estate was speculative. They wanted to make money. Probably Hugh White did too, but his chief aim in turning away his Connecticut surroundings was to get a fresh start for his family. The war had been harsh. White had invested in the currency of the Continental Congress, as had hundreds of others, and this had now, in the 1780s, become largely worthless.

In 1787, White bought Melancthon Smith's share and became the owner of most of the area between Sauquoit and Oriskany Creeks. He was a good salesman, writing many letters to Connecticut friends in which he spoke glowingly of his new home. And each year he sent back some of the biggest ears of corn and largest potatoes from his land.

Therefore the Whites were not alone for long. Amos Wetmore, George Doolittle and Lemuel Leavenworth and their families came to Whitestown in 1785 and 1786. Jedediah Sanger, a young New Hampshire resident, bought 1000 acres in Whitestown in 1788, and quickly became an area leader and the first supervisor of the Town of Whitestown and the founder of New Hartford. In 1790, Jonas Platt, son of Zephaniah Platt, settled in Whitestown. He was then 21, and for the next 30 years was one of the area's and state's prominent citizens – county clerk, member of the state assembly and senate, and a justice of the State Supreme Court. In 1802 Gerrit Lansing bought 400 acres along Oriskany Creek and founded the Oriskany community.

As more settlers arrived, more services were needed. In March 1788, Governor George Clinton and the state legislature redrew the map of the state. Sixteen counties were established. Whitestown became the most westerly town in a new Montgomery County.

Oriskany Monument marks the battlefield as a State and National Historic Landmark. It was erected in 1884 by the Oneida County Historical Society.

Trinkhaus Park is home to the new Oriskany Historical Museum developed through the efforts of Robert Healy. It is an unusual memorial to veterans and those who served aboard the aircraft carrier U.S.S. Oriskany (CVA-34). On display are an A-4 Skyhawk aircraft, the ship's bell, 15 ton starboard anchor and many artifacts in the museum. Also buried at the Park is the Oneida County Bicentennial 50 year time capsule.

Almost immediately, there was clamor for change. A journey to Johnstown, the seat of Montgomery County, for court and legal business, was long and difficult. So Herkimer County was founded in February 1791. Whitestown and Fort Dayton (Herkimer) became centers for court. Sessions were held in Hugh Whites' barn. White, Jedediah Sanger and Amos Wetmore were designated as judges. There was no requirement in that day for a county judge to be a lawyer. To be a respected citizen was enough.

All of this was setting the stage for Oneida County, established in March 1798. Where the county seat should be located immediately became a subject of controversy. Whitestown had strong claim. It was the area's largest settlement. Hugh White offered land for a courthouse and a jail. Finally, a state commission settled the matter by compromise. Whitestown and Rome were designated. This situation continued until the early 1850s when Utica built the first of its courthouses. In 1860, Philo White, grandson of Hugh White, gave the courthouse structure and the land in front of it to the town and village. It remains today a memorial to the family's long, vital role in the areas growth.

Hugh White died at 79 in April 1812. For more than a quarter century he had been the first citizen in the town that bore his name.

By 1830 Whitestown was no longer a giant in size. Its boundaries had become shaped almost as they are today. Its population was almost 6000. New counties, a score of them, had been formed on the north, south and west. Within Oneida County, a dozen towns had been created from land that once was wholly Whitestown. This process began in the early 1790s with the forming of Rome, Westmoreland, Paris and Steuben. It ended with the establishment of the Town of New Hartford in 1827.

And within the town, subdivisions appeared. The Villages of Whitesboro, Yorkville, New York Mills and Oriskany took shape. Whitesboro, on some early maps labeled Whitehall Landing, began talking about a village charter as early as 1811, but did not settle differences of opinion until 1829. S. Newton Baker was Whitesboro's first village president (the term mayor was not used until late in the 19th century). He served only one year and was succeeded by Fortune White, grandson of the founder.

Yorkville probably was incorporated 1902-3, Oriskany in 1914 and New York Mills in 1922.

Village service quickly took form. Whitesboro had a fire department as early as 1831 and Yorkville by 1833. For a 100 years, until 1932, Yorkville firemen fought fires in New York Mills, although by 1850 the Mills had fire equipment, keeping it in the Yorkville fire headquarters. Today the New York Mills firehouse is adjacent to the village hall, built in 1844. The bell in the hall that rang

1910 view of the entrance to Summit Park on the Utica-Rome trolley line, east of Oriskany. (upper photo) Summit Park's natural amphitheater presented a wide range of entertainment from minstrel shows to lectures. (lower photo).

nightly at nine, was originally in the tower of one of the early mills. For years it was curfew – and strictly enforced too. Oriskany has had a fire unit since 1845. The present department was organized in 1900.

Whitesboro's post office dates from 1792 or 1793. Its designation carries the signature of George Washington. Dr. Elizur Moseley was the first postmaster. Oriskany had a post office in 1820, Yorkville in 1828 and New York Mills in 1831.

Whitesboro has had a bank continuously since 1838. All the villages in the town made crude efforts at water systems as a safeguard against fire losses. In Whitesboro and New York Mills they were tied to early industries, dating from the 1820s and 1840s. Village-wide programs were not launched until the 1890s.

Getting places always has been important, and in the pioneer era, difficult. By 1795, Jason Parker, sturdy pioneer from Massachusetts, was operating a stage from Whitestown to Canajoharie, a 12-hour trip. The fare was four cents per passenger per mile. By 1803, Parker had expanded his schedule to include trips from Whitestown to Albany and to Onondaga (Syracuse).

The Erie Canal, started in Rome July 4, 1817, reached Whitestown two years later, following through the Village of Oriskany, the same route that Route 69 and Oriskany Boulevard follows today. Immediately, it gave new momentum to business and industry. It opened a door to the west in a day when roads were either nonexistent or treacherous for travel. In summer, some swam in it, in winter, it was a fun place for skating.

The railroad followed on the heels of the canal. Whitesboro people saw their first train on the Utica and Syracuse line on June 27, 1839, becoming the New York Central in 1853. For 85 cents round trip, a Whitesboro resident could board a train at the brick depot on Railroad Street (now Linwood Place) at 8 in the morning, reach Syracuse at 11, spend two hours, and be home again at 4 in the afternoon. The age of speed had truly arrived. By 1880, 18 passenger trains were stopping at Whitesboro and almost as many in Oriskany.

Then came the trolleys, an era still recalled pleasantly by older residents. They were horse-drawn at first, sometimes not bothering to stay on the tracks. They were unheated. Lamps, in the front and rear, furnished feeble illumination. Tracks ran on the north side of Whitesboro and Yorkville's Main Street on the route to and from Utica. A connecting line extended up to New York Mills' Main Street. Electricity took over in the mid 1890s and service was expanded to a car every half hour. And there was a Rome line which ran along the south fringe of the canal, convenient transportation for workers in the businesses and industries that bordered the canal. This, too, was the

Oneida Historical Society

The buildings of the Whitestown Seminary, Main Street, Whitesboro were adapted for industrial use after 1890. Today the center structure remains, with space leased to several businesses.

route used by hundreds who in summertime, rode in open-air cars to Summit Park in Oriskany, a pleasure spot enjoyed by two generations.

Located on the Oriskany Bluffs – east of Oriskany Creek, the park was a special mecca for trolley riders between 1897 and 1926. Entering through a turnstile gateway, visitors could enjoy a promenade with restaurant, a large dance pavilion, indoor theater, baseball field, observation tower, merry-go-round, a miniature railroad, a roller coaster and a natural amphitheater where many attractions were presented. Below the park, boating was available on a lake created by the State dam for the Erie Canal and the local mill dam.

No chapter in Whitestown's history has changed more dramatically than transportation. The old Erie is long gone. It is now the Barge Canal, moved in the first years of this century from the core of the villages to a new location to the north. Freight is king on the railroad. Passenger trains are operated by the Amtrak system, but they no longer stop at Whitesboro or Oriskany. Trolleys have been replaced by buses.

The four lanes of the New York State Thruway cut through the edge of town. And on the northwest fringe is the Oneida County Airport, dedicated in July 1951, and surrounded by an industrial development area in which the county has high hopes.

Whitestown has a proud educational background. It covers 190 years from the first log school that Hugh White built in 1786-87 on a site just west of today's town hall to today's extensive systems in Whitesboro, Yorkville, New York Mills and Oriskany, which educate more than 9000 young people.

Schools were private at first, financed by tuition and a small amount of state aid. Whitestown Academy was founded in 1813, located first on Moseley Street and then Main Street in Whitesboro. In 1835, when enrollment had reached 261 (203 boys and 58 girls), the parents of sons paid $6 per term and of daughters $3.50. At that time, boys appeared to attend for two terms and girls for one. State aid in 1835 amounted to $623.40, raised by a state lottery. Students at the Academy were mostly between 12 and 20 years old.

After sharp controversy, stemming largely from dislike of the thought of direct taxation, the public school was born. In 1858, Whitesboro residents, for example, taxed themselves $6000 to erect the two-story wooden building that served for 60 years and was familiarly known as the "old green school." Legally, it was the Union Free School District of Whitesboro with a staff of three (a principal and two teachers) paid a total of $57 per month. The "old green" served until 1920 when it was torn down and the present Main Street School was erected.

The Oriskany Hotel erected in the early 1870's at the corner of River and Utica Streets (above) was replaced by the modern Oriskany Library in 1988 (right).

Today's Whitesboro Central School, organized in 1936, is the second largest centralized system in New York State with an enrollment of almost 4000. It includes the high school, built in 1966 in the Town of Marcy, the junior high school (formerly the high school) on Oriskany Boulevard in Whitesboro, and four elementary schools.

New York Mills had a public school in 1827, located in what was known as the Lower Mill. It was operated by the mill management for the children of workers. Today the village program, includes the junior-senior high school, built in 1959, and the elementary school on Main Street (once the high school) which dates to 1916.

Yorkville had a school in 1844, located near the present post office. The brick school on Whitesboro Street was built in 1902 and today serves as part of the Whitesboro Central system.

Oriskany, beginning in 1812 had a series of school buildings. The Oriskany Central School program, extending to the Rome city line and north to the Town of Floyd, includes a high school, built in 1932, and Walbran Elementary School, built in 1961.

Then there was Oneida Institute, later called Whitestown Seminary. This was a church-backed school, established by the Presbyterians in 1827, to prepare young men for the ministry. It was large – 550 were enrolled in the middle of 1850 – stormy in its history, struggling constantly to get enough money to operate.

It was a tough, no-nonsense school at which the day began at four in the morning with work in the fields in summer and in a factory area in winter making pails, buckets and some farm tools. It graduated 2000 young men who became clergymen and missionaries in all parts of the world.

Split over the slavery issue and out of money, the Presbyterians gave up in the mid-1840s, and the Free Will Baptists took over. Less involved in the current events of the times and more flexible in their thinking, they revived the seminary and ran it until it closed in the early 1880s. At its height it had three large buildings and owned 114 acres of land, stretching from Whitesboro's Main Street, between Ellis and Ablett Avenues, to the Mohawk River.

Libraries play an important role in the continuing education of communities. Whitestown has strong ones. Whitesboro's library had its beginning in the mid-1920s. George Dunham, who was publisher of the *Utica Daily Press* (died in 1922) deeded the family home to the village for library use. Today Dunham Library retains the charm of an old residence and with a modern addition has space for volumes plus meeting rooms.

The library movement in New York Mills began in the late 1930s and was climaxed by the opening in March 1940 of a one-room library in the village hall. Today's fine

Trinkhaus Manor and restaurant at Christmas time created a Winter fairy-tale-land in Oriskany until fire destroyed the landmark in 1992.

library on Main Street was opened in April 1973. The Oriskany Village Library started in 1937 in an abandoned gas station, with founders trying to crowd 600 books into a single tiny room. The Oriskany library moved to Utica Street in the summer of 1941. On October 1988, the library opened its new building on Utica Street, located on the site of the old Oriskany Hotel.

The Presbyterians emerged from the Revolution as the strongest religious group in the new country, in numbers and in organization. Connecticut was the principal center of the trend to consolidate older Congregational churches with the more vibrant Presbyterian movement.

Thus, it was natural for Hugh White and those who joined him in Whitestown in the first years to think Presbyterian when they established a church in the new town and called 26-year-old Bethuel Dodd, a Rutgers graduate from Bristol, Connecticut, as pastor, in 1793.

The Rev. Mr. Dodd, who served until his death in 1804, preached in the homes of members until the first church building was erected in 1803. Every third Sunday he traveled to Fort Schuyler, soon to become Utica, to lead services. The present Whitesboro Presbyterian Church was built in 1834 at a cost of $5100.

The Baptists came to Whitesboro in 1796 and built a church two years later. These were religious societies with a reach. The Presbyterian church was the parent of three other Presbyterian societies: Utica (1813), New York Mills (1830) and Oriskany (1832). The Yorkville church established in 1917 had a charter membership of 53, of whom a majority previously had been identified with the Whitesboro and New York Mills churches. The Baptists in Whitesboro furnished momentum for societies in Oriskany, Marcy, Oneida, and Walesville. They also developed an Indian mission in Deansboro.

Catholic services began in Whitesboro in April 1882. The St. Paul's parish church took shape the following year with the appointment of Reverend John B. Mulaney as pastor. St. Paul's was dedicated October 12, 1886. Space limitations necessitated demolishing this building and completion of the present St. Paul's Church in 1972 under Reverend Vincent Donovan.

St. Anne's Catholic Church in Whitesboro began in May 1965. The present church was completed in September of 1966 on land purchased from the Devereux estate.

St. Mary's parish in New York Mills was established in 1910. And in 1923 the Sacred Heart of Jesus Holy Cross Polish National Church of New York Mills was completed.

Growth of the Anglican church was slow after the Revolution because many of those who remained loyal to the Crown had been identified with it. However, there was an early Anglican (Episcopal) movement in the Mohawk

The First Presbyterian Church, Main Street, Whitesboro, was built in 1834. On July 18, 1979, a fire destroyed much of the building including the steeple with its beloved clock that was a village time keeper. The main part of the church was renovated and returned to service in November 1980. In October 1989 work restoring the steeple and clock was completed.

Valley. The first church in Oriskany (1830) was Episcopal. It continued until 1996 when it closed. The Whitesboro church dates from 1844.

The Methodists were early in New York Mills – 1826 – reflecting perhaps the swift development of the mill industry.

Large industry, such as Utica Corporation (Kelsey-Hayes) remains in Whitestown; but the day when Whitesboro, Yorkville, New York Mills and Oriskany were leaders in textile and clothing, in furniture, in tool making and iron products is long since gone.

There are big names to be remembered. In 1806, Dr. Seth Capron, physician by profession, came from Rhode Island, and in the next half dozen years was the force behind the launching of the New York Mills and Oriskany cotton and woolen industries. Benjamin S. Walcott, also a Rhode Island man, followed soon and gave the mill industry in New York Mills the momentum that carried through three generations of his family. In the 1840s, another name, Samuel Campbell, joined in the leadership of this remarkable enterprise.

These were impressive men who not only built mill structures that were among the largest of their type in the country, and created sizeable family fortunes, but also had deep impact on the area in which they lived. The Walcotts built homes, endowed churches and schools, and set standard. The Walcotts, for example, were strict prohibitionists, and New York Mills was without a saloon for years in the 19th century, a time when the drinking spot was common in most localities. The Walcott mills were among the earliest in the state to have a medical program for employees and among the first to build company housing, available for workers for $20 or less a year.

And there were others. B.T. Babbitt, native of Westmoreland, made a fortune in New York City in the manufacture of soap and cleaning powders, and then, at the age of 40, returned to Whitesboro, and as a sort of hobby, established an iron works. His factory on the Erie Canal made products ranging from army cannon to ventilators for Pullman railroad cars.

Babbitt died in 1880, and his industrial property was taken over by a Utica-Whitesboro group headed by Charles Powell. The new ownership made a sharp shift and turned to making of sweaters and underwear. Alliance Knitting, the new firm, employed 400 and enjoyed a nationwide market for its sales.

Sutton and Quigley made rolltop desks and other office furniture for 40 years in Whitesboro. Wybo Wind, a sturdy Dutchman, who settled first in New York Mills, moved in 1888 to Whitesboro and established a bakery whose trucks carried bread and other items throughout much of Upstate New York. To Oriskany in 1880 came Henry H. Waterbury and his four sons to establish the wool felt industry which for almost 100 years has carried the family name and remains today one of the region's strong local industries.

Today Whitestown is a suburban region of 18,900 people where, as in most upstate communities, old and new are blended. Whitesboro, New York Mills, Yorkville and Oriskany reflect the past in their old homes, many reaching back more than a century, in their stately churches, and in some of their business structures.

The Oneida County Industrial Park located at the Oneida County Airport has become an active venue for commercial growth. The Park is home to Metropolitan Life Insurance Co., Bus Industries Manufacturing Co., Metra Health, Bank of New York, and the Federal Reserve Bank. Regular Allegheny Air Line commuter flights service passenger travel from the airport. Current plans for development of the Judd Road highway connector will link Routes 8 and 12 in New Hartford to the Industrial Park, Airport, and City of Rome.

Selected References

Rohaman, D. Gordon, *Here's Whitesboro,* (New York, 1949).

Whitcher, M.L., *A Few Stray Leaves in the History of Whitesboro,* (1884, reprinted 1957 by Clinton Courier, Inc.).

The emblem of the Utica Curling Club marks the location of their new, state of the art facility on Clark Mills Road, Whitesboro.

Timeline

1693	Albany County was formed, including the present area of Oneida County.
1758	Fort Stanwix (Rome) was built by the British at to protect the portage from Wood Creek to the Mohawk River.
1758	Fort Schuyler (Utica) was built as a supply fort by the British near the fording place in the Mohawk River.
1768	The Treaty of Fort Stanwix, negotiated between Sir William Johnson and Iroquois chiefs, fixed the "Line of Property". The boundary between the British lands and Indian lands and ran from Fort Stanwix southward.
1772	Tryon County was formed and included the present area of Oneida County.
1777	Fort Stanwix was besieged by a British army led by Barry St. Leger. During the siege, the Stars and Stripes, the newly adopted flag of the American colonies, flew for the first time in battle.
1777	The Battle of Oriskany was fought on August 6.
1784	Hugh White and his sons established the first permanent settlement in Oneida County in Whitestown.
1786	The Brothertown Indians settled in the Towns of Marshall and Kirkland.
1790	Baron von Steuben settled in the Town of Steuben that he was awarded by New York State.
1793	The Holland Land Company began selling land in Oneida County. During the following decade settlements were begun at Barneveld and Holland Patent.
1792-6	The Western Inland Lock Navigation Company constructed a canal between the Mohawk River and Wood Creek at Rome.
1793	The Whitestown Gazette, the first newspaper west of Albany, was published at New Hartford.
1793	The first mail route from Whitestown to Utica and Canajoharie was established.
1793	Samuel Kirkland, missionary to the Oneida Indians, established the Hamilton-Oneida Academy in the Town of Kirkland to educate Indian and colonist children.
1794	Treaty of Canandaigua between the United States and Indian Nations established Oneida Indian lands.
1794	The Great Genesee Road was authorized by New York State to extend from Old Fort Schuyler (Utica) westward to the Genesee Valley.
1795	First post stage route established by Jason Parker between Whitestown and Canajoharie.
1796	Welsh immigrants began settling in the Towns of Steuben and Remsen.
1798	Old Fort Schuyler was incorporated as the Village of Utica.
1798	Oneida County was formed from Herkimer County and chartered on March 15, 1798.
1799	The Cherry Valley Turnpike (Route 20) was chartered and built from Albany to Cazenovia.
1803	General William Floyd, delegate to the Continental Congress and Signer of the Declaration of Independence, acquired land in the Town of Western and built a summer home.
1807	County Court houses were built at Whitesboro and Rome.
1809	One of the earliest cotton mills in New York State was started at New York Mills.
1811	A woolen mill, believed to be the first in New York State, was opened in Oriskany.
1812	The Hamilton-Oneida Academy was granted a state charter as Hamilton College.
1816	The United States Arsenal was completed on West Dominick Street, Rome.
1817	Construction of the Erie Canal began at Rome on July 4. The Utica-Rome part was completed in 1819.
1819	The Village of Rome was incorporated.
1822	"The Rural Resort" first accommodations for tourists erected at Trenton Falls by Rev. John Sherman.
1825	The entire Erie Canal was completed joining the Atlantic Ocean with the Great lakes.
1832	Utica was chartered as a City.
1833	The Utica and Schenectady Railroad was chartered.
1833	The Chenango Canal was authorized. It was opened in 1836 and its route was from Utica to Binghamton.
1835	The Anti-Slavery Convention was held in Utica.
1837-43	The Utica State Hospital was built as the first state asylum for the indigent mentally ill.

1839	The Utica and Syracuse Railroad was opened.
1846	An early commercial telegraph line was established between New York City and Buffalo. The headquarters was in Utica with Theodore Faxton of Utica as president.
1846	Associated Press originated in Utica by Thomas Faxton.
1851	The first factory in the United States to manufacture cheese was established by Jesse Williams near Rome.
1851	The Black River Canal opened between Rome and Port Leyden.
1852-4	Horatio Seymour of Utica served as Governor of New York State. He served again from 1862 to 1864.
1853	The Black River and Utica Railroad was organized.
1858	John Butterfield of Utica established the Overland Mail Route across the United States.
1860's	Trenton Falls was at its height as a world famous resort.
1867-81	Roscoe Conkling of Utica served as United States Senator.
1870	The City of Rome was incorporated.
1872	Utica Knitting Co. founded, made Utica knit goods capital of the world.
1875-81	Francis Kernan of Utica served as United States Senator.
1875	Central New York State School for the Deaf was established in Rome.
1890's	The Saturday Globe, published in Utica, was the first illustrated newspaper in the United States.
1901	Automobile Club of Utica formed. Led to American Automobile Association in 1902.
1905-09	Elihu Root of Clinton served as Secretary of State in the administration of Theodore Roosevelt. He had been Secretary of War from 1899 to 1905 and then was elected to the United States Senate from 1909 to 1915.
1908-12	James S. Sherman of Utica served as Vice-President of the United States.
1909	The Oneida County Court House in Utica was completed.
1909-18	The Barge Canal was built, replacing the Erie Canal, mostly using the same route.
1916	The City of Sherrill was incorporated.
1926	Broadacres Sanatorium was established with the building completed in 1929.
1936	Munson-Williams-Proctor Institute was opened to the public in Utica.
1941	Air Force Repair and Maintenance Base sited at Rome on 2,000 acres.
1946	Utica College of Syracuse University was established in Utica.
1951	The Oneida County Airport was dedicated at Oriskany.
1961	Oneida County, by popular vote, changed to a charter form of government.
1965	Kirkland College received a charter as a four year college for women in association with Hamilton College.
1966	Representatives to Oneida County Government were elected from reapportioned districts and the name of the body was changed to Oneida County Board of Legislators.
1969	The State University of New York Upper Division College was established. SUNY site in Marcy selected 1981
1970	The Oneida County Office Building was dedicated.
1970	The New York State Office building opened in Utica.
1973	Oneida County Health Department created; County Hospital at Rome, NY, closed.
1974	Oneida County Office for Aging was established.
1974	The Stanley Performing Arts Center took form in Utica.
1974	The Riverside Mall opened in Utica
1976	Fort Stanwix National Monument reconstruction completed in Rome.
1977	Boilermaker 15K Road Race first run with 800 participants.
1979	The Sheraton Inn opened in downtown Utica.
1980	Sangertown Square Mall opened in New Hartford.
1982	Utica celebrates sesquicentennial of incorporation as a city.
1982	Good Old Summertime Festival started.
1993	Former Utica Water Board became a regional authority governed by individuals from City and County.
1994	Oneida County assumed City's aid to Utica Zoo.
1994	Control of Utica Auditorium transferred to an independent authority.
1995	Griffiss Air Force Base was closed resulting in loss of about 5,000 jobs.
1996	Oneida County Economic Development Growth Enterprises (EDGE) and Griffiss Local Development Corp. (GLDC) formed to attract new business.
1997	Bankers Trust Building purchased and renovation started by Harold (Tom) Clark – reopens with business offices and Adirondack Bank operations.
1998	Local investors announce plans to buy and renovate Hotel Utica to original splendor.

Index

～⊗ *EXPLORING* ⊗⌇
200 YEARS OF ONEIDA COUNTY HISTORY

was composed in 11-point Times and leaded two points with display type in Veljovic by Pieshare, Inc.; text printed on 80-pound Utopia Three Blue White matte text with covers adhesive bound with 10-point Carolina by Canterbury Press; and published by

Oneida County Historical Society
Utica, New York